DATE DUE			

THE
ENCYCLOPEDIA OF
CHILD ABUSE

THE ENCYCLOPEDIA OF CHILD ABUSE

Robin E. Clark
and
Judith Freeman Clark
Introduction by
Richard J. Gelles, PhD

Facts On File
New York • Oxford

The Encyclopedia of Child Abuse

Facts On File,® Inc.
460 Park Avenue South
New York, New York 10016

Library of Congress Cataloging-in-Publication Data

Clark, Robin E.
The encyclopedia of child abuse/Robin E. Clark and Judith Freeman Clark;
introduction by Richard J. Gelles
    p. cm.
  Bibliography: p.
  Includes index.
  ISBN 0-8160-1584-8
  1. Child abuse—Dictionaries. 2. Child abuse—United States—Dictionaries.
I. Clark, Judith Freeman. II. Title.
HV6626.5.C57 1989
362.7'044—dc19

88-30880
CIP

British CIP data available on request

Composition by Facts On File, Inc.
Printed in the United States of America

10 9 8 7 6 5 4 3 2 1

This book is dedicated to
the boys of Pine Cottage
Alexander Children's Center, 1975-1976—
Benji, Bobby, Carl, Daryl, Hank
Jamie, Mark, Mickey, Robert, Thomas—
and to all children.

CONTENTS

Preface

Child abuse and neglect have many different dimensions. Though we often think of child abuse only in terms of physical violence, various forms of psychological threats, coercion, sexual exploitation and even folk medicine practices can also produce serious and long-lasting damage. The range of actions classified as child abuse or neglect is constantly changing as a result of social and economic conditions, political ideology, advances in medicine, improvements in communication and melding of cultures. Absence of a single, explicit and universally accepted definition of abuse makes studies of its incidence difficult. Yet, child abuse and neglect are not simply cultural inventions. As international concern for the plight of children grows, those concerned with preventing abuse and neglect are beginning to find more and more common ground for collaboration.

The *Encyclopedia of Child Abuse* reflects the struggle to define, prevent and treat this problem. Entries reflect the range of disciplines (including law, medicine, psychology, sociology, economics, history, education and others) that contribute to our understanding of child maltreatment as well as the scope of debate within and among disciplines. Where there is disagreement on a particular point we have tried to identify the different arguments. Obviously, it is not possible to present an exhaustive discussion of each of the hundreds of topics included in this book. For those who wish to explore a topic in depth we make suggestions for further reading at the end of selected entries. An extensive bibliography is also included at the back of the book.

Space and time considerations forced us to be selective in choosing the topics we discussed. In attempting to present an overall view of child abuse and neglect we chose topics that we felt would give the reader a grasp of the central issues.

Information presented in this book comes from the most up-to-date sources available at the time of writing. We have attempted to present material in clear language that does not require specialized knowledge of medicine, law or other disciplines. Our use of "simple" language should not be construed as simplistic. We believe professionals and general readers alike will find the book contains a wealth of useful information.

Though we have attempted to present child abuse and neglect from an international perspective, readers will notice that most statistical information comes from the United States. This is a reflection of the availability of such information rather than a statement of relative importance. The U.S. is virtually the only country that regularly collects, compiles and reports extensive statistical information on child abuse and neglect.

In selecting entries, we chose not to include biographies of individuals who have contributed to the understanding and/or prevention of child abuse and neglect. The list of these individuals is long and new names are constantly being added. Such a listing, though important, is beyond the scope of this book. Biographical information is included only when it is relevant for the understanding of a particular case, concept or contribution.

Finally, we hope users of this book will be stimulated to learn more about child abuse and neglect. Only through a better understanding of the complex and often misunderstood phenomenon of child abuse can we hope to prevent it.

Robin E. Clark and Judith Freeman Clark
Northampton, Massachusetts

Acknowledgments

Over the months that this book was researched and written, we contacted dozens of organizations to ask for information about child abuse and neglect. In particular, staff at the Clearinghouse on Child Abuse and Neglect Information; the House of Representatives Subcommittee on Children, Youth and Families; staff of the American Association for Protecting Children; and staff of the Incest Survivors Resource Network deserve special acknowledgment. Countless individuals at other public and private sector agencies answered our mail and telephone inquiries and sent us statistics and facts on hundreds of topics. Although it is impossible to mention each person by name, a sincere thank-you goes to these people for their cooperation and assistance.

The reference departments of libraries at Boston College School of Social Work, Brandeis University, Smith College, the University of Massachusetts at Amherst, as well as the Forbes Library, Northampton, Massachusetts, provided us with easy access to information. The graciousness and competence of staff at these libraries cannot be overemphasized; and without the help of experts in the Government Documents Room at the University of Massachusetts, fact-checking would have been tedious indeed.

Kate Kelly, our editor, has been unfailingly cheerful throughout all stages of this project; her suggestions have been thoughtful and her editorial comments helpful. Elizabeth Frost Knappmann of New England Publishing Associates deserves mention for her efforts on our behalf.

Friends and colleagues have been generous with support and encouragement during the time that we researched and wrote this book. Janet Logan and Susan Carter Sawyer are among those who were especially helpful to us.

Members of our family have been patient as we completed our work. We are grateful for their understanding and, in particular, would like to acknowledge the support of our mothers, Martha Clark and Elizabeth Bartlett. Finally, a very special thanks to Tim and Stephanie.

CHILD ABUSE—AN OVERVIEW

Ten years ago 10% of a national sample of Americans considered child abuse a serious problem. In 1982, nine out of 10 people surveyed by Louis Harris and Associates thought that child abuse was a serious social problem. Has the problem increased ninefold, or have Americans just become more aware of the dimensions of the problem of child maltreatment?

Historical Evidence of Child Abuse and Neglect

The rapid increase in public awareness of child abuse has led many people to conclude that abuse and neglect of children is a new phenomenon that has increased in epidemic proportions in the last few years. Child abuse is not new. Throughout the history of Western Society, children have been subjected to unspeakable cruelties. The historian Samuel Radbill (1980) reports that in ancient times infants had no rights until the right to live was ritually bestowed upon them by their fathers. The right to live was sometimes withheld by fathers, and infants were indeed abandoned or left to die. Although we do not know how often children were killed or abandoned, we do know that infanticide was widely accepted among ancient and prehistoric cultures. Infants could be put to death because they cried too much, because they were sickly or deformed, or because they had some perceived imperfection. Girls, twins and the children of unmarried women were the special targets of infanticide (Robin, 1980). Lloyd DeMause (1974, 1975) has examined the history of childhood and notes that by 1526 the latrines of Rome were said to "resound with the cries of children who had been plunged into them." Infanticide continued through the 18th and 19th centuries. Even today, illegitimate children continue to run the greatest risk of infanticide.

Many societies also subjected their offspring to rituals or survival tests. Some Native Americans threw their newborn into pools of water and rescued them only if they rose to the surface and cried. The Greeks exposed their children to the natural elements as a survival test.

Killing children was not the only form of abuse inflicted by generations of parents. From prehistoric times right through Colonial America children have been mutilated, beaten and maltreated. Such treatment was not only condoned, but also often mandated as the most appropriate child-rearing method. Children were hit with rods, canes and switches. Boys have been castrated to produce eunuchs. Our forefathers in Colonial America were implored to "beat the devil" out of their children. Stubborn child laws were passed that permitted parents to put to death unruly children, although it is not clear whether children were actually ever killed (Robin, 1982; Ross, 1980).

Discovering Childhood, Children, and Child Abuse

The historical rights were recognized, but slowly. Six thousand years ago children in Mesopotamia had a patron goddess to look after them. The Greeks and Romans had orphan homes. Some historical accounts also mention the existence of foster care for children. Radbill (1980) reports that child protection laws were legislated as long ago as 450 B.C. At the same time the father's complete control over his children was modified. Anthropologists have noted that nearly every society has had laws and rules regarding sexual access to children.

Michael Robin (1982) reports that the Renaissance marked a new morality regarding children. Children were seen as a dependent class in need of the protection of society. But this was also a time when the family was looked to for teaching children the proper rules of behavior. At the same time, the power of the father increased dramatically.

While society paid more attention to children, this was not without some dire consequences. Puritan parents in Colonial America were instructed by leaders such as Cotton Mather that strict discipline of children could not begin too early.

The enlightenment of the 18th century brought children increased attention and services. The London Foundling Hospital, founded during the 18th century, not only provided pediatric care, but was also the center of the moral reform movement on behalf of children (Robin, 1982).

In the United States the case of Mary Ellen Wilson is almost always singled out as the turning point in concern for children's welfare. An illegitimate child born in 1866 in New York City, Mary Ellen was in the care of foster parents when she was discovered, beaten and neglected, by Etta Wheeler, a charity worker. Wheeler called upon the police and the New York City Department of Charities to help Mary Ellen Wilson but was turned down—first by the police who said there was no proof of a crime and then by the charity agency who said they did not have custody of Mary Ellen. The legend goes on to note that Henry Bergh, founder of the Society for the Prevention of Cruelty to Animals, finally intervened on behalf of Mary Ellen. The courts accepted the case because Mary Ellen was an animal. In reality, the court reviewed the case because the child needed protection. The case was argued, not by Henry Bergh, but by his colleague, Elbridge Gerry.

Mary Ellen Wilson was removed from her foster home and placed in an orphanage. Her foster mother was imprisoned for a year, and the case received detailed press coverage for months. In December of 1874 the New York Society for the Prevention of Cruelty to Children was founded (Nelson, 1984; Robin, 1982).

Protective societies appeared and disappeared during the next 80 years. The political scientist Barbara Nelson (1984) notes that by the 1950s public interest in abuse and neglect was practically nonexistent. Technology paved the way for the rediscovery of child abuse. In 1946 the radiologist John Caffey reported on a number of cases of children who had multiple long bone fractures and subdural hematomas (Caffey, 1946). Caffey used the X ray to identify the fractures, although he did not speculate about the causes. In 1953 P.V. Woolley and W.A. Evans (Woolley and Evans, 1953) speculated that the injuries might be inflicted by the children's parents. Caffey (1957) looked again at his X-ray data and proposed that such injuries could have been inflicted by parents or caretakers. By 1962, physician C. Henry Kempe and his colleagues at the University of Colorado Medical Center were quite certain that many of the injuries they were seeing, and the healed fractures that appeared on X rays, were intentionally inflicted by parents (Kempe et al., 1962).

Kempe and his colleagues' article became the benchmark of the public and professional rediscovery of child abuse. Kempe's article and a strong editorial that accompanied the article in the *Journal of the American Medical Association* created considerable public and professional concern.

Steps to Prevent and Treat Child Abuse

The Children's Bureau, founded in 1912 as an agency in the Department of Labor (later becoming an agency of the Department of Health, Education, and Welfare), addressed the problem of abused children as far back as the 1950s. The Bureau was founded by an act of Congress with a mandate to disseminate information on child development; it also acquired the budget and mandate to conduct research on issues concerning child development. The Children's Bureau engaged in a variety of activities regarding child abuse and neglect, and participated in one of the earliest national meetings on child abuse, sponsored by the Children's Division of the American Humane Association. After the publication of Kempe's 1962 article, the Bureau convened a meeting that drafted in 1963 a model child abuse reporting law. By 1967, all 50 states had enacted mandatory reporting laws based on the model reporting law. In 1974, Congress enacted the Child Abuse Prevention and Treatment Act and located the National Center on Child Abuse and Neglect in the Children's Bureau (Nelson, 1984).

The Definition Dilemma

The earliest and most enduring problem in the study of child abuse has been the development of a useful, clear, acceptable (and accepted) definition of "abuse." The terms—abuse, neglect and maltreatment—are not easily defined. Offenders' views differ from those of victims. Agents of social control (e.g., police or social workers) may have different perceptions from participants. Friends, neighbors and bystanders offer additional perspectives.

Kempe and his colleagues (1962) first defined the "battered child syndrome" as a clinical condition—meaning that diagnosable medical and physical symptoms existed—involving those who have been deliberately injured by a physical assault. Kempe's definition of abuse, which set the stage for the way in which abuse would be defined and studied for a decade, was restricted only to acts of physical violence that produce diagnosable injuries.

As the study of child abuse expanded, discussions of how to define abuse increased in scope and intensity. No conference on child abuse was complete without one or more sessions set aside to produce a definition of child abuse. Far from producing a clear definition, the discussions muddied the already turbid water. One set of debates focused on consequences. Did an act by a parent or caretaker have to produce an injury for it to be defined as abuse? The social policy expert and noted researcher on child abuse, David Gil, responded to this question anecdotally. Gil was the father of twin sons. As a response to the question about consequences, Gil posed another question. "Suppose," he said, "I hold one of my twin sons in each hand. I then throw them to the ground. The son in my right hand falls onto the concrete floor and fractures his skull. The son I hold in my left hand falls on a carpet and is not injured. Am I a right-handed abuser only?" Gil's question forced those in the field of child abuse to recognize that diagnosable injury was not the *sine qua non* of a definition of abuse. Parents could inflict cruel and harsh treatment on their children without necessarily producing a diagnosable clinical condition. Physicians and social workers were quick to recognize that depending on diagnosable injury as the necessary and sufficient condition by which to define an act as abuse would mean always having to react to abuse. For the definition to be useful, it had to allow for diagnosis in advance of injury.

A second focus of attention and debate was on intent. Could one define abuse in such a way that the act had to be intentional? In general, most definitions of abuse require that the act be intentional. Intent, however, is not readily or objectively measured.

The third focus was on whether abuse is limited to acts of physical violence. Kempe and his colleagues did confine their classic definition of the battered child syndrome to injuries caused by physical assault. However, not long after Kempe published his article, social service personnel began to argue quite strongly that physical injury was not the only injury children suffered. Children are starved, sent outdoors into freezing weather with inadequate clothing, deprived of medical attention and the opportunity for an education, medicated and sedated needlessly, subjected to cruel mental and emotional abuse, and are sexually victimized by adult caretakers.

The National Center on Child Abuse and Neglect defines child abuse as:

the physical or mental injury, sexual abuse, negligent treatment, or maltreatment of a child under the age of eighteen by a person who is responsible for the child's welfare under circumstances which indicate that the child's health or welfare is harmed or threatened thereby. (Public Law 93-237)

David Gil (1975) takes this formal definition much further. For Gil, abuse is any act of commission or omission by a parent, or individual, institution or society as a whole, that deprives a child of equal rights and liberty, and/or interferes with or constrains the child's ability to achieve his or her optimal developmental potential.

It is tempting to think that the years of debate and discussion have resulted in a conclusive definition of child abuse. Such is not the case. Debate still rages over the issue of consequence and intent. The broadening of the definition has produced as many problems as it has solved. For example, in the mid 1970s, after all 50 states had adopted definitions of child abuse that were similar to the definition provided by the National Center on Child Abuse and Neglect, a young child was removed from her home by child welfare authorities in a southern state. The authorities argued that the child was a victim of abuse because she was being forced to live in a depraved environment. The environment was labelled depraved because the child's mother was cohabitating with a man to whom she was not married.

Twenty years of discussion, debate and action have led me to conclude that there will never be an accepted or acceptable definition of abuse, because abuse is not a scientific or clinical term. Rather, it is a political concept. Abuse is essentially any act that is considered deviant or harmful by a group large enough or with sufficient political power to enforce the definition. Abuse is a useful term for journalists who want to capture the attention of their readers or viewers. It is a useful political term because it carries such a strong pejorative connotation that it captures public attention. Unfortunately, there is no one set of objective acts that can be characterized as abusive, and what is defined as abuse depends on a process of political negotiation.

What is now considered child abuse is the product of a 20-year effort to educate clinicians, policy makers and the public about what acts and actions are considered harmful to children. Although typically there is consensus that certain acts of physical violence are harmful, even here there is debate. On one side are those who feel that any act of violence, including a slap or a spanking, is harmful. On the other side are those who believe that sparing the rod spoils the child and that not using physical discipline is harmful to the welfare of children. With regard to sexual abuse, some feel that sexual acts with minor children who are not able to give informed consent are harmful irrespective of the physical or emotional consequences. Others claim that such sexual activity is actually beneficial to children and helps provide them with a healthy introduction to sex and sexuality.

Defining neglect also produces debate and dissension that sometimes end up in court. Each year there are a number of instances where Christian Scientist parents engage in battles with medical authorities over treatment of dependent children. Some parents have had their parental rights terminated in order that physicians might be permitted to administer drugs or transfusions to ill children. The newest and most recent battle emerged over treatment of newborns with severe medical disabilities. The classic case is that of Baby Jane Doe. Baby Jane Doe was born in 1983 on Long Island, New York, with spina bifida. Baby Doe's condition involved three major birth defects: an abnormally small head, an incomplete enclosure of the spine and excess fluid on the brain. Baby Jane Doe's parents sought medical advice and, after receiving conflicting opinions, decided against corrective surgery. Without the surgery Baby Jane Doe would live for perhaps two years. With it she might live for two decades, but severely physically and mentally retarded. A Vermont right-to-life activist sued to force the surgery. The case was thrown out of a state appellate court. The federal government intervened, arguing that withholding surgery might violate the infant's civil rights. A federal judge ruled for the parents' decision against surgery. That child abuse is a political concept was underscored when Congress modified the definition of child abuse in 1984 to include instances of withholding food or medical treatment from handicapped infants.

A final testimony to the politics of defining abuse is the raging debate over abortion. On one side is the so-called pro-life contingent, which argues that abortion is child murder. On the other side are the pro-choice groups, which believe that restricting access to abortion is an abuse of women in general and often results in the birth of unwanted children who run a very high risk of abuse and maltreatment.

A precise study of a political concept such as abuse seems ultimately impossible. An intensive examination of the definitions of child abuse and neglect carried out by the social welfare researchers Jean Giovanonni and Rosina Becerra (1979) presented a series of vignettes to professionals and members of the public. Not surprisingly they found considerable variation, across the various professional groups surveyed, in the behaviors defined as abuse. Definitions of abuse also varied by race, social class and occupation.

Although I use the term "abuse" in my writings and in this overview, my proposed solution to the definitional problem is to focus on specific, definable acts of omission and commission that are harmful to individuals in families. Thus, in my own work, I focus on specific acts of violence toward children and other family members.

The interest in cross-cultural research on child maltreatment further illustrates the definitional problems that have been reviewed above. The anthropologist Jill Korbin (1981) points out that since there is no universal standard for optimal child rearing, there can be no universal standard for what constitutes child abuse and neglect. Thus, those who seek to develop cross-cultural definitions of abuse and apply them to cross-national studies of the extent, causes and consequences of maltreatment, face the dilemma between choosing a culturally relative standard, in which any behavior can be abusive or nonabusive depending on the cultural context of the act, or an idiosyncratic standard, whereby abusive acts are those behaviors that are at a variance with normal cultural standards for raising children. Finkelhor and Korbin (1988) explain that a definition of child abuse that could be used internationally should accomplish at least two objectives: (1) it should distinguish child abuse clearly from other social, economic and health problems of international concern; and (2) it should be sufficiently flexible to apply to a range of situations in a variety of social and cultural contexts. They note that some of what is talked about as child abuse in Western societies has very little meaning on other societies.

Finkelhor and Korbin propose the following definition of child abuse for cross-cultural research: "Child abuse is the portion of harm to children that results from human action that is proscribed (negatively valued), proximate (the action is close to the actual harm—thus, deforesting land which results in child malnutrition does not fit this definition), and preventable (the action could have been avoided)."

The Extent of Child Abuse and Neglect

Considerable effort has been expended in discussion, debate and research concerning the extent of child abuse and neglect. Part of this effort is aimed at exploding the myth that child abuse is rare. Another goal has been to convince policy makers, opinion leaders and the public that child maltreatment is extensive enough to bid for a place on the agenda of social problems—especially since one part of the definition of a social problem is that a behavior is found harmful to a *significant* number of people (Merton and Nisbet, 1976).

Sources of Data

Data on child abuse and neglect come from three major sources. Each source has certain advantages and specific weaknesses that influence both the nature and generalizability of the findings derived from the research.

Clinical Samples. The most common source of data are clinical studies carried out by psychiatrists, psychologists and counselors. This is primarily due to the fact that these investigators have the most direct access to cases of abuse and neglect. The taboo nature of the topic and the relatively low base rate make access to cases of maltreatment difficult for nonclinicians. The clinical setting provides access to extensive in-depth information about particular cases of abuse and neglect. The pioneer studies of child abuse were almost exclusively based on such clinical samples (see, for example, Gladston, 1965; Kempe et al., 1962; Steele and Pollock, 1968).

Such studies, while important for breaking new ground and rich in qualitative data, cannot be used to generalize information on incidence of the frequency and strength of factors associated with maltreatment. Such samples are never representative, and few investigators gathering data from clinical samples employ comparison groups.

Official Statistics. The establishment of mandatory reporting laws for suspected cases of child abuse and neglect made case-level and aggregate-level data on abuse available to researchers. Each year since 1976 the American Association for Protecting Children (a division of the American Humane Association) collects data from each state on officially reported child abuse and neglect. In addition, the federal government sponsored its own national survey of officially reported child maltreatment in 1979-1980 (Burgdorf, 1980).

Official report data provide information on an extremely large number of cases. But these cases are limited only to those known by service providers. Incidence rates based on these data are likely to be lower than the true rates, and the data are biased in a number of ways (Finkelhor and Hotaling, 1984). A major problem with all official report data is the selective, biased sample of offenders, victims and violent acts that is produced. As with many other types of official records of deviant behavior, the poor are overrepresented in official records of child abuse, as are ethnic and racial minorities (Gelles, 1975; Newberger et al., 1977).

Turbett and O'Toole (1980) conducted an experiment, the results of which demonstrate the biases inherent in official statistics on child abuse. The researchers presented sample medical records to groups of physicians and nurses. The files contained descriptions of injuries suffered by a child. One trial varied the socioeconomic status of the father of the child described in the medical record while holding constant all other variables, including the nature of the physical condition of the child. The second trial varied the race of the father, but held all the other variables constant. Subjects were more likely to define a case as child abuse if the father was described as having a working class occupation. Furthermore, the clinicians stated that the child of the working class father should be reported as a victim of child abuse. Similarly, injuries to the black child elicited greater definitions of abuse and more inclination to report officially than the case of the white child.

Biases in official data also arise in the process of validation of child abuse reports. A comparison of reports of child abuse that were ruled valid or invalid by a child protection agency indicated that the status of the person making the report, not the nature of the reported injury, influenced whether the report would be found valid. If the reporter was a professional, such as a physician, a report was much more likely to be found valid, even controlling for the nature of the injury to the child or the social status of the alleged abuser (Carr, 1979; Eckenrode, et al., 1988).

Social Surveys. The relatively low base rate of child abuse and the sensitive and taboo nature of the topic pose constraints for those who desire to apply survey research methods to studying child maltreatment. A major problem is to locate a sufficient number of individuals who are involved as offenders or victims in incidents of abuse or neglect. Some investigators cope with the problem of the low base rate by employing purposive or nonrepresentative sampling techniques to identify cases. Some investigators use available, large groups of subjects. Murray Straus's first research studies of family violence collected data by distributing questionnaires to undergraduate students enrolled in introductory sociology courses (Straus, 1974). Similarly, David Finkelhor's first research project on sexual victimization of children collected data from undergraduate students (1979).

Self-report surveys of college students or purposive samples provide considerable descriptive data on the extent and nature of violence in families. However, such surveys are still limited by the nonrepresentative nature of the sample. One cannot generalize about the incidence of child abuse, the correlates, causes or consequences from samples of white, middle class college students, or from those individuals who sought help from either social service agencies or the police. In order to develop a generalizable knowledge base, it is necessary to derive data from representative samples of families.

Estimates of the Extent of Child Abuse and Neglect

Clinical Estimates. Clinical studies do not attempt to gather data on the extent of child abuse. However, clinicians, based on their clinical experience, have presented their own estimates of the extent of the abuse of children. Vincent DeFrancis, testifying before the U.S. Senate in 1973, estimated that there were 30,000 to 40,000 truly abused children in the United States. Henry Kempe (1971) set the figure at 60,000, while the physician Vincent Fontana (1973) placed the figure at 1,500,000 children. None of these estimates, however, was based on research or empirical data.

Official Report Data. Data from official statistics yield higher incidence figures than the clinical estimates. Cohen and Sussman (1975) obtained data on officially reported cases of abuse and neglect from the 10 most populated states and projected 40,104 confirmed cases of child abuse in 1973. Nagi (1975) attempted to compensate for the shortcomings of estimates of child abuse based on official report records by surveying a national sample of community agencies and agency personnel. Nagi estimated that there were 167,000 cases of abuse reported annually, while an additional 97,000 cases went unreported. One of the most detailed attempts to record officially reported cases of child abuse is conducted annually by the American Association for the Protection of Children, a division of the American Humane Association. Beginning in 1976 the agency has collected data on officially reported cases of child abuse from child protection agencies nationwide. Data are collected from each of the 50 states and the District of Columbia.

Data are based exclusively on cases that were identified and reported to the state agency designated by each state's child abuse reporting law.

The most recent data available are for 1986 (American Association for Protecting Children, 1987). During 1986, 2,200,000 abuse and neglect reports were received by state agencies.

A second source of data on the national incidence of child abuse is the National Study of the Incidence Severity of Child Maltreatment conducted for the National Center on Child Abuse and Neglect by Westat (Burgdorf, 1980). The survey assessed how many cases of child maltreatment were known to investigatory agencies (including the protective service agencies used in the American Humane Association census) as well as schools, hospitals, the police, and other social agencies.

The accompanying table presents the results of the national incidence survey. A total of 652,000 maltreated children were known by agencies surveyed in the study (Burgdorf, 1980). Stated in terms of incidence rates, it was estimated that 10.5 children per 1,000 are abused and neglected annually; 5.7 children per 1,000 (351,000) are physically abused.

Surveys. Gelles and Straus have conducted two national surveys of physical violence in families (Straus, Gelles and Steinmetz, 1980; Gelles and Straus, 1988). The first survey,

Estimated Number of Recognized In-Scope Children (per 1000 per year)[1]

Form of Maltreatment and Severity of Injury/Impairment	Number In-Scope Children	Incidence Rate[3] (per 1000)
Form of Maltreatment[2]		
Total, all maltreated children	652,000	10.5
Total, all abused children	351,100	5.7
Physical assault	207,600	3.4
Sexual exploitation	44,700	0.7
Emotional abuse	138,400	2.2
Total, all neglected children	329,000	5.3
Physical neglect	108,000	1.7
Educational neglect	181,500	2.9
Emotional neglect	59,400	1.0
Severity of Child's Injury/Impairment		
Fatal	1,000	0.02
Serious	136,900	2.2
Moderate	410,300	6.6
Probable	101,700	1.6

[1] National incidence estimates by major form of maltreatment and by severity of maltreatment-related injury or impairments.

[2] Totals may be lower than sum of categories, since a child may have experienced more than one in-scope category of maltreatment.

[3] Numerator = estimated number of recognized children; denominator = 61,900, the estimated total number (in thousands) of children under 18 in the United States in December 1979.

Source: Reprinted with permission from K. Burgdorf, *Recognition and Reporting of Child Maltreatment: Findings from the National Study of the Incidence and Severity of Child Abuse and Neglect.* Washington, D.C.: National Center on Child Abuse and Neglect, 1980, p. 37.

conducted in 1975, used the Conflict Tactics Scales (Straus, 1979) to measure physical violence in 2,146 households. One part of the study involved measuring violence toward children in the 1,143 homes with children at home between the ages of 3 and 17. (The inclusion criteria of children 3 to 17 years of age was established for the purposes of studying sibling violence.) Nearly 40 parents in 1,000 (3.6%) engaged in one act of abusive violence during the year prior to the survey. Projecting this rate to all children three to 17 years of age who lived at home in 1975 means that 1,400,000 children experience acts of abusive violence each year (Gelles, 1978; Straus, Gelles and Steinmetz, 1980). The detailed breakdown of the data is found in the following table.

FREQUENCY OF PARENTAL VIOLENCE TOWARD CHILDREN
Percentage of Occurrences
in Past Year

Violent Behavior	Once	Twice	More Than Twice	Total	Percentage of Occurrence Ever Reported
Threw something	1.3	1.8	2.3	5.4	9.6
Pushed, grabbed or shoved	4.3	9.0	18.5	31.8	46.4
Slapped or spanked	5.2	9.4	43.6	58.2	71.0
Kicked, bit or hit with fist	0.7	0.8	1.7	3.2	7.7
Hit or tried to hit with something	1.0	2.6	9.8	13.4	20.0
Beat up	0.4	0.3	0.6	1.3	4.2
Threatened with knife or gun	0.1	0.0	0.0	0.1	2.8
Used a knife or gun	0.1	0.0	0.0	0.1	2.9

Source: Gelles (1978).

Because two groups of high risk children, those under three years of age and children of single parents, were excluded from the survey, the study findings likely underestimate the true rate of physical abuse.

Even with the underestimate, the results of the First National Family Violence Survey confirm Burgdorf's (1980) notion that only about one-third of child maltreatment incidents are reported to official agencies.

No national surveys have been conducted that focus on either child neglect or sexual abuse of children, thus there are no comparable incidence data to the data on physical violence collected in the two National Family Violence Surveys.

Estimates of the Changing Rates of Child Abuse
Since the early 1960s, when child abuse became an issue of major professional and public concern, there has been a wide-spread belief that the rates of child abuse and violence toward children have been increasing. This belief has been partially supported by the fact that the number of cases of child abuse that are reported to social service agencies has been rising at a rate of about 10% each year since the mid-seventies (American Association for Protecting Children,

1987). Overall, for all forms of reportable child maltreatment, the American Humane Association study found a 223% increase in child maltreatment reporting from 1976 to 1986, the last year of data that has been analyzed to date (American Association For Protecting Children, 1987). The largest yearly increase was from the first year of the study (1976) to the next—an increase of 24.2%. The actual rate of increase has declined since 1980 and has been somewhat stable for the last few years.

A drawback of the American Humane Association tabulations lies in the state-to-state variation in the method of enumeration. Some states use the family as the unit of analysis. This underrepresents the amount of abuse since there may be more than one maltreated child per family. The second drawback to these data is more obvious. Child abuse reports are not the same as incidents of child abuse. Given that so much attention has been focused on child abuse and neglect in the last two decades, and that there has been a considerable increase in state and local efforts (and funding) to increase reporting, it would be amazing if the number of reports had not increased since 1976. Laws have been revised in each state, intake systems have been redesigned, 24-hour hot lines for reporting are now commonplace, and there have been state and national media campaigns (including television docudramas) that have been designed to spur reporting.

In contrast to the increase in the rate of child neglect and abuse found in the official report data collected by the American Humane Association, the Second National Family Violence Survey found that parent reports of physical child abuse had declined 47% between 1975 and 1985, from 3.6% to 1.9% (see accompanying table).

Has the rate of severe and abusive violence toward children really dropped? There are three logical explanations for the results. First, the change could be the result of parents becoming unwilling to report violence to researchers. Second, the change could be due to some other methodological artifact. Lastly, the findings could reflect an actual change in behavior. It is unlikely that the change is due to methodological differences in the two studies (Gelles, Straus, and Harrop, 1988). It is possible that increased attention to child abuse and neglect has indeed made people less willing to report abuse to interviewers. The most likely explanation, however, is that the rate of violence and abuse did in fact decline.

There have been significant changes in family organization since 1975. The average age when having a first child has increased, the number of children per family has decreased, and the number of unwanted children has declined. Parents in 1985 are among the first generation to be able to choose a full range of planned parenthood options (including abortion) to plan family size. All these factors are related to lower rates of violence and abuse.

The economic climate of the country is better in 1985 than in 1975 (at least for the population that was examined—intact families). The rate of unemployment and inflation is down compared to 10 years ago. The one-year referent period that we used for the survey (1985) coincided with one of the more prosperous economic periods in the past decade. Thus, the lower level of economic stress that families experienced in 1985 may explain the decline in severe violence.

Finally, new and innovative prevention and treatment programs have been implemented to deal with the problem of child maltreatment. States have enacted reporting laws for abuse and neglect, and public and private social services have been developed to try to treat and prevent abuse. While there have been few rigorous evaluations of the effectiveness of these programs, they do at the very least fill the gaps in protective services that existed prior to the 1970s.

PARENT-TO-CHILD
A COMPARISON OF RATES

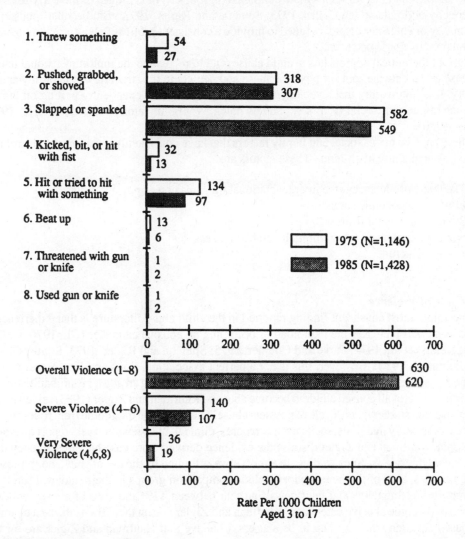

1. Threw something   54 / 27
2. Pushed, grabbed, or shoved   318 / 307
3. Slapped or spanked   582 / 549
4. Kicked, bit, or hit with fist   32 / 13
5. Hit or tried to hit with something   134 / 97
6. Beat up   13 / 6
7. Threatened with gun or knife   1 / 2
8. Used gun or knife   1 / 2

1975 (N=1,146)
1985 (N=1,428)

Overall Violence (1–8)   630 / 620
Severe Violence (4–6)   140 / 107
Very Severe Violence (4,6,8)   36 / 19

Rate Per 1000 Children
Aged 3 to 17

Source: Gelles and Straus, 1988.

Patterns and Causes of Child Abuse

Factors Associated With Child Abuse

The first research articles on child abuse and neglect characterized offenders as suffering from various forms of psychopathology (see, for example, Bennie and Sclare, 1969; Gladston, 1965; Steele and Pollock, 1974). Thus, the initial approach to explaining and understanding maltreatment was to identify the personality and character disorders that were thought to be associated with abusers.

Although numerous articles attempted to present the psychological profiles of abusers, the research efforts were limited by methodological design problems, including small, nonrepresentative samples and lack of appropriate comparison groups. (For critiques of the early research projects on child abuse see Gelles, 1973; Spinetta and Rigler, 1973.) Studies that focused on personality or character disorders failed to provide a consistent profile of abusers and thus failed to explain why abuse occurred.

Current theoretical approaches to child abuse tend to recognize the multidimensional nature of abuse and locate the roots of physical abuse and neglect in the structure of the family and/or society. It is noteworthy that a sociologist and a psychiatrist, independently writing on family violence, agree that social factors explain as much as 90% of family violence (Steele, 1978; Straus, 1980).

There are five major social and family factors that have consistently been found to be related to the physical abuse of children. These factors are:

1. The cycle of violence—the intergenerational transmission of physical abuse
2. Low socioeconomic status
3. Social and structural stress
4. Social isolation and low community embeddedness
5. Family structure

The Cycle of Violence

The single most consistent finding reported in the child abuse literature is that experiencing abuse as a child increases the likelihood of becoming an abusive caretaker (Gil, 1970; Gelles, 1973; Kempe et al., 1972; Parke and Collmer, 1975; Spinetta and Rigler, 1973; Straus, Gelles, and Steinmetz, 1980). However, this is not a perfect association. Potts and Herzberger (1979) point out that the relationship between being abused and becoming an abuser is probabilistic, not deterministic. Not all abused children become abusers. Kaufman and Zigler (1985) reviewed the major research studies on the cycle of physical abuse. They note that data come from four primary sources: case study materials, social agency records, clinical interviews and self-report questionnaire data. Kaufman and Zigler dismiss the evidence derived from case histories, agency data and clinical interviews. Such studies are almost always limited by the use of small, nonrepresentative samples. Few of the investigators include comparison groups in their studies. Data from self-report questionnaires and interviews find that between 17% and 70% of abused children grow up to become abusive caretakers. Kaufman and Zigler reason that 30% is the best estimate of abused children who grow up to be abusers. I believe that Kaufman and Zigler are far too quick to abandon the cycle of violence hypothesis. A rate of 30% abusive behavior is far greater than the rate of less than 4% of abusive behavior found among the general population (Burgdorf, 1980; Straus, Gelles, and Steinmetz, 1980). Exposure to violence does appear to be a significant factor related to the likelihood of later abusive behavior, even if less than half of abused children grow up to become abusers.

Kaufman and Zigler suggest that the most appropriate question to ask is not, "Do abused children grow up to be abusers?" But rather, "Under what conditions do abused children grow up to be abusive?"

Egeland, Jacobvitz and Papatola (1987) have followed 267 high-risk mothers from the last three months of their pregnancies to the time when their children were in kindergarten. Seventy percent of the mothers who were seriously abused were abusive to their children. Those mothers who were seriously abused but who did not become abusive shared a number of characteristics, including having at least one parent or foster parent who provided love and support when they were children. As adults, these mothers had husbands who provided a supportive home environment and a stable source of income. Hunter and Kilstrom (1979) report that parents who broke the cycle of abuse had more extensive social supports, fewer ambivalent feelings about their pregnancies, and healthier babies. The nonabusive, abused parents displayed more open anger about their abusive experiences and were able to describe these experiences freely. Typically, they were abused by only one parent while the other parent provided support.

Both studies, which have examined the conditions under which violence and abuse is repeated, point to the fact that the link can be broken if present support—both psychological and social—is available.

Low Socioeconomic Status

The first researchers who studied child abuse noted that they thought social, economic and demographic factors were irrelevant to the actual act of abuse (see, for example, Steele and Pollock, 1974). Indeed, child abuse may be found among all socioeconomic groups. Yet, a disproportionate number of cases of abuse come from low-income families (Elmer, 1967; Gil, 1970; Gelles, 1973; Maden and Wrench, 1977; Parke and Collmer, 1975; Pelton, 1978; Straus, Gelles, and Steinmetz, 1980).

There is a need for caution in interpreting data on the relationship between child abuse and social class. As we noted earlier, that caution stems from the fact that lower-class families are much more vulnerable to being publicly recorded for abusive behavior.

Data collected directly by questionnaire or interview are less subject to the biases of official report data, and these data do confirm the higher rates of abuse among the lower class. This difference between social classes, however, is not nearly as great as it would seem from the data collected from official agency or case study sources.

Social Stress

Researchers agree that the mechanism through which low socioeconomic status works to bring about child abuse is social stress. Abusive and neglectful families are reported as experiencing more stressful life events than non-maltreating families (Elmer, 1967; Gil, 1970; Gelles, 1973; Parke and Collmer, 1975; Straus, Gelles and Steinmetz, 1980).

One of the more significant social stressors related to abuse and neglect is unemployment. Among families in which the father is unemployed or employed part-time, the risk of abuse is higher than in other households, where the father has full-time work (Galdston, 1965; Gil, 1970; Straus, Gelles, and Steinmetz, 1980).

Poor housing conditions and larger than average family size are also risk factors for maltreatment (Gil, 1970; Johnson and Morse, 1968; Straus, Gelles, and Steinmetz, 1980). Other stressful life conditions found to be related to abuse include a new baby present in the home, presence of a handicapped person in the home, illness, death of a family member, and child care problems.

Stress produced by child-related factors can also lead to abuse. Low birthweight babies, premature children and handicapped, retarded or developmentally disabled children are at higher risk for abuse than children without these conditions (Elmer, 1967; Friedrich and Boriskin, 1967; Gil, 1970; Newberger et al., 1977; Parke and Collmer, 1975).

Social Isolation and Low Community Embeddedness

Parents who abuse their children tend to be socially isolated from both formal and informal social networks (Elmer, 1967; Garbarino and Gilliam, 1980). Smith (1975) found that abusive mothers have fewer contacts with their parents, relatives, neighbors or friends, and engage in fewer social or recreational activities.

The lack of formal or informal social networks deprives abusive parents of support systems that would aid them in dealing with social or family stress. Moreover, the lack of community contacts makes these families less likely to change their behavior to conform with community values and standards (Steinmetz, 1978). Thus, they are particularly vulnerable to violent responses to stress while at the same time not perceiving their behavior as deviant.

Family Structure

Certain family structures are common among abusive and neglectful families. There is a general belief that single parents are at higher risk to abuse their children. Unfortunately, it is difficult to separate the effects of youth and poverty from the impact of the single parent family structure—many single parent homes are those of young mothers who live in poverty.

Within intact homes, inequality is a major structural feature found related to the use of abusive violence toward children. Straus and his colleagues (1980) found that the rate of severe violence toward children was highest in homes where there was little shared decision-making. Those homes in which either the husband or wife dominated the decision-making and where little family equality existed were among the most violent.

Explaining the Abuse of Children

The study of child abuse abounds with simplistic models. The earliest research advanced a psychopathological model: Mental illness caused people to abuse their children. Other intra-individual models proposed that abuse was caused by alcohol and/or drugs.

The major theoretical approaches to child abuse have been reviewed extensively elsewhere (Gelles, 1980; Gelles and Straus, 1979). Here I review some of the more complex theories that have been applied to explaining the abuse of children. These theories include an economic model, a sociocultural explanation, an ecological model and an exchange theory approach.

An Economic Model

The economic or social-structural model explains that violence and abuse arise out of socially structured stress. Stress, such as low income, unemployment and illness, is unevenly distributed in the social structure. When violence is the accepted response or adaptation to stress, stress leads to violence and abuse (Coser, 1967).

A Sociocultural Explanation

Students of violence have explained the occurrence of family violence, including child abuse, by drawing on sociocultural attitudes and norms concerning violent behavior. Societies, cultures, and subcultures that approve the use of violence are thought to have the highest rates of domestic violence and abuse of children (Straus et al., 1980).

An Ecological Model

Garbarino (1977) has proposed an ecological model of child maltreatment. The model rests on three levels of analysis: the relationship between organism and environment, the interacting and overlapping system in which human development occurs, and environmental quality.

Garbarino proposes that maltreatment arises out of a mismatch between parent/child/family and neighborhood and community.

Exchange Theory

Exchange theory (Gelles, 1983) proposes that family violence and child abuse are governed by the principle of costs and rewards. Abuse is used when the rewards are higher than the costs. The private nature of the family, the reluctance of social institutions and agencies to intervene—in spite of mandatory child abuse reporting laws—and the low risk of other interventions reduce the costs of abuse and violence. The cultural approval of violence as both expressive and, in the case of disciplining children, instrumental behavior raises the potential rewards for violence.

Summary

The comparative recency of child abuse and neglect as an area of study and the fact that the first decade of research was dominated by the psychopathology model, has resulted in a limited level of theoretical development in this field. Yet, despite the rather primitive level of theory building and theory testing, one conclusion is inescapable. Researchers have found that no one factor can explain the presence or absence of child abuse. Characteristics of the child, parent, family, social situation and community all have a relation to which children are abused and under what conditions, and individual caretakers and community factors are moderated and influenced by family structure and family situations. Although there are indeed multiple factors related to the abuse of children, all operate through the structure and function of the family group.

The Consequences of Maltreatment

While much of the research, and most of the public attention, has focused on the question of whether or not abuse experienced as a child leads to violent behavior later in life, less attention has been given to the more subtle developmental consequences of violence. Victims of child maltreatment are thought of as innocent and defenseless. Those who are harmed by the abuse do not remain innocent and defenseless for long. The image of the cute and cuddly battered baby is a myth. Therapists and foster parents have found these children to suffer from numerous deficits, which often make them extremely difficult children to raise and nurture.

Our knowledge about the long-term effects of abuse during the early years of life is quite limited. In almost no case has an investigator followed abused infants and children from early childhood through adolescence and into adult life. Most of what we know comes from studies that obtain retrospective histories from older children, teenagers and adults who speak of past abuse and present troubles.

Despite the methodological limitations, a number of investigators have collected data that suggest that growing up in a violent home compromises the intellectual development of abused children. Children who have experienced violence and neglect are reported to have achieved lower scores on formal intelligence tests than peers from nonabusive homes. In addition, other researchers have found that abused and maltreated children exhibit learning problems. There is some evidence that maltreatment experiences translate into poorer school performance and lower grades (Baher et al., 1976; Elmer and Gregg, 1967; Elmer, 1967; Martin, 1972; Martin et al., 1974; Morse et al., 1970; Sandgrund et al., 1975). Research conducted by Roy and Ellen Herrenkohl (1984) found that children from families in which a child welfare agency had found indications of physical abuse were more likely to have experienced academic failure, attended special classes, and have learning disabilities.

Researchers and clinicians list several characteristics that have been found among abused children, including such symptoms as bed wetting, poor self concept, a tendency to withdraw and become isolated, and a pattern of hyperactivity and tantrums (Martin et al., 1974). E. Milling Kinard (1979) reviewed much of the literature on the psychological consequences of abuse and found other traits, such as an inability to trust others, difficulties relating to both peers and adults, and a generalized unhappiness. The psychiatrist Brandt Steele (1978) notes that many abused children see themselves as ugly, stupid, inept, clumsy or somehow defective.

Growing up in an abusive home may dramatically compromise the developmental and personal competence of children. Many maltreated children enter adolescence with severe personal deficits. It should be no great surprise that many of these children are prone to juvenile delinquency.

A variety of data point to the fact that abused children, especially boys, have a much greater chance of becoming involved in juvenile crime than children from nonabusive homes (Alfaro, 1977; Bolton et al., 1977; Smith et al., 1980). A number of social scientists point to the fact that what we call juvenile delinquency, including acts such as running away, is a logical form of expression for the maltreated child who has a damaged self-concept and a persistent need to belong to something or do something that will improve the shattered ego. Running away serves the important function of fleeing maltreatment, even though technically it is a status offense and a delinquent act. Delinquent groups and gangs can provide approval. Delinquent and antisocial acts are a form of direct and indirect revenge against maltreating caretakers or a society that is powerless to protect the injured child.

One investigation in New York State (Alfaro, 1977) tracks children who had contact with official agencies for child maltreatment in the 1950s. The investigators examined records of juvenile justice agencies to see if the maltreated children had later contact for delinquency. A second group of juveniles who had contact for delinquency in 1970 were traced backwards in time to determine if they had prior contact for child maltreatment. Overall, the records of more than 4,000 children were examined, tracked and traced. The investigators found that one in five children with contact for maltreatment had later reported instances of delinquency. Similarly, one in five delinquents had prior contact for maltreatment. More importantly, the kind of maltreatment related to the form of delinquency. If the maltreatment was physical abuse, the delinquency tended toward violent crime rather than status offenses, such as running away or truancy.

Data from the Second National Family Violence Survey (Gelles and Straus, 1988) found that, across the board, children who experience severe violence are more likely to have personal troubles (temper tantrums, trouble making friends); school problems (failing grades, discipline problems); and aggressive and violent flareups with family members and people outside the home. These children are three to four times more likely than children from nonviolent homes to engage in illegal acts—vandalism, stealing, drinking and taking drugs—and to be arrested.

Future Trends

The study of child abuse and neglect is relatively new. Much has been accomplished in the last 25 years, and yet it is clear that those who study, treat and attempt to prevent child maltreatment are still struggling with definitional issues, methodological constraints and problems, and assessing which prevention and treatment programs are the most effective in reducing the risk of abuse and neglect. Few theories of child maltreatment have actually been tested using appropriate methods and samples. Even fewer prevention and treatment programs have been properly assessed.

The study of child maltreatment is an interdisciplinary effort that involves psychologists, sociologists, anthropologists, physicians and social workers. In the future we should expect to see continued efforts to study child maltreatment across subcultures and cultural groups. Such research studies will help illuminate the societal and structural forces that lead to the abuse of children. Additional research is needed on the factors related to abuse and neglect, but more importantly, we need to examine the social and psychological processes that lead to the maltreatment of children. Lastly, evaluation research on prevention and treatment strategies is needed.

Richard J. Gelles
University of Rhode Island

A

AAPC *See* AMERICAN ASSOCIATION FOR PROTECTING CHILDREN.

abandonment Legally, abandoned children must generally be considered victims of actual parental intent to abandon. In the United States, parents who abandon the home can, in some cases, be charged with neglect. Each state has its own, different statute with regard to the legal definition of abandonment; these statutes apply not only to infants and small children but to adolescents as well. There are legal precedents for abandonment charges to be brought against parents who lock their teenage children out of the house.

abdominal injuries Abdominal trauma is a common but often overlooked result of physical abuse. Such trauma includes damage to kidneys, blood vessels, stomach, duodenum, small bowel, colon, pancreas, liver or spleen. Frequently more than one organ is affected. Because there are few outward signs of abdominal injuries, they may go untreated for extended periods of time, subjecting the child to a great deal of pain and sometimes resulting in death.

Injuries to the abdomen are usually caused by one of three forces: compression, crushing or acceleration. A blow to the midsection can compress organs filled with fluid or gas, causing them to rupture. Compression injuries most often affect the stomach and colon. Crushing of internal organs can occur when a blow to the front of the abdomen presses the organ against a hard structure such as the spinal column or rib cage. Rupture of the kidneys, pancreas, spleen or liver may result from such crushing. Rapid acceleration, such as when a child is thrown or struck so forcefully that he or she is knocked down, can tear connective tissue, resulting in hemorrage or perforation of the small intestines.

A thorough screening for abdominal trauma is recommended when children show evidence of having been physically abused or when abuse is suspected. (*See also* GASTROINTESTINAL INJURIES.)

Norman S. Ellerstein, *Child Abuse and Neglect: A Medical Reference* (New York: John Wiley and Sons, 1981).
Alejandro Rodriguez, *Handbook of Child Abuse and Neglect* (Flushing, N.Y.: Medical Examination Publishing Co., 1977).

abduction *See* CHILD STEALING.

abuse, adolescent *See* ADOLESCENT ABUSE.

abuse, cycle of *See* INTERGENERATIONAL CYCLE OF ABUSE.

abuse, drug *See* SUBSTANCE ABUSE.

abuse, emotional *See* PSYCHOLOGICAL MALTREATMENT.

abuse, incidence of *See* INCIDENCE OF CHILD ABUSE.

abuse, indicators *See* INDICATORS OF CHILD ABUSE AND NEGLECT.

abuse, institutional *See* INSTITUTIONAL ABUSE AND NEGLECT.

abuse, neurological manifestations *See* NEUROLOGICAL MANIFESTATIONS OF ABUSE AND NEGLECT.

abuse, passive *See* PASSIVE ABUSER.

abuse, physical *See* PHYSICAL ABUSE.

abuse, prediction of *See* PREDICTION OF ABUSE AND NEGLECT.

abuse, psychological *See* PSYCHOLOGICAL MALTREATMENT.

abuse, psychopathological   *See* PSYCHOPATHOLOGY.

abuse, sexual   *See* SEXUAL ABUSE.

abuse, sibling   *See* SIBLING ABUSE.

abuse, situational   *See* SITUATIONAL ABUSE AND NEGLECT.

abuse, social   *See* SOCIAL ABUSE.

abuse, spouse   *See* SPOUSE ABUSE.

abuse, substance   *See* SUBSTANCE ABUSE.

abuse, verbal   *See* VERBAL ABUSE.

abused children, placement   *S e e* PLACE-MENT OF ABUSED CHILDREN.

abusive parents   *See* CHARACTERISTICS OF ABUSING AND NEGLECTFUL PARENTS.

acting-out   The term acting-out is often used to refer to aggressive or socially undesirable behavior displayed by children or adults. Some mental health professionals see such behavior as an outward manifestation of internal (intrapsychic) conflict. According to psychodynamic theory, individuals may act out feelings that, because of their highly sensitive emotional content, are difficult to discuss directly. In some cases these feelings may be unconscious.

Psychodynamic theorists and practitioners often attribute abusive behavior of parents to the expression of repressed or unconscious feelings. Abusive behavior directed toward a child may be traced to internal conflicts that have little direct connection with the child. Based on this theoretical model, treatment of abusers focuses on helping the patient to become aware of internal conflicts and to address these problems in a more effective and socially acceptable manner.

Acting-out may partially explain the behavior of abusers. When displayed by a child, however, it may help to identify him or her as a possible victim of abuse. Though antisocial behavior is a feature of normal child development some behaviors are associated with maltreatment.

Sexually abused children may display sexual knowledge and aggressiveness beyond that expected for their age. Conversely, some child victims may display fear and/or aggression toward all males. Behaviors that have no apparent rational basis may lead the trained child protection worker to question the child further.

In adolescents, running away from home and sexual promiscuity are often connected to abuse. Studies of runaways show a high incidence of incest and other forms of abuse.

Physically abused children sometimes display extreme aggression toward other children. This behavior may be seen as an attempt by the child to gain control over his or her life. A child, defenseless against physical attacks by an adult, may become abusive toward other children as a way of acting-out aggressive feelings that cannot be expressed safely in the presence of the abuser.

Most child development experts agree that a certain amount of acting-out is to be expected of children. These experts caution, however, that such behavior should be examined closely when it is persistent and extreme.

addiction, infantile   Infants born to drug-addicted mothers are at great risk of being addicted at birth. Approximately one-half of all infants born to heroin-addicted mothers experience moderate to severe withdrawal symptoms. Eighty-five percent of newborns whose mothers are addicted to methadone show moderate or severe symptoms. Withdrawal symptoms usually appear during the first 24 hours following birth. Severity of symptoms is proportional to the quantity of any drug used on a daily basis by the mother. Symptoms frequently observed in infants experiencing narcotic withdrawal are listed in the following table.

While most acute symptoms of infantile addiction disappear within 10 days of birth, follow-up studies have shown that these infants continue to appear irritable, restless and unresponsive for up to a year. They need frequent feeding, tend to regurgitate often and require almost constant attention. These characteristics increase the likelihood that the infant will be physically abused by the primary caretaker. (*See* "AT RISK" CHILDREN.)

Table 1

Neonatal Withdrawal Symptoms

Tremors

Irritability

Tachypnea (unusually rapid respiration)

Muscular rigidity

Diarrhea

Watery stools

Vomiting

Shrill crying

Excessive perspiration

Sneezing

Yawning

Fever

Myoclonic jerks (erratic muscular spasms)

Convulsions

addiction, maternal *See* MATERNAL DRUG DEPENDENCE.

adjudicatory hearing Once charges of abuse or neglect have been filed, a court hearing is held to determine the extent to which these charges are supported by admissible evidence. If insufficient evidence is presented, a judge may decide not to proceed with a trial. A trial may be scheduled if, in the judge's opinion, there is sufficient evidence to warrant further consideration of the charges.

An adjudicatory hearing may also be called a "fact-finding" hearing. (*See also* EVIDENCE.)

adolescent abuse Abuse of adolescents has attracted less public attention than maltreatment of children. Many assume that the age of the child is relatively unimportant or, since adolescents are better able to defend themselves, that adolescent abuse is less serious.

Available data indicate that adolescent abuse is, in many ways, significantly different from abuse of children under the age of 12. Psychological and sexual abuse levels are higher among adolescents. Adolescents receive less serious injuries as a result of abuse, reflecting both fewer physical assaults and a greater ability to protect themselves.

Boys are at greatest risk of abuse during early childhood, becoming less susceptible as they grow older. Conversely, girls are more likely to be abused as they grow older.

Some abuse of adolescents is a continuation of an abusive pattern that began in early childhood. In other cases abuse of adolescents is a new phenomenon brought on by a complex set of factors. Children may outgrow methods of parental control that rely heavily on use of physical force, indulgence or intrusion. Abusive families may be less able to adapt to these changes, thereby increasing the level of conflict.

Adolescents at high risk of abuse often have more poorly developed social skills and display more negative behavior than their peers. The combination of an aggressive or defiant adolescent with a harsh or inappropriate parenting style greatly increases the likelihood of abuse.

High-risk families are more likely to include stepparents. A national survey conducted in the United States in 1981 revealed that 40% of maltreated adolescents lived with a stepparent. The nationwide average of children living with stepparents is 12% to 15%.

Overall, the rate of abuse is higher for adolescents than for younger children. Maltreatment of younger children appears to be more strongly associated with a low family income. Abuse of adolescents is more evenly distributed among families at all income levels.

Abuse is also connected to other problems of adolescence. A disproportionate number of adolescents who run away from home are victims of abuse. Studies show that abused adolescents tend to run farther from home and stay away longer than those with no history of maltreatment. Further, the act of running away greatly increases the likelihood of sexual abuse for both boys and girls. Runaways, particularly those who have been sexually abused, often fall into prostitution as a means of supporting themselves. One study found that 60% of runaways involved in prostitution had been sexually abused at home. Another study of adolescents housed in a Canadian runaway shelter found that 38% of boys and 73% of girls had been sexually molested.

Not all adolescent runaways leave home by choice. Statistics show that 10% to 25% of adolescents housed in runaway programs had been put out of their homes by their parents. These adolescents are considered victims of parental neglect, just as infants who are abandoned by their parents. (*See also* ABANDONMENT.)

James Garbarino, C. Shellenbach, J. Sebes and Associates, *Troubled Youth, Troubled Families* (Hawthorne, N.Y.: Aldine, 1986).

adolescent perpetrator network   This multidisciplinary group, based at the Kempe National Center at the University of Colorado School of Medicine (*See* APPENDIX 1 for complete listing), was conceived as a way of providing support for professionals working with adolescent offenders. Currently, the Network serves over 300 individuals who work specifically with adolescent perpetrators of SEXUAL ABUSE. Information about Network services can be found in a newsletter, *Interchange*. An annotated bibliography prepared by the Network contains material on adolescent sex offenders and their treatment. (*See*

also ADOLESCENT PERPETRATORS OF SEXUAL ABUSE.)

adolescent perpetrators of sexual abuse
The extent of SEXUAL ABUSE perpetrated by adolescents is unknown; however, many who work with adult sex offenders believe it to be a serious problem. Adolescent perpetrators may engage in sexually abusive or exploitative behavior toward dates or friends or while employed as babysitters. Like adult child molesters, adolescent offenders are predominantly male and usually known to their victims.

The amount of sibling-to-sibling abuse is thought to be greatly underreported. Parents may view it as harmless sexual play or may be embarrassed to talk about it with others outside the family. In some cases, sexual abuse by a sibling can have more harmful effects on the victim than an incident involving an extrafamilial offender, especially if allowed to continue over an extended period of time. Sexual abuse by a sibling often involves a high degree of coercion. As with other forms of INCEST this type of exploitation may make it difficult for the victim to form trusting relationships and may result in marital difficulty and a sexual dysfunction later in life.

Sexual abuse by adolescents is often passed off as experimentation or diagnosed as an adolescent adjustment reaction. Many professionals who work with adolescents are reluctant to label them as sex offenders. Adolescents who sexually molest children or other adolescents are seldom brought to court.

Recent evidence indicates that many incarcerated adult sex offenders began their sexually abusive behavior as adolescents. Some professionals who work with sex offenders believe that the seriousness of adolescent sexual assault has been minimized. Some argue that the failure of court- and youth-serving institutions to intervene effectively in such behavior has prevented young offenders from receiving treatment at a critical period. Repeat adult offenders have proven to be especially resistant to treatment. Treatment providers believe that these adult offenders may have been more amenable to intervention at an earlier age.

Another problem associated with the failure to recognize the seriousness of sexual abuse perpetrated by adolescents is that offenses often go undocumented. In the absence of a record of past assaults each offense may be treated as an isolated incident. Young offenders can sometimes engage in a number of assaults before being charged with a criminal offense.

A large number of adolescent sexual offenders are themselves victims of sexual abuse. This fact suggests that, like PHYSICAL ABUSE, there may be a cyclical pattern to sexual abuse. Most psychotherapists believe early intervention with victims as well as offenders is an effective way to break the CYCLE OF ABUSE.

Though relatively little research has been done on the problem of adolescent sex offenders, most treatment providers agree that it is important for them to be held accountable for their behavior. Further, most providers believe treatment should be specific to the problem and should combine individual treatment with peer group and family counseling. Court involvement can be helpful in making sure offenders follow through with treatment recommendations.

Gail Ryan, "Annotated Bibliography: Adolescent Perpetrators of Sexual Molestation of Children," *Child Abuse and Neglect* (10:1986, pp. 125-131).

Adoption Assistance and Child Welfare Reform Act of 1980 (P.L. 96-272)

Concerned about large numbers of children living in foster care, the United States Congress amended the Social Security Act to include specific guidelines for out-of-home placement and to remove barriers to adoption. Congress hoped to encourage adoption of those children in foster care who, due to physical or mental disability or other factors, are least likely to be adopted. The act made special provisions for medical assistance and other payments to families who adopt such children.

The practices of protective service workers were affected significantly by requirements in the act relating to conditions under which a child could be placed in FOSTER CARE, the nature of the placement, and review of foster placement cases. The new law required that preventive services such as HOMEMAKER SERVICES, CRISIS INTERVENTION, counseling, day care and other supports be made available to families before a child is voluntarily or involuntarily removed from home. Except for EMERGENCIES, a child could not be involuntarily removed from home unless a judge determined that: (1) the child is in substantial and immediate danger, which could not be addressed by preventive services; (2) preventive services were available and had either been refused or had failed to improve the situation; or (3) the child was guilty of a delinquent offense.

When children are placed in foster care the law requires that they be placed in the "least restrictive setting," which, taking their special needs into consideration, approximates a family setting as closely as possible. Children must be placed with a relative when appropriate. Placements should be within reasonable proximity to the original home. States are also required to offer family reunification services designed to "ensure the swiftest possible return of the child to his home."

The act allows any party to a foster placement to request and receive a review of the placement decision by an impartial hearing officer. Each child must have a case plan outlining services to be provided to the child and family, a description of the foster placement, how the state plans to facilitate the child's return home or permanent placement, and other relevant information. Case plans must be reviewed at least once every six months.

Adults Molested As Children United (AMACU)   Self-help group for adults who were sexually abused as children. Affiliated with PARENTS UNITED. For more information, *see* APPENDIX 1.

advisement   After arguments of both sides are presented in a court of law the judge or jury takes evidence under advisement. Advisement takes place before rendering of an opinion and includes consideration of evidence presented and consultation among jurors.

advocacy   For most children, a parent acts as an advocate. Various needs, including physical, psychological, educational and emotional, are met by the parent or parents so that children are nurtured and protected until they are able to care for themselves. For children who are the victims of neglect or abuse, however, advocacy extends to institutions, groups and individuals in society who are best able to provide for children whose needs are not met by their parent(s).

In the United States at different times a variety of efforts have constituted child advocacy. Among these, the report in 1969 from the Joint Commission on the Mental Health of Children recommended that a child advocacy system be put in place in order to guarantee that children be represented adequately no matter what their family situations. Some decades earlier, in 1909, as a result of the first WHITE HOUSE CONFERENCE ON CHILDREN, the CHILDREN'S BUREAU was established by the federal government to meet this goal of advocacy for children.

According to some experts, there are certain factors that characterize effective child advocacy. These include: (1) the making of connections among the different units (family, society etc.) of a child's life, (2) addressing child development; (3) conflict resolution; (4) fact-finding; (5) interdisciplinary teamwork; and (6) legal protection for CHILDREN'S RIGHTS. Ideally, combinations of all these fac-

tors exist when a group or individual works on behalf of the needs of children.

In legal proceedings where a child's welfare is concerned, an advocate is often appointed by the court. Recognizing that the child's interests may differ from those of the parents and the state, the court seeks to have the child represented by a competent adult who functions independently of other parties to the case. This advocate may represent the child in other proceedings as well (i.e., case conferences, administrative hearings etc.). (*See also* GUARDIAN AD LITEM, COURT APPOINTED SPECIAL ADVOCATE [CASA].)

affidavit   In legal proceedings, a written, sworn statement known as an affidavit is sometimes introduced as evidence. The document must bear the seal of a notary public who has administered a legal oath to the signer. False statements contained in an affidavit are subject to penalties for perjury. Affidavits are frequently used in juvenile court hearings.

Africa   Experts generally agree that various forms of child abuse, neglect and maltreatment are widespread in many African nations. However, researchers, cognizant of the cross-cultural aspect of their work, use carefully defined criteria when gathering data on these subjects. The size of the African continent (the world's second-largest land area) and the diversity of the African population (more than 800 groups divided according to custom and language) make most observations general at best. There have been very few studies of child care practices among African peoples so that definitions of abuse, neglect or maltreatment may be limited to data available on small groups or individual countries or cultures.

Most experts concur that internationally applicable standards used to define child abuse, neglect or maltreatment should include indictments of practices that result in serious physical harm, whether or not the practices are part of locally accepted norms. Actions leading to developmental impairment or death are often included in discussions of African child abuse, neglect or maltreatment. Such cultural-ly acceptable practices as, for example, scarification or genital mutilation, would fall under the heading of abusive treatment in Western nations and so are included in studies of its incidence in Africa. In 26 African countries, CLITORIDECTOMY is a common practice involving girls who are generally be-tween ages three and eight years but it some-times involves infants only several days old.

Some African nations and some tribal groups identify certain behaviors as abuse, neglect or maltreatment according to the standards of their culture. These behaviors might include excessive disciplinary actions taken by an angry parent toward a child, or a child-slavery incident that results in govern-ment intervention. However, other practices, such as child marriage, are considered part of the socialization process and are culturally acceptable.

Political violence in some areas of Africa results in abusive treatment of children. Numerous reports of injury, death and im-prisonment of minors in South Africa reflect the sweeping nature of criminal legislation in that nation. In 1986, a U.S.- based legal group reported to the *New York Times* that, in one year alone, over 200 South African children had been injured by police actions in which "tear gas, birdshot, rubber bullets . . . and even live ammunition" were used. It was also reported that children as young as seven years had been arrested and detained. (*See also* CHILDREN'S RIGHTS, DISCIPLINE, INITIATION RITES, SLAVERY.)

Jill E. Korbin, *Child Abuse and Neglect: Cross-Cultural Perspectives* (Berkeley: University of California Press, 1981).

Defense for Children International–USA Collec-tive, *The Children's Clarion, Database on the Rights of the Child, 1987* (Brooklyn, N.Y.: DCI–USA, 1987), Record No. 736.

aggressor, identification with   *See* IDEN-TIFICATION WITH THE AGGRESSOR.

aid, categorical   *See* CATEGORICAL AID.

alcoholism   *See* SUBSTANCE ABUSE.

allegation   Legal proceedings related to child abuse or neglect are initiated by state-ments, called allegations, of what a particular party seeks to prove. These allegations are usually contained in a petition that outlines specific charges of maltreatment against the defendant. Both parties may introduce evidence to support or disprove allegations.

Alopecia, traumatic   Alopecia refers to hair loss in both children and adults, usually as a result of disease. Traumatic alopecia is a term used to describe hair lost as a result of pulling. While traumatic alopecia may occur by accident as well as by deliberate abuse, it is a symptom that generally calls for further investigation. Close examination by a trained physician can generally determine the cause of hair loss.

American Association for Protecting Children (AAPC)   A division of the AMERICAN HUMANE ASSOCIATION, which was founded in 1877, the AAPC provides training, evaluation and assistance to community and state agencies in the area of child maltreat-ment. The AAPC publishes materials detail-ing various aspects of child protection, including *Protecting Children*, a quarterly newsletter. The AAPC acts as an advocate for child protection legislation and maintains a data base of reports on abuse and neglect. For more information, *see* APPENDIX 1.

American Humane Association   T h i s group was founded in 1877 as the first national organization of locally based societies for the prevention of cruelty to children. Today, the society maintains two divisions: one promotes humane treatment of animals; the other is known as the AMERICAN ASSOCIATION FOR PROTECTING CHILDREN (formerly the Children's Division). For more information, *see* APPENDIX 1.

anatomically correct dolls   *See* NATURAL DOLLS.

apathy-futility syndrome   Based on studies of families in southern Appalachia and Philadelphia, Norman Polansky, a professor of social work at the University of Georgia, developed a diagnostic description of mothers who tended to be most neglectful. These mothers appeared passive, withdrawn and lacking in expression. In his description of the apathy-futility syndrome, Polansky de-emphasizes the role of poverty, pointing to the majority of poor families in which there is no abuse or neglect. Extreme apathy exhibited by some mothers is compared to the sense of futility displayed by individuals suffering from characterological disorders or schizophrenia.

Major features of the apathy-futility syndrome include the following traits:

- a feeling that nothing is worth doing (futility)
- emotional numbness similar to deep psychological depression
- development of superficial, clinging interpersonal relationships, often accompanied by intense loneliness
- unreasonable fear of failure resulting in an unwillingness to attempt new tasks and leading to a lack of competence in many tasks of daily living
- passive-aggressive expression of anger
- stubborn negativism
- limited verbal communication, making it difficult to engage in meaningful dialogue and limiting problem-solving capability
- an uncanny skill in bringing to consciousness the same feelings of futility in others— a trait interpreted as a defense against change, which appears very threatening to the parent

Though mothers suffering from the apathy-futility syndrome are severely and chronically neglectful of their children, they are unlikely to abandon them outright. Little information is available concerning the father/husband's role in the family. They are described as typically "the first or second man who showed interest in [the mother] and . . . ill equipped in education and in vocational skills."

Often limited in intellectual ability, these mothers tend to be lacking in basic knowledge of child-rearing. Polansky cites the mother's own deprived childhood as evidence for an INTERGENERATIONAL CYCLE OF ABUSE.

Norman A. Polansky, Mary Ann Chalmers, Elizabeth Buttenwieser and David P. Williams, *Damaged Parents* (Chicago: University of Chicago Press, 1981).

appeal   Any party to a child abuse or neglect case has the right to request that the procedures followed and decision reached be reviewed by a higher court. In cases where accurate records are not available (e.g., some juvenile courts) the appeal may involve a rehearing of all evidence, including testimony. At the second hearing a record is kept from which an appeal can be filed.

Upon reviewing court transcripts, the court to which the appeal was made may: (1) uphold the lower court's decision; (2) reverse the decision and return the case to the lower court; or (3) in the event of a procedural or DUE PROCESS violation, order a new trial.

asphyxia   *See* CENTRAL NERVOUS SYSTEM INJURIES.

assault   Any violent act, physical or verbal, may be called assault. The term assault is sometimes used as a euphemism for sexual molestation or rape.

Legally, assault is defined as "an intentional or reckless threat of physical injury." Aggravated assault implies an intent to carry out the threat. Simple assault refers to a threat without intent actually to commit the act. If an act is not attempted the threat is considered a simple assault.

Assault and BATTERY often appear together in legal charges related to PHYSICAL ABUSE or SEXUAL ABUSE OF CHILDREN.

assessment Following an initial INVESTIGA-TION to verify that a child has been abused or neglected, an assessment is conducted. The primary function of this process is to determine why abuse occurred and identify specific areas where intervention is needed. Assessment is the basis for development of a SERVICE PLAN. While assessment serves a purpose separate from investigation the two terms are sometimes used interchangeably. In practice, gathering of information for assessment often begins during an initial investigation to determine the validity of a report of suspected abuse. The investigatory process includes an assessment of immediate risk to the child. This ·initial evaluation serves as the basis for emergency intervention on behalf of the child and is followed by a more thorough social assessment.

The social assessment is based on the child protection worker's direct observation of the child's home environment and family interaction patterns. Important information is also obtained from interviews with the family, teachers, physicians, neighbors and others who have special knowledge of the child's living situation. Under certain circumstances a psychological, psychiatric or medical examination may be required for a thorough assessment.

The United States' National Center on Child Abuse and Neglect (Part of HHS, formerly HEW) recommends the following information be included in a social assessment:

- Factual information on the family—names, ages, occupations of members of the immediate family, existence of extended family
- A brief summary of the family's contact with other agencies, as part of the investigation
- The family's perceptions of the incidence of abuse and neglect, the worker's perceptions, and notations of any discrepancies between the two
- Strengths and weaknesses in the family
- Ways in which the family interacts

- Significant historical data about the parents' upbringing that describe events that formed their ideas of child-rearing, parent-child relations, appropriate behavior for children etc.
- A listing of the family's needs that should be met to assure the health and safety of the child

The result will be a report summarizing family problems related to abuse and neglect, family strengths and the type of help families will need. Information is usually gathered by a single social worker; however, a MULTIDIS-CIPLINARY TEAM often assists in reviewing and interpreting data gathered.

U.S. Department of Health, Education and Welfare, Office of Human Development Services, Administration for Children, Youth and Families, Children's Bureau, National Center on Child Abuse and Neglect, *Child Protective Services: A Guide for Workers* (Washington, D.C.: 1979; (OHDS) 79-30203).

"at risk" children A variety of personal, familial and environmental factors serve to place some children at greater risk of abuse or neglect than others. Even prenatal occurrences such as parental substance abuse or an unwanted pregnancy can predispose a child to maltreatment.

Usually the presence or absence of a particular trait is less important than the perception that it exists. Perpetrators of abuse may attempt to explain their behavior as a response to a characteristic of the child. Such characteristics, in some instances, may be seen as contributing factors. They are never considered as justification for abuse.

Infants born prematurely have been shown to have a significantly greater chance of subsequent abuse than those carried to full term. Studies of abused children have identified from 12% to 33% as prematurely born. These children tend to have a low birth weight and may be more restless, distractible, unresponsive and demanding than the average child. Child-specific factors when combined with a parent who is inexperienced or easily frustrated greatly increase the risk of abuse.

Age is also an important characteristic in determining the likelihood and type of maltreatment. A nationwide study conducted by the Children's Division of the American Humane Association noted that, in general, younger children are at greater risk than their older peers. Young children are especially likely to experience neglect. Reports of sexual and emotional maltreatment, however, increase as children get older. And, while abused children of all ages show high rates of physical injury, older children are the most frequently reported victims.

Mentally retarded, physically handicapped, mentally ill and emotionally impaired children all have an increased chance of being singled out for abuse. Developmentally delayed children require more attention from caregivers and often do not respond to parental direction and affection as quickly as others. Parents may become frustrated or embarrassed by these behaviors. In such cases the risk of abuse is increased, especially if the parent is inadequately prepared or under a great deal of stress.

A child or adolescent's gender is also a contributing factor. Girls are over five times more likely to be sexually abused than boys.

Characteristics of parents play an important role in determining the likelihood of abuse. A child whose primary caregiver is under 18 years old, e.g., a teenaged parent, is more likely to be abused or neglected. Children of parents who were themselves abused are at risk. Parental substance abuse, mental retardation, social isolation, marital discord, mental illness and rigidity are all associated with child abuse and neglect.

Divorce increases the likelihood that girls will be abused. This phenomenon is attributed to increased contact with unrelated adult males as a result of the mother's dating. Statistics also show that stepfathers are more likely than natural fathers to assault the daughter sexually.

Inexperienced parents may have unrealistically high expectations of their children. Children are often punished for not meeting these expectations. When the child has a disability, unrealistic expectations can be intensely frustrating to the caregiver and damaging to the child.

Other environmental stresses can increase the risk of abuse or neglect. Over 40% of all reported abuse and neglect cases involve families receiving public assistance. Many researchers and clinicians have noted the role of POVERTY in child maltreatment. In some cases poverty may prevent a parent from providing for basic needs of food, shelter, clothing, medical and educational care. More often poverty is seen as a source of family stress that combines with other factors to create a climate conducive to maltreatment.

Many students of family violence point to cultural norms that condone and even promote violence as a tool for child rearing. They argue that culturally sanctioned familial violence places all children at risk and is an underlying factor in most child abuse.

Any child may be at risk of abuse from time to time. No one factor or combination of factors make abuse or neglect inevitable. Most low-income families are free of abuse; many disabled children receive adequate and loving care. The majority of stepfathers are not child molesters. Nevertheless, the presence of these and other factors does place children at greater risk of maltreatment.

In evaluating the potential for abuse it is important to consider the number of risk factors present, the severity of each factor and the length of time the child is at risk. To date, there is no foolproof method for evaluating the level of risk.

Australia Child abuse and neglect in Australia has a history dating back, at least, to the years when the British established the nation as a penal colony. The First Fleet arrived in Australia in 1788, carrying among its passengers 36 children who were subsequently abandoned. According to one historian, there were 1,832 children in Australia in 1806. At least 1,000 of these children were illegitimate and abandoned.

Child welfare groups became active in Australia during the 19th century and worked to save some of the most desperate cases, like five-year-olds who were often forced into prostitution or other crime. In 1864, the Neglected and Criminal Childrens Act set up industrial schools to take care of poor children who were either abandoned or neglected, in many instances as a result of the gold rushes of the period. Children were sometimes removed from their homes by the state and sent to institutions, where overcrowding and unsanitary conditions provided little in the way of relief from the neglect to which they were previously subject under their parents' care. By the 1930s, children had been recognized by the government as an important national resource and funding was provided to establish research centers that focused on child development issues, although these centers did relatively little to alleviate social problems identified as causes of abuse and neglect.

During the 1970s, the Commonwealth Royal Commission into Human Relationships detailed child abuse as a topic in need of further investigation. Too, in recent years, various groups in Australia have met and held conferences to discuss child abuse and neglect, its prevention and treatment as well as its parameters. At present, there are slightly different definitions of child abuse and neglect in each of the Australian states. Each has its own Department for Community Welfare, which is responsible for child protection services; currently, mandatory reporting of child abuse exists only in New South Wales.

Since the 1960s, some attention has been focused on the incidence of INCEST in Australia. Results of some surveys show that incest is a problem that is reported more frequently now than in the past. In the state of Western Australia, the Department for Community Welfare Survey in 1978 revealed that 127 cases of incest came before the courts or

to professional attention during a five-month period. Of these cases, 86% were against female children. South Australia showed similar findings.

There are a range of services and programs, both government-run and private, that address issues of child abuse and neglect. In 1974, the first shelter for battered women and their children was founded in New South Wales, others have followed in neighboring states. Parents Anonymous is one self-help group that was established in Australia in 1973 by concerned mothers who sought professional guidance but who found that peer counseling and support was helpful to them as well. Some voluntary parent aide programs have been established also, modeled after similar programs in the U.S., which were based on work done by C. Henry Kempe. These parents aides act as peer support for abusing parents, generally in cases of physical or emotional abuse. In addition, public opposition to the use of corporal punishment in Australian schools prompted establishment of Parents and Teachers Against Violence in Education (PTAVE) in 1978. As a result of its lobbying actions, guided by PTAVE founder Jordan Riak, an American who was living in Sydney during the 1970s, corporal punishment by educators is now illegal in some parts of Australia. The Australian states of new South Wales and Victoria—in which nearly 1.5 million children attend school—now prohibit use of cruel, degrading and humiliating treatment in schools.

Carol O'Donnell and Jan Craney, eds., *Family Violence in Australia* (Melbourne: Longman Cheshire Pty. Ltd., 1982).

autoptic evidence   *See* EVIDENCE.

autopsy Postmortem examination by a forensic pathologist is recommended whenever abuse or neglect is the suspected cause of a child's death. The forensic medical specialist often works with a team of law enforcement and social work personnel in investigating circumstances surrounding the death.

A careful autopsy includes information gained from an examination of the child's environment. Assessment of the cleanliness and adequacy of the child's physical surroundings and interviews with family members, neighbors and others to learn more about family relationships, discipline patterns etc., often provide useful information.

The autopsy begins with a thorough external medical examination. Items such as the child's clothing, cleanliness, height, weight and apparent nutritional state are noted. A careful inspection of the skin for evidence of trauma or neglect includes a search for bruises, cuts, scars, swelling, untreated or infected lesions, parasitic infestation and severe diaper rash. Physical evidence that might lead to identification of the assailant is carefully labeled and preserved.

The medical examiner is also alert to attempts to conceal abuse. Appearance of severe diaper rash on a freshly washed, carefully scrubbed body suggests an attempt to conceal previous neglect. Close inspection of the soles of the child's feet sometimes yields evidence of abuse such as cigarette burns or bruises, at the hands of a caretaker attempting to avoid detection.

Internal examination includes thorough examination and description of all organ systems, with careful photographic documentation of pathology. When neglect is the suspected cause of death the examiner is alert for evidence of chronic disease that might provide an alternative explanation of starvation or nutritional deficiency. Careful attention is given to determining when the trauma occurred. Dating of injuries may be helpful in establishing evidence of long-standing abuse and may help identify the perpetrator. Toxicological screens are also used to identify any poisons or medication that might have contributed to death. A thorough SKELETAL SURVEY is always conducted to detect fractures and separations of the bones.

An autopsy may reveal evidence of serious internal injury such as liver or spleen damage when there is scant external evidence of trauma. Examination of the galea (area between the scalp and the cranium) sometimes shows well-defined hemorrhages that reflect the outline of the weapon used to strike the child.

Comparison of evidence obtained from an autopsy with the caretaker's explanation often serves as the basis for criminal charges. By carefully establishing and documenting the probable cause of death an autopsy can support or call into question such an explanation. In combination with other evidence, medical evidence can help convict a child abuser and possibly protect other children from abuse or neglect by the same perpetrator.

James T. Weston, "The Pathology of Child Abuse and Neglect," in C. Henry Kempe and Ray E. Helfer, eds, *The Battered Child*, 3rd Edition (Chicago: University of Chicago Press, 1980).

aversive conditioning Painful measures such as spanking or electric shock have been used in the treatment of certain psychiatric disorders as a way of controlling behavior considered dangerous or socially undesirable. This mode of treatment has often been abused and is the subject of continuing debate among advocates, practitioners and lawyers. Nevertheless, aversive conditioning continues to be used, especially in the treatment of autism.

In 1975, the National Society for Autistic Children detailed guidelines for the use of aversive measures in treatment. The society stated that use of painful stimuli was permissible as a way of controlling behavior that "threatens the child's safety or survival in an optimal environment."

Sharon R. Morgan, *Abuse and Neglect of Handicapped Children* (Boston: College-Hill Press, 1987).

avitaminosis A condition caused by a deficiency of one or more essential vitamins. This condition may occur in children suffering from nutritional neglect. Also called hypovitaminosis.

Some examples include children whose diets contain insufficient levels of vitamin C. These children are at risk of developing SCURVY, a disease that is characterized by multiple hemorrhages. Also, children with vitamin D-deficient diets may develop RICKETS, in which stunted growth and skeletal deformities are common. Vitamin A deficiency often denotes a general malnourished state. Children who lack sufficient intake of vitamin A are at risk for a range of eye problems, including, in cases of severe vitamin A deficiency, blindness.

John Marks, *The Vitamins, Their Role in Medical Practice* (Lancaster, England: MTP Press Limited, 1985).

B

Baby Doe   A controversial court case in the United States illustrates the difficulty in defining child abuse. In October of 1983 a baby, known simply as Baby Jane Doe, was born in a New York hospital. In addition to an exposed spine (spina bifida), Baby Doe suffered from excess fluid on the brain and an abnormally small head. Corrective surgery could add several years to her life but could not correct her severe mental and physical retardation. After consulting with several physicians, the parents decided not to give permission for an operation to enclose the spine. Baby Doe was treated with nonsurgical techniques, including antibiotics and measures to encourage natural enclosure of the spine.

The U.S. Department of Health and Human Services, reeling from public criticism for failure to intervene in a similar case in Indiana, filed a child abuse complaint with the New York Child Protection Services. When NYCPS did not substantiate the complaint, a private citizen from Vermont filed suit to force the parents to give permission for surgery. Again the parents' decision was upheld. HHS then attempted to enforce newly developed regulations that forbade withholding medical treatment or nutrition on the basis of an infant's impairment. The Department appealed the case to the U.S. Supreme Court, arguing that disabled infants were entitled to protection from discrimination under the Rehabilitation Act of 1973. In 1986, the Supreme Court ruled the new regulations unconstitutional. Baby Doe continued to receive nonsurgical medical treatment.

Concern over this and similar cases led the U.S. Congress to amend the CHILD ABUSE PREVENTION AND TREATMENT ACT to include withholding of medically indicated treatment as a form of abuse. Subsequent regulations allowed parents to deny permission for treat-

ment if it is judged ineffective in improving or correcting a life-threatening condition, if it only prolongs dying, or if the infant is irreversibly comatose. This expanded definition of child abuse is similar in content to the regulations struck down by the U.S. Supreme Court.

In no case have parents in the United States been convicted for withholding extraordinary medical care.

baby farms   The practice of nursing or rearing children in exchange for money was widespread in 19th-century England. Working mothers often entrusted infants to a caretaker for a lump sum payment. Unscrupulous "nurses" were known to accept large numbers of infants at prices far lower than what was necessary to provide adequate care. Needless to say, these "baby farms" provided substandard care and were often filthy.

In 1868, Ernest Hart, editor of the *British Medical Journal* decried the practice of professional adoption, saying ". . . many of these women carried on the business [of adoption] with a deliberate knowledge that the children would die very quickly and evidently with a deliberate intention that they should die." Hart's attempts to regulate baby farms were largely unsuccessful until a celebrated case known as the "Brixton Horrors" was brought to light in 1870.

Investigating a large number of abandoned infant corpses found in various parts of the city, police discovered a baby farm run by a Margaret Waters and her sister, Sarah Ellis. Evidence found at the Waters home showed that infants were fed only limewater and that many had been drugged, poisoned or starved to death.

Subsequent investigations of other baby farms uncovered additional horror stories. It was estimated that 80% to 90% of the infants entrusted to the care of "professional nurses" perished.

Public outrage stimulated the passage of the INFANT LIFE PROTECTION ACT in 1872.

Though it was an important first step, the act was largely ineffectual in curbing the abuses found in baby farms. Twenty-five years later the act was amended to increase protections for adopted children

Baker v. Owen, 1975   The issue of schools' use of CORPORAL PUNISHMENT has been the subject of a great deal of litigation and public debate in recent years. United States courts have consistently ruled in favor of a school's right to use physical punishment as a means of discipline as long as certain safety precautions are followed.

In the case of *Baker v. Owen*, the United States Supreme Court upheld a teacher's right to punish a child physically in spite of a parent's wishes to the contrary. The case involved a sixth grade student in a North Carolina school. A school official punished the child after his mother had submitted a note forbidding the official to do so.

BAPSCAN   *See* BRITISH ASSOCIATION FOR THE PREVENTION AND STUDY OF CHILD ABUSE AND NEGLECT.

battered child syndrome   The late C. Henry Kempe, a professor of pediatrics at the University of Colorado School of Medicine, is credited with coining the term "battered child syndrome." Concerned by the number of abused infants and children receiving medical care who were misdiagnosed or improperly treated, Dr. Kempe sought to bring the problem of child abuse to the attention of physicians. Using his position as president of the American Academy of Pediatrics, he organized a symposium on the subject in 1961. The name battered child syndrome was chosen, in part to create public interest in a phenomenon many people considered repugnant. The symposium generated a great deal of interest and was followed a year later by a much-quoted article of the same name published in *The Journal of the American Medical Association*. In the article, Kempe and others outlined the basic features of the syndrome.

Though many of the symptoms had been outlined previously by John Caffey, Frederick Silverman and other pediatric radiologists, the Kempe article was the first to bring together information on clinical/radiologic manifestations, psychiatric factors, evaluation and incidence.

The battered child syndrome as originally described included a range of physical abuse suffered by children primarily under age three. Later definitions have expanded the age to five years and even older. Specific symptoms may include: general poor health, evidence of neglect, poor skin hygiene, multiple soft tissue injuries, malnutrition, a history suggesting parental neglect or abuse, marked discrepancy between clinical evidence and information supplied by the caretaker, subdural hematoma and multiple fractures in various stages of healing. Symptoms can be present in different combinations but the last two were particularly important to physicians. Due to advances in pediatric radiology, physicians were able to verify the presence of subdural hematomas and, more importantly, to distinguish between bone fractures caused by accidental injury and those typical of inflicted abuse. Kempe wrote: "To the informed physician, the bones tell a story the child is too young or too frightened to tell."

Linking verifiable clinical/radiological phenomena to child abuse was a particularly important step in encouraging physicians to pursue adequate measures for protecting children from further abuse. Indeed the general reluctance on the part of physicians, social workers and others to acknowledge child abuse is still a cause for concern. However, willingness to identify and report child abuse has increased somewhat as a result of mandatory reporting laws in many areas.

Though not widely used today, the term battered child syndrome played an important role in refocusing public attention on child abuse. By making child abuse a medical phenomenon, the considerable influence of physicians was brought to bear on a problem that many had chosen to ignore. Increasing concern over abuse has shifted the focus from protection of parents and caretakers to an emphasis on the rights and welfare of the child. This approach attributes most child abuse to a poorly functioning family system or to individual pathology on the part of parents or caretakers.

C. Henry Kempe, N. Frederick Silverman, Brandt F. Steele, William Droegemueller and Henry K. Silver, "The Battered-Child Syndrome," in *Journal of the American Medical Association* (181:1962, 17-24).

battering child   Attacks from other children represent a small percentage of reported child abuse. These attacks may range from relatively harmless sibling rivalry (*see* SIBLING ABUSE) to attempted murder.

Abuse by a child outside the family is more likely to be reported to authorities than sibling abuse. Parents are often reluctant to report abuse that occurs at the hands of an older brother or sister. In such cases, parents may be afraid to acknowledge that a child's behavior is beyond their control. Rather than taking steps to protect the victimized sibling, parents attempt to placate the aggressor and downplay the extent of the abuse. Some psychotherapists have suggested that child batterers are acting out the parents' unconscious wish to be rid of a younger child.

A parent or caretaker's failure to protect children from harmful assaults by another child constitutes, at a minimum, neglect. In particularly serious cases, caretakers may be considered coconspirators in the abuse.

Ironically, mental health professionals, like parents, have tended to focus more attention on the treatment needs of the abuser than those of the abused child. Victims of sibling attacks, lacking parental support or fearing further abuse, are reluctant to participate in psychotherapy. This being the case, they frequently require extended treatment before improvement is seen.

Battering children attack others for a variety of reasons. These include jealousy, emotional disturbance or a history of being abused themselves. As mentioned earlier, abusive children are sometimes acting out a parent's wishes. Older children are sometimes given too much responsibility in caring for younger brothers and sisters. Children may misunderstand a parent's idle threats to strangle a crying child and actually attempt to carry out such a punishment.

battery   Illegal contact, especially physical violence, with a person is known as battery. The term is most often used in reference to beating.

For contact to be considered illegal it must take place without the consent of the victim. Since a minor cannot give legal consent, any offensive or violent contact with a child can be considered battery. Acts of battery may be classified as either aggravated or simple. Aggravated battery refers to intentional acts of violence. Unintentional acts or acts that do not cause severe harm may be called simple battery. (*See also* ASSAULT.)

bedwetting   *See* ENURESIS.

behavior   *See* SEDUCTIVE BEHAVIOR, SELF-DESTRUCTIVE BEHAVIOR.

best interests of the child   It has long been held that parents usually act in the best interests of children. In cases of child abuse or neglect, however, this benevolent parental action is found lacking and judicial intervention on behalf of the children is necessary.

The legal standard of a child's best interest was developed in response to a need to establish guidelines in safeguarding children's rights. The standard of best interest of the child takes into consideration the many variables of a child's life, including the fitness of parent(s) or legal guardian. Aside from abuse and neglect cases, it is a standard invoked most frequently in cases of custody or placement, when a court is obliged to determine with whom a child should make his or her home.

In recent years, the best interest standard has been challenged on the grounds that it places too much emphasis on an unattainable ideal. A suggested substitute, the "least detrimental alternative," holds that a court's determination should be based on careful weighing of many alternatives open to discussion. According to proponents of the least detrimental alternative standard, placement made on the basis of best interest generally seeks to find a solution without negative ramifications for the child. It is against this ideal of "best" interest that critics argue.

Joseph Goldstein, Anna Freud and Albert J. Solnit, *Beyond the Best Interests of the Child*, new ed, (New York: The Free Press, 1979).

beyond a reasonable doubt This is a legal standard of proof required in criminal trials and, frequently, for termination of parental rights. *See* EVIDENTIARY STANDARDS.

biting Human bites leave distinctive, crescent-shaped bruises containing tooth marks. In some cases the bruise marks may join to form a ring. Bite marks on children may be self-inflicted or the result of an attack by a playmate or caretaker. Careful measurements of the space between the canine teeth can determine whether the perpetrator has permanent teeth (greater than 3 cm) or not (fewer than 3 cm). Location of bite marks in areas that would be difficult for the child to reach is also an indicator of suspicious origin. Since bite marks usually leave a distinct impression, they can sometimes be traced to the abusers by comparing them to wax dental impressions taken from suspected perpetrators. The attacker's blood type can sometimes be identified from small amounts of saliva surrounding the wound.

blaming the victim A common rationalization of child maltreatment is that the victim of the abuse is in some way responsible for the abuse. Abusive parents often have unrealistic expectations of their children and punish them for behavior that may be natural for children of a given age. Punishing children for behavior over which they have little control is not only ineffective but may cause further negative behavior. Thinking the child has not learned his or her lesson, immature parents may increase punishment to the point of physical or emotional injury. Frustrated caretakers often label the child sick or bad and use these judgments as excuses for further abuse.

Blaming the child for the parent's abusive behavior is a form of denial that prevents parents from accepting responsibility for their own actions. Sometimes abusers are able to convince others that a child's extreme behavior justifies severe punishment. Family members and friends may engage in a conspiracy of denial to avoid acknowledging abuse. In such instances perceptions of the child as the initiator of abuse are reinforced, increasing the likelihood of further abuse.

Often parents choose particular traits of the child as justification for abuse. Low birthweight infants may cry incessantly, developmentally disabled children may not respond to parents' demands, or children may simply be defiant. These and other characteristics of children may make parenting more difficult. They do not, however, justify abuse. Responsibility for abuse rests with the abuser's own inability to manage his or her actions.

Children often come to believe that they are indeed responsible for their own abuse. Even when abuse is unprovoked a child may feel that he or she must have done something to deserve punishment. Internalized feelings of guilt and negative self-worth become deeply ingrained in the child's psyche and respond slowly to treatment. Often, long-term psychotherapy is recommended to help abuse victims overcome self-blame.

Abusers must learn to accept responsibility for their own actions before they can make full use of treatment services. Repeat sexual offenders can be particularly persistent in blaming children for being seductive or for initiating sexual contact. Their inability to ac-knowledge the child's vulnerability and to accept their own responsibility as adults makes them particularly slow to respond to treatment.

bonding   *See* BONDING FAILURE.

bonding failure   Several studies have demonstrated a link between failure to develop a strong parent-infant attachment or emotional bond and subsequent FAILURE TO THRIVE SYNDROME and battering. Research indicates that the type and amount of parent-child interaction during the first two to three days following birth are crucial in determining the strength of the parent-child bond.

Mothers who have extensive early contact with their infants during the first three days of life tend to show more interest in the child's health and are more likely to soothe the child when upset. An early separation of parent and infant increases the risk that the child will later be maltreated. One researcher found that abused children were significantly more like-ly than their siblings to have been separated from their mothers for a period of two days or more immediately following birth.

Illness of a parent or infant may hinder the development of a strong bond. Infants born prematurely are often placed in incubators that prevent, or severely limit, parent-infant con-tact. Statistics indicate that children born prematurely and those who were separated from the mother at birth for other reasons are overrepresented among victims of abuse and neglect.

Newborns who suffer from developmental disabilities may not respond to parents' at-tempts to communicate. Parents sometimes reject infants who, for these and other reasons, fail to meet expectations. Very young parents are more likely to have unrealistic expecta-tions of an infant and fail to establish a strong bond.

Many experts believe that the foundation for a strong parent-child bond is laid prior to birth. During pregnancy parents must prepare themselves emotionally as well as intellec-tually to receive the child. First-time parents may benefit from training programs that prepare them for the birthing and care of an infant. Several perinatal coaching programs begin training prospective parents before their child's birth and continue into the first year of life. These programs offer prenatal support services, group preparatory classes, prenatal health care, assistance during birth, coaching to enhance parent-infant communication beginning shortly after birth, postnatal health care and follow-up.

Recent research has shown that newborns have more advanced sensory capabilities than previously thought. Newborns can focus on close objects and can follow movement with their eyes. Infants respond to human speech and as early as 36 hours after birth can imitate facial expressions. By six days of age new-borns can recognize their mother's scent.

Not only do babies respond to adults' com-munications, they seem to evoke speech. Ob-servations in hospital nurseries indicate that adults begin speaking to newborns (not just making sounds) from the first day of life. The newborn's ability to evoke and respond to human communication is an important part of the bonding process. During such early com-munication parents usually develop a strong emotional attachment and come to view the infant as a separate, yet very dependent, per-son. Abusive or neglectful parents may have unrealistic expectations of the parent-child relationship and fail to develop such an attach-ment.

Recognition of the bonding period's im-portance has led many professionals to focus prevention efforts on the perinatal period (the time surrounding birth). Many hospitals have changed policies to allow fathers to be present during birth and to increase both the amount and quality of parent-infant contact during the first hours of life.

brain damage   *See* CENTRAL NERVOUS SYS-TEM INJURIES.

Britain The government of England and Wales has a clearly defined position on child abuse and neglect—it administers and provides referral, treatment and prevention services via the National Health Service and a network of voluntary, charitable and self-help organizations. A concrete response to child welfare needs occurred in Britain during the 19th century, although awareness of the needs of neglected, abused or maltreated children had developed as early as the 17th century in England. Services that parallel British offerings are found in Scotland and are administered there under the auspices of the Scottish Development Department and the Scottish Home and Health Department.

Parliament has passed a variety of legislation dealing with three separate categories: juvenile offenders, children in need of care and protection, and children beyond parental control. Issues of abuse, neglect or maltreatment generally fall into one of these three categories and are addressed by appropriate laws. Generally speaking, all local health and social service authorities make prevention of child abuse a priority, with the result that cases are dealt with in reasonably effective fashion. Recent studies indicate that sexual abuse victims now benefit from specially-designed programs and therapeutic strategies via hospital-based services and mental health units. In 1986, a national campaign in Britain entitled "Forgotten Children" targeted child neglect. It was sponsored by the National Society for the Prevention of Cruelty to Children.

The National Health Service runs a number of programs for detection and treatment of child abuse and neglect, as well as prevention and education projects. Although provisions of legislation regarding child maltreatment are complex, it is useful to note some Acts of Parliament, pertaining most specifically to child abuse and neglect: the Children's Acts, Children and Young Persons Acts, Adoption Acts, and the Child Care Act of 1980.

The British established a National Society for the Prevention of Cruelty to Children in the late 1800s. Currently, voluntary services

doing work in the area of child abuse and neglect, and in general child welfare, receive some government financial support as well as referrals from state agencies. There are also a number of charitable and self-help groups for parents and families, organizations that often aid directly in prevention of abusive treatment or in support and respite services for situations in which abuse or neglect has been an issue in the past. These nonstatutory, voluntary organizations include: Church of England Children's Society; Dr. Barnardo's; Family Service Units; Family Welfare Association; National Society for the Prevention of Cruelty to Children; the Rainer Foundation; Save the Children Fund; Organization for Parents Under Stress; National Association for Young People in Care.

Juvenile courts hear cases dealing with care or delinquency involving children aged 14 years or less and young persons between the ages of 14 and 17 years. Cases of family violence, which comprise physical abuse or sexual abuse, are under the jurisdiction of several different courts.

Shelters for mothers and children are operated by the Women's Aid Federation (England) and the Welsh Women's Aid (Wales). These organizations both have affiliated groups that receive some government support as well as private donations.

George K. Behlmer, *Child Abuse and Moral Reform in England, 1870-1908* (Stanford, Calif.: Stanford University Press, 1982).

J.P. Gallagher, *The Price of Charity* (London: Robert Hale, 1975).

Emmeline W. Cohen, *English Social Services* (London: Robert Hale, 1975).

Family Welfare Association, *Guide to the Social Services 1988*, 76th ed. (London: The Family Welfare Association, 1988).

———, *Guide to the Social Services 1987*, 75th ed. (London: The Family Welfare Association, 1987).

Benedict Nightingale, *Charities* (London: Allen Lane/Penguin, 1973).

Nigel Parton, *The Politics of Child Abuse* (New York: St. Martin's Press, 1985).

British Association for the Prevention and Study of Child Abuse and Neglect (BAPSCAN)   Due to the increased frequency of child abuse and neglect cases, concerned individuals formed BAPSCAN to urge that professionals pay strict attention to all aspects of abuse. In one instance, BAPSCAN's actions worked to bring the issue of child sexual abuse into discussion when it had been omitted from government documents dealing with child abuse and neglect. By monitoring policies and procedures of government agencies, BAPSCAN tries to ensure that important issues not be overlooked and that both the public and the professional workers are kept abreast of new developments that may affect delivery of services to children.

bruises   Easily recognizable as discolored patches of skin, bruises are caused by bleeding beneath the skin. They are perhaps the most common observable indicator of child battering. For purposes of easier description bruises are divided into three categories.

Petechiae: very small bruises caused by broken capillaries. These lesions may be caused by trauma such as bumps or blows or may be the result of a clotting disorder. Clotting factor tests are sometimes conducted to determine the origin of bruises.

Purpura: the term purpura may refer to a group of petechiae or a small bruise up to one centimeter in diameter.

Ecchymosis: refers to any bruise larger than one centimeter in diameter.

Bulgaria   *See* SOVIET EASTERN EUROPE.

burden of proof   In a court of law the petitioner or plaintiff is responsible for producing evidence establishing the truth of allegations made against the defendant. This duty is referred to as the burden of proof or, in Latin, *onus probandi*. The burden of proof in child abuse and neglect cases rests with the governmental unit charged with enforcing such laws, usually the state. Depending on the nature of the charges different standards of proof may be required (*see* EVIDENTIARY STANDARDS).

Burden of proof can also refer to the "burden of going forward with the evidence," which may shift back and forth between the two parties. Under this meaning of the term either party may be required to raise a reasonable doubt concerning the existence or nonexistence of a particular fact.

burnout   Staff burnout is a frequent problem among child protection services (CPS) workers. The work is demanding and the benefits of staff efforts often cannot immediately be seen by the staff. Typically, CPS workers carry caseloads that are too large to permit satisfactory attention to each case. Time pressures, hostile reactions of parents and children, and inadequate support from supervisors also take their toll on workers.

Frustration with working conditions has led to a high rate of turnover among CPS staff. Some workers who do not leave their jobs may become apathetic or angry. In addition to the obviously negative consequences of burnout for workers, frequent turnover and worker apathy also diminish the effectiveness of the child protection system.

Apathy and frustration associated with burnout can be reduced and in some cases prevented. Thorough, ongoing training plays an important role in reducing burnout. Well-trained workers feel more confident and are better prepared to handle the inevitable stresses they encounter in their work.

Competent and accessible supervision is essential. Regular feedback and emotional support from the supervisor is especially important for CPS workers. Peer support and consultation from specialists may also help reduce stress when workers must make difficult decisions concerning a child's well-being. Many child protection agencies have found that regularly scheduled meetings of workers are important ways of encouraging peer support and exchanging professional information.

Finally, the CPS worker must be careful to set limits between his or her personal and professional activities. The intense nature of child abuse investigation and the dedication of many workers often cause them to bring job-related problems home. Workers who have a variety of interests outside of work are often better able to avoid burnout than those who have few outside supports.

burns   One of the leading causes of accidental death to children, burns are also a frequent method of abuse. Treatment of burns is painful and permanent scarring may result from third degree burns.

Records show that 10% of all physically abused children suffer from burns. One researcher has estimated that more than 90% of abused children exhibit skin findings such as bruises and burns. Children who are burned abusively are most likely to be victims of scalds, the most common type of burn injury in children. Contact burns are the second most common type of burn and may result from cigarettes or heated objects being placed against the skin. Contact burns also occur when a child is held against a heated surface, such as a stove burner or heater. Chemical burns occur when acid, lye or other caustic substances are thrown on the child's skin. In some cases, children have been forced to drink such substances, causing internal lesions. Friction burns are sometimes observed on the wrists and ankles of children who have been bound with rope or cord.

Abuse by burning is often detected when the nature of the burn is suspicious or when caretakers offer implausible stories for a burn's occurrence. Intentional cigarette burns are easily distinguished from accidental burns. Location of burns in areas that are usually clothed is also an indicator of possible abuse.

Burns are usually inflicted in conjunction with other forms of PHYSICAL ABUSE. When burns arouse suspicion of child abuse, medical personnel seek to obtain independent accounts of the incident from all caretakers. A SKELETAL SURVEY may be obtained to determine evidence of fractures or separations, which also may be indicative of abuse.

C

Caffey-Kempe Syndrome *See* PARENT-IN-
FANT TRAUMATIC SYNDROME (PITS).

Caffey's Disease *See* INFANTILE CORTICAL
HYPEROSTOSIS.

caida de mollera *See* FALLEN FONTAN-
ELLE.

callus A meshwork of new bone tissue
develops (usually beneath the periosteum) as
a result of a fracture. The new tissue, called
callus, forms along the pattern of the original
clot caused by the injury. Callus shows up as
a hazy, undifferentiated mass on X rays.
Presence of callus sometimes provides confirmation of battering injuries not immediately
observable at the time of occurrence. Later in
the healing process, the new bone tissue
thickens and is incorporated into the cortex or
shaft of the damaged bone.

Canada As in the United States, widespread
interest in child protection had its origins in
19th century concern over the plight of urban
poor children. In Toronto, Ontario, the first
Children's Aid Society was founded in July
1891, and its establishment was followed two
years later by protective legislation (see
below), the first of the early provincial laws
passed to address child welfare issues.

Currently, there are child welfare statutes
containing mandatory reporting provisions
for child abuse in all of Canada, except for the
Northwest Territories, which has no legal requirements for reporting. Each province's
statute separately distinguishes the
parameters of abuse or neglect and these
definitions vary in complexity and scope.
Some provincial statutes include requirements for maintaining a registry of reported
cases; again, these vary depending on the area.

There is no overall reporting law encompass-
ing all of Canada.

Statutes dealing with Canadian child welfare and protection were enacted or amended
at different times, the earliest being Ontario's
Act for the Prevention of Cruelty to, and Better Protection of, Children, 1893. This served
as a basis on which Canadian children's aid
societies were established in other regions.
Another, more recent, piece of legislation,
Alberta's Child Welfare Act of 1970, was the
first to deal specifically with cases of child
abuse and neglect. (See appendix for list of
child welfare statutes in Canada.) In general,
these recent statutes were passed in response
to the growing body of information about
child abuse and neglect compiled in the
United States beginning in the 1960s.

Few studies have been done concerning
child abuse and neglect nationwide in Canada.
Most available discussions comprise data
taken from a single province or territorial
region.

Corinne Robertshaw, *Child Protection in Canada*,
discussion paper (Ottawa: Social Services
Division, Department of National Health and
Welfare, 1981).
Mary Van Stolk, *The Battered Child in Canada*
(Toronto: McClelland and Stewart, 1978).

caning As part of an established disciplinary tradition, teachers have, for centuries,
caned students. To implement this CORPORAL
PUNISHMENT, adults most generally use a
flexible rod made of rattan or bamboo, which
is usually about 3 feet long and 0.5 inches in
diameter.

Caning in British public schools (the
equivalent of U.S. private, independent
schools) has long been an accepted practice;
masters and students alike proclaim its ef-
ficacy both as a deterrent and as a disciplinary
technique. In 18th- and 19th-century America,
teachers widely employed caning as a means
of maintaining classroom order.

Numerous accounts by educators and
pupils attest to the fear and injury resulting
from caning. Currently, caning is merely one

of the many legal forms of corporal punishment that continue to be carried out in the 20th century. (*See also* PADDLING; *INGRAHAM V. WRIGHT.*)

Irwin A. Hyman and James D. Wise, eds., *Corporal Punishment in American Education* (Philadelphia: Temple University Press, 1979).

Cao Gio Often, practices considered therapeutic in one culture are considered abusive in another. *Cao Gio*—a Vietnamese folk medicine practice believed to cure fever, chills and headaches—is an example of this phenomenon. Meaning literally, "scratch the wind," *Cao Gio* is thought to rid the body of "bad winds." The procedure involves rubbing hot oil on the skin of the afflicted child, then stroking the area with a heated metal object, usually a coin. BRUISES may result from this procedure and cause it to be reported as suspected child abuse.

It is not clear how painful this practice is or whether it presents a significant health risk to the child. The cultural origins and practices of the family generally must be taken into consideration in evaluating suspected abuse and neglect.

CASA *See* COURT APPOINTED SPECIAL ADVOCATE.

case plan *See* SERVICE PLAN.

castration Though often condemned, the castration of young boys was widely practiced in earlier times. In the Middle and Far East castration produced eunuchs to serve in harems, in the military and as servants. Trade in castrated boys continued into the 20th century in some countries. In western culture, boys were routinely castrated as a way of preserving high-pitched singing voices until Pope Clement XIV (reigned 1769-1774) effectively ended the practice by forbidding these castrati from singing in church.

categorical aid Government financial aid provided to individuals in different categories, e.g., children in low-income families or disabled individuals, is known as categorical aid. Categorical aid is one response to societal child abuse and neglect.

In the United States, most categorical aid available to children and their families is authorized under the Social Security Act. Title IV of the act provides for payments to low-income families with children. This program, known as Aid to Families with Dependent Children (AFDC), is designed to allow single parents to care adequately for children in their own homes. During 1984 the federal government paid over $14 billion to AFDC recipients. Payments averaged $110 per person or $322 per family.

celiac syndrome A condition in which gluten, a protein found in grains, is incompletely absorbed by the intestines. Symptoms of celiac syndrome can include diarrhea, GROWTH FAILURE, anorexia, irritability and a distended abdomen. Celiac disease is one of several malabsorption problems that can cause organic FAILURE TO THRIVE SYNDROME in infants.

Center for the Study of Parental Acceptance and Rejection Based at the University of Connecticut, this nonprofit center was founded in 1981. Staff and visiting scholars study causes, correlates and consequences of acceptance/rejection of children by parents— e.g., child abuse and neglect. The Center provides a locus for independent research projects concerning families and children, of both a national and international nature. For more information, *see* APPENDIX 1.

central nervous system injuries Damage to the central nervous system (CNS) is the leading cause of child abuse-related death. Injury to the brain and spinal cord can be caused by shaking as well as by a direct blow. CNS injuries include hemorrhaging, skull fracture, cerebral contusion, subdural hematoma and spinal cord injury.

The rapid acceleration and deceleration of the head that occurs when a child or infant is shaken can tear blood vessels inside the cranial cavity and can cause contusion of the brain. Severe brain swelling resulting from contusion is difficult to treat and can be fatal. Brain injury not resulting in death may cause atrophy or scarring, and produce seizures and/or permanent neurologic deficits.

The thin, soft skull of the infant, with its open fontanelle, is particularly susceptible to trauma. A blunt blow directly to the skull can cause immediate trauma to the brain or result in intracranial swelling that may not be noticeable for a period of weeks. Skull fractures are sometimes indicated by bleeding from the nose or ears. In some cases, ecchymosis (*see* BRUISES) behind the ear indicate fracture; in others, bone trauma can only be detected by X ray.

Spinal cord injuries may result from twisting or shaking of a child or infant. Because the vertebral column of the infant is cartilaginous it can withstand a good deal of trauma without permanent damage; however, the spinal cord, located inside the vertebral column, is easily damaged. X rays often do not reveal spinal cord damage; therefore, this type of injury may be overlooked in infants and young children. Indications of possible spinal cord damage include development of kyphosis (abnormal curvature of the spine) without adequate explanation of trauma, tenderness in the area of the spine, pain in the extremities when moved, difficulty walking, sudden development of quadriplegia or paraplegia, urinary retention and progressive neurologic deficits.

Asphyxia, a combination of too little oxygen and too much carbon dioxide in the bloodstream, is also a cause of CNS damage in children. Lack of oxygen in the brain can result in seizures, neurologic deficit, increased pressure within the cranium, coma and death. Unless the victim is forcibly strangled it may be difficult to establish child abuse as the cause of asphyxia. Physicians and investigators often must rely on implausible or inconsistent explanations by the caretaker, or indicators of past maltreatment, as aids in detecting abuse.

Norman S. Ellerstein, Ed., *Child Abuse and Neglect: A Medical Reference* (New York: John Wiley, 1981).
Alejandro Rodriguez, *Handbook of Child Abuse and Neglect* (Flushing, N.Y.: Medical Examination Publishing Co., 1977).

central register   Child protection agencies and law enforcement authorities in many countries maintain a central register of reported abuse and neglect. In the United States registers are kept by the state agencies charged with investigation of child abuse.

Information contained in a register usually includes the names of children who have been the subject of child protection reports, names of suspected or verified perpetrators of maltreatment, and the results of past investigations and interventions.

Central registers serve several different purposes. One of the most important of these is the documentation of past allegations of abuse and the results of previous investigations. Parents or other persons responsible for the care of children often seek to avoid detection by moving frequently, bringing the child to different hospitals or physicians for treatment of injuries (*see* HOSPITAL HOPPING), and giving inaccurate or misleading information to investigators. By checking a central register a child protection worker can identify patterns of maltreatment that may otherwise have gone undetected.

Other uses of a central register include improving coordination of treatment and prevention efforts, monitoring the performance of child protection agencies, and providing data for research and planning.

Some critics have opposed central registries because of their potential for misuse. While all collected information is protected by laws that make such information confidential, the potential for misuse exists. Many fear that the reputations of persons who are wrongly accused of child abuse may be damaged if such information is carelessly or maliciously revealed.

central reporting agency   Most areas designate one agency to receive all reports of suspected abuse or neglect. A central reporting agency is responsible for conducting an investigation of alleged abuse or assigning that duty to another appropriate agency.

In the United States each state and territory has designated an agency to receive reports of child abuse. Most jurisdictions designate a social service department; however, some have designated juvenile courts or law enforcement agencies.

See APPENDIX 3 for a list of central reporting agencies in the United States.

cerebral palsy   A number of brain syndromes that interfere with motor function are grouped under the inclusive name cerebral palsy. These syndromes may be the result of genetic traits or may be acquired through trauma, illness or nutritional deficiency. Conditions that give rise to cerebral palsy can occur before or during birth or in infancy. Low birth weight and premature birth are often contributing factors.

In addition, cerebral palsy may be induced through head injuries caused by battering or shaking. Extreme nutritional deficiency caused by neglect can also damage brain tissue, causing cerebral palsy. Victims of cerebral palsy frequently become targets for abuse by caretakers because of adults' reactions to symptomatic muscular control problems, feeding difficulty and need for additional care.

characteristics of abusing and neglectful parents   Each case of child abuse is unique. There is no specific type of parent who abuses or neglects a child. Factors such as psychological stress, poverty, illness or substance abuse often contribute to child abuse. The National Center on Child Abuse and Neglect has compiled a list of characteristics

that may indicate that a parent is abusive. The list was developed from information obtained from a large number of cases. Observation of one or more indicators does not prove that a parent is abusive. The presence of such characteristics simply suggests that further investigation by a trained child protection worker should be considered.

Abusive parents:
- seem unconcerned about the child
- see the child as "bad," "evil," a "monster" or "witch"
- offer illogical, unconvincing, contradictory explanations or have no explanation of the child's injury
- attempt to conceal the child's injury or protect the identity of person(s) responsible
- routinely employ harsh, unreasonable discipline that is inappropriate to the child's age, transgressions and condition
- were often abused as children
- were expected to meet high demands of their parents
- were unable to depend on their parents for love and nurturance
- cannot provide emotionally for themselves as adults
- expect their children to fill their emotional void
- have poor impulse control
- expect rejection
- have low self-esteem
- are emotionally immature
- are isolated; have no support system
- marry a non-emotionally supporting spouse, and the spouse passively supports the abuse

Neglectful parents:
- may have a chaotic home life
- may live in unsafe conditions (no food; garbage and excrement in living areas; exposed wiring; drugs and poisons kept within the reach of children)
- may abuse drugs or alcohol
- may be mentally retarded, have low IQ or have a flat personality

- may be impulsive individuals who seek immediate gratification without regard to long-term consequences
- may be motivated and employed but unable to find or afford child care
- generally have not experienced success
- had emotional needs that were not met by their parents
- have little motivation or skill to effect changes in their lives
- tend to be passive.

See also INCEST.

U.S. Department of Health, Education and Welfare, Office of Human Development Services, Administration for Children, Youth and Families, Children's Bureau, National Center on Child Abuse and Neglect: *Child Protective Services: A Guide for Workers* (Washington, D.C.: Government Printing Office, 1979; [OHDS] 79-30203).

chickenhawk   A slang expression for men who seek young boys as sexual partners. The boys on whom these pederasts prey are known as "chickens."

Chickenhawks represent a broad cross section of society, including both professional and working-class men. Their boy victims often come from poor families and are lured by money or gifts; some work for prostitution rings.

Organizations such as the North American Man/Boy Love Association (NAMBLA) and Great Britain's Pedofile Information Exchange have sought to legalize sex between men and boys, claiming children have a civil right to such activities.

Several newsletters with names such as *Hermes* and *Straight to Hell* help match chickenhawks with groups through which they can meet boys. In some Asian and Middle Eastern countries boys as well as girls are openly sold into white slavery. Boys are commonplace in the brothels of these countries. Prepubic boys who are feminine in appearance are usually preferred; however, many adolescent boys

also serve as prostitutes. (*See also* CHILD PROSTITUTION, PEDERASTY.)

chickens   A slang name for boys used by pederasts. The term usually refers to boys who have not yet reached puberty. (*See also* CHICKENHAWK.)

child   The term child is used generally to refer to a person, from birth to the legal age of maturity. Age of legal maturity varies from state to state and from country to country. Some states consider anyone who has a developmental disability—regardless of age—as a child. In the United States, the CHILD ABUSE PREVENTION AND TREATMENT ACT OF 1974 defines a child as anyone under age 18.

child, removal of   *See* DISPOSITION, PLACEMENT OF ABUSED CHILDREN.

child abuse   There is no universally agreed upon definition of child abuse. In its broadest sense the term refers to any harm, physical or emotional, done intentionally to a CHILD. Abuse may include physical assault, sexual exploitation, verbal or emotional assault.

There are many different interpretations of exactly what constitutes harm. In the United States and Britain spanking for disciplinary reasons is generally not considered abuse; however, in Sweden spanking is specifically prohibited by law. In attempting a cross-cultural definition of child abuse sociologist David Finkelhor (University of New Hampshire) and anthropologist Jill Korbin (Case Western Reserve University) emphasize the harm resulting directly from human actions that are negatively valued, directly related to the child's suffering, and preventable.

Traditionally, child abuse has been limited to actions of a parent/guardian or other person responsible for a child's welfare. Crimes committed against children by strangers or by other children were not, strictly speaking, known as child abuse. More recently statutes have expanded to include teachers, day-care workers and others responsible for out-of-home care of children.

The age of the victim is an important part of legal definitions of abuse. Most laws state that the victim must be under the age of legal majority, usually 18 years; however, many areas allow minors to consent to sexual relations before they reach majority. In such cases, sexual exploitation after the age of consent may be dealt with as a criminal offense.

For additional information *see* ADOLESCENT ABUSE, BATTERED CHILD SYNDROME, CHARACTERISTICS OF ABUSING AND NEGLECTFUL PARENTS, CULTURAL FACTORS, INCEST, PHYSICAL ABUSE, PSYCHOLOGICAL MALTREATMENT, MUNCHAUSEN SYNDROME BY PROXY, SEXUAL ABUSE, SIBLING ABUSE and VERBAL ABUSE.

Richard Bourne and Eli H. Newberger, eds., *Critical Perspectives on Child Abuse* (Lexington, Mass.: Lexington Books, 1979).

Vincent Fontana, *Somewhere a Child is Crying: Maltreatment—Causes and Prevention* (New York: Macmillan, 1973).

C. Henry Kempe and Ray E. Helfer, eds., *The Battered Child*, 3rd ed. (Chicago: University of Chicago Press, 1980).

Jeanne M. Giovannoni and Rosina M. Becerra, *Defining Child Abuse* (New York: Free Press, 1979).

Pamela Mayhall and Katherine E. Norgard, *Child Abuse and Neglect* (New York: Macmillan, 1986).

child abuse, continuum model of   *See* CONTINUUM MODEL OF CHILD ABUSE.

child abuse, media coverage   *See* MEDIA COVERAGE OF CHILD ABUSE.

Child Abuse Prevention and Treatment Act of 1974 (P.L. 93- 246)   This act, introduced into Congress by Sen. Walter F. Mondale, was signed into law on January 31, 1974. Its purpose was to establish the NATIONAL CENTER ON CHILD ABUSE AND NEGLECT (NCCAN) as part of the federal CHILDREN'S BUREAU, and to appropriate annual funding for NCCAN. The federal monies provided by this act support research into causes and consequences of child abuse and neglect, and also provide a clearinghouse for information on the incidence of child abuse in the United States. Training materials used in prevention programs, and various technical assistance, as well as some direct support to state programs, is also funded by P.L. 93-246. See APPENDIX 14 for full text of the act.

Barbara J. Nelson, *Making an Issue of Child Abuse* (Chicago: University of Chicago Press, 1984).

child, battering   *See* BATTERING CHILD.

child, best interest of   *See* BEST INTERESTS OF THE CHILD.

Child Find   Established in 1980 in the United States, Child Find is a private, non-profit organization that serves as a link between missing children and their parents. Child Find's services include a toll-free telephone number (1-800-I-AM-LOST) for use by missing children and others who may have information leading to the location or recovery of a missing child. The organization also seeks to publicize the problem of missing children and maintains a directory, the *Child Find of America Directory of Missing and Abducted Children*, which contains photographs and physical descriptions of children who have been reported as missing.

A mediation program administered by Child Find maintains a toll free number, 1-800-A-WAY-OUT, to help those concerned with child abduction and works to establish communication between parents and to reconcile disputes. Affiliate groups, known collectively as Friends of Child Find (FOCF), work to raise public awareness about missing children at state and local levels. Among the activities sponsored by FOCF are fingerprinting sessions and programs aimed at educating the public about parental and stranger abduction. Child Find publishes a newsletter and an

annual report. For more information, see AP-
PENDIX 1.

Child Keyppers' International   Founded
in 1982, this group exists to help recover
missing children, prevent child abuse and
educate people concerning the dangers of
child abduction. It supports identification of
children through such methods as fingerprinting, advocates legislation addressing
children's issues, publishes teaching manuals
and varied materials aimed at promoting child
safety, prevention, education. It maintains a
missing children's data bank, and publishes a
quarterly and a missing child directory. For
more information, *see* APPENDIX 1.

child labor laws   The incidence of child
labor in the United States had always been
high when, in the 19th century, vigorous
reform efforts were aimed at passage and
enforcement of legislation against such practice. Available statistics from 1880 indicate
that over one million children ages 10 to 15
years worked—fully one-sixth of all
American children in that age bracket. It was
not until the early 20th century that any
effective legislation against child labor was
passed. In general, these laws were proposed
to eliminate exploitation of children, and to
make possible their education, as well as to
protect young people from hazardous
workplace conditions. Particularly in the
earlier part of the 20th century, the number of
children who benefited from child labor laws
remained low.

Historically in the U.S. the experience of
children with regard to work was affected by
a number of factors that helped determine
expectations about a child's function within
the family unit. Children in urban areas had
vastly different labor experiences when compared to those living in rural locations. The
latter group, part of an agrarian economy that
required youthful participation in various
farm tasks, was expected to perform work that
would today be considered far beyond the
physical capacities of a child.

City children, generally the offspring of
laboring class parents who in many cases were
foreign immigrants, were expected to contribute to the family economy either by working or by caring for younger siblings while
their parents worked. In virtually all cases,
19th century child labor was a function of
economic class, ethnicity, race or a combination of these.

Only in relatively recent times have activities by state and federal officials focused
on elimination of child labor. During the early
to mid-1800s, efforts to control or eliminate
child labor stemmed largely from concerns
over children's educational needs. In fact, the
growth of opposition to child labor coincided
with state and federal efforts to establish compulsory public education

On the eve of the Civil War, a handful of
states required several months of school annually for children working in factories. In
1913, a Connecticut law established regulations concerning education for children who
worked in specific manufacturing concerns.
By 1930, fully 38 states had passed laws requiring a minimum of education for working
children under age 15. By this time also most
states limited the number of hours children
could work each day and specified as well a
minimum age for employed children.

Efforts to control child labor were spearheaded by a number of individuals and organizations at the federal level as well as in
individual states. As early as 1902, New York
state had established a Child Labor Committee that attempted to control various street
trades primarily employing children
(newspaper selling, flower selling etc.). And
in 1904, the federal government had established a National Child Labor Committee to
report on child labor conditions and to sponsor
legislation on behalf of child workers.

The federal CHILDREN'S BUREAU was
founded in 1912 in part to lobby against child
labor. By 1916, with support from the
Children's Bureau, the National Child Labor
Committee had successfully pushed for passage of the KEATING-OWEN BILL (the Child

Labor Act of 1916), which abolished factory and mine work for children under the age of 16. Despite its initial passage, however, the bill was short-lived and was struck down two years later as unconstitutional when the Supreme Court ruled on *Hammer v. Dagenhart.*

The same year that Keating-Owen was abolished, another attempt was made on behalf of limiting child labor. The Child Labor Tax Act of 1918 was designed to impose a 10% tax on items manufactured by children, but this, too, was repealed soon after passage. Reformers then attempted to gain support for an amendment to the U.S. Constitution that would protect children—the Child Labor Amendment, which was approved by Congress and sent to the states for ratification in 1924. By 1938 the amendment had garnered only minimal support in the form of ratification by six states. Opposition to this unpopular amendment was great—38 states had rejected it by 1931. Later attempts to resurrect this child labor amendment were consistently unsuccessful as well.

During the New Deal administration of President Franklin D. Roosevelt, however, several laws with provision for child labor protection were passed, including the Fair Labor Standards Act. Others were the National Recovery Act (1933), which established minimal codes to protect child workers; the Federal Sugar Act; and the Fair Labor Standards Act, which barred interstate commerce in goods produced by individuals under age 16 in jobs considered hazardous to health or general welfare. Despite the intentions of the latter, however, this legislation was worded so broadly that estimates indicate that only 50,000 of working children under age 16 were covered by its provisions, although in 1938 there were an estimated 850,000 such youth employed in the United States.

Currently, each state has legislation that controls child labor, although regulations vary widely. In general, these laws affect commercial activities, although some in the nonprofit sector are also governed by child labor legislation.

Limits on the number of hours worked, age minimums and restrictions with regard to hazardous or unhealthy working conditions figure prominently in each state's child labor laws. In a large number of states, work permits are required as well. Too, parents are prohibited from arranging work contracts for their children if those contractual agreements conflict with the protection given to the child under the law. (*See also* LATIN AMERICA; ISRAEL; SLAVERY, CHILD.)

child molester A child molester is any significantly older person who engages in sexual activity with a child. The molester may be a stranger or may be known to the victim, as in the case of intrafamilial SEXUAL ABUSE.

The term child molester encompasses a wide spectrum of offenders and types of sexual exploitation. Molestation can range from verbal sexual stimulation or exhibitionism to forced rape. Contrary to the popular image of the child molester as a "dirty old man" obsessed with PEDOPHILIA, the term applies equally to customers of child prostitutes, single and repeat offenders, male and female perpetrators. Though many child molesters are pedophiles a significant number are not. Some child molesters actually prefer sex with adults, preying on children only because they are more readily available or more vulnerable.

Mental health professionals may differ from law enforcement officials in their application of this term. The former sometimes make a distinction between the child molester who attempts to coax or lure the child into sexual activity and rapists who use violence or physical force. Law enforcement officials are more likely to refer to a child molester as anyone who engages in legally prohibited sexual activity with children

child pornography The issue of where art ends and pornography begins has been, and continues to be, widely debated. Generally, pornography is taken to be the presentation of sexually related subject matter solely for the stimulation of the viewer. Pornography may include written material, photographs, drawings, film and video. Child pornography may vary from photographs of children presented in a provocative manner to pictures and descriptions of children engaged in sexual acts with adults.

Public concern over child pornography increased in the United States during the mid and late 1970s. In 1978 Congress enacted the PROTECTION OF CHILDREN AGAINST SEXUAL EXPLOITATION ACT, an effort to aid in prosecuting those who produce and sell child pornography. The problem continues to be the subject of congressional hearings and investigations.

Although some anti-pornography groups have asserted that child pornography is a $500,000,000 business in the United States, government officials estimate the figure to be much lower. Economic measures of the extent of child pornography may, however, be misleading. Because of strong social and legal sanctions against child exploitation, pedophiles (see PEDOPHILIA) tend to trade pornographic material privately among themselves. Many convicted child molesters have been found to have extensive private collections.

Law enforcement experts consider child pornography to be directly linked to sexual molestation and PROSTITUTION. Since pedophiles are the largest producers and buyers of such material investigators often identify and track potential sexual offenders through various pedophile information exchange publications. Increased efforts by postal inspectors to monitor the exchange of child pornography have caused consumers to look for other means of making contact. Computer bulletin boards are now widely used as a way for pedophiles to contact one another. For as little as $10 to $20 pedophiles in many areas can subscribe to a computer network that will put them in touch with others who have similar interest.

Pornography serves a number of functions for the pedophile. It may be used as a fantasy aid in masturbation. Exchange of material with other pedophiles serves as reassurance that the pedophile is not alone in his preoccupation. Photographs of children engaged in sexual acts are often employed as a means of convincing a child to pose and/or engage in a sexual act with the adult. The molester hopes to convince the child that it is all right to engage in these acts because other children do it too. Later, photographs taken by the molester may be used as blackmail to prevent the child from telling others about the exploitation. As the child grows older and is no longer attractive to the pedophile, photographs may be exchanged with other pedophiles as a means of gaining access to other children.

Because of increased activity by law enforcement officials in the United States, child pornography has become much more difficult to obtain. This fact has led to increased importation of pornographic materials from other countries. U.S. Customs records show that the majority of child pornography seized comes from Sweden, Denmark and the Netherlands. All three countries have begun to work with United States officials to investigate sellers of pornographic materials involving children.

The crackdown on child pornography has also affected the ability of pornographers to obtain material for their publications. Several police experts have noted that photographs sold in recent publications are often recycled from earlier publications. This paucity of new material has forced some publications to go out of business and has raised the price of remaining publications.

Arguments for legalization of child pornography put forth by organizations promoting pedophilia assert that pornographic material in itself is harmless when used privately. One group argues that depictions of adult-child and child-child relations are not harmful as long as prophylactics are used. Most law enforcement officers and mental health professionals strongly disagree with this assertion. Almost all pornographic material requires that children engage in or simulate an illegal act. Many studies have documented the harmful effects, both immediate and long term, of SEXUAL ABUSE. Finally, sexual exploitation is, by definition, an abuse of power on the part of the adult. Though some children may appear to participate willingly they are usually not in a position to evaluate the possible future consequences of their actions.

Many experts argue that child pornography is not only a product of exploitation but that it encourages future sexual abuse as well. Potential child molesters may be stimulated by such material and led to believe that sexual relations with children are desirable. Pornographic material may also be used to convince children that sexual relations with adults are harmless or even pleasurable.

Child pornography is becoming an increasingly important international concern. Several European countries have recently enacted tougher anti-pornography laws and are engaging in cooperative efforts with other countries to stop international trade in child pornography. Still, penalties imposed on pornographers vary greatly. There is increasing evidence that child pornographers in developing countries may be moving in to fill the gap left by stricter enforcement of laws in industrialized nations.

child prostitution Childhood prostitution is a problem in cities throughout the world. SOS Enfants, a French child advocacy organization, estimates that 5,000 boys and 3,000 girls work as prostitutes in Paris. Thailand has an estimated one million prostitutes, the majority of whom are adolescents.

There are no accurate estimates of the number of child prostitutes in the United States. Some experts in the United States speculate that approximately 600,000 children are engaged in prostitution. One study of 200 prostitutes conducted in San Francisco during the 1970s found that 70% were under the age of 21. Sixty percent were under the age of 16

and some were as young as 10 years old. Another study of prostitutes in New York found the majority had been sexually abused at home. Eighty-two percent had engaged in sexual intercourse before the age of 13.

Throughout history children have been sought out as prostitutes. In ancient Rome and Greece prepubescent boys were especially popular in brothels. Captain Cook, the British explorer, forbade sexual relations between members of his crew and young Polynesian women when the trading of iron nails for sexual favors threatened to destroy his ship. A sensational scandal involving child prostitution in England during the late 19th century caused Parliament to raise the legal age of sexual consent. In the early 20th century citizens of the United States became very disturbed over reports of unscrupulous traders who kidnapped young girls and shipped them to foreign countries where they were in great demand as prostitutes. Newspaper accounts estimated 60,000 girls were lost to white slavery each year. Today youthful prostitutes are still in the greatest demand. Most prostitutes begin their careers as adolescents and by age 30 are in greatly reduced demand.

Almost as long as there have been prostitutes there have been laws against prostitution. Legal penalties have usually been imposed on those who operate prostitution rings and the prostitutes themselves. Anti-prostitution laws are often enforced halfheartedly or not at all. It is only recently that penalties have been imposed on customers. Some countries prohibit prostitution in any form while others attempt to regulate it by imposing minimum age limits on prostitutes and requiring their registration. Both practices have resulted in various attempts to circumvent laws, including creating false identification for young prostitutes to make them appear to be of legal age, and transportation of children across governmental boundaries for purposes of exploitation.

Customers of child prostitutes are most often adult men between the ages of 40 and 65. Many, but not all, are pedophiles (*see*

PEDOPHILIA) who have an exclusive desire for sex with children. These men may go to great lengths and take significant risks to engage in sex with children.

Though sexual traffickers in some locations may demand higher prices for sex with a young child, children in many parts of the world may be sold into prostitution for less than $50. Child prostitutes in the United States frequently earn $20 to $40 per trick; however, many children who are not part of organized sex rings may prostitute themselves in exchange for smaller amounts of money, gifts, drugs, alcohol or simply companionship. Contrary to the popular image of prostitutes as exclusively female, child prostitution claims approximately equal numbers of boys and girls.

Runaways are particularly at risk of involvement in prostitution. Unable to obtain legal employment and often lonely, runaways are easy targets for recruitment by pimps and sexual traffickers. Studies of runaways show a high percentage have been sexually victimized at home. Ironically, these children may actually be running from one sexually exploitative situation to another.

There appears to be a close connection between CHILD PORNOGRAPHY and prostitution. Some underground publications advertise tours expressly designed to take pedophiles to cities and countries where child prostitutes are easily obtainable. One guide listed 378 places in 59 U.S. cities where child victims could be located. Other publications list guides who match customers with prostitutes in cities such as Bangkok, Manila and Seoul.

There is little evidence to support the popular myth of the happy prostitute. Child prostitutes often see the selling of sexual favors as the only way they can survive in the adult world. In developing countries, impoverished children may be lured into prostitution by promises of marriage to a wealthy foreigner. In some cases children are sold for a small fee by parents.

Though some may be lured into the practice by promises of money and an exciting lifestyle, most young prostitutes suffer a great deal of abuse, unhappiness and poor health. Drug addiction, violence and suicide claim the lives of many prostitutes. Those who manage to avoid serious physical harm are likely to bear significant psychological scars, including depression, extreme feelings of worthlessness and difficulty forming close relationships.

See also CHILD SLAVERY.

child protection team   *See* MULTIDISCIPLINARY TEAM.

child slavery   In the New World, child slavery existed among African slaves as early as the 17th century, although this was clearly a practice imposed by slave owners and not endemic to the African culture from which the slaves came. These children did not represent a significant percentage of the slave population in the U.S. until the 1800s (slavery was abolished in Caribbean colonial holdings in 1832), when slave families had grown in number and stability. Most of these children lived in Maryland, Virginia and other Southern Colonies. Contrary to some beliefs, the majority of these slave children were not segregated from their families but lived with their parents until about age 10.

While child slavery is now uncommon (and illegal) in almost all countries, there have been isolated incidents in which some forms of enslavement have surfaced in various parts of the world. In the 1960s, Kenyan government officials put a stop to the practice of fathers in the Kisii District selling their young sons into forestry work in Tanzania. There are reports that in Bolivia and Colombia today, very young Indian girls are adopted by white families so that they will perform domestic tasks without pay. In China, according to a United Nations report in the mid-1980s, school children had been forced to work while in school, earning money to supplement the school's budget. In India, there are reports of children being kidnapped, maimed, then forced to work as beggars, collecting money for those who seized them. Another report from India, in 1986, described a case in which several children between the ages of seven and 14 had been bonded to work for a carpet shed owner and forced to work over 12 hours a day for no wages.

In countries such as Malaysia, Jamaica, Morocco, the Philippines, Thailand and Mexico, weakly-enforced or nonexistent child labor legislation results in exceptionally negative working conditions for children, who often receive only a few pennies per day in wages. These children work on sugar planta- .tions, in factories, sweatshops, rug factories, as domestic workers and as dump pickers. The International Labor Organization, the United Nations, and various antislavery and anti-child labor organizations view many of these situations as forms of child slavery.

Publicity concerning the current sex trade in countries such as Thailand, Peru, the Philippines, Sri Lanka, Brazil and Bangladesh, has revealed that young girls (and sometimes young boys) are reportedly being sold into prostitution by parents or other relatives. In India, this form of child slavery involves girls who are sold as Devadasis—females forbidden to marry for religious reasons, but dedicated to sacred prostitution.

Another well-publicized form of child slavery involves prostitution rings, many of which are involved in international sex tourism schemes. These involve both boys and girls, some reportedly as young as six years old, who are either kidnapped or sold as prostitutes. (*See also* TRAFFICKING, SEXUAL.)

Defense for Children International-USA Collective, *The Children's Clarion, Database on the Rights of the Child, 1987* (Brooklyn, New York: DCI-USA, 1987).

child stealing Primarily as a result of child custody disputes, large numbers of children are victims each year of parental abduction. This phenomenon is known as child stealing

or, less accurately, child snatching, to differentiate it from third-party abduction or kidnapping. Until fairly recently, it had been estimated by various sources to occur between 25,000 and 100,000 times annually in the United States. However, this figure was not empirically based and according to more current research may substantially underestimate the true incidence of child stealing.

In 1983, Richard J. Gelles, a sociologist who specializes in family violence, published survey results indicating the probability that between 459,000 and 751,000 such abductions per year occurred among American families. Further, Gelles's research suggested that large numbers of child stealing cases involve more than one child per family. He also indicated that households other than that of the child and the parent are often involved. These other households typically include grandparents, uncles, aunts and other relatives and may include professionals such as lawyers, teachers, police officers, private detectives.

As a result, separate states have adopted the UNIFORM CHILD CUSTODY JURISDICTION ACT, and the U.S. Congress has worked to support individual states' efforts at cutting down on parental child stealing by passing the Federal Parental Kidnapping Prevention Act. Because of the latter, the Federal Bureau of Investigation reportedly assisted in nearly 1,400 parental kidnapping cases in 1985.

In addition to domestic child stealings, experts say there has been an increase during the past few decades in international child abductions. These typically involve child custody disputes. Few reliable statistics are available concerning these international cases. Despite the dearth of empirical evidence concerning these abductions, however, experts agree that child stealing across the borders of different nations is an issue of growing proportions.

The disruption in a child's life that results from abduction by a parent or other family member is considered by most experts to be quite serious and to have a long-term, negative effect. Besides a child's home life, his or her school life and general social development are seriously affected by the abrupt and invariably confusing incidents surrounding parental abduction. Some children who are taken from, but subsequently retrieved by, the custodial parent are described as hostile, frightened and physically unhealthy following their return to the custodial home.

In 1980, the Hague Convention on the Civil Aspects of International Child Abduction was devised as a way to facilitate return of children who have been abducted across international boundaries. To date, a handful of nations, including Canada, France, Hungary, Luxembourg, Portugal, Switzerland and the United Kingdom have adopted the convention. And the United States Congress was expected to implement the Convention before the end of 1988. (*See also* KIDNAPPING.)

Michael W. Agopian, *Parental Child Stealing* (Lexington, Massachusetts: Lexington Books, D.C. Heath, 1981).
Phyllis Chesler, *Mothers on Trial, the Battle for Custody and Children* (New York: McGraw-Hill, 1986).
Richard J. Gelles, "Parental Child Snatching: A Preliminary Estimate of the National Incidence," in *Journal of Marriage and the Family* (August 1984), pp. 735-739.
Sanford N. Katz, *Child Snatching: The Legal Response to the Abduction of Children* (Chicago: ABA Press, 1981).
Bobbi Lawrence and Olivia Taylor-Young, *The Child Snatchers* (Boston: Charles River Books, 1983).

Child Welfare League of America A privately supported, not-for-profit organization incorporated in 1920, the CWLA is described in a recent annual report as "devoting its efforts to helping deprived, neglected and abused children and their families." The CWLA provides information, conducts research and develops standards for children's services. Its membership comprises 450 children's agencies with 125,000 staff members and 1,000 affiliates, throughout the United States and Canada. The organization currently serves two million children annually. The CWLA publishes a bibliography of its numerous publications, including articles from *Child Welfare*, a bimonthly journal of the CWLA. For more information, see APPENDIX 1.

Childhelp USA Established in 1983, Childhelp USA is a nonprofit organization that serves the needs of neglected and abused children. It operates the National Child Abuse Hotline (1-800-4-A-CHILD), disseminates literature, posters, and other materials related to prevention of child abuse, provides treatment and evaluation services, operates a residential treatment center for children between the ages of two and 12, and funds research related to child abuse and neglect. For more information, see APPENDIX 1.

Childhood Level of Living Scale Unlike some forms of PHYSICAL ABUSE that are easily recognized, child neglect is difficult to define. Though various statutes have attempted to define neglect, such legal definitions are often vague and too broadly defined to be of use to the average person. One reason for the difficulty in defining neglect is the absence of agreed-upon standards for child rearing. In an attempt to measure the quality of child care more accurately Norman Polansky, a professor of social work at the University of Georgia, and others have developed a scale for assessing child care.

The Childhood Level of Living Scale (CLL) was adopted for use in urban areas. It is divided into two parts, which focus on physical care and emotional/cognitive care. Part A, physical care, consists of 47 items broken down into five subcategories: general positive child care, state of repair of house, negligence, quality of household maintenance, and quality of health care and grooming. Emotional/cognitive questions, part B, focus on: encouraging competence, inconsistency of discipline and coldness, encouraging superego development, and material giving (to the child). Part B contains 52 items.

Families are evaluated on each item by an independent scorer. Maximum possible score on the CLL is 99. A score of 62 or less is considered indicative of neglect. Acceptable child care begins at 77. A score of 88 or higher is judged as good.

In addition to its use as a research tool, the CLL has been used by protective service workers in several areas to assess the quality of child care in a family where neglect is suspected.

For the full text of the CLL see: Carolyn Hally, Nancy F. Polansky and Norman A. Polansky, *Child Neglect: Mobilizing Services* (Washington, D.C.: Government Printing Office, 1980; DHHS, OHDS 80-30257).

Norman A. Polansky, Mary Ann Chalmers, Elizabeth Buttenwieser and David P. Williams, *Damaged Parents* (Chicago: University of Chicago Press, 1981).

childhood, loss of   *See* PARENTIFIED CHILD.

children as property   Traditionally, the law has treated children not as individuals with legal standing equal to that of adults but as the property of their parents or the state. When viewed as property, children have no rights to self-determination.

In earlier times, children were viewed as an economic asset. Families often depended upon their children's labor for survival. In 19th-century England and in North America children were treated in much the same way as farm animals. They could be placed in servitude, beaten and, if they consistently disobeyed, even killed by their parents. Though communities did occasionally condemn parents for cruel treatment of their children, the children themselves had no legal standing to complain about maltreatment. Indeed, some of the first child protection cases in both England and America were brought by societies organized to prevent cruelty to animals. No child protection societies existed in the U.S. or in Britain before the latter half of the 19th century.

Abused and neglected children still cannot directly petition the court for protection. Child protection agencies and the courts typically make decisions in what they believe to be the BEST INTERESTS OF THE CHILD. The child is often consulted but has little recourse if he or she disagrees with a decision.

Recent decisions by the United States Supreme Court have established that children do have some legal standing under the Constitution. *TINKER V. DES MOINES*, for example, held that children have a right to free speech under the First Amendment. Still, the relationship between children under the age of legal majority and their parents is heavily tilted in favor of parents.

Some child advocates favor treating children and adults equally under the law. Others believe parents need legal power in order to protect children adequately from their own immature judgments. In the United States, courts and lawmakers have attempted to give children a status above that of property but below that of parents. (*See also* CHILDREN'S RIGHTS, PARENTS' RIGHTS, PARENS PATRIAE.)

Children's Aid Society   This organization was founded in BRITAIN in 1856, one of numerous voluntary societies that addressed the welfare of disadvantaged, underrepresented and powerless groups. Children's Aid Societies also were established in CANADA during the 19th century.

Children's Bureau   Until the late 19th century, children in the United States were afforded little legal protection from abuse and neglect. A variety of factors contributed to the formation of federal government policies concerning child welfare in the United States, factors that converged during the Progressive Era. Increased legislative reform during this period resulted in federal involvement in social welfare issues.

Chief among these progressive reforms was formation of the United States Children's Bureau in 1912. The bureau was founded in the wake of activities at the first WHITE HOUSE CONFERENCE ON CHILDREN in 1909 and was part of the Department of Commerce and Labor. The Children's Bureau, with only a small staff, investigated and reported on issues concerning children. By 1938, the Children's Bureau had been instrumental in passage of federal legislation prohibiting child labor. Concerns over infant mortality rates in the United States led the bureau, shortly after its formation, to formalize registration of infant births and deaths nationwide. The bureau also published a variety of pamphlets aimed at educating parents about the care of young children.

Strong supporters of and contributors to establishment of the Federal Children's Bureau included Florence Kelley and Lillian Wald, both social workers. Along with Julia Lathrop (the first chief of the Children's Bureau, from 1913 to 1921) and Grace Abbott (chief from 1921 to 1934), these and many other Children's Bureau workers promoted systematic, broad support of child welfare in the United States. (*See also* CHILD LABOR LAWS KEATING-OWEN BILL, SHEPPARD-TOWNER INFANCY AND MATERNITY ACT.)

Joseph M Hawes and N. Ray Hiner, *American Childhood, A Research Guide and Historical Handbook* (Westport, Conn.: Greenwood Press, 1985).
Barbara J. Nelson, *Making an Issue of Child Abuse* (Chicago: University of Chicago Press, 1984).

Children's Charter *See* PREVENTION OF CRUELTY TO AND PROTECTION OF CHILDREN ACT OF 1889 (BRITAIN).

Children's Defense Fund The Children's Defense Fund is a privately supported, non-profit organization founded in the United States in 1969. It gathers data and provides information about programs and policies affecting children and provides "long-range and systematic advocacy on behalf of the nation's children."

The CDF has offices in Ohio, Mississippi, Texas, Minnesota and Virginia, and has na-

tional headquarters in Washington, D.C. Among its major interests are: adolescent pregnancy prevention, early screening and diagnosis to prevent medical problems, support for federal projects such as Headstart, and other health care, job training, foster care and child support programs. The CDF annually publishes a variety of books and reports, including several volumes concerning the civil rights of children, the public schools, children in jail, and handbooks addressing handicapped children's rights, education of minority children, children's health care, homeless children and availability of services to children provided under Title XX of the Social Security Act.

The CDF lobbies for legislation that takes into account the best interests of children in the United States. Viewing children's welfare as a prime responsibility of public agencies, the CDF encourages support for local child advocacy groups and programs, and seeks to establish an effective, 50-state network for children. The Fund works as well toward establishment of efficient fundraising sources for its many projects and activities.

The CDF has a board of directors made up of child advocates who represent a variety of national public interest groups. Marian Wright Edelman is founder and director of the Children's Defense Fund. For more information, see APPENDIX 1.

Children's Division of the American Humane Association *See* AMERICAN AS-SOCIATION FOR PROTECTING CHILDREN.

Children's Petition of 1669 (Britain) This appeal to the British Parliament was the first formal attempt in Britain to place legal limitations on CORPORAL PUNISHMENT of children in schools. A sequel to the petition came in 1698-1699, and it contains the passage, "There is nothing but an Act of Parliament about the education of children can deliver the nation from this evil."

children's rights When speaking of children's rights, advocates often combine the concepts of legal and moral rights. Claims for children's moral rights are usually broad statements of principle such as "All children have a right to develop to their full potential." Moral rights often are not enforceable under existing laws. Rather, they are principles whose existence is often debated. Legal rights are entitlements under existing law. The right to vote is an example of a legal right.

Children's legal rights vary from state to state and from country to country. In the United States the ages at which children may marry, obtain a driver's license, purchase alcohol or quit school differ according to locale.

In Scotland legal rights and responsibilities of children are spelled out very specifically, including such items as when the child may go to the cinema (age 7), when he or she may be given alcohol at home (age 5) and when the child is considered capable of committing a criminal offense (age 8). A legal distinction is made between prepubescent children, called "pupils," and adolescents, who are known as minors. Girls obtain minority at age 12 while boys must wait until they are 14 to be termed minors. Different treatment of girls and boys is apparently based on differences in physical maturation, although both males and females attain legal adulthood at 18 years of age.

In many countries children are treated as the property of their parents and, as such, have no legal rights. Not until the 1960s did courts in the United States begin to consider children as individuals having constitutional rights of their own.

The first Supreme Court case to clearly establish constitutional protections for children was in *IN RE GAULT*.

In this 1967 ruling involving a delinquency hearing for an Arizona youth, the high court ruled that children are entitled to procedural due process under the 14th Amendment. Specific due process protections include proper notice of charges, the right to counsel, the right to confront and cross-examine witnesses, privilege against self-incrimination,

the right to a transcript of the proceedings and the right to an appellate review of the case.

The right to political expression was affirmed two years later in *TINKER V. DES MOINES*. Subsequent rulings in some states have invoked due process protections for dependent children who are committed to a mental institution against their wishes. Some states now allow children to sue parents for willful acts of physical violence that go beyond the limits of reasonable discipline.

Despite these protections, children are far from having legal status equal to that of adults. In *Ginsberg v. New York* the Supreme Court affirmed that children's rights can be restricted in some instances.

Internationally, the United Nations issued a DECLARATION ON THE RIGHTS OF THE CHILD in 1959. This document spells out 10 basic rights and freedoms of children throughout the world. Among the rights claimed for children by the United Nations declaration are the right to grow and develop in a healthy manner and freedom from abuse and neglect. Though the declaration, as well as the U.N. CONVENTION ON THE RIGHTS OF THE CHILD, which was proposed in 1978, represent important philosophical and political statements, neither document affords children specific legal status or protection. (*See also* CHILDREN AS PROPERTY, PARENTS' RIGHTS.)

Bob Franklin, *The Rights of Children* (Oxford: Basil Blackwell, 1986).

C.A. Wringe, *Children's Rights* (London: Routledge & Kegan Paul, 1981).

Children's Trust Funds Beginning in 1980 the NATIONAL COMMITTEE FOR PREVENTION OF CHILD ABUSE spearheaded an effort to establish trust or prevention funds in each state. The United States Congress authorized a challenge grant program in 1985 to encourage states to establish and maintain trust funds. By 1988, 44 states had established such trusts.

The goal of the effort is to make available to community-based child abuse services a dependable source of funding. Money placed in the trust fund is usually earmarked specifically for child abuse prevention and cannot be used for other purposes. Though sources of revenue for trust funds vary, many states generate income for these projects by increasing fees for marriage licenses or divorce decrees. Since funds are held in trust, they are less susceptible to changes in government funding policy.

Children and Young Persons Acts (Britain)
Between 1908 and 1969, the passage of several parliamentary acts evolved a range of policies, procedures and agencies to meet the needs of children and youth. The first, the Children and Young Persons Act of 1908, set up a juvenile court system. The Children and Young Persons Act of 1933 brought closer together the provisions for care and treatment of delinquent as well as deprived, abused or neglected children, since delinquent children and youth had previously been viewed as a separate group with entirely separate problems. The 1933 act also established a system of alternative living arrangements for children in need of care and protection.

In 1948, the Children and Young Persons Act made it possible for the court to order specific placement for children, i.e., send a child to an approved school, place a child with a local authority or other fit person, place a child in the care of a probation officer or order a child's parent or guardian to promise proper care. The act also empowered local authorities to set up Children's Departments, which now are part of the local Social Services Department. These Children's Departments were made responsible for homes, hostels, remand homes, reception centers and special schools into which children in need of different categories of care were placed. The act shifted the courts' focus away from the punishment of abusive parents and toward enhancing the welfare of the child. It allowed voluntary placement of children by parents and guardians as a preventative measure for "at risk" children. This eliminated the need to convict

parents of a criminal act in order for children to be placed out of the home. Social workers became more active in working with families of abused children as a result of expanded roles granted them under this act.

In recognition of the importance of family in a child's life, the Children and Young Persons Act of 1963 enabled local authorities to take steps to prevent the breakdown of families, such as providing financial assistance when needed. Several years later, the Children and Young Persons Act of 1969 eliminated the approved school orders and fit person orders laid down by the 1948 act. By so doing, it placed care orders in the hands of the local authorities, leaving the court with the power to remove a child from the home but relinquishing the power to determine under whose care the child should be placed. This act also helped develop a system of community homes and facilities to replace the schools and homes designated under the 1948 act.

The Children and Young Persons Act of 1975 was an outgrowth of the much publicized inquiry into the death of Maria Colwell, a seven-year-old Brighton girl who, despite protective intervention, was beaten to death by her stepfather. It made sweeping changes in the way children under the care of the government were treated. Parliament placed increased emphasis on the use of community (foster) care and gave greater control to local authorities. Emphasizing the needs of the child over those of the parent, the act made it easier to sever parental ties, and also made it less difficult for abused children to be adopted. As a result of this act, children received separate representation in court proceedings for the first time.

China, People's Republic of　*See* PEOPLE'S REPUBLIC OF CHINA

chylous ascites When chyle, a milky substance normally absorbed during the process of digestion, accumulates in the peritoneal cavity, the resulting condition is known as chylous ascites. This condition can occur as a result of physical anomalies, obstruction of the thoracic duct or injury. It is sometimes observed in children who have experienced abdominal trauma as a result of battering.

circumstantial evidence   *See* EVIDENCE.

civil court   *See* COURT.

civil proceeding   Sometimes referred to as a civil action, this term describes any lawsuit that is not a criminal prosecution. Juvenile court cases and family court (or domestic relations court) cases fall under the general description of civil proceedings, as do probate court cases. Child abuse and neglect cases can be civil or criminal proceedings. Criminal proceedings concern punishment of abusers while civil proceedings usually focus on matters pertaining to the child's well-being. Each state handles abuse and neglect cases differently, assigning a case to a court depending on a variety of judicial factors or criteria. (*See also* COURT.)

clear and convincing evidence   *See* EVIDENTIARY STANDARDS.

clitoridectomy   Sexual mutilation of females is practiced in many countries throughout the world. Clitoridectomy is one form of painful mutilation widely practiced in African countries. Specifically, this ritual involves removal of the clitoris and accompanying labia minora. Among the Gusii, an African tribe, young girls have their clitoris removed in a brutal ceremony, which also includes other extremely painful and humiliating rituals. Originally performed in late adolescence, victims now average eight to 10 years of age. Young girls who wish may postpone participation in the ritual. However, due to the great cultural significance attached to it, virtually all females eventually submit to the practice. To refuse is to be denied status as an adult member of the tribe.

The procedure is typically performed by older women on children, beginning as early as age three. In some areas, removal of the clitoris is performed, ostensibly as a medical procedure, in hospitals. Wherever it takes place, it is an extremely painful and dangerous procedure. Children often die from shock, excessive bleeding or infection following such operations. Survivors may experience a number of painful complications later.

Origins of this practice are unclear. Though some explain it as a religious rite there is little evidence that any religion specifically requires such a procedure. All major religions are represented in groups that practice clitoridectomy. Other explanations include custom, prevention of female promiscuity and a host of "health" reasons. As recently as the 1940s clitoridectomy was practiced in the United States and Great Britain as a cure for child masturbation, insomnia and other ills.

Although approved of within many subcultures the practice of clitoridectomy is widely condemned around the world as a cruel and abusive practice. Many groups that formerly engaged in this painful ritual have now abandoned it. (*See also* CULTURAL FACTORS, INITIATION RITES, INFIBULATION.)

clotting factor   When child battering is expected, one of the laboratory tests sometimes used by physicians is a test for clotting factor. Clotting factor refers to the length of time it takes for the blood to clot. Children with the hereditary condition known as hemophilia have a very low clotting factor. These children tend to bruise easily and may appear to have been subjected to battering when in fact their bruises are the result of normal daily activities.

Colwell, Maria   The unfortunate death of Maria Colwell and the resulting inquiry into the handling of her case had far-reaching effects on the protective service system in Great Britain. Maria, born on March 25, 1965, was one of nine children. Authorities placed her in foster care with an aunt for more than five years. Shortly before her seventh birthday, Maria was returned home to live with her mother and her stepfather, Mr. Kepple, in Brighton, England. Despite concerns expressed by a school teacher and neighbors over the ill-treatment she received, Maria was allowed to remain at home until she was beaten to death by her stepfather early in January of 1973. Maria had achieved only about 75% of the expected normal height and weight for a child her age.

Maria Colwell's stepfather, Mr. Kepple, was sentenced to eight years in prison on manslaughter charges and the case sparked a public inquiry that ultimately revealed numerous faults in Britain's existing child protection system. This inquiry eventually resulted in parliament's passage of the Children Act of 1975.

Nigel Parton, *The Politics of Child Abuse* (New York: St. Martin's Press, 1985).

Commission on Children's Rights 1978 (Sweden) As early as 1920, Swedish legislation made provision for the rights of parents to punish their children. By 1949, the Parenthood and Guardianship Code used the term "reprimand" as a substitute for the previous word "punish" in reference to parental behavior toward children. Until 1957, the Swedish Penal Code exempted a parent from liability in the event that offspring sustained minor injury as a result of disciplinary action. By 1966, the Parenthood and Guardianship Code had removed the right of parents to beat their children, and the handling of parents who continued to beat their children was placed under the jurisdiction of the Criminal Code. In this situation, parents who beat their children would receive the same consideration as if they had acted violently toward another adult or a child who was not a member of the family.

In 1978, the Swedish Commission on Children's Rights proposed that parents be further prohibited from spanking their children as a means of discipline. The commission suggested that this prohibition be incorporated as part of the Parenthood and Guardianship Code, with jurisdiction of cases to fall to civil, rather than criminal courts. On July 1, 1979, when this recommendation became law, spanking children became illegal in Sweden.

Community Council for Child Abuse and Neglect The concept of a multidisciplinary council was developed in the United States for the purpose of maximizing efforts to prevent child abuse. Composed of community members from a variety of disciplines, the central role of the community council is to coordinate community education, protective services and treatment providers.

Depending upon the specific needs of the community the council may: coordinate case consultation, present or assist in the development of educational programs, identify gaps in services and encourage the development of new services, stimulate research, assess the overall effectiveness of programs serving abused and neglected children and/or advocate for legislative and procedural reforms to improve services to victims of abuse.

The term community council is sometimes used in reference to the program coordination component of a COMMUNITY TEAM.

community education Education is an important tool in the prevention of child abuse. Efforts to educate citizens about child abuse often focus on identification and reporting of abuse. However, parent education programs also play an important role in preventing abuse.

Community education efforts that heighten public awareness of the nature and extent of child abuse lay the groundwork for future efforts to treat and prevent maltreatment. Recent surveys indicate that, in the United States, public knowledge about child abuse has risen dramatically over the past two decades. Heightened awareness of child abuse has contributed to increased reporting of suspected abuse and to expansion of services to families. (*See also* MEDIA COVERAGE OF CHILD ABUSE.)

community neglect The term community neglect assumes that members of a community, and the government that represents them, have a collective responsibility to provide an environment that promotes healthy growth and development for the community's children. Communities that fail to provide adequate support for families and children are considered neglectful of their responsibility to children. Examples of community neglect include: condoning or failing to control activities that are illegal or discriminatory; failure to provide adequate social services for the support of children and families; and failure to provide adequate educational opportunities for all children. Unlike individuals, communities cannot be legally prosecuted for neglect. The absence of widely accepted standards for social support services hampers efforts to eliminate community neglect.

community team A community team consists of three components. The first is a multidisciplinary team of professionals responsible for diagnosis, crisis intervention and initial treatment planning for all child abuse and neglect cases. The second or long-term treatment component is made up of representatives of all programs involved in treatment of children or their families, of child advocacy groups and supportive services. This group reviews the treatment progress of cases on a regular basis. A third component, also known as the COMMUNITY COUNCIL, is responsible for education, training and public relations.

complaint This is a legal term that is used, variously, in reference to a written or oral assertion. It can describe a statement made orally when charging criminal, abusive or neglectful conduct toward a child. The term may be used in describing a document employed by a district attorney to begin a criminal prosecution. Further, it is employed when referring to a document that begins a civil proceeding, although it is generally referred to as a PETITION in either juvenile or family court. Less often, the term complaint is used in some jurisdictions instead of the term report, in cases of suspected abuse or neglect.

compliance When state legislation conforms to the requirements detailed in the CHILD ABUSE PREVENTION AND TREATMENT ACT OF 1974, as well as certain Department of Health & Human Services regulations, it is said to be in compliance. This compliance therefore allows for federal funding of state-sponsored child abuse and neglect activities.

The term is also used to describe the behavior of children who are anxious to please an abusive or neglectful parent. Compliant children are more than ordinarily yielding and biddable in the face of demands made by the abusing or neglectful adult.

comprehensive emergency services (CES)
In order to respond effectively to a variety of child protection emergencies some communities have developed a comprehensive system of services. Such services are usually available around the clock and can be reached by telephone. Components of these systems may include availability of a child protection worker at all times, homemaker services, crisis nurseries, family shelters and emergency foster care. (*See also* EMERGENCIES.)

conciliation, court of *See* COURT.

conditioning, aversive *See* AVERSIVE CONDITIONING.

confidentiality Reports of suspected child abuse or neglect as well as the results of investigations are usually considered confidential and specifically protected by law. In the United States the confidentiality of child protection records is required under the CHILD ABUSE PREVENTION AND TREATMENT ACT. In most states unauthorized disclosure of such information is a misdemeanor.

Many areas specifically restrict access to child protection records to the agency legally mandated to investigate cases of suspected

maltreatment. Some states allow all MAN-
DATED REPORTERS access to the CENTRAL
REGISTER, a practice that has been criticized
by some as compromising the right to privacy.

The confidentiality of communications between certain professionals and religious
leaders is specifically protected by law. A
breach of confidentiality by a professional can
result in legal action on behalf of the client,
patient or communicant. Laws requiring these
parties to report suspected child abuse and
neglect supersede laws that provide for
privileged communication. Not only are mandated reporters allowed to share with child
protection workers information that is normally considered confidential, they are also subject to legal action if they fail to do so.

continuum model of child abuse   S o m e
experts suggest there is no fundamental
difference between abusive and nonabusive
parents. In contrast to others who view abuse
as evidence of psychopathology, proponents
of this model see parental behavior on a
continuum from affectionate, loving interactions at one end to extreme abuse or murder at
the other. The specific point at which behavior
becomes abusive is hard to determine and is
often interpreted differently. All parents are
seen as potential abusers. Whether or not a
parent actually batters or otherwise abuses a
child depends on environmental and familial
factors.

Based on this model, treatment of abusive
parents focuses on management of stress and
development of a sense of which behaviors are
appropriate and which are not. Behavioral
therapy and educational techniques are sometimes used. The continuum model eliminates
some of the stigma that attaches to abusers
under a psychopathological approach.

contusion   *See* BRUISES.

**Convention on the Rights of the Child
(U.N.)**   In order to address more completely
the rights of all children under international
law, in 1978 the government of Poland

submitted a draft Convention on the Rights of
the Child to the United Nations General
Assembly. This draft was one of many
contributions made by various national
governments in conjunction with observances
of the International Year of the Child.

Previously, children's rights had been encompassed most principally by adoption in
1959 of the U.N. DECLARATION ON THE RIGHTS
OF THE CHILD. The 1978 draft is different from
other U.N. conventions because it specifies
not only social and economic rights of
children, but their political and civil rights as
well. It has yet to be determined which of the
many children's rights detailed in the convention are mandatory on the part of states/parties
affected by the convention when it is made
part of international law.

In 1979, the draft Convention on the Rights
of the Child was referred for consideration by
a group that is part of the U.N. Center on
Human Rights. This group has been meeting
annually to work on the provisions included
in the convention. The group has also been
discussing means of implementing the convention. Currently, most members of the
working group favor establishment of a formal committee on the rights of the child to
review the convention on a periodic basis and
to report to the General Assembly on compliance etc., once the convention is made law.

There are indications that the draft convention will be completed by early 1989 with the
intention that it might be presented to the
General Assembly in late 1989, where its acceptance would be determined by vote. After
acceptance, the convention would require
ratification by a predetermined number of
member states. Currently, the Polish suggestion is that the convention would become law
"six months after the deposit [with the
Secretary-General] of the fifteenth instrument
of ratification or accession." (*See* APPENDIX 13
for the text of this convention.)

cord injuries   The use of electrical cords as
instruments for punishing children is particularly dangerous due to the high potential

for severe laceration and permanent scarring. In one study, 95% of all children who had been struck with electrical cords had visible lacerations or scarring. In the remaining 5% the skin was marked but unbroken. Particularly distressing is the finding, in the same study, that 96% of the parents who used electrical cords to strike their children saw nothing wrong with the practice.

Electrical cords leave easily recognizable linear or hook-shaped lacerations, bruises and scars. Children between the ages of six and 13 consistently appear most likely to be victims of this method of abuse.

corporal punishment Broadly defined as the inflicting of bodily pain, loss or confinement as a response to an offense, corporal punishment of children has been commonplace for centuries. The issue is most generally discussed in connection with children in public institutions, namely schools. When children are the subjects of corporal punishment in the home, there is less public controversy surrounding the issue. According to sociologist Richard J. Gelles, "the normal kind of violence such as spanking…is typically dismissed by clinicians as being part of family relations." It is true, however, that extreme forms of corporal punishment administered by parents are often labeled a form of child abuse. Another researcher, Ralph S. Welsh, has defined Severe Parental Punishment (SPP) as "any type of physical discipline utilizing an object capable of inflicting physical injury. Included are belts, boards, extension cords, fists or the equivalent. Excluded are open hands, switches and minor forms of corporal punishment."

In ancient Greece and Rome, as well as in Egypt, students were regularly beaten for a variety of infractions. Medieval Europe saw a continuation of this practice, which also has biblical precedents. The books of Proverbs, Chronicles, Joshua and Kings in the Old Testament positively sanction violence against children and have provided moral defenses for

those accused of being too harsh with children.

One of the more significant references to corporal punishment in modern times came in 1669 with the CHILDREN'S PETITION, in Britain. This appeal to the British Parliament was the first formal attempt to place legal limitations on corporal punishment of children in schools. A sequel to the petition came in 1698-1699, although neither effected any change in the practice of corporal punishment.

Corporal punishment was not limited to European schools. As a means of keeping order in the classroom, corporal punishment was widely employed in Colonial America. There exist specific references to various types of corporal punishment used by parents and community officials as well as by educators, in the interest of maintaining social order. In fact, obedience was so prized by the Puritans that laws governing corporal punishment made provision for capital punishment as well. According to the 1642 records of the Massachusetts Bay Colony,

If a man have a stubborn or rebellious son, of sufficient years and understanding, viz, 16, who will not obey…then shall his father and mother…bring him to the magistrate assembled in Court, and testify unto them…that this son is stubborn and rebellious, and will not obey their voice and chastisement, but lives in sundry notorious crimes, such a son shall be put to death.

Thus, from its inception American law viewed corporal punishment as an effective and acceptable means of maintaining order, in and out of the classroom.

Corporal punishment has been the subject of criticism as well as being an accepted practice. Educators, parents and civil authorities in the United States and elsewhere have long debated the ultimate effectiveness of corporal punishment. As well, its inherent morality (or immorality) and long-term effects on the child victim have been the focus of discussion. But not until the mid-19th century was any legal action taken against perpetrators of corporal punishment in American schools.

In 1867, New Jersey banned corporal punishment in public school classrooms. More than 100 years passed before another state, Massachusetts, made corporal punishment illegal in schools, although many cities and towns, including New York and Chicago, prohibit corporal punishment of students.

In 1977, legal challenges to policies of corporal punishment resulted in a clear message to children and adults alike. That year, the United States Supreme Court upheld the constitutionality of corporal punishment in *IN-GRAHAM V. WRIGHT*, a case involving a student whose physical injuries resulted from paddling by school authorities and who required hospitalization for treatment of these injuries. The court determined in this ruling that corporal punishment remains an acceptable means of maintaining discipline in the schools. In a related case, *BAKER V. OWEN*, the United States Supreme Court ruled that the school has authority over parents in issues involving discipline. This case upheld the constitutional authority of schools over parents, despite a parent's objection to the corporal punishment of a child. These two cases, as well as some others, clearly establish acceptability of legal violence toward children in institutional settings in the United States.

Some groups—notably the National Education Association in the United States—have repeatedly called for elimination of corporal punishment in schools. Despite this objection, however, children continue to be subjected to various corporal punishments.

In addition to PADDLING or spanking the buttocks, corporal punishments include a wide range of other forms of assault and battery. According to Jordan Riak, founder of PARENTS AND TEACHERS AGAINST VIOLENCE IN EDUCATION—a nonprofit group that works to prohibit corporal punishment of children—these practices also comprise slapping, cuffing, grabbing, yanking, shaking, dragging, shoving, kicking, banging a child against the wall, shutting a child in a box or closet, wash-ing a child's mouth with noxious substances, not allowing a child to use the bathroom, allowing or encouraging bullies to torment a child, deliberately provoking a child to violence, taping a child's mouth shut, tying a child to the desk, forcing a child to do push-ups or run laps, denying a child normal movement, denying adequate free time for recess and lunch, striking with leather straps, requiring maintenance of uncomfortable postures for long periods, forcing ingestion of nonfood substances such as cigarettes.

Despite the severity of damage resulting from corporal punishment (CNS hemorrhage, spinal and whiplash injuries, sciatic nerve damage), such practices remain legal, albeit hotly debated, public school procedures in 41 out of the 50 states in the United States. As of early 1988, 11 states had anti-paddling legislation pending. A recent survey published by the U.S. Department of Education indicated that, between 1985 and 1986, over one million students were paddled in the nation's schools. Of this number, almost 80% were in the South.

Other nations widely and routinely prohibit corporal punishment in schools. Among those countries that have outlawed these practices are: Austria, portions of Australia, Belgium, Cyprus, Denmark, Ecuador, France, Finland, Holland, Iceland, Italy, Israel, Japan, Jordan, Luxembourg, Mauritius, Norway, Poland, Qatar, Sweden, Portugal, the Philippines and the U.S.S.R. In 1979, Sweden passed a law prohibiting all corporal punishment of children, by teachers or parents, in any setting, home or school. (*See also* CANING, CORD INJURIES.)

Irwin A. Hyman and James D. Wise, eds., *Corporal Punishment in American Education* (Philadelphia: Temple University Press, 1979).

cot death *See* SUDDEN INFANT DEATH SYNDROME.

court Most child abuse and neglect cases are handled outside the court system. When legal action is necessary child abuse cases may appear in different types of court depending on the purpose of the hearing. Alleged perpetrators of child abuse or neglect may be tried in a *criminal court*. The purpose of criminal courts is to determine guilt or innocence and, if guilty, assign appropriate punishment. *Civil court* proceedings focus primarily on the child's welfare.

Criminal Proceedings

Perpetrators of abuse or neglect are often prosecuted under criminal codes that apply to a wide range of behavior such as ASSAULT, BATTERY and homicide. Some states have separate laws dealing with criminal aspects of child maltreatment. Criminal courts typically operate in a more formal manner than civil courts and require a higher standard of proof (i.e., BEYOND A REASONABLE DOUBT).

The defendant in a criminal hearing is entitled to: trial by jury, strict adherence to EVIDENTIARY STANDARDS, cross-examination of WITNESSES, appointed legal representation if necessary and a speedy and public trial. Evidence that may be admissible in a civil court proceeding may not meet stricter evidentiary standards imposed in criminal courts. Criminal courts can sentence those convicted of child abuse or neglect to penalties ranging from probation and counseling to incarceration or, in some areas, death.

Child victims are often called on to testify in criminal court, but such courts deal only with punishment and rehabilitation of the offender. Issues related to the child's welfare are handled through a variety of noncriminal courts.

Civil Proceedings

Legal questions related directly to a child's welfare are decided through a civil court process. States vary in the names they assign to civil courts as well as the jurisdiction assigned to each court. Cases related to child abuse may be tried in any of the following courts:

Domestic Relations—hears divorce and custody cases.

Court of Conciliation—a division of domestic relations court that seeks to promote reconciliation in divorce and custody disputes.

Juvenile Court—often handles issues such as protective custody, adjudicatory hearings to establish that a child has been abused and is therefore "dependent" (i.e., in need of state care of protection), dispositional hearings related to the family's ability to care for the child and recommendations for treatment and/or placement, periodic review of dependency cases and termination of parental rights for the purpose of freeing the child for adoption. Juvenile courts also hear cases involving alleged delinquent behavior of minors and children or families in need of court-supervised services for reasons other than child abuse and neglect.

Family Court—may combine domestic relations, juvenile and probate functions into one court. In some areas family courts hear criminal cases involving family relations.

Probate Court—processes adoption and guardianship cases and handles matters related to the estates of deceased persons

The largest number of child abuse-related cases are heard in family or juvenile courts. Civil courts are usually more informal than criminal courts and require less stringent standards of proof (evidentiary standards). In some situations a case may be the subject of both criminal proceedings against the alleged abuser and civil proceedings related to the child's welfare. Recently the number of child abuse cases heard in United States criminal courts has increased substantially.

U.S. Department of Health and Human Services, Office of Human Development Services, Administration for Children, Youth and Families, Children's Bureau, National Center on Child Abuse and Neglect, *Child Protection: The Role of the Courts* (Washington, D.C.: Government Printing Office, 1980; [OHDS] 80—30256).

court, civil   *See* COURT.

court, criminal   *See* COURT.

court, family   *See* COURT.

court, juvenile   *See* COURT.

court, probate   *See* COURT.

court appointed special advocate (CASA)
Judges often appoint an adult to represent a child's interests. The advocate should be someone who has no personal stake (i.e., is independent of parents and state), knows the legal and child welfare systems, is sympathetic to the child and has the time necessary to research and present the child's interests. CASAs are usually volunteers with special training. Court appointed advocates need not be lawyers but should have access to independent legal counsel. (*See also* GUARDIAN AD LITEM.)

court of conciliation   *See* COURT.

crib death   *See* SUDDEN INFANT DEATH SYNDROME.

criminal court   *See* COURT.

criminal prosecution   Persons who abuse or neglect children may be subject to criminal as well as civil charges. Alleged child abusers are often prosecuted under statues that deal with contributing to the delinquency of a minor, ASSAULT, BATTERY, homicide or RAPE. Some jurisdictions have separate criminal laws written specifically for child abuse.

Criminal proceedings are conducted for the sole purpose of determining the guilt or innocence of the alleged perpetrator. Convicted abusers are subject to a range of penalties including probation and incarceration. Legal questions concerning the victim of child abuse or neglect are decided in civil court.

Typically, criminal proceedings afford defendants far greater legal protection than civil trials. In the United States defendants have rights to trial by jury, to cross-examine witnesses, to free legal counsel and to a speedy public trial. Criminal courts adhere more closely to rules of evidence than civil courts. The highest standard of evidence, proof beyond a reasonable doubt, is required to convict someone of a criminal offense.

Prosecution of child abusers is often made more difficult by the absence of credible evidence. Young children may not be allowed to testify or may have their credibility challenged by the defendant. Testifying in court can be a traumatic experience for a child, particularly when the defendant is a family member.

Despite the difficulty of successfully prosecuting child abusers, the number of criminal cases brought to trial in the United States has risen substantially over the past 10 years. Many states have enacted laws that permit children to testify in the judge's chambers, on videotape or closed circuit television. Use of NATURAL DOLLS as an aid to testimony for young victims of sexual abuse is also widely accepted in courts. (*See also* EVIDENTIARY STANDARDS, COURT, TESTIMONY.)

crisis intervention   A speedy response may be necessary to protect a child who is being abused. In other cases prompt intervention may prevent abuse or neglect. For further discussion of crisis intervention, see EMERGENCIES.

crisis nursery   In some areas specialized nurseries are available to relieve parental stress that might lead to abuse. Crisis nurseries provide short-term child care for parents temporarily unable or unwilling to care for their children. A child may attend a crisis nursery for periods ranging from a few hours to several days. Parents who have requested the service or who have been identified as likely to abuse their children are encouraged to seek child care relief as a preventative measure. Such services are particularly important for parents who are isolated from friends and relatives.

cruelty, mental   *See* MENTAL CRUELTY.

cultural factors   Patterns of child rearing vary widely from culture to culture. Parental practices considered normal and necessary in some societies may be looked on with horror by members of another society.

The Western practice of allowing infants and children to sleep alone in their own beds, often in separate rooms, is seen as cruel and neglectful by parents in other parts of the world. Likewise, Westerners are frequently shocked by various disciplinary and folk medicine practices of other cultures. The traditional Vietnamese remedy for chills and fever, known as CAO GIO, sometimes leaves multiple bruises on a child's body. In the United States concerned teachers and neighbors have reported Vietnamese children to child protection agencies as suspected victims of physical abuse. Child protection workers are placed in the difficult position of having to decide whether the parents' actions, which were actually intended to relieve the child's suffering, constitute abuse. Such folk practices are generally not defined as abuse unless they severely endanger the health or well-being of the child.

Cultural values and practices must be taken into consideration when determining whether a specific act constitutes child abuse. This does not mean, however, that any action that stems from a specific cultural belief should be condoned. Experts generally agree that some forms of child maltreatment are so damaging and so abhorrent that they should be prohibited anywhere in the world. CLITORIDECTOMY and INFIBULATION of young girls are frequently cited as examples of practices that are abusive in spite of cultural justifications. Torture, murder and the use of young children to clear minefields are examples of wartime activities that, despite al-

leged approval by some political regimes, are widely held to be cruel and abusive.

Increasingly, experts are turning their attention to international issues in child abuse and neglect. One of the most difficult tasks in studying and in combatting child abuse on a global level is arriving at an acceptable definition of abuse. To achieve acceptance a definition must be sensitive to cultural differences yet must not condone practices that are clearly harmful to children. In a 1988 article in *Child Abuse and Neglect: The International Journal* David Finkelhor and Jill Korbin offer a cross-cultural definition of child abuse that attempts to address this problem.

According to Finkelhor and Korbin, "child abuse is the portion of harm to children that results from human action that is proscribed, proximate, and preventable." By focusing on human action, such a definition distinguishes child abuse from such unfortunate events as disease, flood or drought. Accidental harm to children is eliminated by confining the definition to "proscribed" (negatively valued) behavior. This part of the definition takes cultural norms into account and allows for some variation from society to society in the specific acts that constitute abuse. Practices that are condoned in one culture but thought by a consensus of other countries to be abusive should be clearly defined. "Demonstrable serious physical harm" is considered a primary criterion for distinguishing such acts. The term "proximate" limits the definition to behaviors that directly cause injury. Various acts such as war or inadequate nutrition resulting from government policy may indirectly result in harm to children but are eliminated from this definition of abuse. Finally, only acts that could reasonably have been prevented are considered abusive.

Until recently, many observers considered child abuse to be a "culturally relative" term. Recent work, such as that by Finkelhor and Korbin, is changing this attitude and may lead to a worldwide campaign against child abuse. Still, some experts fear such efforts will result in powerful countries imposing their cultural beliefs on weaker nations. (*See also* FALLEN FONTANELLE, TOE TOURNIQUET SYNDROME.)

David Finkelhor and J. Korbin, "Child Abuse as an International Issue," in *Child Abuse and Neglect: The International Journal*, 12:1 (1988), pp. 3-23.

cunnilingus   Oral stimulation of the female genitals. In the case of SEXUAL ABUSE, the child may be the subject of the stimulation or may be forced to perform the act on an adult or another child.

custody   Primary responsibility for the care of a child usually rests with the biological parents. If both parents die, become incapacitated or otherwise unable to discharge adequately their parental responsibility the court may award custody to another person or persons. In cases of abuse and neglect a state protective services agency or juvenile probation department usually assumes custody. Court-awarded custody may be temporary, for example, while the parent seeks psychological treatment, or permanent, upon formal TERMINATION OF PARENTAL RIGHTS. Temporary custody places control of the child in the hands of the state but does not relieve parents of the duty to provide financial support.

The state's right to assume custody of an abused or neglected child stems from the doctrine of PARENS PATRIAE. During the late 19th and early 20th centuries, removal of maltreated children from parents was the primary intervention used by child protection workers. More recently, concern over inadequate treatment of children in institutions and by foster families has caused child advocates to be more cautious. Many experts now believe even temporary removal of children from the home may have long-term psychological consequences that must be weighed carefully against the risk to the child of staying at home. (*See also* BEST INTERESTS OF THE CHILD, DETENTION, EMERGENCIES, EMERGENCY CUSTODY, PROTECTIVE CUSTODY.)

Phyllis Chesler, *Mothers on Trial, The Battle for Custody and Children* (New York: McGraw-Hill, 1986).

custody, emergency   *See* EMERGENCY CUSTODY.

custody, protective   *See* PROTECTIVE CUSTODY.

cycle of abuse   *See* INTERGENERATIONAL CYCLE OF ABUSE.

D

Daughters and Sons United (DSU)

Daughters and Sons United is a self-help group for victims of intrafamilial child SEXUAL ABUSE. DSU is affiliated with PARENTS UNITED, a similar self-help organization for families of sexually abused children. At weekly meetings, children are given emotional support and helped to cope with the initial crisis. Group meetings are designed to help victims understand their feelings about the abuse, improve communication skills and learn how to prevent future sexual assaults. Children between the ages of five and 18 years are accepted as members. For more information, see APPENDIX 1.

de homine replegando   This legal proceeding is an English writ invoked in the 1874 case in the United States involving Mary Ellen Wilson, an eight-year-old New York girl abused by her stepparents (*see* WILSON, MARY ELLEN). The proceeding was unique for this type of case at that time. It provided a means by which a child could be removed from the custody of the home without prior parental consent. Initially, an inquiry into Mary Ellen Wilson's situation was brought to the attention of Henry Bergh, founder of the American Society for the Prevention of Cruelty to Animals. Later, in the courtroom, Mary Ellen Wilson's lawyer, Elbridge Gerry, successfully argued that a child deserved protection in the same way that animals required protection from cruel owners. The landmark case eventually led to Gerry's helping to establish the New York Society for the Prevention of Cruelty to Children. This New York group was the first charitable group of its kind in the United States and was a forerunner of the American Humane Association.

De homine replegando, a judicial order delivering a person out of prison or out of the custody of another person, has been superseded by a writ of habeas corpus but is still used in an amended or altered form in some areas of the United States.
See EMERGENCY CUSTODY.

Declaration on the Rights of the Child

See UNITED NATIONS DECLARATION ON THE RIGHTS OF THE CHILD.

defect model of child abuse   A great number of treatment, prevention and research efforts are guided by the belief that child abuse is the result of a defect inside the perpetrator. This approach has also influenced thinking about differences in educational achievement, mental illness and poverty. The tendency to abuse children may be seen as genetic or biological inferiority, a malformed personality structure or moral weakness. Repeated efforts to identify a particular trait or defect that makes an individual more likely to abuse children have been unsuccessful.

The defect model leads practitioners and policymakers to focus on individual problems, often at the cost of ignoring larger societal factors that may be related to abuse and neglect. This approach represents one extreme in a long-standing debate over the origins of child abuse and other forms of deviance. An opposing view seeks to explain social problems wholly in terms of societal forces. Most experts now agree that abuse and neglect are the result of many different factors, some individually based, others not.

Defense for Children International—U.S.A. (DCI-USA)

DCI-USA is the United States section of Defense for Children International (Defense des Enfants International) and is a national advocacy organization that aims to protect children from exploitation, abuse and neglect. It publishes "The Children's Tribune" and maintains *The Children's Clarion*, the printed version of a computer data base on international child abuse. DCI-USA provides court representation on behalf of children and investigates child abuse and neglect. DCI-USA holds consultative status with UNICEF and at the United Nations. For more information, see APPENDIX 1.

demonstrative evidence *See* EVIDENCE.

denial Failure to acknowledge reality plays an important role in the psychodynamics of abuse and neglect. Parents who neglect their children may unconsciously deny their existence. Such parents cut themselves off from their children emotionally and sometimes physically. Denial of children is often seen in parents who have a great deal of difficulty naming a child.

The psychological process of PROJECTION may contribute to denial. The parent, seeing the child as the personification of his or her own negative self-image, wishes to avoid or deny existence of the child. When confronted with their own neglect, parents may blame the child for rejecting them. In this case, denial represents a defense mechanism protecting parents against their own unconscious desires.

Abusive families also practice denial. Incest is often referred to as "the family secret." Frequently, several nonparticipating family members are aware of sexual abuse but deny its existence to outsiders. Denial may reflect embarrassment or a feeling that "things like this should not be discussed outside the family." Also, other family members may derive secondary benefits from the abuse and therefore wish it to continue. Mothers are sometimes accused of being silent partners to father-daughter incest in order to avoid sexual relations with their own husbands or to protect themselves from abandonment or abuse.

Finally, BLAMING THE VICTIM is a form of denial in which abusers try to avoid responsibility for their actions by accusing the child of provoking the abuse. Children may be portrayed as seductive or evil. By investing the child with negative intentions, abusers hope to convince others that maltreatment is excusable or even necessary. Many self-help and treatment groups place a great deal of emphasis on cutting through denial and get-

ting abusers to accept responsibility for their own actions.

Denmark Historically, Denmark's record of physically abusive behavior toward children bears similarities to many other Western nations. In particular, corporal punishment as a means of maintaining control within the family was long an accepted practice. In 1683, King Christian V declared that parents had the right to strike their children or their servants with a stick, as long as the beatings did not affect the victims' health. However, parents were forbidden to use weapons to beat children and servants.

Since the 17th century, Denmark has passed a variety of legislation concerning behavior toward children. Under the supervision of the ministry of Family Services, local child and youth welfare committees serve municipalities with populations of up to 130,000 people, overseeing care and protection of children and ensuring compliance with the law, which includes mandatory reporting of abuse.

In 1934, a law prohibited parents from punishing children for bedwetting, and also forbid them to cut a child's hair as a means of punishment or discipline. Three years later, in 1937, physical punishment in child care institutions was permitted only as a procedure of last resort. By 1967, physical punishment of children in schools and child care institutions was totally banned.

Following the model of a ban on spanking passed in SWEDEN in 1979, Denmark amended its parental code in 1985, dictating that parents should protect their children from physical and emotional violence or other forms of abuse and neglect.

In large part, contemporary professional concern over child abuse and neglect in Denmark focuses on diagnosis and treatment issues. According to some observers, sexual abuse of children in Denmark is not a topic that receives a great deal of attention. Compared to other developed nations, there appears to be less consensus in Denmark over definitions of child abuse. Some experts feel that this may result from the lack of a perceived problem with child abuse in Danish society.

Denver model A multidisciplinary approach to identification and treatment of child abuse and neglect developed in Denver, Colorado, served as a model for many other programs. The model is based on close cooperation between hospital and community-based programs.

depression Clinical depression is marked by deep feelings of hopelessness in combination with physical symptoms such as changes in appetite and sleeping too much or too little. It is often cited both as a factor contributing to

Table 2

The Denver Model

Time	Task	Performed By
Within first 24 hours	Identification of the child as a suspected victim of child abuse or neglect	Community
	Admission of child to hospital	Hospital
	Telephone report to protective services agency	Hospital
	Home evaluation	Community (Protective Services)
Within first 72 hours	Dispositional conference	Hospital and Community
	Court becomes involved (if necessary)	Community
Within first two weeks	Dispositional plan is implemented	Hospital and Community
Six to nine months	Case management	Community
	Long-term treatment is provided	Hospital and Community
	Child goes home after it is safe	Hospital and Community

Adapted from: U.S. Department of Health and Human Services, *Interdisciplinary Glossary on Child Abuse and Neglect*; and C.H. Kempe and R. Helfer, *Helping the Battered Child and His Family* (Philadelphia: Lippincott, 1972).

maltreatment and as the result of abuse and neglect. Deep depression may immobilize a parent, rendering him or her unable to meet parental responsibilities and so contribute to neglect. Poor IMPULSE CONTROL is sometimes linked to depression. The depressed parent often lacks sufficient ego strength to cope with the inevitable stresses of childrearing and may impulsively lash out at the child in frustration.

Psychological depression of child abuse and neglect victims is well documented. Depression in later life is sometimes attributed to a sense of "learned helplessness" acquired by the child who feels trapped in a painful situation with no hope of escape. Indeed the sense of being unable to control one's situation is a pervasive characteristic of psychologically depressed people. Abuse-related depression may last well into adulthood. Studies of adults who were sexually abused as children often reveal unusually high levels of clinical depression.

Treatment for depression often employs a combination of drug therapy and psychotherapy. Given adequate treatment over a period of time, most people can recover from the debilitating effects of psychological depression.

deprivation *See* EMOTIONAL NEGLECT, SLEEP DEPRIVATION.

deprivation/failure to thrive syndrome *See* FAILURE TO THRIVE SYNDROME.

detention A public authority may take a child into temporary custody pending a hearing to determine whether it is safe for him or her to return home. Children may be detained in an emergency shelter, foster home or hospital. (*See also* EMERGENCY CUSTODY.)

diagnostic team *See* MULTIDISCIPLINARY TEAM.

Diphenylhydantoin Diphenylhydantoin, also known as Dilantin, is a seizure suppressing drug that has been used with limited

success in the treatment of extremely abusive parents.

direct evidence *See* EVIDENCE.

discipline Methods of child discipline have varied widely over the centuries and across cultures, but their purposes have generally aimed at proper socialization. Effective discipline will result in the child's being able to fill his or her role in the culture.

Nevertheless, the means by which this goal of socialization is achieved is fraught with controversy. U.S. history alone is filled with examples of adult behavior that appears, to contemporary eyes at least, to have overstepped the bounds of disciplinary punishment and emerged as abuse—physical, emotional or psychological. In other countries, even in the mid-20th century, disciplinary practices sometimes appear either useless or dangerous or both.

There are also benign examples of discipline used by adults whose sole intent seemed to be to educate and to instill a sense of reason in a child. Most child advocates have been encouraged by the growing international trend to condemn violent forms of discipline in favor of methods that teach children to identify inappropriate behavior and to prevent it from happening in the first place. Perhaps the culmination of this attitude can be seen in a 1979 law passed in Sweden that forbids parents to use corporal punishment when disciplining their children. Most international child welfare specialists applauded the actions of the Swedish government in legislating against what its own society viewed as an ineffective disciplinary measure.

There are supporters of harsh disciplinary measures, as well as educators, parents and others who draw correlations between aberrant behavior in later life and excessive discipline in childhood. Most experts agree that parents who resort to disciplinary measures such as spanking, yelling, humiliation, or restricting a child's freedom or action, do so as a way of asserting their own power over the

child. Power-assertive parents who vigorous-
ly act out through punishment differ from
non-power-assertive parents, who use withholding of affection and turning away as a
means of disciplining children. The latter
group may refuse to speak to a disobedient
child as a way of punishment. Experts tend to
agree that neither method is in the best interests of the child's health development. Further, no matter which disciplinary approach is
used, it is clear that an adult who disciplines a
child as soon as possible after an infraction is
more successful in preventing recurrent disobedient behavior. A child disciplined some
time after an infraction is less able to associate
the punishment with the disobedience. Because of this, discipline is less effective, since
it fails to achieve the desired goal—to imbue
a child with a sense of appropriate behavior.

The most effective means of discipline has
proven to be inductive in nature. That is,
parents who explain negative effects of unwanted behavior immediately after the behavior occurs are thought to have a better
chance at success in disciplining children than
parents who either assert their power through
physical means or who withhold and turn
away from the disobedient child.

In other cultures, there are differing standards by which disciplinary measures are
viewed. For example, based on norms in the
Sub-Saharan African Chaga tribe, a parent is
considered overwrought if he punishes a child
for disobedience by beating him, rubbing salt
in his wounds and placing him in a bag of
stinging weeds. In Taiwan, a child in need of
discipline is often forced to kneel as an exercise in psychological humiliation that is, if
carried out for a long period of time, physically painful as well. In some rural Indian villages, hanging a disobedient child by the
hands is considered an effective, if severe,
form of discipline. Research indicates that this
punitive measure is sometimes augmented by
a simultaneous beating.

In New Guinea, discipline of children
under age seven is unusual because of the
general concept of a young child being unable

to understand the difference between "good"
and "bad" behavior. According to one researcher, adults in New Guinea value in-
dividualism and tolerance of varying views
and actions and extend this attitude to children
as well as to other adults. In Turkey, discipline
of children is shared among all adults. Corporal punishment as a means of discipline is
common since most families are fairly
authoritarian in structure, although studies
show that it is not administered harshly, especially to very young children. Traditional
Turkish society has been described as providing a warm emotional atmosphere for child-
rearing, within which corporal punishment
(mostly spanking) occurs naturally. Researchers have termed this atmosphere as
restrictive-permissive.

dismissal *See* DISPOSITION.

disposition In addition to questions of fact
surrounding alleged child abuse or neglect,
civil courts must decide what actions should
be taken on behalf of the child. This type of
decision, known as a disposition, is equivalent
to sentencing in a criminal case.

Dispositional choices available to judges
are different in different jurisdictions. Most
dispositions related to child abuse or neglect
fall into one of the following categories: dismissal, adjournment in contemplation of dismissal, suspended judgment, issuing an order
of protection, removal of the child from the
caretaker or termination of parental rights.

Dismissal. When evidence is not sufficient
to prove child abuse or the child is no longer
in danger a judge may terminate or dismiss the
case. No further action may be taken following dismissal.

*Adjournment in Contemplation of Dismiss-
al.* Parties to a case may agree to a specific
court order (e.g., a family treatment program)
before the court makes a decision concerning
the facts. Compliance with the agreement is
monitored for a specified period of time after
which the court may decide that the child is no
longer in danger and dismiss the case. If, after

a hearing, the court determines that all parties have not complied with the agreement it may then proceed to a DISPOSITIONAL HEARING without completing a full fact-finding hearing.

Suspended Judgment. In some areas a court may issue specific orders to the parties and delay its decision for a specified period of time. During this time (usually six months to a year) the court monitors compliance. At the end of the time period the court may decide to dismiss the case, extend the monitoring period or, in the case of noncompliance, issue an order based on the evidence presented at the original adjudicatory hearing.

An order of suspended judgment is issued after all evidence has been heard. Adjournment in contemplation of dismissal may take place before fact-finding.

Order of Protection. The order of protection allows a child to remain at home under the supervision of a designated agency. Conditions that must be met by the caretakers are carefully spelled out in the order. Failure to comply with provisions of the order may result in caretakers being held in contempt of court. The order of protection may be used in conjunction with other dispositions.

Removal of the Child. When less drastic measures fail, the abused child may be removed from home and placed in the custody of a public or private agency. Placement orders usually specify time limits and the conditions necessary for the child to return home. In the United States the ADOPTION ASSISTANCE AND CHILD WELFARE REFORM ACT requires regular review of out-of-home placements.

Termination of Parental Rights. In extreme cases where it appears that parents will never be able to care adequately for the child the court may permanently sever the parents' rights to serve as legal guardians of the child. Many states require that separate hearings be held when termination of parental rights is at issue.

(*See also* DISPOSITIONAL HEARING.)

dispositional hearing The dispositional hearing is held to determine what actions should be taken on behalf of the child. In most areas the dispositional hearing is a separate proceeding that follows the ADJUDICATORY HEARING or fact-finding hearing.

Information taken into consideration at the hearing may include medical and mental health evaluations, social assessments and similar materials as well as specific recommendations of the probation officer or child protection worker. (*See also* DISPOSITION, ASSESSMENT, COURT.)

doctrine of sovereign immunity A professional child protection worker in the United States often works for a state or for a state-sponsored agency. As a MANDATED REPORTER of suspected child abuse or neglect, a professional so employed cannot always expect legal immunity from lawsuits stemming from such reports or cases. Although the agency (or the state itself) may be free of legal liability under the doctrine of sovereign immunity, the individual employee is not. In more than a few situations, however, all professionals who work for the state or state agency receive unqualified immunity. Some individual state provisions for modification in the immunity laws exist as well. (*See also* APPENDIX 1.)

Doe, Baby Jane *See* BABY DOE.

dolls, anatomically correct *See* NATURAL DOLLS.

domestic relations *See* COURT.

drug dependence, maternal *See* MATERNAL DRUG DEPENDENCE.

due process Due process refers to the fundamental fairness of the law and the procedures by which it is administered. There are two types of due process. *Substantive due process* requires that a law be reasonable, not arbitrary or capricious. *Procedural due* *process*, more often an issue in child abuse cases, deals with the right of each person to a fair trial. Fairness is often defined in terms of three basic rights: privacy, proper notice of the hearing and an impartial hearing.

Investigations of suspected abuse or neglect often give rise to concerns that the alleged abuser's right to privacy has been violated. The line between a reasonable investigation and invasion of personal privacy is often unclear. Some actions that would normally be construed as privacy violations are permissible if they are clearly in the interest of the child's welfare. For example, it may be necessary for a protective service worker to enter a private home without permission in order to prevent further harm to a child. In general, invasions of privacy are permissible only if an overriding public interest is at stake.

Parties to a child abuse hearing are entitled to timely notice of the hearing. The notice should inform them of the charges, names of the parties involved, where and when the hearing is to be held.

Several rights are subsumed under the general right to a fair hearing. These include the right to be represented by counsel, to confront and cross-examine witnesses, the right to a jury trial and family integrity. Actual application of these rights may vary depending upon the type of proceeding (i.e., civil or criminal), the court in which the case is tried (criminal, juvenile etc.) and the specific charges made. Criminal proceedings usually adhere closely to due process procedures; juvenile courts are often less strict in adherence.

In keeping with the right to counsel, most states specifically provide for the appointment of a GUARDIAN AD LITEM to represent the interests of the child. The guardian ad litem must act independently of attorneys for both the prosecution and defense.

The right to confront one's accusers and to cross-examine witnesses is often problematic in child abuse trials, particularly when the victim is very young. Normal court procedures may be intimidating to the child; tes-timony and cross-examination can subject the child to additional trauma. Many courts now allow videotaped or closed-circuit television testimony. Others allow testimony IN CAMERA. Whatever methods are used, provisions for cross-examination must be made.

Some states do not permit trial by jury in juvenile court proceedings. In others a judge may, at the request of one or both parties, make a jury trial available.

United States law requires that reasonable attempts be made by the state to maintain family integrity by offering rehabilitative services. Before PARENTS' RIGHTS can be terminated, the state must prove that attempts have been made to keep a child at home or that the child is in immediate danger. (*See also IN RE GAULT*, CHILDREN'S RIGHTS, ADVOCACY, TERMINATION OF PARENTAL RIGHTS.)

due process, procedural   *See* DUE PROCESS.

due process, substantive   *See* DUE PROCESS.

dwarfism   Prolonged abuse or neglect can inhibit the body's secretion of the growth-producing hormone somatotropin, which causes significant physical, emotional and intellectual retardation. This syndrome is known by several names, including: psychosocial dwarfism, abuse dwarfism, deprivation dwarfism, reversible hyposomatotropinism, reversible growth failure, and post-traumatic hypopituitarism.

Diagnosis is based on the observation of a significant slowdown in physical growth after infancy. Skeletal growth is severely retarded, and height is below the third percentile as compared to children of the same chronological age.

Endocrinological tests demonstrate a lack of somatotropin (growth hormone) production before the child is removed from the unhealthy environment. The factor that distinguishes these symptoms from other organically induced growth failure is the rapid reversal seen when children are hospitalized. Significant increases in pituitary secretion have been observed as rapidly as two weeks following removal of the child from the abusive situation. Other symptoms may take much longer to improve. SUBDURAL HEMATOMA, often a result of shaking or battering, has also been identified as a cause of hypopituitarism.

Psychosocial dwarfism is in some ways similar to the FAILURE TO THRIVE syndrome seen in infants. The major distinction between the two is the age of the child at onset. A generally, but not universally, accepted demarcation point is age three. Growth failure occurring prior to that point is known as failure to thrive, afterward as psychosocial dwarfism.

In addition to a background of especially cruel or neglectful treatment at home, children suffering from pychosocial dwarfism may present a history of unusual behavioral symptoms. They may exhibit an exaggerated desire for food or drink, sometimes eating from trash cans or drinking from toilet bowls. Bouts of excessive eating may be followed by self-starvation or vomiting. These children often lack age-appropriate control of urination and bowel movements, and may throw aggressive tantrums or appear socially withdrawn.

Sleep appears to play an important part in producing the growth failure seen in psychosocial dwarfs. Unusual patterns of sleep and wakefulness are frequently observed. Research has shown a direct correspondence between the normalization of sleep patterns and the growth spurt experienced by children when they are removed from the abusive situation.

Retarded motor and intellectual development is frequently present in the psychosocial dwarf. Like skeletal growth, these symptoms usually show remarkable improvement when the child is moved to a healthy living environment. Improvements in IQ scores up to as much as 55 points have been recorded. When deprivation continues into adolescence, a delay in the onset of puberty is usually observed. The exact cause, or causes, of somatotropin deficiency in the psychosocial dwarfism syndrome is not clear. As mentioned earlier, sleep patterns seem to be related to production of the growth hormone, however there is no consistent explanation for the sleeping difficulties. Significant increase in somatotropin production is usually observed when the child is removed from the home in which the initial symptoms occurred. The relative rarity of psychosocial dwarfism coupled with the difficulty of collecting accurate information about the child's treatment prior to intervention has left many questions about this syndrome unanswered.

Gertrude J. Williams and John Money, eds., *Traumatic Abuse and Neglect of Children at Home* (Baltimore: Johns Hopkins University Press, 1980).

E

Early and Periodic Screening, Diagnosis and Treatment (EPSDT) The Early and Periodic Screening, Diagnosis and Treatment (EPSDT) program was enacted in 1967 by the Congress of the United States as part of the MEDICAID program. Medicaid is jointly funded by the states and the federal government to provide medical care to low income families and individuals.

EPSDT was specifically designed to detect potentially disabling physical or mental conditions in poor children. Screening begins in infancy and may continue up to age 21. In addition to screening, the program provides treatment of any medical problems and transportation to and from the medical facility.

All states are required to provide this service to Medicaid eligible children. Welfare departments are responsible for administration of EPSDT in most areas.

Regular monitoring can help identify cases of maltreatment that might otherwise have gone undetected. Screening programs such as EPSDT can also help reduce the incidence of SITUATIONAL ABUSE AND NEGLECT. (*See also* POVERTY.)

Eastern Europe *See* SOCIALIST EASTERN EUROPE.

ecchymosis *See* BRUISES.

edema Bumps or BRUISES can result in edema, a swelling of body tissue caused by an excessive collecting of fluid in the body tissue. Such swelling is a possible indicator of battering but may also be the result of various diseases, malnutrition or allergies.

education, community *See* COMMUNITY EDUCATION.

education, parent *See* PARENT EDUCATION.

educational neglect The National Center on Child Abuse and Neglect offers the following definition of educational neglect:

> Failure to provide for a child's cognitive development. This may include failure to conform to state legal requirements regarding school attendance.

Little information is available on the incidence of this problem. Most child protection agencies do not keep separate statistics on this form of neglect. Because educational neglect is not considered life-threatening, it may receive less attention from child abuse experts than other forms of abuse and neglect.

In recent years several proposals have been made that would penalize parents of children who are chronically truant from school. Proposed penalties range from fines and imprisonment to reductions in welfare assistance. These proposals illustrate a growing tendency to deal with the problem of school attendance outside of the child protection system.

emergencies Abused or neglected children may need immediate intervention to protect them from further severe maltreatment or to ensure proper treatment of injuries. All areas of the United States are covered by HOTLINES that provide around-the-clock telephone screening of potential child abuse emergencies. These phone services are usually operated by, or have a direct link with, local child protection agencies and law enforcement authorities.

Assessment of danger to the child is the first and perhaps the most important step in the screening and investigatory process (*see* INVESTIGATION). The United States' National Center on Child Abuse and Neglect defines potential emergencies as:

- all complaints of severe physical abuse
- all complaints of sexual abuse

- complaints alleging that children under the age of eight have been left alone
- complaints alleging that children and their parents are in need of food or housing
- complaints alleging that parents of young children are psychotic, behave in a bizarre manner or act under the influence of drugs or alcohol
- complaints alleging bizarre punishment (e.g., locking a child in a closet)
- complaints alleging that children or adolescents are suicidal
- complaints involving abandonment
- complaints from hospital emergency rooms concerning children under their care
- self-referrals from parents who state they are unable to cope, feel that they will hurt or kill their children, or desire their children's removal and placement away from home
- cases in which protective custody is authorized

U.S. Department of Health, Education and Welfare, Office of Human Development Services, Administration for Children, Youth and Families, Children's Bureau, National Center on Child Abuse and Neglect. *Child Protective Services: A Guide for Workers* (Washington, D.C.: 1979; [OHDS] 79-30203).

If the child is determined to be in immediate physical or emotional danger several alternatives are available. PARENT AIDES or HOMEMAKER SERVICES may be called to assist the family and ensure proper treatment of the child. The abusing adult may be voluntarily or involuntarily removed from home. When abuse is discovered in a hospital emergency room, the child may be placed on HOSPITAL HOLD for his or her protection.

Removing a child from home is usually the least preferable of emergency interventions. Emergency removal may place additional strain on a child who has already suffered severe emotional trauma. Children often find it difficult to adjust to abrupt changes brought on by out-of-home placement. Emergency placement further disrupts families and may reduce parents' willingness to cooperate with

subsequent efforts to protect the child. When emergency removal of a child is necessary, trauma to the child and family may be reduced by placing the child with a friend or relative. Placement in an emergency shelter or foster home is considered only if no suitable alternatives are available.

Most developed countries make legal provisions for placing children in protective custody. In the United States, children may be removed from parents' custody by court order or, in an emergency, by state authority. Many states allow police to take a child into protective custody without prior court approval. When children are removed without a court order, a HEARING must be held to review the decision. Court supervision of protective custody focuses on rights of the child, parents and the state.

emergency custody Virtually all states have legal provisions for an authorized person to remove a child from a dangerous or abusive situation. This immediate removal into emergency custody can occur either with or without a court order, although states have varying requirements governing this action; some states require that a court order be obtained before emergency custody without parental consent is effected. In addition, each state has different definitions of who is authorized to take emergency custody action.

Despite the clear necessity of emergency custody in some cases, most experts currently agree that, in general, every effort should be made to avoid unnecessary removal of a child from the home. The entire concept of interfering with what has been termed the "sanctity of the home and family" is one that has received increasing judicial scrutiny in recent years.

emergency room Most severely abused children and many with less serious physical injuries are brought to hospital emergency rooms for treatment. Specialized training both in detection of child abuse and in crisis intervention is considered essential for emergency room personnel.

Emergency room physicians and nurses must often work without benefit of adequate social or medical histories of the child who receives treatment. In urban areas, emergency room personnel must be alert to HOSPITAL HOPPING, a practice employed by some chronic abusers.

Metropolitan hospitals may see 50% to 65% of reported cases of abuse as opposed to the 2% to 5% treated by private physicians. Figures such as these have led some observers to speculate that private physicians tend to underreport abuse. Statistics also indicate that low income families rely heavily on hospital emergency rooms for treatment. In theory, this increases the likelihood that abuse in families of lower socioeconomic status will be detected and reported.

emotional abuse   *S e e* PSYCHOLOGICAL MALTREATMENT.

emotional neglect The NATIONAL CENTER ON CHILD ABUSE AND NEGLECT defines emotional neglect as "failure to provide the psychological nurturance necessary for a child's psychological growth and development."

Numerous studies have documented the crucial importance of a warm, safe and loving relationship with an adult for the healthy physical and emotional development of children. Early studies of HOSPITALISM in infants separated from their mothers at birth documented physical and cognitive impairment. These deficits appeared to result from a lack of physical contact and emotional interaction. Institutionalized infants in the studies received adequate food, shelter and medical care yet appeared undernourished, listless and withdrawn. In many cases the condition of these infants continued to worsen and eventually resulted in their death. Their FAILURE TO THRIVE was attributed to impersonal care received in the hospital. Overburdened nurses had little time to hold or interact with the infants. The sterile hospital environment offered little sensory stimulation. Conversely, infants in another ward who received a good deal of loving attention in a sensory-rich environment appeared happier and followed normal developmental patterns. Similar characteristics have been observed in children who receive insufficient parental attention at home.

Tactile stimulation (touching) appears to be especially important for both cognitive and emotional development of infants and children. Infants whose parents are physically undemonstrative may reach out indiscriminately to strangers at a time when others their age normally exhibit a fear of strangers.

Emotionally neglected children often show signs of psychopathology in later life. As children they may appear depressed and withdrawn or may engage in frantic ACTING-OUT in the hopes of attracting some type of attention from caretakers. Norman Polansky, a professor of social work at the University of Georgia, has described a phenomenon that he calls the APATHY-FUTILITY SYNDROME, in which neglected children develop a form of emotional numbness and immaturity that may later result in their becoming neglectful parents.

Despite the potentially devastating effects of emotional neglect, many areas do not specifically identify it as a condition to be reported to child protection agencies. Legal definitions of emotional neglect, when they exist, arc often so vague as to be useless in a court of law. Further, while the results of emotional neglect can be observed, it is often difficult to prove that parental neglect, rather than other factors, was the cause.

encopresis Repeated involuntary defecation (soiling) occurring in children over the age of four years is termed encopresis. Boys are over three times more likely than girls to suffer from this condition. Encopresis is usually accompanied by chronic constipation. Physical causes of encopresis include neurogenic megacolon, a nerve deficiency that inhibits peristalsis in the bowel, and anatomic megacolon, the obstruction of the bowel by a tumor or lesion. When no physiological cause is found encopresis is sometimes interpreted as the child's attempt to express hostility or resolve conflict. Many encopretic children live in families where open conflict is avoided at all costs.

Some psychotherapists have observed similarities between a parent's somatic concerns and those of the child. For example, the encopretic child may have a parent who suffers from irritable bowel syndrome or from chronic constipation.

Fecal soiling may be seen as both a precipitant and a consequence of abuse. Caretakers find an encopretic child extremely frustrating and enraged parents may resort to harsh punishment in an effort to stop the behavior. Harsh treatment can actually prolong the problem and is almost never helpful.

In a child who has been toilet trained for over one year encopresis sometimes is seen as indicative of internal conflicts that the child cannot address directly. These conflicts may be related to abuse.

A careful assessment, beginning with a thorough medical examination, is recommended as the first step in treating encopresis.

Charles E. Schaefer, *Childhood Encopresis and Enuresis: Causes and Therapy* (New York: Van Nostrand Reinhold Company, 1979).

End Violence Against the Next Generation (EVAN-G)   This group was founded in 1971 and works to eliminate CORPORAL PUNISHMENT from schools and other institutions. One of several organizations that oppose corporal punishment, it publishes a quarterly, *The Last Resort*, and maintains both a speakers bureau and a library aimed at educating the public on the effects of corporal punishment. Its membership comprises educators, lawyers, social service workers, parents and other interested adults who disseminate information about corporal punishment. EVAN-G provides counseling and consultation services for school boards and produces articles for publication in scholarly journals. For more information, see APPENDIX 1.

England   *See* BRITAIN.

enuresis   Repeated involuntary discharge of urine in a child over three years of age. Enuresis is derived from the Greek word meaning "I make water." Approximately 10% of children between the ages of six and 10 in the United States are enuretic.

A number of myths have grown up around the problem of enuresis. Many caregivers believe that bedwetting is done out of spite, although psychotherapists strongly oppose this interpretation. Most believe enuresis is related to anxiety, usually due to situational stress.

Another myth is that enuretic children are emotionally disturbed. Though the incidence of emotional problems is slightly higher among this group, many of these problems vanish as the enuresis is controlled.

Many cruel and inhumane remedies have been tried in an effort to cure enuresis. Seventh-century parents forced bedwetters to drink a pint of their own urine. Other "cures" included beating, tying a string around the penis, placing the child's buttocks on a hot stove, making the child wear wet garments, shaming or ridiculing the child. All of these methods are ineffective and abusive. There is no evidence that punishment is an effective treatment for enuresis.

Physicians and psychologists generally attribute non- physiologically based enuresis to situational stress. Punishment usually exacerbates the problem in these cases.

As with ENCOPRESIS, treatment of enuresis should begin with a thorough medical examination.

Charles E. Schaefer, *Childhood Encopresis and Enuresis: Causes and Therapy (New York: Van Nostrand Reinhold, 1979).*

EPSDT   *See* EARLY AND PERIODIC SCREENING, DIAGNOSIS AND TREATMENT.

EVAN-G *See* END VIOLENCE AGAINST THE NEXT GENERATION.

evidence Statements by various parties, written documents, material objects and the opinions of experts may all serve as evidence in an investigation of suspected child abuse or neglect. Not all such evidence is allowed in court hearings. Courts have rules that govern the kinds of evidence that may be considered. Types of evidence allowed may differ according to the type of hearing. Preliminary or pretrial hearings are held for the purpose of issuing temporary orders. Evidence allowed at a preliminary hearing may not meet the rules of evidence applicable to a later court proceeding.

Adjudicatory or "fact-finding" hearings usually require that evidence conform to the legal rules of evidence and have a direct bearing on the issue before the court. In general four kinds of evidence are allowed.

Direct evidence is based on the witness's own observations and perceptions and does not depend on proof of any other facts. A neighbor's account of having watched the accused beating the child is direct evidence.

Real, demonstrative or autoptic evidence is concrete physical evidence. A child's injuries, X rays showing broken bones, instruments used to harm a child, and photographs are examples of real evidence.

Circumstantial evidence includes observations that allow the court to reach a specific conclusion, for example, testimony that a parent was shouting, threatening and visibly enraged at a child shortly before the alleged abuse occurred.

Expert or opinion evidence is usually given by someone who has special skills or expertise beyond that of the court. Opinions of expert witnesses are admissible only if they are related to an expert's area of expertise. Physicians are often called upon to give expert testimony concerning the nature and extent of a child's physical injuries.

Evidence that is not based on a witness's direct observations or experience is called "hearsay" and is generally not admissible in a fact-finding hearing. (*See* TESTIMONY for special cases where hearsay evidence may be allowed.)

In most court proceedings certain conversations such as those between a physician and patient or between psychotherapist and client are considered "privileged" and therefore may be excluded from testimony. Many states have laws specifically abrogating these privileges where child abuse or neglect is involved. Such communications can serve as important evidence in court.

evidence, autoptic *See* EVIDENCE.

evidence, circumstantial *See* EVIDENCE.

evidence, clear and convincing *See* EVIDENTIARY STANDARDS.

evidence, demonstrative *See* EVIDENCE.

evidence, direct *See* EVIDENCE.

evidence, expert *See* EVIDENCE.

evidence, opinion *See* EVIDENCE.

evidence, preponderance of. *See* PREPONDERANCE OF EVIDENCE.

evidence, real *See* EVIDENCE.

evidentiary standards Different types of court cases require different levels or standards of proof. The three most common standards are: a fair preponderance of the evidence; clear and convincing evidence; and proof beyond a reasonable doubt.

Jurisdictions differ in the particular evidentiary standard applied to specific types of cases. If a standard is not specified by law, the preponderance of evidence standard is usually applied.

Preponderance of evidence is the least restrictive, or easiest, standard. To meet this standard a party must simply give a greater amount of credible evidence than that provided by the opposing party. Evidence presented may leave some degree of doubt in the minds of the judge or jury. When all evidence presented in court is considered a jury must decide if one side has presented more credible evidence in support of its case than has its opponent. The preponderance of evidence standard is used most often in civil court proceedings.

Clear and convincing evidence requires more confidence on the part of the decision-maker than a simple preponderance of evidence. This standard is usually applied to removal of a child from home due to child abuse or neglect. By requiring a somewhat higher standard of proof courts seek to strike a balance between parents' interests in maintaining their children at home and the child's need for protection.

Beyond a reasonable doubt, the highest standard, is applied in criminal court proceedings. Evidence must support a party's contentions to a moral certainty. There must be no "reasonable" doubt in jurors' minds. The word reasonable implies a comparison of the jurors' standards for absolute certainty to those of the average person. This standard is particularly challenging to prosecutors of child sexual abuse cases who often must rely on circumstantial evidence and/or testimony from very young children to prove a case.

Proof beyond a reasonable doubt is also required for TERMINATION OF PARENTAL RIGHTS.

ex parte Crouse   In Pennsylvania in 1838, a court ruling upheld the right of the state to determine whether a young girl, Mary Ann Crouse, should remain in the Philadelphia House of Refuge, outside the custody of her parents. Crouse had been remanded to the House of Refuge at her mother's request, although without her father's knowledge or approval. In an attempt to obtain custody of his daughter, the father demanded Mary Ann's release on the grounds of the Sixth Amendment, which provides for due process of law.

The institution countered that the young girl was ineligible for such protection since she was a minor and the Pennsylvania Supreme Court subsequently ruled against the father. Mary Ann Crouse was the first juvenile in the United States whose custody was determined by a court that successfully invoked the doctrine of PARENS PATRIAE as a way of removing her from parental jurisdiction.

excited utterance   Courts usually do not accept hearsay testimony (observations concerning statements made by someone other than the witness) as evidence. An exception to this rule may be made when a person under great stress (usually the victim of a crime) makes a statement. In such instances a person who heard the statement may be allowed to testify concerning the victim's original exclamation.

The excited-utterance exception to the hearsay rule is frequently applied in trials involving child abuse. Because the credibility of a young child's testimony is often questioned, corroborating testimony from an adult is considered important evidence. Some states require that testimony of a young child be supported by testimony from an adult. A child's statements made shortly after an incident of alleged abuse and in the presence of a child protection worker, teacher or other adult are allowed under the ancient rule of *res gestae*. This rule may be interpreted literally as "things done." It extends to things said, gestures made and thoughts expressed that are so closely related to the occurrence of an event as to be considered a part of the event.

Excited utterances are justified by the theory that a victim's statements immediately following a crime are likely to be truthful because the victim is under stress and unable to construct a false account of events. The victim's mental state (i.e., excitement and the length of time that elapses between the event in question and the victim's statement) are of crucial importance.

Acceptance of excited utterance testimony from children is controversial. Courts are sometimes criticized for allowing this type of testimony when several hours, even days, have passed between the incident and the excited utterance. Another problem associated with reliance on excited utterance testimony is that children often delay reporting abuse out of fear or shame. Very young children may fail to understand an event and therefore do not become upset immediately following abuse. In such cases the child's statements would fail to meet the criterion of being under stress. (*See also* TESTIMONY.)

exhibitionism   Exposure of the sex organs as a means of sexual gratification. Some experts also refer to flaunting of past abuse as exhibitionism.

Sexual Exhibitionism

One-third of all reported sex offenses involve exhibitionism. Research indicates that only 17% of all exhibitionistic episodes are referred to the police.

Victims of exhibitionism include both children and adults but are almost always female. Girls at or near the age of puberty are the most frequent victims. The majority of victims show no long-term effects though a small proportion may be significantly traumatized.

Perpetrators of sexual exhibitionism are most likely to be young adult males with interpersonal difficulties but without serious psychopathology. Exhibitionists usually do *not* progress to more serious sex crimes.

Almost three-fourths of all exhibitionism takes place outdoors. Most incidents occur in streets, alleys and parking lots. Only 5% take place in public parks or school playgrounds. About 14% of exhibitionist incidents occur at home.

Many states have statutes that impose harsher penalties against offenders when the victim is a child.

Children who have been subjected to repeated sexual abuse sometimes engage in

seductive or exhibitionistic behavior toward adults. Incest victims may behave seductively as a means of getting love or attention when their emotional needs cannot be met in more conventional ways. These children come to view themselves as dehumanized sexual objects in much the same way that they have been treated by their abusers. Such behavior has contributed to the damaging myths that children enjoy sexual relations with adults and that children are the seducers.

Other Forms of Exhibitionism

A second and rather rare form of exhibitionism has been observed in abused children following their removal from the abusive situation. Displaying an eagerness to describe their abuse to others these children have developed an identity centered around their history of abuse. Self-labeling is used as justification for current negative behavior or as a means of gaining special consideration from others. For example, a child may blame all failures to comply with the wishes of teachers or foster parents on his or her status as an abused child, e.g., "I can't do it because I was abused by my parents." This form of exhibitionism should not be confused with a normal, healthy desire to understand past abuse by talking about it with others.

Daniel J. Cox and Reid J. Daitzman, *Exhibitionism: Description, Assessment and Treatment* (New York: Garland Press, 1980).

exhibitionism, sexual   *See* EXHIBITIONISM.

expert evidence   *See* EVIDENCE.

expert witness   In any court situation, a witness is called upon to testify according to first-hand knowledge of an event or series of events. Some witnesses may have special education, experience or skills that are valuable in a child abuse or neglect case. These witnesses contribute either to the defense or to the prosecution, or are important in terms of general edification of the court. This type of witness may be asked to comment upon details of the case and to give an opinion based on the specialized training or background he or she has in a specific area. In this situation, the witness is called upon to do more than simply state facts as seen or heard. Some expert witnesses in child abuse or neglect cases are physicians, psychiatrists, psychologists and social workers. (*See also* WITNESS.)

exploitation, physical   *See* CHILD LABOR LAWS, CHILD SLAVERY.

exploitation, sexual   *See* SEXUAL EXPLOITATION.

exposure   This procedure is a form of *infanticide* in which a newborn is abandoned to die from such indirect causes as hypothermia or starvation. Some ancient cultures positively sanctioned or encouraged exposure of weak, premature or deformed infants. Believing that such children would pass their deformities along to their offspring, Aristotle recommended that rearing of disabled or deformed children be forbidden by law.

Roman law allowed exposure of infants born in cases where marital infidelity was suspected, a practice that continued until outlawed by the Emperor Valentinian III in 434 A.D. Exposure was practiced by many other cultures as well. In 19th-century China, female infants were routinely cast into a river or left to die.

expungement   Judges may order the destruction or expungement of court records. In many states records of juvenile court proceedings are expunged after a predetermined number of years. Some jurisdictions allow either party to a child abuse case to apply for expungement. When requesting expungement a convicted defendant must satisfy the court that he or she has been rehabilitated, i.e., no longer engages in the conduct that lead to conviction.

Expungement of unverified reports of abuse has been a hotly debated issue among proponents and critics of child abuse reporting laws. Those in favor of expungement argue that an individual's reputation can be severely harmed by such information, even though an investigation has determined the report to be unfounded. Some child advocates believe it is important to maintain such information for use in future investigations. State policies differ regarding expungement of unverified reports.

eye injuries   Vision problems and eye injuries are important and usually easily recognizable indicators of abuse. Close examination of the eyes by a trained physician using an ophthalmoscope can sometimes reveal evidence of trauma and internal injuries that would otherwise have gone unnoticed.

Abuse-related eye injuries can be caused by a number of different kinds of trauma. Sharp objects can lacerate eyelids, cornea and sclera. Subsequent scarring from these cuts can permanently impair vision. Harsh chemicals introduced into the eye can cause burns and scarring. A direct blow from a fist or other blunt object can cause retinal damage as well as external damage to the cornea. Force transferred through the vitreous (jellylike substance inside the eye) to all parts of the eye applies sudden and extreme pressure to delicate internal structures and may damage the optic nerve. Collection of blood and damaged tissue inside the eye following trauma can also impair vision.

Blows to the front of the head may injure the visual cortex, causing blindness or other visual problems. Damage to the optic nerve can occur when head trauma causes cranial bones to splinter or when swelling applies pressure. Gouging can separate the optic nerve from the eye, resulting in permanent vision loss.

A sudden blow to the chest may produce a rapid increase in pressure within the blood vessels, causing retinal hemorrhaging. This condition, known as PURTSHER RETINOPATHY, is common among young children who have been battered. Though retinal hemorrhages are often found in abused children they can also occur as a result of other childhood activities, such as participation in contact sports or gymnastics.

An ophthalmoscopic examination is an important part of a thorough medical assessment of PHYSICAL ABUSE.

Norman S. Ellerstein, *Child Abuse and Neglect: A Medical Reference* (New York: John Wiley, 1981).

Alejandro Rodriguez, *Handbook of Child Abuse and Neglect* (Flushing, N.Y.: Medical Examination Publishing Co., 1977).

F

failure to bond   *See* BONDING FAILURE.

failure to grow   *See* GROWTH FAILURE.

Failure to Thrive Syndrome (FTT)   A child who, during the first three years of life, experiences a marked retardation or cessation of growth is said to suffer from the failure to thrive syndrome. The most frequently used technical criterion for diagnosing FTT is when the child's weight falls below the third percentile on a standard growth chart. At this level of physical retardation, the child has a serious and often life- threatening condition.

Cases of FTT are divided into two major categories: organic and nonorganic. Organic FTT may be the result of genetic predisposition, constitutional factors, chronic illness or diseases that affect the intake, absorption or utilization of food.

Nonorganic FTT—a lack of adequate nurturing are also known as deprivation DWARFISM and the maternal rejection syndrome—may stem from any one of a long list of environmental conditions, including: the parents' lack of knowledge about child rearing, inadequate technical advice or support for mothers who breast-feed their babies, nutritional deficiencies caused by extended breast-feeding as the sole source of nourishment, rigidity in feeding practices, maternal depression, and anxiety over the ability to care for the infant. In some cases the primary caretaker feels that the child is in some way damaged, retarded or intractable and uses this as a basis for rejection. BONDING FAILURE resulting from maternal illness or a difficult birth may also contribute to a lack of proper nurturance or to rejection.

Though some researchers attribute nonorganic FTT solely to insufficient nutritional intake, others believe it may also be due to a neuroendocrine disturbance that occurs when an infant or child is deprived of emotional nurturance.

Mothers of nonthriving infants have been characterized as cold, rejecting, aggressive, anxious and inadequate. They are frequently undernourished themselves and live a life of social isolation with little or no help from friends, family or neighbors. In addition, fathers of these nonthriving children are often absent from the home.

Children suffering from FTT usually appear emaciated, weak, irritable, listless or apathetic. At the same time, infants may display a kind of HYPERVIGILANCE—looking to anyone who approaches for nurturance, devoid of the customary wariness of strangers exhibited by other children of their age. Infants suffering from the sensory deprivation associated with FTT often maintain a posture in which the arms are held out, flexed at the elbow with the hands up and legs drawn in. This position of apparent surrender is held for long periods of time.

Some children may not appear to be malnourished at first glance, but upon careful examination may have poor muscular development, dull or pale skin, sparse, dry hair or similar evidence of poor nourishment. Young victims of FTT often show a remarkable growth spurt upon hospitalization, with rapid gains in both weight and head circumference. Behavioral manifestations are slower to improve and may linger for some time after the child has regained an adequate rate of physical growth.

Unfortunately the rapid improvement experienced during hospitalization is often reversed when the child is returned home. Unless significant changes are made in the quality of care provided at home the child may continue to suffer from retarded physical, psychological and intellectual development.

Follow-up studies of children hospitalized for FTT show that about half of them remain below the third percentile in height and weight. Additionally, many of these children are intellectually retarded and experience a higher-than-average number of educational and emotional problems.

Ernesto Pollitt and Rudolph Leibel, "Biological and Social Correlates of Failure to Thrive," in *Social and Biological Predictors of Nutritional Status, Physical Growth and Neurological Development*, Lawrence Green and Francis Johnston, eds. (New York: Academic Press, 1980).

fallen fontanelle (caida de mollera)
Traditional medicine in many Latin American countries, as well as among Mexican-Americans, holds that fallen fontanelle (the soft cranial bones) in infants can result in listlessness, diarrhea and vomiting. There is no evidence, however, that these symptoms are attributable to displacement of the cranial bones.

The traditional cure for this condition is to turn the baby upside down, place the top of the head in water, and shake the infant to return the fontanelle to its proper position. Though this practice can produce RETINAL HEMORRHAGE, or even SUBDURAL HEMATOMA if applied too forcefully, it is not considered abusive since it is a widely held, culturally based belief.

Families Anonymous *The National Center for the Prevention and Treatment of Child Abuse and Neglect* often refers to self-help groups for abusive parents as Families Anonymous. These groups are similar to PARENTS ANONYMOUS but, unlike P.A., are not affiliated with a nationwide network of similar organizations. Families Anonymous is also a name used in the substance abuse treatment field for self-help groups that focus on the members of a drug or alcohol abuser's family.

family court *See* COURT.

family violence The term family violence includes physical attacks on a child, spouse or sibling by another member of the family unit. Attacks by or on an unmarried live-in partner may also be referred to as family violence.

Research suggests that inappropriate or excessive use of force frequently occurs in more than one form in a family. Child abuse and sibling abuse is often present in families where there is spousal abuse and vice versa. Countries also differ in the characteristics and levels of familial violence. Though Western industrialized countries appear to have higher levels of family violence it is a problem in all countries.

National surveys conducted in the United States in 1975 and 1985 indicate that the level of severe violence (kicking, hitting with a fist, biting, beating, use of a gun or knife) may be decreasing. The 1985 survey estimated that 19 of every 1,000 children were victims of severe violence, a 47% decrease from 1975 estimates. The study did not include children under the age of three years.

In contrast to physical child abuse, which may be declining, spousal abuse remained relatively stable. Estimates in 1985 of husband-to-wife abuse were 30 couples out of every thousand. Wife-to-husband levels of severe violence were 44 per thousand. Overall, at least one severe assault occurred among 58 of every thousand couples during 1985.

Though wives may attack husbands more frequently, many of these attacks are in self-defense. Because their average size and strength is greater, men are more likely to inflict serious injury.

Violence between siblings may be the most frequent form of family violence. Unfortunately, little information is available on the incidence or effects of sibling-to-sibling attacks. SIBLING ABUSE is thought to represent a significant proportion of child abuse; however, it is the type of family violence least likely to be reported to authorities.

Richard J. Gelles, a sociologist specializing in child abuse and family violence, identifies four factors that are related to family violence. The first is the intergenerational nature of abuse. An abused child is more likely to become an abusive adult than a child who has not been abused.

Poverty is also related to violence in families. Though the majority of families with incomes below poverty guidelines are not violent, rates of child abuse and spouse abuse in poor families are higher than in families with substantially higher incomes.

A third characteristic of violent as well as neglectful families is social isolation. These families are observed to have infrequent contacts with friends and relatives, participate in few community activities and move often.

A final factor, social stress, may combine some of the three previous factors with other stressful circumstances. Unemployment, low levels of education, high-stress jobs, marital conflict, poor living conditions and many other factors can increase the level of family stress.

Eli Newberger and Richard Bourne, eds, *Unhappy Families* (New York: PSG Publishing Co., 1985).

David Finkelhor, Richard J. Gelles, Gerald Hotaling, Murray Straus, eds, *The Dark Side of Families* (Beverly Hills, Calif.: Sage Publications, 1983).

James Garbarino and G. Gilliam, *Understanding Abusive Families* (Lexington, Mass: D.C. Heath, 1980).

Richard J. Gelles and Claire Pedrick Cornell, eds, *International Perspectives on Family Violence* (Lexington, Mass.: Lexington Books, 1983).

Richard J. Gelles and Murray Straus, *Intimate Violence* (New York: Simon and Schuster, 1988).

Federal Republic of Germany *See* GERMANY, FEDERAL REPUBLIC OF.

fellatio This term refers to oral contact with the male genitals. Fellatio is a form of sexual abuse when a child is forced or encouraged to perform, submit to or observe the activity. Children are sometimes forced to engage in fellatio with another child for the sexual stimulation of a pedophile. In such cases the adult is responsible for the behavior even though he or she is not physically engaged in the act itself. (*See also* SEXUAL ABUSE.)

felony Crimes punishable by death or by imprisonment for longer than one year are called felonies. In common law, murder, mayhem, arson, rape, robbery, burglary, larceny, escape from prison and rescue of a convicted felon were considered felonies.

Criminal acts of abuse or neglect may be classed as either a felony or a MISDEMEANOR, depending on the severity of the act. Jurisdictions may vary in the specific acts they consider felonies; however, a felony is always a more serious crime than a misdemeanor.

fetal alcohol syndrome Heavy alcohol consumption during pregnancy can lead to a condition known as fetal alcohol syndrome (FAS). Infants born with FAS exhibit growth retardation, facial disfigurement and central nervous system damage. Children suffering from FAS are often recognizable by the low placement and posterior rotation of their ears, by epicanthic folds, thin lips, a small upturned nose, and other facial malformations. They are also likely to suffer from mental retardation and other neurological abnormalities.

Evidence shows that women who drink heavily are twice as likely to abort spontaneously as those who do not. Heavy drinkers may also be at greater risk for stillbirth. In recent years some states have begun to require the reporting of conditions such as maternal alcoholism and drug addiction that may endanger the health of a child before it is born. It is difficult, however, to establish and enforce minimum standards of prenatal care.

A 1981 decision by a Canadian court may have set a precedent for intervention in extreme cases. The court ruled that a mother whose child was born with FAS, and who had ignored her physician's repeated advice to seek treatment for her alcoholism, was guilty of PHYSICAL ABUSE. The child was removed from the mother's custody under provisions of the Child Welfare Act.

It is not clear what effects moderate and low alcohol consumption have on the fetus. Some physicians caution that even small amounts of alcohol may be detrimental to the developing fetus. Alcohol is passed directly to the fetus in the same concentration as in the mother's blood. Due to the undeveloped metabolic and elimination capabilities of the fetus, alcohol remains in the system longer and has a more toxic effect. The National Institute on Alcohol Abuse and Alcoholism (NIAAA) recommends complete abstinence during pregnancy since severe and lasting damage to a child's health can occur as a result of heavy consumption of alcohol by the mother during pregnancy. The National Institute on Alcohol Abuse and Alcoholism has determined that the consumption of three or more ounces of alcohol at any one time presents a serious health risk to the fetus. Other studies suggest that even smaller amounts of alcohol can have detrimental effects. Heavy consumption of alcohol during critical developmetal periods can lead to physical malformation, retarded growth and impaired neurological development.

Ernest L. Abel, *Fetal Alcohol Syndrome and Fetal Alcohol Effects (New York: Plenum Press, 1984)*.
Moira Plant, *Women, Drinking and Pregnancy* (London: Tavistock, 1985).

filicide   Murder of a child by the parent is termed filicide. Statistics from 1985 show that 3% of all homicides reported in the United States during that year were filicides. This figure may underestimate true incidence, however, because many child abuse–related deaths are reported as accidents. Over twice as many children are killed by their parents than parents killed by their children.

fixated offender   This type of male sexual offender presents a pattern, beginning in adolescence, of being sexually attracted to children. Though he may occasionally engage in sexual activity with adults, such an offender rarely initiates the activity. The fixated offender actively seeks the company of children and fantasizes about sexual contact with them.

PEDOPHILIA is deeply ingrained in the psyche of the fixated offender. Unlike regression, fixation is not the result of a frustrated desire for sex with an adult or similar situational cause, and the offender rarely shows any remorse for his sexual attacks on children. Often compared to an addiction, this pattern of abusive behavior is particularly resistant to treatment.

Though the terms fixated and regressed have been widely used to differentiate perpetrators of child sexual abuse, it has been suggested recently that the motivation of the offender can be better understood as a continuum ranging from appropriate display of affection to brutal rape. David Finkelhor, a noted researcher of child sexual abuse, has suggested that the two major factors that differentiate pedophiles are: (1) the exclusivity of their attraction to children, and (2) the strength of that attraction. This idea is known as a CONTINUUM MODEL OF CHILD ABUSE.

fondling   In the context of child SEXUAL ABUSE, fondling refers to touching of the genitals, breasts or buttocks. Fondling may be a prelude to more extensive sexual activity or an end in itself. Adults are most frequently the fondlers; however, some sexual abuse involves encouraging or coercing children to fondle adults.

As is the case with other forms of sexual abuse, men are more likely to be reported for fondling. While men are the most frequent sexual aggressors, some writers speculate that women's role of primary caretaker of children permits inappropriate fondling to go unnoticed. Reports of nurses and childcare workers who routinely use fondling as a way of quieting upset infants appear with reasonable frequency but are often difficult to document.

fontanelle, fallen   *See* FALLEN FONTANELLE.

forensic medicine   In cases of suspected child abuse or neglect specialized medical knowledge is often necessary to answer

Table 3
Reports of Fatalities for 29 States
Providing Complete Information, 1984–1985

State	1984	1985
Arkansas	19	9
Colorado	20	12
Connecticut	18	7
Florida	7	9
Hawaii	2[a,b]	1[a,b]
Idaho	6	1
Illinois	88[c]	115[c]
Indiana	31	29
Iowa	11	9
Kansas	5	9
Kentucky	22	10
Louisiana	33	40
Maine	2	1
Maryland	10	9
Massachusetts	38	27
Missouri	32	24
Nevada	3	6
New Jersey	21	20
New York	136	130
North Carolina	16	8
Oklahoma	16	16
Oregon	3	5
Pennsylvania	42	35
South Carolina	6	21
Utah	5	8
Vermont	0	0
Virginia	16	14
Wisconsin	17	9
Wyoming	0	3
Total	625	587

[a] Figures represent substantiated reports.
[b] No figures available (for 1981–1982).
[c] Figures represent fiscal years, not calendar years.

questions of law. A physician may be asked to examine a child and to testify in court whether, in his or her professional opinion, the child has been abused. When a child dies under suspicious circumstances a medical examiner, usually a pathologist, is called upon to conduct an autopsy to determine the probable cause of death. Both of these physicians are practicing forensic medicine.

Forensic medicine requires special training in gathering medical evidence and providing expert court testimony. With respect to child abuse, forensic specialists must have thorough knowledge of various methods of abuse and must be able to distinguish between accidental injuries and those likely to be intentionally inflicted. In such cases the physician is often asked to determine the validity of a caretaker's explanation of the injury. Through careful examination and application of specialized knowledge the physician is often able to find evidence to support or refute the caretaker's claim.

The ability to date injuries is particularly important in determining who was responsible for the child at the time of injury and also in establishing evidence of a pattern of abuse. Physicians frequently rely on microscopic examination of damaged tissue and use of X rays to determine the approximate date of the abuse. Applying knowledge of the normal healing process, the examiner is able to determine the amount of time that has elapsed since the injury. Multiple injuries, fractures for example, in various stages of healing are usually indicative of abuse over an extended period of time. Such evidence belies explanations of a "freak accident" or a single episode of abuse.

When neglect is a suspected cause of death the forensic examiner's task is somewhat different. In addition to looking for evidence of abuse and neglect, the physician must also rule out other medical explanations for the death. Some chronic diseases can inhibit the normal absorption of nutrients, causing a child to die of starvation despite being fed a healthy diet. In some cases, such as SUDDEN INFANT DEATH SYNDROME, no satisfactory explanation of death can be determined.

Evidence presented by the forensic medical examiner is usually presented in combination with other evidence concerning the child's psychosocial history, the parent's history, the current family situation, reports from teachers, neighbors etc. (*See also* RADIOLOGY, PEDIATRIC.)

foster care   A relatively small percentage of abused and neglected children are placed in foster care. Foster placement is intended to provide short- term substitute care until a child can return home. Most foster care is provided by families licensed by a state agency. Typically, foster parents receive a small stipend to defray the cost of food and clothing. In the United States children in foster care are eligible for MEDICAID coverage.

Unfortunately, many children remain in foster care much longer than originally intended. Long periods of out-of-home placement are difficult for the child, natural parents and the foster family. Children in placement are sometimes reluctant to form a close bond with their foster families because they expect to be returning home soon. As time passes they may find themselves cut off emotionally from both natural parents and foster family. In other cases the child may form an immediate bond with the foster parents and may be reluctant to return home.

Due to changes in the foster family's status, incompatible matches and agency practices, children who remain in foster care for any length of time are often subject to frequent moves. The potentially negative effects of foster placement have led to attempts to limit its use.

In 1980, the United States Congress passed the ADOPTION ASSISTANCE AND CHILD WELFARE REFORM ACT in an attempt to address the problem of extended foster placements. The act requires that extensive efforts be devoted to maintaining the child at home if at all possible. When foster placement is considered necessary, a judge must review the decision.

All foster children must have a CASE PLAN. Plans are subject to an independent administrative review at least once every six months. Finally, the act attempts to make it easier for children to be freed for adoption when it appears that they will not be able to return to their biological parents.

Despite its problems, foster care is an important resource for abused children. The majority of foster families offer competent, warm and loving care. Under good conditions, foster families receive adequate support from case workers and in turn provide a stable environment for the child. To be effective, foster care must be part of a comprehensive system of treatment involving the child, natural family and foster family. (*See also* PLACEMENT OF ABUSED CHILDREN.)

founded report   Reports of suspected child abuse or neglect are considered founded if verified by an investigation. The process of verifying reports is called SUBSTANTIATION.

Statistics from several states indicate a wide variation in the percentage of reports that are founded. Differences in rates of substantiation may reflect legal definitions of abuse and neglect or variations in protective service agencies policies.

foundling hospital   The first known foundling hospital for unwanted children was established in 787 A.D. by Datheus, Archpriest of Milan. During the late 19th century, a large foundling hospital in St. Petersburg, Russia, handled an average of 25,000 babies annually.

Although they were established to care for large numbers of unwanted babies who were being killed or abandoned by their parents, the foundling hospitals themselves often provided inadequate care or engaged in exploitation. About one in every four babies placed in early foundling hospitals died there. Early studies of the FAILURE TO THRIVE SYNDROME by Rene A. Spitz, John Bowlby and others were conducted in foundling hospi-

tals. These studies concluded that even when infants were provided with excellent physical and medical care they often became listless, failed to grow at the normal rate, and sometimes died—apparently as a result of inadequate emotional nurturance.

New methods of birth control, legalized abortion, the availability of public financial support for the poor, and an expanded interest in adoption have combined to reduce the need for foundling hospitals in most Western nations since World War II.

fractures   The ability of physicians to identify and date fractures was greatly enhanced by advances in the use and interpretation of X rays. Employing X-ray technology, pediatric radiologists are able to tell approximately when a fracture occurred and often what type of force caused the fracture. By comparing this information with the caretaker's explanation of an injury the physician can often identify cases of suspected abuse.

While certain types of fracture are indicative of abuse, a diagnosis of abuse requires information about the child's environment, how the injury occurred, the child's caretakers and medical history. Some childhood diseases can render the bones brittle and thus more susceptible to injury. Conditions such as OSTEOGENESIS IMPERFECTA and congenital insensitivity to pain must be ruled out in the process of diagnosing child abuse. It is not uncommon for infants, particularly breech deliveries, to sustain fractures during childbirth. As a general rule, fractures incidental to childbirth will be visible on X rays by the eleventh day of life. Bone trauma appearing after this time is assumed to have occurred following birth.

In evaluating the possibility of child battering, consideration of the child's age is important. While it is quite possible for a child to sustain certain types of fracture while learning to walk, the presence of a transverse (crosswise) or spiral fracture in a child who is not yet able to walk may arouse suspicion.

Bone fractures related to child abuse are caused by a direct blow, twisting (usually of a limb), shaking or squeezing. The particular kind of force used may produce a characteristic type of fracture. A direct blow often produces a transverse or spiral fracture to the shaft of a long bone. Blows to the head often produce internal injuries in addition to fractures of the cranium, mandible and maxillary bones. Swelling due to increased pressure inside the cranium can cause the sutures of the skull to separate.

Twisting forces may produce spiral fractures in the long bone shaft. This type of fracture, like those resulting from direct blows, occurs frequently from accidental causes. A spiral fracture of the tibia (one of two bones in the forearm) is somewhat more likely to be the result of abuse than similar fracture of other bones.

Fractures at the epiphyseal-metaphyseal junction are also produced by twisting and are more frequently related to abuse. The epiphysis, the cartilaginous end of a child's long bones, can be detached from the relatively stronger metaphysis by twisting or vigorous jiggling of a child's limbs. This type of injury is difficult to identify in the early stages of healing. In some cases a fragment of bone or cartilage may be visible on an X ray, in others the only visible sign is swelling of tissues around the joint. Epiphyseal-metaphyseal injuries to the hip and shoulder sometimes cause the joint space to fill with blood. Widening of

Table 4

Fractures Associated With Battering

Transverse —Long Bones	often accidental in children who are old enough to walk, rarely accidental in nonambulatory children; may result from a direct blow
Spiral —Long Bones	can be caused by twisting or a direct blow; often accidental in older children
Fractures of the Cranium	young children and infants are especially susceptible to these injuries; may result in macrocephaly, separation of the cranial sutures, CNS damage
Vertebral Fractures, —*Compression, Notching*	often caused by shaking; may also be associated with CNS injury, subdural hematoma, internal organ damage
Epiphyseal-Metaphyseal Injury—Long Bones	caused by twisting forces; most frequently associated with battering; may not be immediately detectable on X rays
Rib Fractures	may result from squeezing of the chest; sometimes associated with shaking injuries; frequently concomitant with internal organ injury

the hip or shoulder joint space usually indicates this type of injury. As healing progresses formation of CALLUS becomes visible in X rays, allowing easier identification of the injury.

Violent shaking of a child can cause spinal damage as well as epiphyseal-metaphyseal fractures. Spinal fractures usually follow hyperflexion (exaggerated twisting or bending) of the vertebral column. Typical injuries are compression, notching and/or dislocation of the vertebrae.

Squeezing injuries usually involve rib fractures. Fractures resulting from squeezing are usually bilateral, caused by an adult grasping both sides of the chest and applying pressure. When rib fractures are detected internal injuries may also be present.

Dating of fractures is especially important in detecting child abuse. By comparing physical evidence of the fracture's age with the caretaker's explanation of the accident the physician can detect discrepancies that might lead to a suspicion of battering. Presence of multiple fractures in various stages of healing is a hallmark of the BATTERED CHILD SYNDROME.

Determination of the age of a particular fracture usually depends on observation of soft tissue changes, observation of a visible fracture line, formation of CALLUS around the fracture and ossification of the periosteum (membrane covering the bone, which is usually damaged by trauma and the resulting bleeding). Immediate soft tissue manifestations of a fracture are EDEMA and swelling. Four to five days after the injury the first stages of new bone growth begin. Actual calcification is not visible on X rays until 10 to 14 days following the injury.

While a fracture line may be immediately visible following the injury some fractures are difficult to detect and are identifiable only after calcification begins to occur. Bone resorption along the line of the fracture during the first few days following the injury usually makes the fracture easier to detect. Most long bone fracture lines remain visible on X rays for four to eight weeks.

Detection of child battering involves the use of information obtained from several sources. When bone fractures are detected information from visual and X-ray examination can help determine the type of force that caused the injury and the approximate date of its occurrence. A SKELETAL SURVEY can also detect the presence of other fractures that may not have been reported. Medical information is then compared to accounts of the injury provided by the caretaker, other witnesses and the child (if old enough). Use of clinical data increases the accuracy with which a diagnosis of child battering can be made. Increased accuracy of diagnosis can help prevent further abuse as well as false accusations of caretakers.

France   Currently, child abuse and neglect in France receives a great deal of attention and is the subject of a wide array of preventive efforts. Both private and government agencies cooperate in providing services for abused children and their families, with the government making policy determinations. General child protective services form a basis on which specialized programs dealing with child maltreatment are built, although specific delineation of child abuse has received less attention than programs that serve all maltreated children. This is due in part to some reluctance to separate abuse from the larger issue of child maltreatment.

French welfare policies and services are established with the intention of serving the broad interests of families; a maternal and child health program is an important component of government-sponsored child welfare offerings in France. This maternal and child health service includes periodic physical examinations. Ninety-five percent of children aged three to five or six years are enrolled in preschool programs that include physical health exams. Court intervention in family situations where neglect or abuse occurs is permitted in France, although parents are not automatically held guilty as a result of a necessary emergency intervention.

Certain diagnostic methods help detect child abuse or child battering, procedures that have been employed in France since the late 1960s. Sexual abuse of children, and sexual violence in French institutions are areas in which some research attention has recently been focused. Also, recent French studies have focused on the possible negative effects of institutional care on child development.

frustration-aggression theory One explanation of physically abusive behavior focuses on the link between biological factors, characteristics of the particular situation and learned response patterns. Seymour Feshbach, a leading proponent of the frustration-aggression approach, focuses primarily on situational factors and learned responses in his explanation of abuse. Aggressive biological impulses are mentioned only as innate impulses to strike out when provoked.

Situational factors that contribute to abusive behavior are broken down into three subgroups: intent, responsibility and perceived justification. Immature or inex-perienced parents often have unrealistic expectations of children. A parent may believe an infant intentionally soils a clean diaper or purposely refuses to go to sleep at the appointed time. The parent believes the child is responsible for these actions in the same way an older child or adult would be accountable. Finally, instead of seeing the situation as a normal part of child-rearing the abusive parent feels treated unfairly by the child. These three perceptions combine to intensify the parent's frustration.

Feshbach credits social learning for increasing the likelihood of an aggressive response. Abusive parents learn, through various means, aggressive ways of dealing with frustration. While frustration does not automatically trigger aggression, parents who have learned aggressive responses are more likely to be abusive.

Following the frustration-aggression approach, treatment of the abusing parent would focus on changing unrealistic perceptions and expectations of the child's behavior and on learning new ways of responding to frustration. Many treatment programs incorporate these elements.

G

gastrointestinal injuries   The stomach and intestines are frequently damaged by forceful blows to the child's abdomen. Hollow organs, particularly the stomach and colon, are most susceptible to injury when they are filled with gas or partially digested food. Rapid compression of these viscera resulting from a blow to the abdomen can rupture organ walls. Such damage to the stomach causes its contents to spill into the peritoneal cavity. Hydrochloric acid from the stomach is highly irritating to other body tissue and can cause a child to go into shock. If the peritoneal cavity is not cleansed, spillage of stomach contents may cause abscesses to develop. Surgical repair of stomach and intestinal ruptures is necessary to prevent further contamination of the peritoneal cavity.

Rapid acceleration when a child is thrown or pushed is likely to tear connective tissue attaching the small intestine to the abdominal wall. Such injuries may cause hemorrhaging of damaged blood vessels.

HEMATOMA (buildup of blood) of the duodenum may result from a blunt blow to the abdomen. This type of injury occurs when the duodenum, with a rich blood supply, is crushed against the vertebral column. The resulting buildup of blood in the walls of the bowel obstructs normal flow of material through the gastrointestinal tract. Indicators of duodenal hematoma include vomiting of greenish material and complaints of tenderness in the upper abdomen. Laboratory tests and X rays are required to confirm the diagnosis.

This type of injury can usually be treated without surgery. With proper medical treatment the hematoma usually dissipates in 10 to 14 days. (*See also* ABDOMINAL INJURIES.)

gatekeepers   Professionals, agencies and institutions in frequent contact with children are the "gatekeepers" of child protection services. Gatekeepers are often mandated by state or federal law to report cases of suspected child abuse or neglect. Doctors, teachers, child care workers, social workers, counselors, psychologists, dentists and others are often the first to identify and report abuse. Unfortunately, many individuals in these positions lack adequate training in detection and reporting of suspected abuse and neglect. Widespread efforts are underway in many areas to provide training to those who work with children on a regular basis.

Gault   *See* IN RE GAULT.

genital mutilation   *See*   CASTRATION, CLITORIDECTOMY and INFIBULATION.

Robin Morgan and Gloria Steinem, "The International Crime of Genital Mutilation," in *Ms.* (March 1980).

German Democratic Republic   *See*   SOCIALIST EASTERN EUROPE.

Germany, Federal Republic of   In addressing concerns over abuse and neglect of children, West Germany puts a primary emphasis on PHYSICAL ABUSE, although there is no clear-cut definition of what constitutes abuse. Neglect of children is more specifically detailed in laws concerning the overall maltreatment of children and the responsibility of parents. While parents' rights in West Germany are treated with a great deal of consideration, in the mid-1970s the government nevertheless enacted legislation depriving parents of custody of their children if convicted of child abuse or neglect and sentenced to six months or more in prison. One researcher notes that, as a result, few parents are sentenced for more than five months in these cases.

Education programs aimed at reducing the incidence of child abuse and neglect were set up by the Senate in Bonn after a series of abuse cases resulted in the death of a number of children. Also, national health insurance provides a limited number of voluntary, no-cost medical exams for children between birth and four years of age. About 75% of preschool-age West German children (three to six years old) are examined by health care professionals as part of public education programs, enabling officials to detect cases of abuse and neglect that might otherwise go unnoticed or unreported.

There is no mandatory reporting legislation for child abuse or neglect in the Federal Republic of Germany. As a matter of historical note, while corporal punishment of children is illegal in West Germany today, in the 1930s the Nazi government in Germany reinstated legally permissible CORPORAL PUNISHMENT in schools and institutions, although it had earlier been banned as inappropriate behavior.

gonorrhea The most common venereal disease, gonorrhea, is caused by a bacterium commonly known as gonococcus. It infects the mucus membranes causing them to become inflamed. A discharge of pus is also common to cases of gonorrhea.

Gonococcus bacteria are spread through direct contact, predominantly during sexual intercourse. In addition, infants may contract gonorrhea at birth when passing through the vagina of an infected mother. If so infected and left untreated, infants can be blinded by the disease. As a part of a complete physical examination for child SEXUAL ABUSE, cultures are obtained from the genitals, rectum and throat of victim children—regardless of reported method of sexual contact. These cultures are then examined for gonococcus bacteria, which, if present, may indicate sexual abuse.

Great Britain *See* BRITAIN.

Greece In the late 1970s, work related to prevention and treatment of child abuse and neglect first became the subject of concerted professional effort in Greece. Currently, at the Institute of Child Health in Athens, as well as at various child welfare agencies throughout Greece, abuse and neglect of children is generally examined in the light of cultural pressures.

Traditionally, Greek society has placed greater expectations on sons, rather than daughters, leading child abuse experts to surmise, for example, that harsh or abusive disciplinary practices directed toward boys can often be attributed to the higher value that boys and men represent. Similarly, the closely knit family structure in traditional Greek society obligates the child and parent in ways that can produce tensions leading to abusive behavior.

CORPORAL PUNISHMENT within the home appears to be standard practice in Greece; one recent study of maternal attitudes toward discipline revealed that 10% of mothers surveyed spanked their children and 40% either shout at their children, isolate them in a darkened room, or subject them to some other form of verbal discipline. Further, there has been some concern over the treatment of Greek schoolchildren. Investigations into behavior of children in their school environment has suggested to researchers that some level of emotional abuse may occur regularly in Greek schools.

As one means of addressing growing concern about child abuse and neglect, the first European Congress on Child Abuse and Neglect was held in early 1987 in Greece. It was organized by the Greek Institute of Child Health working together with the INTERNATIONAL SOCIETY FOR THE PREVENTION OF CHILD ABUSE AND NEGLECT (ISPCAN) and several other Greek organizations, including the Greek Ministries of Culture and Health and Welfare.

growth failure Failure to meet age-appropriate milestones for physical development is primarily caused by inadequate nutrition. A number of organic problems, such as malabsorption of vital nutrients, genetically linked characteristics, disease or infection can interfere with a child or infant's maturation. In some cases, inadequate nutrition is linked to nonorganic factors, such as lack of knowledge by parents, rigid feeding practices or parental neglect and rejection.

Between birth and age three, significant growth failure is most often referred to as FAILURE TO THRIVE SYNDROME. After age three, growth retardation is known as DWARF-ISM.

Though Rene A. Spitz, John Bowlby and other researchers hypothesized that growth failure could result directly from a lack of emotional nurturance, it is now believed that this phenomenon is primarily related to poor nutrition. However, emotional factors frequently contribute to inadequate nutrition. Clinical evidence shows that when children suffering from psychosocial dwarfism are removed from the abusive situation, they experience a rapid growth spurt. This is also true of infants suffering from nonorganic failure to thrive syndrome.

growth failure, reversible   *See* DWARFISM.

guardian   An adult other than the biological parent may be appointed by a court of law to serve as a child's guardian. A guardian has virtually the same legal powers and respon-sibilities as a parent; however, guardianship is subject to change or termination by the court. In some cases the guardian may not have actual CUSTODY of the child. (*See also* GUARDIAN AD LITEM.)

guardian ad litem   In a child protection case involving suspected abuse or neglect, a child is granted an adult advocate, usually but not always an attorney. This individual represents the child for the duration of the litigation, with primary responsibility to ensure that procedural aspects of the case are legally correct. A guardian ad litem is appointed by the court when circumstances dictate that the best interests of the child would be served by so doing.

State laws differ concerning the right to counsel in juvenile proceedings. However, some state courts have found that in cases of child abuse or neglect, the right to counsel is required by the United States Constitution, which calls for due process and equal protection. The guardian ad litem—literally, guardian at law—is charged with protecting only legal rights. This differs from a guardian of the person, whose responsibility is to safeguard the physical and emotional well-being of a child in abuse or neglect proceedings.

H

Hague Convention on the Civil Aspects of International Child Abduction   In order to address issues of concern relative to return of abducted children and international visiting rights, on October 6, 1980, delegates and representatives of 36 nations convened in the 14th session of the Hague Conference on Private International Law. Their intent was to submit to their governments a comprehensive statement concerning the protection of children in matters relating to custody. On October 24, the assembly adopted the Hague Convention, which was subsequently signed by the United States on Dec. 23, 1981.

The stated desire of the convention was to "protect children internationally from the harmful effects of their wrongful removal or retention." Among other things, the convention establishes a central authority in each country to help individuals who seek return of children abducted from or retained outside the nation in which they are legal residents. In 1986, the United States Senate gave "advice and consent" to the Hague Convention and in 1987 legislation was introduced to implement policies and procedures outlined in the international document.

hairpulling   Hairpulling may result in traumatic ALOPECIA (hair loss) and SUBGALEAL HEMATOMA.

Head Start   A nationwide, comprehensive educational program for disadvantaged preschool children that is funded by the United States government, Head Start provides a range of educational enrichment services to young children. Recent studies have shown it to be an effective tool in countering the effects of poverty on children's educational readiness.

As a matter of federal policy, all Head Start staff are MANDATED REPORTERS of child abuse and neglect.

health visitor   In BRITAIN, National Health Service provisions include education and prevention programs and general promotion of good health through the services of a health visitor. Most generally, a health visitor's primary concern is with preschool children and their families. In this capacity, the health visitor may be involved in surveillance of child health and welfare, making regular and routine exams of children. British law requires that newborns be seen by a health visitor at least once during the first 12 months of life; high-risk cases are visited more often.

In the United States, there is no permanently established health visitor system, although a short-term experimental lay health visitor program was established at the Department of Pediatrics of Colorado General Hospital in the late 1970s. Specifically designed to offer routine support and after-care in pediatric cases, this program provided services to families in which parenting problems were considered either to exist or to be at risk of developing. (*See also* PARENT AIDES.)

hearing   Any proceeding where evidence is considered for the purposes of determining an issue of fact is known as a hearing. Usually a hearing takes the form of a formal trial; however, administrative hearings may take place outside of the court process.

Judicial hearings may be held for the purpose of issuing temporary orders (preliminary hearing), fact-finding (adjudicatory hearing) and to determine what action should be taken (dispositional hearing). Emergency removal of a child from home and changes in custody also require hearings. In emergencies a hearing must take place within a specified period of time following removal of the child. (*See also* ADJUDICATORY HEARING, DISPOSITIONAL HEARING, EMERGENCY CUSTODY, CUSTODY.)

hearing, adjudicatory   *See* ADJUDICA-TORY HEARING.

hearing, dispositional   *See* DISPOSITIONAL HEARING.

hebephelia   Sexual desire and responses directed exclusively toward pubescent children by an adult are termed hebephelia. Hebephiles are often mislabled as pedophiles, adults who are sexually attracted to prepubescent children (see PEDOPHILIA). The hebephile usually shows little interest in young children and will engage in sexual activity with adults or children only when adolescents are unavailable. (*See also* ADOLESCENT ABUSE, CHILD MOLESTER and SEXUAL ABUSE.)

helpline   Telephone counseling services are often called helplines. Usually staffed by trained volunteers, helplines offer information, referral and paraprofessional counseling. Unlike HOTLINES, which are frequently connected to protective service agencies, helplines usually do not directly report suspected abuse or neglect. Calls to these services are often anonymous. If abuse or neglect is suspected the callers are encouraged to seek help on their own.

Helplines can serve an important early intervention function. By helping families cope with stress and relieving the social isolation many parents feel, these services can prevent abuse and neglect.

hematemesis   The vomiting of blood, usually as a result of abdominal trauma. Hematemesis can be indicative of internal battering injuries when no external signs are observable.

hematoma, jejunal   *See* JEJUNAL HEMA-TOMA.

hematoma, subdural   *See* SUBDURAL HE-MATOMA.

hematoma, subgaleal   *See* SUBGALEAL HEMATOMA.

hematuria   Trauma to the kidneys or bladder can frequently be detected by the presence of hematuria—blood in the urine. Hematuria is a sign of serious internal injury. Children who present this symptom should be examined by a knowledgeable physician for other evidence of abuse when battering is suspected.

hemoptysis   Spitting or coughing of blood, usually caused by damage to the lungs. Hemoptysis is sometimes observed in battered children.

hemorrhage, intradermal   *See* INTRADER-MAL HEMORRHAGE.

hemorrhage, retinal   *See* RETINAL HEMOR-RHAGE.

herpes, genital   Herpes simplex is an inflammatory disease that causes clusters of small vesicles to form on the skin. Genital herpes or herpes simplex of the genitals is characterized by blisters or sores on the penis or vagina. Herpes simplex is not curable but alternates between periods of inflammation and remission. During periods of remission when there are no skin lesions the disease is not considered transmissible.

Observation of genital herpes, or any venereal disease, in a prepubertal child is likely to be the result of SEXUAL ABUSE. Children with this disease should be screened by a physician for other evidence of sexual abuse.

homelessness   Lack of adequate, stable shelter is a significant problem for children in industrialized as well as developing countries. In the United States families comprise over 25% of the homeless population. Most of these families are headed by a young single mother with two to three young children. The typical child in a homeless family is subject to a great deal of poverty, stress and disruption.

One study of children in Massachusetts temporary shelters for the homeless found that many had been abused. Almost half of children five years of age and younger were developmentally delayed in some way. Results of psychological tests indicated that approximately 50% of all homeless children studied were in need of psychiatric care. Only 9% were actually receiving such care.

Fathers were absent in 90% of the families studied. Of the mothers, one-third reported having been abused as children, two-thirds came from families in which there was a major disruption during their childhood. In the year prior to being housed in the shelter the families had moved an average of four times.

Homeless children suffer from poverty, abuse and neglect in addition to instability and lack of adequate housing. In some developing countries homeless children, abandoned by their families, must live on their own, supporting themselves by whatever means are available. Because of its connection to POVERTY, homelessness may be seen as a form of SOCIETAL or SOCIAL ABUSE. Responsibility for such abuse is often seen as resting with the society, which denies children the basic requirements for healthy development. (*See also* LATIN AMERICA, INDIA.)

Ellen Bassuk and Lenore Rubin, "Homeless Children: A Neglected Population," in *American Journal Orthopsychiatry*, 57:2 (April 1987) 279-286.

Jean I. Layzer, Barbara D. Goodson and Christine deLange, "Children in Shelters," in *Children Today*, (March-April 1986) 6-11.

homemaker services—home health aide services The origin of homemaker-home health aide programs in the United States can be traced at least as far back as the 1920s. There are also some reports detailing groups in the late 19th century that provided in-home care to children and families. These were often affiliated with a religious organization, e.g., the Little Sisters of the Poor, a Roman Catholic order, or the Jewish Welfare Society in Philadelphia. In general, these early services were available to new mothers who needed help with infants, or to mothers too ill

to convalesce and care for their families simultaneously.

Not until the 1960s was there any large-scale federal funding for regular in-home care to children and families. In 1965, Title XVIII of the Social Security Act included benefits for homemakers-home health aides under Medicare.

The range of services that homemaker-home health aides provide includes help for families in which situational neglect has been identified. This neglect is often the result of an overburdened caretaker. Respite care is another role assumed by the homemaker-home health aide. In families where a child is disabled, terminally ill, retarded, or mentally disturbed, such respite care can alleviate parental stress. The homemaker-home health aide can both teach and assist, in order to alleviate the parental stress and the neglect to children. Also, in cases of suspected or known abuse, homemaker-home health aides play multiple roles. These may include observation and reporting, as well as the above-mentioned assistance and education. In cases of suspected child abuse and neglect, the homemaker-home health aide may be asked to provide TESTIMONY in court.

Many professionals recognize the value of homemaker-home health aide services as an alternative to less costly forms of care. Foster care or other out-of-home care for children is also less desirable, since it is disruptive to family life. Homemaker-home health aides can play an important part in diminishing potential disruption in family settings, particularly those in which real or suspected abuse and neglect may already have caused disruption.

Guidelines and accreditation for training and employing homemaker-home health aides are advocated by the National Home-Caring Council, an organization that had its inception in the early 1960s. The Council's standards, for example, require that if any homemaker-home health aide program does not have a social worker or a nurse "on staff, the expertise of that professional must be available through a written contract or agreement." The council's address is: 519 C Street NE, Washington, DC 20002.

Hong Kong   No laws mandate reporting child abuse and neglect in Hong Kong. Independent agencies, however, sometimes collect data on child abuse cases and this has provided a basis for occasional studies of abuse. Among the records available, there is clear evidence that physical abuse of children between the ages of six and 13 years is most prevalent in Hong Kong. These records, from several hospitals and agencies, indicate that slightly over 50% of these cases involved boys. Because physical abuse was defined as "unreasonable bodily harm" in one territory-wide survey, much subsequent analysis has also focused on physical rather than other forms of abuse.

One of the most common forms of injury in physically abused children results from CANING, a standard disciplinary practice in Hong Kong society. Children were also found to have been beaten with fists, flogged or chained, all in the name of discipline. Experts have not considered these reports surprising since physical punishment of children has been acceptable in Chinese society for hundreds of years. Extreme disciplinary actions are therefore seen as the primary sources of physical abuse of children in Hong Kong. (*See also* DISCIPLINE, TAIWAN, PEOPLE'S REPUBLIC OF CHINA.)

Garythe M. Samuda, "Child Discipline and Abuse in Hong Kong," in *Child Abuse and Neglect*, 12(1988), pp. 282-287.

hospital hold   In many areas hospitals are granted broad powers to hold children in custody for up to 24 hours when, in the opinion of the administrator, a child's safety is in danger or the parents may leave before a protective service worker can make a home visit. A hospital hold is used as an interim measure to protect abused children who are brought to hospital EMERGENCY ROOMS for treatment. The procedure allows child protection agencies sufficient time to act on cases when a child is in immediate danger.

hospital hopping   Abusive parents and caretakers often go to great lengths to avoid detection. Chronic child abusers sometimes engage in an evasive practice called hospital hopping. Fearing detection, the abuser will avoid using the same hospital or doctor twice when seeking medical care for the abused child. Medical personnel have greater difficulty recognizing a pattern of abuse when they are unfamiliar with the child's medical and social history.

hospitalism   High mortality rates among infants in European and American hospitals became a cause for concern during the early part of the 20th century. The FAILURE TO THRIVE SYNDROME observed in institutionalized infants, known as hospitalism, was initially attributed to poor nutrition and infection. Later, physicians began to suspect that lack of social and sensory stimulation might be related to this plight of institutionalized infants.

A well-known study conducted by Rene Spitz during the 1940s compared four groups of infants—three raised by their mothers in different settings and a fourth group raised in a FOUNDLING HOSPITAL. Infants who were cared for by their mothers all received similar types of attention. The foundling hospital provided a much different kind of care. Infants in this setting spent their days in cribs located in separate cubicles. Human contact was limited to brief visits from custodial and medical staff. After the first year of life infants reared by their mothers were within normal developmental limits. Foundling infants were retarded in their physical development, withdrawn, apathetic, less active and scored poorly on infant intelligence tests (these characteristics are sometimes referred to as MARASMUS).

Later studies of maternal deprivation showed that infants raised at home by severely neglectful mothers exhibited characteristics similar to those of the foundling infants. Subsequent research showed that retardation of physical growth was more likely related to inadequate feeding habits rather than lack of physical and emotional stimulation. Intellectual, developmental and emotional impairment associated with the deprived infants appeared to be more closely related to the lack of social and sensory stimulation.

Rene A. Spitz, "Hospitalism," in *The Psychoanalytic Study of the Child*, 1(1945): 53.
————, "Hospitalism: A Follow-up Report," in *The Psychoanalytic Study of the Child*, 2(1946): 113.

Hotlines   Hotlines play an important role in child protection. These telephone services provide around-the-clock information and referral for victims and reporters of suspected child abuse or neglect.

Telephone crisis services were originally designed to facilitate a quick response to emergencies that required a child to be removed immediately from an abusive situation. Many hotlines now provide non-emergency information and referral as well.

Hotlines are an important part of a comprehensive child protection system. Most government-sponsored child protection programs around the world maintain some form of 24-hour availability, usually in the form of a telephone hotline. Hotlines are usually staffed by professional child protection workers or trained volunteers backed up by an on-call professional. Workers are trained to screen reports and to respond appropriately to emergency situations. By necessity, hotline workers are called upon to provide counseling to callers in crisis. However, unlike HELPLINES, which are intended to provide telephone counseling, the role of the hotline worker is to match the caller to the appropriate service. This requires workers to be skilled in assessing calls quickly and knowledgeable concerning the range of resources available.

In the United States, most state-affiliated child protection agencies operate hotlines with 24-hour availability. In addition, there are two national hotlines that provide toll-free services to callers from anywhere in the country. (*See also* NATIONAL CHILD ABUSE HOTLINE and PARENTS ANONYMOUS.)

Hungary   *See* SOCIALIST EASTERN EUROPE.

hydrocephaly Enlargement of the head caused by a buildup of cerebrospinal fluid. Increased pressure within the cranial cavity can result in permanent CENTRAL NERVOUS SYSTEM INJURY and death.

Hydrocephaly can develop as a result of disease or trauma. Child abuse should be considered as a possible cause in cases where explanation of the head trauma seems implausible and where no evidence of disease is present.

hypervigilance Severely abused children may become hypervigilant as a result of the random nature of past abuse. These children are watchful and withdrawn, constantly on guard, lacking an ability to trust others yet seeking emotional nurturance. Lengthy treatment and much patience on the part of the therapist and caretaker are usually required to overcome this manifestation of abuse.

A form of hypervigilance is also observed in infants suffering from FAILURE TO THRIVE SYNDROME. These infants sometimes lack the wariness of older children, seeking affection indiscriminately from anyone who approaches. (*See also* WITHDRAWAL.)

hyphema Hemorrhage in the front portion of the eye is known as hyphema. Observable as a "bloodshot" eye, hyphema may be the result of a blow directly to the eye or other head trauma.

hypopituitarism, post-traumatic *See* DWARFISM.

hyposomatotropinism, reversible   *See*   DWARFISM.

hypovitaminosis   *See* AVITAMINOSIS.

I

identification with the aggressor
Psychoanalytic theory explains aggressive
behavior of abused children as an ego defense
mechanism. In an attempt to cope with
feelings of powerlessness the abused child
often adopts a violent mode of relating to
others. Rage that cannot be expressed toward
the abuser for fear of retaliation is redirected
at other, less powerful individuals. Identification with the aggressor may explain the high
degree of SIBLING ABUSE in families where
one or both parents are abusive.

Though adopting an aggressive self identity may give the child a temporary sense of
control over a situation that is largely beyond
control, it ultimately causes the child to feel
even worse. In becoming the aggressor the
child may also internalize negative feelings
toward the abuser. When others condemn the
child for violent acts the child, remembering
anger at the abuser, feels that he or she is also
hopelessly bad. The child becomes trapped in
a cycle in which feelings of low self-worth
lead to acts of aggression that, in turn, bring
confirmation of the child's badness from
others.

identification with the victim   Passive, dependent behavior of abused children may
result from identification with a parent who is
also the victim of abuse. Though this form of
ego defense appears to be less common than
IDENTIFICATION WITH THE AGGRESSOR it can
be observed in many children who are
withdrawn and who appear to be perpetual
victims.

Psychoanalytic theorists believe identification with the victim is likely to occur
when the child forms a strong early attachment to a passive-dependent parent. Identity
as a victim offers a clearly defined, though
maladaptive, role. Unlike the child who identifies with the aggressor, the child who copes

with abuse in this way may be less burdened
by feelings of guilt. Both types of ego defense
are likely to lead to deep, long-lasting feelings
of low self-esteem.

immunity, legal   Most jurisdictions that
have laws specifically requiring individuals to
report suspected abuse and neglect also
protect reporters from legal liability for such
reports. MANDATED REPORTERs are typically
granted immunity from criminal and civil
charges arising from a report made in good
faith. In many areas all reports are presumed
to be in good faith unless it can be proven that
the reporter knowingly filed a false report.
Immunity from criminal and civil prosecution
removes a significant legal barrier to reporting
suspected abuse and neglect.

Critics of immunity for reporters argue that
it leads to overreporting and abuse of reporting laws. In particular, opponents argue that
the difficulty of proving a report was filed in
bad faith encourages divorced parents to use
false reports as a tactic in custody disputes.
Some states have attempted to address this
problem by increasing penalties for false
reports. (*See also* APPENDIX 7; DOCTRINE OF
SOVEREIGN IMMUNITY.)

Douglas J. Besharov, "Child Welfare Liability: The
   Need for Immunity Legislation," in *Children
   Today* (Sept.-Oct. 1986).

impetigo   A highly contagious skin disease
occurring primarily in young children and
infants, impetigo produces rapidly spreading
red blisters. Severe cases of impetigo are often
indicators of neglect and unsanitary living
conditions.

impulse control   Poor impulse control may
be both a precipitant and a result of abuse.
Parental immaturity, reflected in an inability
to separate emotions from actions, is often
blamed for abuse. Impulse control is lacking
when the parent's frustrations and emotional
needs are translated directly into action. In
psychoanalytic terms, impulsive behavior

reflects a weak superego (internal control mechanism).

When parents become frustrated or angry they may lash out at the first convenient target—usually the child. Though they may later regret their actions, abusive parents often lack sufficient control to avoid impulsive maltreatment of their children. Pedophiles and repeat sexual offenders are also cited as having poor control over sexual impulses. Development of internal controls is an important goal in psychoanalytic treatment of abusers. Until sufficient internal controls are developed, protection of the child may depend on external controls exercised by another adult or a child protection agency.

Learning to control aggressive impulses is a normal task in child development. Children of abusive parents usually lack adequate role models for controlling or sublimating anger. Though a child may develop a kind of pseudo-impulse control founded on fear of punishment, this mechanism quickly breaks down under stress. The resulting behavior often takes the form of unpredictable temper tantrums. Failure to master aggressive impulses leads the child to feelings of hopelessness and negative self-worth. If the abused child does not later develop adequate internal controls, he or she may grow up to be an abusive parent.

in camera   In some cases of suspected child abuse or neglect, a legal hearing is held in the judge's chambers. This closed hearing is described by "in camera," the Latin term meaning, literally, in secret.

in loco parentis   Literally, in place of the parents—this term is applied when either the state or a court-appointed individual acts on behalf of a child in cases of suspected abuse or neglect.

in re Gault   Due to the lack of a clearly defined body of legal rights for children, the United States Supreme Court in 1967 established basic principles governing those rights.

In re Gault, the legal case that prompted the court's decision, concerned itself with the rights of juveniles charged with delinquency. Specifically, the case involved a 15-year-old Arizona boy, Gerald Francis Gault, who was accused of making an obscene telephone call to a neighbor. After an informal hearing in juvenile court, he was committed to a state institution for juvenile delinquents until age 21. Had he been an adult he would have received DUE PROCESS protections and a maximum incarceration of two months. The Supreme Court overturned the juvenile court's decision and found that juveniles—who could possibly be jailed if found guilty—had the right to notice, counsel, confrontation and cross-examination. They were protected as well against self-incrimination.

Establishing this precedent in the Gault case meant that the traditional PARENS PATRIAE view taken by juvenile court was no longer viable. Gault provided judicial guarantees that children's rights would be protected in the same way that adults' rights were preserved under the Constitution. This ruling bears directly on child abuse and neglect cases, since legal rights of children in such court proceedings can be considered independent of those of their parents.

Robert H. Mnookin, *Child, Family and State: Problems and Materials on Children and the Law* (Boston: Little, Brown, 1978).

incest   Contrary to the popular image of the child molester as a stranger lurking in a park, most perpetrators of SEXUAL ABUSE are known to the child. A great deal of sexual abuse involves incest, the sexual assault of family members by other family members. Stepfathers and fathers are, by a substantial margin, the most frequent molesters. Despite almost universal cultural, religious and legal prohibitions against father-daughter incest, studies show that it accounts for three-quarters of all intrafamily sexual assault. Girls who have stepfathers are five times more likely to be sexually assaulted than those who do not.

While stepfathers themselves account for a significant portion of this increased risk, stepdaughters are also more likely to be assaulted by other men as well. One explanation for this phenomenon is that the mother's dating prior to marriage often brings the daughter into close contact with a number of adult men to whom she is not related. These men may have fewer inhibitions concerning sexual relations with the daughter than her male relatives may have. Obviously, increased divorce and remarriage rates during the past three decades have placed girls at greater risk for this type of abuse. On the other hand, the increased viability of divorce as an option may have made it possible for some mothers and their daughters to escape abusive situations more easily than in previous times.

Father-son incest ranks a distant second to father-daughter incest in number of cases reported. Mother-son incest accounts for an even smaller proportion of incest, while cases of reported mother-daughter incest are the least frequently documented. Incest involving siblings as both perpetrators and victims is less likely to be reported than incidents involving parent-child exploitation. This may reflect an attitude that such occurrences are less serious, or a parental preference for handling such matters within the family.

Reports of intrafamily sexual abuse have increased at an alarming rate in recent years. American Humane Association statistics showed a 200% increase in reports during the eight-year period ending in 1984. Some of this increase has been attributed to heightened awareness of the problem. Many experts believe, however, that such factors as decreased family stability, increased economic stress, and changing sex roles and sexual norms have contributed to a real increase in the number of sexual assaults within the family.

The phenomenon of incest has a long and complex history. The story of Oedipus, who unknowingly married his own mother, is often cited as an example of early attitudes toward incest. When finally faced with the knowledge that he had married his mother, Oedipus gouged out his eyes. His mother committed suicide. Both acts illustrate the extreme shame and disgrace felt as a result of a strong cultural prohibition against incestual relations.

Biblical references to incest range from sympathetic, in the case of Lot—who engaged in sexual relations with his daughters after the death of his wife—to a strong injunction against incest in the book of Leviticus. Among ancient Egyptian royalty, marriage between brothers and sisters was expected as a way of maintaining the purity of blood lines. Generally, however, sexual relations between close relatives have been looked upon with disgust and have been subject to strong negative sanctions throughout history.

Explanations for the incest taboo have ranged from the now-refuted idea that biological barriers to incest are inherited, to sociological, psychological, moral, legal and economic reasons. One theory states that the incest taboo serves the function of promoting interdependence between families through marriage, encouraging important economic and social exchange.

A great deal of debate has taken place concerning the genetic consequences of incest; however, the actual supporting evidence for predicting substantially increased risk of genetic defects is unclear. Perhaps the most compelling argument is found in more recent clinical evidence that points to the lasting psychological damage suffered by many child incest victims. While such damage is not inevitable, the fact that many prostitutes, drug addicts and convicted sexual offenders were incest victims strongly supports the idea that intrafamily sexual abuse can be very damaging.

Incest that begins during, or continues into, adolescence appears to be more likely to have severe and lasting effects than incest that ceases prior to the onset of puberty. Though sons are much less likely to be victimized than daughters, some researchers believe sons are both more likely to be seriously affected and less likely to overcome the psychological effects of incest.

The following list of characteristics compiled by the NATIONAL CENTER ON CHILD ABUSE AND NEGLECT (NCCAN) suggests some commonalities of parents who sexually abuse their children. The presence of one or more of these characteristics does not prove that a parent is sexually abusive; it merely suggests that further investigation may be useful.

Characteristics of Sexually Abusive Parents

Both parents:

- have low self-esteem
- had emotional needs that were not met by their parents
- have inadequate coping skills
- may have experienced the loss of their spouse through death or divorce
- may be experiencing overcrowding in their home
- may have marital problems causing one spouse to seek physical affection from a child rather than the other spouse (a situation the "denying" husband or wife might find acceptable)
- may abuse alcohol
- lack social and emotional contacts outside the family
- are geographically isolated
- have [different] cultural standards that determine the degree of acceptable body contact

Adult male:

- is often a rigid disciplinarian
- is passive outside the home
- does not usually have a police record nor is he known to be involved in any public disturbance
- does not engage in social activities outside the home
- is jealous and protective of the child

- often initiates sexual contact with the child by hugging and kissing, which tends to develop over time into more caressing, genital-genital and oral-genital contacts

Adult female:

- is frequently cognizant of the sexual abuse but subconsciously denies it
- may hesitate reporting for fear of destroying the marriage and being left on her own
- may see sexual activity within the family as preferable to extramarital affairs
- may feel that the sexual activity between the husband and daughter is a relief from her wifely sexual responsibilities and will make certain that time is available for the two to be alone
- often feels a mixture of guilt and jealousy toward her daughter

U.S. Department of Health, Education and Welfare, Office of Human Development Services, Administration for Children, Youth and Families, Children's Bureau, National Center on Child Abuse and Neglect. *Child Protective Services: A Guide for Workers* (Washington, D.C.: 1979; [OHDS] 79-30203).

Wendy Maltz and Beverly Holman, *Incest and Sexuality* (Lexington, Mass.: Lexington Books, 1987).

Domeena C. Trenshaw, *Incest: Understanding and Treatment* (Boston: Little Brown, 1982).

Brenda J. Vander Mey and Ronald L. Neff, *Incest as Child Abuse* (New York: Praeger, 1986).

Incest Survivors Anonymous (ISA) This self-help group was founded in 1980 with the "sole purpose . . . to help the incest survivor who wants to stop negative behavior (get out of the victim role)." The organization, a private, nonprofit group, is patterned (with permission) after Alcoholics Anonymous. Members of ISA provide peer support at meetings nationally. The group runs a speakers' bureau, and disseminates ISA-published information on incest written and donated by incest survivors and pro-survivors. For more information, see APPENDIX 1.

Incest Survivors Resource Network, International   An educational resource service of the Task Group on Family Trauma, New York Yearly Meeting of the Religious society of Friends (Quakers). Members help promote education, professional therapeutic intervention and self-help to help incest survivors resolve trauma. For more information, see APPENDIX 1.

incidence of child abuse   No one knows exactly how many children are abused or neglected. Attempts to determine the incidence of child abuse have been hampered by use of retrospective data, varying definitions of abuse and other research problems. Casual observers often confuse reported abuse with incidence. Though approximately 737,000 confirmed reports of child abuse and neglect were received by United States agencies in 1986, most experts believe the actual number of children who suffer from these problems is much greater. Some estimate that only one-half of all physical abuse is reported. Reports of child sexual abuse are thought to represent less than one-third of all victims.

Actual estimates of the incidence of abuse vary widely. Different studies have estimated the incidence of SEXUAL ABUSE to range from 6% to 62% for females and from 3% to 31% for males in the United States. In a survey of family violence conducted in 1975 and again in 1985, family violence researchers Murray Straus and Richard J. Gelles estimated that the rate of very severe violence (kicking, biting, hitting with a fist, beating, using a gun or knife) toward children declined from 3.6% to 1.9%. Their study did not include children under the age of three and thus underestimates the true incidence of PHYSICAL VIOLENCE. Still, this study is one of the few that manages to overcome definitional problems in studying the incidence of abuse.

Outside the United States even less information is available on incidence. Many observers believe violence toward children is more common in Western, developed countries. Scandinavian countries are thought to have a lower rate of violence, as also China, Russia, Poland, Japan and Italy. Unfortunately, few data exist to confirm or refute these beliefs.

Murray A. Straus and Richard J. Gelles, "Societal Change and Change in Family Violence From 1975 to 1985 As Revealed by Two National Surveys," in *Journal of Marriage and the Family,* 48(August 1986), 465-479.

U.S. Department of Health and Human Services, Office of Human Development Services, Administration for Children, Youth and Families, Children's Bureau, National Center on Child Abuse and Neglect. *Executive Summary: National Study of the Incidence and Severity of Child Abuse and Neglect* (Washington, D.C.: Government Printing Office, 1981; [OHDS] 81-30329).

Indecency with Children Act 1960 (Britain)   Provisions of this act of Parliament specifically dictate the criminal nature of sexual behavior toward children. The acts states that, "Any person who commits an act of gross indecency with or towards a child under the age of 14, or who incites a child under that age to such an act with him or another, shall be liable on conviction."

indenture   In previous centuries, those in Europe and colonists in America devised a way to handle neglected children. This was to place them in the care of a family who provided food and shelter in exchange for a legal promise that the children would act as servants until a certain age or, in the case of girls, until marriage. Many children placed in indenture were either orphans or from poor families who could not afford to provide food and shelter.

The indenture system originally was formalized in the 17th century to permit adults without money a means of immigrating to the North American colonies. These individuals would enter an agreement, similar in some ways to an apprenticeship, in which they contracted with an employer for a specific period.

This system soon accommodated children, many but not all of whom were orphans, who had no other means of support.

Indentured servants were under the absolute control of a master or mistress, who was bound by law to provide for the indentured servant's basic needs. In 17th-century North America, the usual term of labor for an indentured servant was about five years, after which the servant received his or her freedom. Terms of indenture and conditions under which servants were bound varied widely from colony to colony. In some areas, indentured servants were treated quite harshly, in others they received fair and reasonable treatment.

In 19th- and early 20th-century Canada, nearly 100,000 poor children under the age of 14 were sent from Britain to serve terms of indenture on farms and as household servants. This trend reflected concerns of philanthropic reformers who wanted to save children from working in mines and factories under conditions considered unsafe and unhealthy. Eventually, other reformers agitated for changes in these programs, which essentially deprived school-age children of their education and placed many of them in situations devoid of comfort, where they performed menial and arduous agricultural or domestic tasks. By 1925, indenture arrangements effectively ended when British policies were changed to prohibit emigration of children under age 14 not accompanied by parents.

India   The constitution of the Republic of India addresses children's needs as well as the responsibility of society in meeting those needs. Nevertheless, there is widespread neglect of children in India, particularly with respect to nutritional needs, and many cases of infant mortality and childhood morbidity, as well as serious instances of exploitation of children. The India Council of Child Welfare and the Department of Social Welfare have established community programs to provide for physical, emotional and social care of children. Likewise, begging has been prohibited in some Indian states, child labor is regulated by law, and health care services in both rural and urban areas are designed to promote child well-being.

These protective measures aside, India appears to present a clear example of the connection between poverty and illiteracy and Western concepts of child abuse and neglect. Estimates indicate that about 40% of Indian children live under the poverty level and that the illiteracy rate in the urban population is near 60%.

Research also indicates that nutritionally-deprived children are commonplace in India. Poor economic conditions account for this, in both rural and urban settings. The high rate of disease-related deaths among children in India is a social problem, due also in large part to economic conditions and the lack of sufficient health services for children and families. Inadequate public health safeguards are a significant contributor to child mortality and morbidity.

A facet of traditional Indian society, the different social value ascribed to males and females, has often been cited as a contributing factor in the abuse of female children, especially in cases of INFANTICIDE. The latter was historically practiced with some regularity in almost all areas of India; it was outlawed by the British during the early 19th century although some researchers believe infanticide persisted into the 20th century. (*See also* CHILD SLAVERY.)

Jill E. Korbin, *Child Abuse and Neglect: Cross-Cultural Perspectives* (Berkeley: University of California Press, 1981).

Indian Child Welfare Act of 1978 (P.L. 95-608)   The Indian Child Welfare Act was designed to prevent the breakup of Native American families in the United States by: (1) shifting authority for out-of-home placement from the state to the tribe; (2) establishing minimum standards for the removal of Native American children from their families; and (3) encouraging the development of programs to assist families and children in distress.

According to a 1976 study 25% of all such children were in foster homes, adoptive homes or boarding schools. Native American children were found to be from five to 25 times more likely to be placed outside their home than other children. Reasons cited for the large number of Native American children removed from their homes included a tendency of welfare agencies to confuse poverty with neglect, blatant discrimination, and lack of understanding of Native American culture by public and private child protection workers. In hearings on the act, Senator James Abourezk, chairman of the Select Committee on Indian Affairs stated, "Because of poverty and discrimination Indian families face many difficulties, but there is no reason or justification for believing that these problems make Indian parents unfit to raise their children, nor is there any reason to believe that the Indian community itself cannot, within its own confines, deal with problems of child neglect when they do arise."

Legislators were also concerned about adoption practices that seemed to favor non-Native American families. As a result of what were termed abusive child removal practices tribal councils were given jurisdiction over child custody proceedings involving tribal members.

The act also provided grants to tribes for establishing and operating child and family service programs. These programs were funded for the purpose of helping Native American children remain either at home or with families of their own tribe.

Indian Child Welfare Act of 1977, hearing before the U.S. Senate Select Committee on Indian Affairs, 95th Congress, 1st Session on S. 1214 ("To Establish Standards for the Placement of Indian Children in Foster or Adoptive Homes, To Prevent the Breakup of Indian Families, and for Other Purposes"), (Washington, D.C: Government Printing Office, August 4, 1977).

indicators of child abuse and neglect
Various signs and symptoms, alone or in combination, may be helpful in identifying an abused or neglected child. The chart lists several such indicators of abuse. The presence of one or more indicators suggests that a child *may* be a victim of abuse or neglect. Further assessment is usually necessary to determine whether or not the specific sign or symptom was related to maltreatment or to some other cause.

Indicators such as those listed below are useful in identifying possible abuse and neglect. Actual determination (substantiation) of whether a child is suffering from abuse requires more extensive evaluation by someone with special training in assessment techniques.

indictment Criminal prosecution for child abuse begins with a written accusation known as an indictment. The document is prepared by a public prosecuting attorney and submitted, under oath, to a grand jury for review. Members of the grand jury must determine whether the accusations, if proven true, would be sufficient to convict the accused of a crime. An indictment approved by a grand jury is known as a true bill.

Indictments serve as formal notices to parties accused of crimes. Charges must be spelled out clearly enough to allow the defendant to prepare an adequate defense. (*See also* PETITION.)

Infant Life Protection Act, 1872 (Britain)
The 19th-century practice of "baby farming" gave rise to the Infant Life Protection Act. Mothers unable or unwilling to care for their children often entrusted their care to women who ran BABY FARMS. These infants were frequently subjected to cruel treatment, and were even sold by women who ran these farms. In two cases of such maltreatment, involving Margaret Walters and Sarah Ellis, such a public outcry was raised that Parliament passed the act.

Although by itself a somewhat ineffective statute, it received a great deal of publicity and set the precedent for a series of reforms affecting the care and well-being of infants. Among

Table 5
Indicators of Child Abuse and Neglect

Category	Child's Appearance	Child's Behavior
Physical Abuse	—Bruises and welts (on the face, lips, or mouth; in various stages of healing; on large areas of the torso, back, buttocks, or thighs; in unusual patterns, clustered, or reflective of the instrument used to inflict them; on several different surface areas). —Burns (cigar or cigarette burns; glove or sock-like burns or doughnut shaped burns on the buttocks or genitalia indicative of immersion in hot liquid; rope burns on the arms, legs, neck or torso; patterned burns that show the shape of the item [iron, grill etc.] used to inflict them). —Fractures (skull, jaw or nasal fractures; spiral fractures of the long [arm and leg] bones; fractures in various states of healing; multiple fractures; any fracture in a child under the age of two). —Lacerations and abrasions (to the mouth, lip, gums, or eye; to the external genitalia). —Human bite marks.	—Wary of physical contact with adults. —Apprehensive when other children cry. —Demonstrates extremes in behavior (e.g., extreme aggressiveness or withdrawal). —Seems frightened of parents. —Reports injury by parents.
Neglect	—Consistently dirty, unwashed, hungry, or inappropriately dressed. —Without supervision for extended periods of time or when engaged in dangerous activities. —Constantly tired or listless. —Has unattended physical problems or lacks routine medical care. —Is exploited, overworked, or kept from attending school. —Has been abandoned.	—Is engaging in delinquent acts (e.g., vandalism, drinking, prostitution, drug use etc.) —Is begging or stealing food. —Rarely attends school.
Sexual Abuse	—Has torn, stained, or bloody underclothing. —Experience pain or itching in the genital area. —Has bruises or bleeding in external genitalia, vagina, or anal regions. —Has venereal disease. —Has swollen or red cervix, vulva, or perineum. —Has semen around mouth or genitalia or on clothing. —Is pregnant.	—Appears withdrawn or engages in fantasy or infantile behavior. —Has poor peer relationships. —Is unwilling to participate in physical activities. —Is engaging in delinquent acts or runs away. —States he/she has been sexually assaulted by parent/caretaker.
Emotional Maltreatment	—Emotional maltreatment, often less tangible than other forms of child abuse and neglect, can be indicated by behaviors of the child and the caretaker.	—Appears overly compliant, passive, undemanding. —Is extremely aggressive, demanding, or rageful. —Shows overly adaptive behaviors, either inappropriately adult (e.g., parents other children) or inappropriately infantile (e.g., rocks constantly, sucks thumb, is enuretic). —Lags in physical, emotional, and intellectual development. —Attempts suicide.

U.S. Department of Health and Human Services, Office of Human Development Services, Administration for Children, Youth and Families, Children's Bureau, National Center on Child Abuse and Neglect, *Interdisciplinary Glossary on Child Abuse and Neglect* (Washington, D.C.: Government Printing Office, 1980; [OHDS] 80-30137, p. 22).

Caretaker's Behavior
—Has history of abuse as a child.
—Uses harsh discipline inappropriate to child's age, transgression, and condition.
—Offers illogical, unconvincing, contradictory, or no explanation of child's injury.
—Seems unconcerned about child.
—Significantly misperceives child (e.g., sees him as bad, evil, a monster etc.).
—Psychotic or psychopathic.
—Misuses alcohol or other drugs.
—Attempts to conceal child's injury or to protect identity of person responsible.
—Misuses alcohol or other drugs.
—Maintains chaotic home life.
—Shows evidence of apathy or futility.
—Is mentally ill or of diminished intelligence.
—Has long-term chronic illnesses.
—Has history of neglect as a child.
—Extremely protective or jealous of child.
—Encourages child to engage in prostitution or sexual acts in the presence of caretaker.
—Has been sexually abused as a child.
—Is experiencing marital difficulties.
—Misuses alcohol or other drugs.
—Is frequently absent from the home.
—Blames or belittles child.
—Is cold and rejecting.
—Withholds love.
—Treats siblings unequally.
—Seems unconcerned about child's problem.

them were registration of homes in which infants were cared for, compulsory registration of births and deaths, and more stringent regulations governing burial of stillborn infants.

infanticide Murder of infants has been practiced throughout history and in virtually every society. Infanticide may take the form of violent trauma, such as strangulation or battering; exposure, wherein the child is left to die of starvation or hypothermia; or ritual sacrifice for religious purposes.

History is rife with accounts of infanticide. Biblical accounts of mass murder of infants include the pharaoh's order that all male children be drowned and Herod's attempt to slaughter all Jewish males under the age of two. Ancient Roman law permitted the destruction of unwanted infants. Aristotle advocated infanticide as a way of dealing with disabled or deformed infants.

Until the 19th century the Indian practice of casting female infants into the Ganges River was widespread. Polynesians expected mothers of lower social status to destroy all newborns immediately following birth. Babies born to upper-class mothers were protected from slaughter. In ancient Norway, Viking brothers were obligated to kill their sister's infant if she died during childbirth. A particularly brutal form of infanticide is said to have been practiced in rural Ireland in the 20th century. Changeling babies, infants who were born with congenital anomalies or who were simply unattractive (because these children were thought to be bewitched), were roasted alive over an open fire.

Though prevalent, infanticide was by no means condoned. In 18th-century Prussia, infant murderers were punished by sacking. Sewn into a cloth sack and weighted with heavy rocks, perpetrators were thrown into a river to drown. Sacking was forbidden by Frederick the Great, who thought decapitation more appropriate. Other punishments included burning at the stake and impaling.

In 1871, the infant death toll in BABY FARMS had reached such proportions that the British House of Commons appointed a special committee to investigate the problem. As a result of the inquiry the INFANT LIFE PROTECTION ACT was passed. For the first time, minimum standards for child care were established.

Some societies did not consider an infant a person until ritually confirmed. In ancient Rome, a newborn was placed on the floor in front of the mother's husband. If he picked the child up, it was considered his offspring, if not, the child was often killed. The Romans viewed this as a way of protecting the purity of their race. Vikings presented the male infant with a spear. If the infant grasped the spear, he was allowed to live. Medieval English society protected the child's right to live only after it had consumed earthly nourishment. Many early Christians did not consider a child fully human until baptized and children who died before baptism were not allowed to be buried in sanctified ground. Excluded from church cemeteries, these children were given the same burial afforded a domestic animal.

In some civilizations, infants were placed in building foundations or in dikes to ensure the structure's strength. Brazilian tribes have been reported, as recently as 1977, as casting children from a high ledge into the ocean. The stated purpose of this ritual slaying was to ensure a bountiful harvest.

Infanticide has long been practiced as a means of population control. Native Hawaiian tribes were known routinely to kill infants born to a mother after her third or fourth child. Australian aboriginal mothers have been reported to kill a child when there was insufficient food or water to sustain the family. This phenomenon is not limited to historical or primitive cultures. Numerous infanticides committed by unwed mothers have been documented in Japan, the United States and other industrialized countries. The United States Federal Bureau of Investigation statistics listed 190 infanticides in 1985.

Statistical studies have indicated an inverse relationship between a country's positive sanction of abortion and the incidence of infanticide. Opponents of legalized abortion argue, however, that the procedure is simply another form of infanticide. Though the ethics of abortion are hotly debated, many countries use access to abortion as one means of controlling population growth. China, attempting to limit growth, has made abortion easily available. Rumania, fearing population decline, has recently repealed laws that legalized abortion. (*See also* NEONATICIDE.)

S. Radbill, "A History of Child Abuse and Infanticide," in Ray Helfer and C. Henry Kempe, eds., *The Battered Child*, 3rd ed. (Chicago: University of Chicago Press, 1980), pp. 3-20.

infantile addiction   *See* ADDICTION, INFANTILE.

infantile cortical hyperostosis   A condition, also known as Caffey's Disease, in which new bone forms beneath the periosteum of infants. A healed lesion of infantile cortical hyperostosis is similar in appearance to a fracture suffered during battering. In 95% of cases of this condition, the mandible (jaw bone) is affected—a bone unlikely to be fractured as a result of battering.

infibulation   This brutal ritual is practiced on young females in many cultures but is particularly prevalent on the African continent. It involves the complete removal of the clitoris and labia. The sides of the vulva are then sewn together leaving only a small opening for discharge of fluids. At marriage, infibulated females have their vaginas reopened to permit intercourse and childbirth. The main function of this procedure is to ensure that the female will be a virgin at the time of marriage.

Some have linked CLITORIDECTOMY and infibulation to the widely practiced custom of male circumcision; however, both infibulation and clitoridectomy are more extensive and more dangerous. Removal of the clitoris effectively eliminates the female's capacity for sexual stimulation. Many young girls die or suffer painful, chronic problems as a result of these operations. Though the practice is defended by some as an important cultural, religious or social ritual, it is widely condemned around the world. Elimination of sexual mutilation has been the topic of several international health conferences. (*See also* CULTURAL FACTORS, INITIATION RITES.)

Ingraham v. Wright An important United States Supreme Court decision in 1977 held that CORPORAL PUNISHMENT in schools was not inherently cruel or abusive. This ruling was based on common-law precedents establishing disciplinary corporal punishment in public schools. The case, *Ingraham v. Wright*, was one that received a great deal of public attention, as it was argued and decided on the basis of the Eighth Amendment, which provides for protection against cruel and unusual punishment.

The plaintiff in the case, James Ingraham—a 14-year-old junior high school student—received hospital treatment for bruises received after being "struck repeatedly by a wooden instrument." The school principal responsible for Ingraham's corporal punishment was absolved of legal responsibility by the court ruling. The court held that "the administration of corporal punishment in public schools, whether or not excessively administered, does not come within the scope of Eighth Amendment protection."

Many child abuse and neglect experts denounced this finding as one that further validates violence against children—and legalizes child abuse—in one of the nation's most influential social institutions, its public schools.

Robert H. Mnookin, *Child, Family and State: Problems and Materials on Children and the Law* (Boston: Little, Brown and Company, 1978).

initiation rites Virtually all cultures have rituals to mark the transition to adulthood. These events are sometimes referred to as puberty rites or rites of passage. Though initiation rites are often harmless ceremonies, rituals practiced by some primitive societies have been widely denounced as forms of institutionalized child abuse.

In New Guinea for example, boys are subjected to a series of increasingly painful rites before they can be officially recognized as adults. Bloodletting plays an important role both as a cleansing ritual and as a symbol of the male's ability to withstand pain. Passage to manhood may also include ritual scarification of the back, face or chest, sleep deprivation, burning, forced vomiting and verbal harassment. Some New Guinea tribes, the Sambia and the Keraki for example, force boys to serve as sexual partners for older initiates. These practices are attributed to a cultural belief that ingestion of semen is necessary for boys to acquire strength. By contrast initiation of girls into womanhood appears much less abusive. The traditional ritual of defloration, once practiced by tribal elders, appears to have ended in New Guinea.

Conversely, some African tribal groups engage in brutal mutilation of females. CLITORIDECTOMY and INFIBULATION are still practiced as initiation rites among remote tribes like the Gusii. Both males and females are expected to endure mutilation and other extremely painful acts unflinchingly.

Though Western child abuse experts classify many initiation rites as abusive, these practices may be seen as normal, even essential, in the societies where they are practiced. Practices such as clitoridectomy and infibulation, and sexual exploitation, are almost universally condemned. However, experts are less likely to agree that practices such as scarification and psychological humiliation constitute abuse. Some even speculate that these institutionalized forms of abuse are responsible for a lower incidence of idiosyncratic (deviating from cultural norms) abuse in non-Western societies. (*See also* CULTURAL FACTORS.)

injuries, abdominal *See* ABDOMINAL IN-
JURIES.

injuries, central nervous system *See*
CENTRAL NERVOUS SYSTEM INJURIES.

injuries, cord *See* CORD INJURIES.

injuries, eye *See* EYE INJURIES.

injuries, gastrointestinal *See* GASTROINTES-
TINAL INJURIES.

injuries, mental *See* MENTAL INJURY.

injuries, mouth *See* MOUTH INJURIES.

innoculation Since the development of
modern vaccines, the innoculation of children
against life-threatening and debilitating disease has become standard practice. Innoculation against disease has significantly reduced
child mortality and increased the average life
span. Many pediatricians now recommend
that children be innoculated by 18 months to
two years of age. Some consider failure to
innoculate by age two to be MEDICAL
NEGLECT.

This form of prevention has proven so effective that a majority of states and countries
have laws requiring that all children be vac-
cinated against certain diseases. Legally required innoculation has not, however, been
without controversy. Some parents dispute
such requirements on the basis of religious
beliefs. Others believe such vaccinations are
dangerous or an infringement on their right to
do what they think is best for their children.

In the United States, laws requiring innoculation vary from state to state. Most states
tie innoculation to school attendance.
Children are denied entry into the school system until they can produce evidence that they
have received the required vaccinations.
Parents who refuse to allow their children to
be innoculated may be charged with MEDICAL
and/or EDUCATIONAL NEGLECT. In some cases
physicians, educators or child welfare

workers can petition the court to order the
parents to have their child innoculated.

Though widely practiced, mandatory innoculation continues to be a controversial subject in many areas.

institutional abuse and neglect Sometimes
social policies and institutions designed to
help children do more harm than good. As the
number of children enrolled in day care,
treatment facilities, correctional institutions
and foster care increases so does concern with
institutional maltreatment.

Some child advocates argue that any in-
stitutionalization of children is abusive. Placement of children with adults in jails,
correctional facilities or treatment centers
puts children at significant risk of abuse and
is prohibited in many areas.

Children placed in treatment and correctional facilities must be given a label. Desig-
nation as retarded, delinquent, emotionally
disturbed or mentally ill can enable a child to
receive special services that may benefit him
or her. Such a label also places a child at
significant risk of subsequent maltreatment.
Some advocates say that institutional labeling
is itself a form of abuse. Others point to the
deprivation of freedom and denial of legal
protection that often goes with institutional
care.

Abuse within institutions may take several
forms. Residents of full-time, 24-hour
residential institutions may suffer physical
neglect associated with poor nutrition, lack of
exercise and idleness due to a lack of
programmed activities. Medical abuse and
neglect may also occur when health problems
go untreated or when medication is dispensed
without adequate monitoring or controls.

Many institutions, due to their age or lack
of adequate funding, do not meet minimal
standards for safety. Children living in these
institutions may suffer burns from un-
protected radiators, lacerations or fractures
from poorly designed or defective buildings
and furnishings, and numerous other environ-
mentally-induced injuries.

Children in institutional settings may suffer physical abuse at the hands of staff, other residents or outsiders. Some children suffering developmental disabilities or mental illness must be protected from self-inflicted injuries.

In recent years a number of child sexual abuse cases in residential facilities and day care centers have received media attention. Historical accounts indicate that sexual exploitation of children in institutions has long been a problem. Recent publicity has caused institutions and lawmakers to consider new ways of protecting children from sexual abuse outside the family.

Problems associated with institutional abuse stem from many different sources. Treatment and correctional facilities are often inadequately funded. Lack of funds may lead to neglect of physical facilities and inadequate supervision of children. Poor recruitment procedures for child care workers and foster families also share blame for the increased risk of maltreatment. Finally, many institutions have simply failed to realize or acknowledge real or potential abuse.

Residential facilities have a responsibility to protect children from abuse. Most governmental, licensing and accreditation authorities require specific procedures for investigation of alleged maltreatment of children. Institutions are typically required to involve a neutral third party, in most cases a child protection or licensing agency, in the investigation of all such complaints. Recent civil suits have forced child care facilities to screen applicants for employment more carefully and to develop more thorough procedures for ensuring safety of children.

interdisciplinary team   *See* MULTIDISCIPLINARY TEAM.

intergenerational cycle of abuse   Numerous studies have documented the increased risk that abused children will become abusive parents when they reach adulthood. Though estimates vary, roughly one-third of parents with a history of childhood abuse also abuse their children. Children of such parents are six times more likely to be abused than their peers.

Despite these sobering figures, the connection between childhood victimization and later abusive behavior is far from inevitable. While there is no doubt that the experience of abuse increases the likelihood of becoming abusive this experience is but one of many factors contributing to child abuse. Other contributing factors include poverty, stress, social isolation and characteristics of the child.

Abused children are not condemned to become abusive parents. However, under stress the parent with a history of abuse appears to be more likely to lash out at a child than to find other ways of expressing frustration and anger.

Many parents who were abused as children find ways of breaking the cycle of abuse. The approximately two-thirds of parents who do not repeat the abuse they received as children appear to have more extensive social supports (friends, family etc.), have fewer negative feelings about pregnancy, give birth to healthier babies and are better able to express anger over their past abuse. These parents are also more likely to have suffered abuse from only one parent, and have frequently reported a satisfactory relationship with the non-abusive parent.

Many mental health professionals agree that early intervention with abused children is an effective way to break the cycle of abuse. In the absence of such intervention it is still possible for parents with a history of abuse to avoid maltreating their children by developing a network of friends and family to call on in time of crisis, by developing appropriate ways of expressing anger and frustration, and by learning new child rearing techniques.

Many self-help organizations such as PARENTS ANONYMOUS seek to help parents break the cycle of abuse by providing social support on a 24-hour basis. Groups such as PA have proven to be particularly effective in preventing further child abuse.

International Society for Prevention of Child Abuse and Neglect Based at the KEMPE NATIONAL CENTER FOR THE PREVENTION OF CHILD ABUSE AND NEGLECT, the International Society provides a worldwide forum for disseminating information on child abuse and neglect. The society holds international congresses on a biennial basis and publishes *Child Abuse and Neglect: The International Journal.* For more information, see APPENDIX 1.

intervention, voluntary *See* VOLUNTARY INTERVENTION.

intradermal hemorrhage Bleeding within the skin. (*See also* BRUISES.)

intraocular bleeding Bleeding inside the eye can be caused by a blow directly to the eye or head. In the case of PURTSCHER RETINOPATHY, sudden compression of a child's chest due to hitting, shaking or squeezing can cause a hemorrhage of the retina. The most common cause of intraocular bleeding is head trauma. Retinal hemorrhage is frequently a symptom of child battering, although it may be caused by accidental injury or participation in sports such as football and gymnastics. Studies of battered children have shown that the presence of bleeding inside the eye—especially the retina—is an indicator that SUBDURAL HEMATOMA may also be present. Small clots that appear in the retina as a result of trauma generally last approximately two weeks. Other forms of intraocular bleeding may indicate serious damage to the eye, possibly resulting in blindness.

investigation Once a report of suspected child abuse or neglect has been made, an investigation is necessary to determine: (1) if the report is accurate and (2) if the child is in danger. Investigations of suspected abuse and neglect are typically conducted by child protection workers; however, in some areas law enforcement officers are responsible for investigation of such reports.

The first responsibility of the investigator is to assess the level of danger to the child and, if necessary, take immediate steps to ensure the child's safety. Situations such as those listed below suggest a child is in immediate danger:

- The maltreatment in the home, present or potential, is such that a child could suffer permanent damage to body or mind if left there.
- Although a child is in immediate need of medical or psychiatric care, the parents refuse to obtain it.
- A child's physical and/or emotional damage is such that the child needs an extremely supportive environment in which to recuperate.
- A child's sex, age, physical or mental condition renders the child incapable of self-protection—or for some reason constitutes a characteristic the parents find completely intolerable.
- Evidence suggests that the parents are torturing the child or systematically resorting to physical force, which bears no relation to reasonable discipline.
- The physical environment of the home poses an immediate threat to the child.
- Evidence suggests that parental anger and discomfort with the investigation will be directed toward the child in the form of severe retaliation against him or her.
- Evidence suggests that the parent or parents are so out of touch with reality that they cannot provide for the child's basic needs.
- Evidence suggests that the parent's physical condition poses a threat to the child.
- The family has a history of hiding the child from outsiders.
- The family has a history of prior incidents or allegations of abuse or neglect.
- The parents are completely unwilling to cooperate in the investigation or to maintain contact with any social agency, and may flee the jurisdiction.
- Parent or parents abandon the child.

The investigation centers on allegations specified in the report of suspected abuse. While evidence of other maltreatment may be collected in the course of an investigation it is important to determine the accuracy of each allegation contained in the original report.

A typical investigation begins with a check of available records to see if the child or family has been the subject of other investigations. The child protection worker may then interview the child, family, the alleged abuser (if not a family member) and others who may have special knowledge of the child or family.

Interviewing the Child

It is usually best that a child be interviewed alone to minimize embarrassment or intimidation; however, in some cases a parent or other trusted adult may facilitate questioning. Though parental permission is not required to interview a child concerning suspected abuse or neglect, a parent should be notified that the child will be interviewed. When sexual abuse is suspected it is recommended that the interviewer and child be of the same gender.

Children are frequently reluctant to discuss alleged abuse with a stranger. Interviewers should make every attempt to put the child at ease. A child may need to be reassured that he or she has done nothing wrong and will not be punished. Criticism of the parent(s) may cause the child to become defensive and uncooperative with the interviewer. As much as possible, children should be allowed to tell their own story in their own words, without leading questions, prompts or undue pressure. Some child protection workers have found anatomically correct dolls useful in interviewing young children who are thought to have been sexually abused.

Reliving abuse through an interview can be traumatic for a child. Often child protection workers, law enforcement officers, lawyers and judges can combine questioning into one interview, thereby reducing trauma to the child. In some cases videotaped interviews may be used as evidence in court.

Direct observation of any injuries is an essential part of an interview. If it is necessary for the child to remove his or her clothing care should be taken to explain the reasons for disrobing in a nonthreatening, careful manner. In some cases it may be necessary to have the child examined by a physician to determine the existence and extent of injury.

Care must be given to explain to the child both the purpose of the interview and what to expect next. The child's questions should be answered truthfully and in language appropriate to his or her age.

Interviewing Adults

Adults should be informed of the reason for the interview and their legal rights with regard to the investigation. When possible, family members should be interviewed both separately and as a group. Separate interviews allow the child protection worker to compare accounts of an incident and may encourage the interviewee to share information more freely. Observing the family together often supplies important data on family interaction patterns.

Parents accused of abuse and neglect are often hostile and uncooperative. Interviewers who convey a neutral attitude toward the alleged abuse and who avoid direct confrontation are often successful in securing a reasonable level of cooperation. Keeping the focus on the child's welfare and asking open-ended questions are also useful strategies for soliciting necessary information. The child protection worker must be supportive of parents without appearing to condone inappropriate behavior.

Other Methods of Obtaining Information

Direct observation of a child's environment can supply useful information. Cleanliness of the home, presence of nutritious food, cooking and sanitary facilities, adequate sleeping arrangements, lighting, heat and water are all important.

Behavior of the child and family members should also be observed. An angry outburst or emotional coldness toward a child may belie a parent's description of a close relationship with the child.

Secondary information may be obtained from medical, school and police records. These kinds of data can help verify information obtained from interviews and observation.

A medical or mental health evaluation of a child may help identify or confirm evidence of abuse or neglect.

Observable physical evidence of injury should be documented with carefully taken photographs. Photographs should be identified accurately (name of subject, time, location, age etc.) and should include distinguishing features that allow identification of the child as well as a clear view of the injury itself. Color film is preferred to black and white. Infrared film may increase visibility of injuries where dark skin coloring inhibits clear observation of trauma. Production of photographs that are acceptable as evidence in court requires the careful attention of a skilled photographer.

Outcome of the Investigation

After all relevant information has been collected the investigator must make a decision concerning the accuracy of the alleged abuse or neglect and the need for further intervention.

The investigator may conclude that abuse or neglect exists, does not exist or that further information is necessary to make a determination. When abuse or neglect is substantiated interventions vary depending on the level of risk to the child, the child's needs and the family's willingness to cooperate. If the family refuses to cooperate a court order may be necessary to ensure treatment. In some cases the investigator may conclude that abuse or neglect does not exist but that service should be offered to the family.

U.S. Department of Health, Education and Welfare, Office of Human Development Services, Administration for Children, Youth and Families, Children's Bureau, National Center on Child Abuse and Neglect. *Child Protective Services: A Guide for Workers* (Washington, D.C.: 1979; [OHDS] 79-30203).

isolation   *See* SOCIAL ISOLATION.

Israel   There are currently no laws dealing specifically with child abuse in Israel. Rather, the prevailing opinion is that abused or neglected children should receive the same concern afforded maltreated children under conventional child protection legislation.

Israel provides free or low-cost child health services that act as a screen for possible child abuse and neglect. Children are seen at clinics virtually from birth.

Child Labor laws in Israel specifically prohibit children under age 16 from working unless they have special permission. In 1986, the chief of Israel's Labor Ministry commented on the prevalence of child labor despite prohibitive legislation, and noted the difficulty in finding and prosecuting those who break child labor laws.

In Jerusalem, according to a recent *Jerusalem Post* article, a children's ombudsman has worked to protect the rights of children who, statistics show, make up 40% of the city's population. The ombudsman's role is to hear complaints, oversee weaknesses in the legal system and raise public awareness about children's rights.

Italy   There is an Association for the Prevention of Child Abuse and Neglect in Italy, and a Family Crisis Center in the city of Milan. However, many experts who specialize in international perspectives on child abuse concur on the lower level of awareness of child abuse and neglect in Italian society compared to some other European nations. In one Italian study, however, physical abuse was targeted as a major problem. Information gathered during research into child maltreatment in Italy suggested there was a need for better definitions of child abuse and neglect, and recommended both legislative reform and upgrading of Italian social services as ways of dealing more effectively with child abuse. As in many other countries, cultural perceptions of children in Italy influence the way abusive behavior is seen, understood and acted upon.

J

Japan   Most research reports dealing with Japan indicate that there is virtually no perception of child abuse as a social problem. Statistics indicate that Japanese culture is less violent than, for example, that of the United States. One researcher indicates that low child abuse reporting rates in Japan are a fairly accurate reflection of reality. Physical punishment of, or violence toward, children in Japan is rare, although occasional newspaper accounts of abuse or neglect do appear. Japanese schoolchildren are subject to biannual physical examinations, during which signs of physical abuse would most likely be detected. The apparent lack of child maltreatment in Japan may be due in part to different cultural definitions of abuse, a common issue when discussing international aspects of abuse and neglect.

According to available research, more common or apparent forms of child abuse or neglect involve young children and infants. Infanticide would appear to be more prevalent, for example, than severe physical abuse of a child. The assumption is that a parent (and Japanese statistics show it is more often the child's mother) resorts to killing her infant rather than letting the child live and abusing or neglecting the child later. In the mid-1970s, a Japanese government survey on child abuse, abandonment and murder revealed that abuse or neglect represented slightly over 6% of all cases reported during one year. Abandonment made up nearly 33% of reports. The combined categories of murder (including infanticide) or murder-abandonment (when an abandoned child died before being discovered) represented 45.2% of cases. Joint suicide, where a parent kills the child before committing suicide, made up nearly 16% of reports in the government study.

Jill E. Korbin, ed., *Child Abuse and Neglect: Cross-Cultural Perspectives (Berkeley: University of California Press, 1981).*

jejunal hematoma   The collection of blood in the jejunum or middle part of the small intestine. Usually the result of a blow to the abdominal area. (*See also* ABDOMINAL INJURIES and GASTROINTESTINAL INJURIES.)

Johnson and Wife v. State of Tennessee   In the 1830s, a Mr. and Mrs. Johnson were convicted of excessively punishing their daughter. This case was one of the earliest recorded occasions where parents in the United States were tried for child maltreatment. The conviction was later overturned because an overzealous judge issued an improper charge to the jury.

juvenile court   *See* COURT.

juvenile court movement   The origins of the juvenile court in the United States date to the early 19th century. At that time, children over age 14 were treated as adults by the court systems, arrested, brought to trial, sentenced and punished according to criminal laws framed with adult offenders in mind. Even children between the ages of seven and 14 years were not always guaranteed immunity from criminal prosecution. It was the state's prerogative to hold a child legally accountable in criminal court if it preferred to do so, and judicial mechanisms for this purpose existed prior to establishment of a juvenile court.

Juvenile court system supporters worked to make judicial law more responsive to the needs of children. In recognition of these needs, by 1875 New York state prohibited placement of children with adults in almshouses for more than 60 days. Proponents of separate and special judicial treatment for children urged use of psychology, social work and medical science when sentencing, treating and rehabilitating youth. As a result, the first juvenile court in the United States was established in 1899 in Chicago, Illinois.

By the early 1900s, the juvenile court movement had been successful in permanently establishing this separate arena where the child's unique needs were taken into account. Wanting to guard the child against societal dangers. the juvenile court movement emphasized rehabilitation rather than retribution. Establishment of a juvenile court system was also to keep children separate from adult offenders. Much earlier, New York City had founded the House of Refuge in 1825, a correctional facility that segregated children from older, more hardened criminals. The juvenile court movement supported this and also sought more informal court procedures, as compared to the legalistic formality of a criminal court. The juvenile court movement desired also that the court consider each child's needs separately. More specifically, the juvenile court movement recognized that children must be protected if they are unable to seek and find their own protection. The juvenile court, therefore, was charged with acting as a substitute parent.

Juvenile Justice Standards Project   This project, completed in 1979, was sponsored by the American Bar Association and the Institute of Judicial Administration. The final report was a 21-volume set of recommendations to each state. Basically, these recommendations would eliminate juvenile court jurisdiction over most status offenses (an action that is an offense because it is committed by a minor, not because of the act itself) in cases of noncriminal misbehavior. This change is intended to encourage more extensive use of voluntary services and especially to make more room in juvenile courts for cases involving abused and neglected children.

K

Keating-Owen bill   As a general result of Progressive Era protective legislation, in 1916 this child labor law was passed as a response to pressure from various groups opposing child labor in the United States. In particular, the Keating-Owen bill was designed to protect children under the age of 16 from long hours and dangerous working conditions in factories and mines. Despite widespread acknowledgment of abusive child labor practice, the Keating-Owen bill was declared unconstitutional two years after its passage.

Kempe National Center for the Prevention of Child Abuse and Neglect   The center was named for one of the foremost U.S. experts on child abuse and neglect, C. Henry Kempe. Affiliated with the Department of Pediatrics of the University of Colorado Medical School since its establishment in 1972, the center also serves as the United States Department of Health and Human Services National Child Abuse and Neglect Clinical Resource Center. According to its program guide, this is a facility providing "training, consultation, program development and evaluation and research in all forms of child abuse and neglect." Affiliated organizations include Hope for the Children, a diagnostic and treatment center; the KEEPSAFE project; the National Association of Counsel for Children; the International Society for Prevention of Child Abuse and Neglect; and the Colorado Child Protection Council. For more information, see APPENDIX 1.

key masters   *See* UNDERGROUND NETWORKS.

kidnapping   Any unlawful seizure of a person and detention against that person's will is generally described as kidnapping. In modern times and in most nations of the world, kidnapping is a crime punished by death or lengthy imprisonment. In the United States, federal laws governing kidnapping were amended following the 1932 abduction and subsequent murder of aviator Charles A. Lindbergh's infant son. The Lindbergh baby kidnapping was the most famous among numerous early 20th-century abductions, many of which involved wealthy or well-known families and a large number of which had extortion as a key factor. The notoriety surrounding the Lindbergh case led directly to federal legislation that imposed the death penalty for anyone convicted of transporting a kidnap victim across state lines. When a noncustodial parent resorts to this type of action in order to secure unlawful custody of a child or children, it is termed CHILD STEALING.

Historically, abducting female children or young women for the purpose of selling them into prostitution was considered in many cultures a form of kidnapping. (*See also* CHILD STEALING; MANN ACT; PARENTAL KIDNAPPING PREVENTION ACT OF 1980; CHILD SLAVERY.)

kinky hair syndrome   *See* MENKE'S KINKY HAIR SYNDROME.

L

laboratory tests   Several routine tests are used by doctors to aid in diagnosis of child abuse. Included are:

Partial Thromboplastin Time and *Prothrombin Time* tests measure blood clotting factors. Knowledge of clotting time helps distinguish between bruising and bleeding associated with hemophilia and trauma-induced injuries.

Urinalysis helps detect sugar, protein, blood or other substances in the urine. Blood in the urine is evidence of internal injury that may not be immediately apparent to the casual observer.

A complete *blood count* yields information about the level of red and white blood cells. This test may give evidence of poor nutrition or infection.

The *Rumpel-Leede* or *Tourniquet* test is used to measure the plasticity of capillaries. Fragile capillaries may cause a child to bruise more easily than other children. Abusive parents frequently claim "the child bruises easily." This test helps verify claims of bruisability.

Landeros v. Flood   This 1976 ruling by the California Supreme Court established the liability of physicians and hospitals when they negligently fail to diagnose and report child abuse.

Gita Landeros, the plaintiff, was severely and repeatedly beaten by her mother and her mother's common-law husband. When brought to the San Jose Hospital for treatment the infant showed clear evidence of suffering from BATTERED CHILD SYNDROME, including a fractured tibia and fibula (apparently from severe twisting) and multiple bruises and abrasions. The physician, A.J. Flood, failed to perform a full SKELETAL SURVEY and therefore did not discover a skull fracture. In failing to properly diagnose the child's condition the physician also did not report the case to the proper law enforcement and child protection authorities.

The child was returned to the mother and her partner who continued to abuse her until she was brought to another hospital for treatment of blows to her eyes and back, puncture wounds, bites on her face and burns on a hand. At the second hospital a physician properly diagnosed the child's condition and reported the case to local authorities who took her into protective custody.

The court reversed a dismissal by a lower court and held the physician and the hospital responsible for failing to diagnose and report child abuse. This ruling opened the door for future malpractice suits against physicians and medical institutions who fail to report suspected child abuse.

Robert H. Mnookin, *Child, Family and State: Problems and Materials on Children and the Law* (Boston: Little, Brown, 1978).
Irving Sloan, *Child Abuse: Governing Law and Legislation* (New York: Oceana Publications, 1983).

Latin America   The diverse cultural groups that make up the countries of Central and South America show similar diversity in terms of abuse and neglect of children. In general, however, it can be said that among indigenous peoples, many of whom are isolated from Western culture, many child-rearing practices exist that would be considered abusive by Western standards. This is particularly true of tribes that inhabit the Amazon region, where primitive lifestyles embrace a generally harsh, subsistence-level existence. Some of these practices persist in nonaggressive tribal cultures where deliberate maltreatment of children is not intentional. Bathing infants in scalding water to drive out anger, scraping a child's skin during puberty rites to ensure stamina against pain, or dipping a baby in a river to force it to stop crying are carried out by generally nonviolent tribes, which apparently seek to strengthen children, physically and psychologically, for a life of relative hardship.

Other native groups characterized as aggressive and violent in their general behavior are known to give hallucinogenic drugs to children, spank disobedient children with nettles, and leave very young children (of one year or less) alone and unattended for hours at a time. Researchers explain that these tribal practices toward children are representative of general social patterns among adults rather than manifestations of abuse or neglect aimed specifically at their children.

While observers can sometimes dismiss abusive practices among primitive societies as exotic aberrations, it is also true that most countries in Central and South America show high rates of abuse and neglect in their modern communities. In urban areas of Latin America child abuse, neglect and maltreatment is common. This is due not only to the huge number of people living below the poverty level but also to social attitudes, economic circumstances and political environments that accept or encourage abusive practices, i.e., child disappearance, torture, child prostitution and child labor.

Reports from international groups, like the United Nations and Amnesty International, as well as domestic human rights organizations, describe a range of situations that embody extreme abuse and neglect of children. In Argentina between 1976 and 1979 many thousands of people, including infants and children, were abducted by the military. Large numbers were never heard from again although in some cases the "disappeared," as they are called, were given to other families and have been raised as their own children. In Chile, Colombia, Guatemala and Peru, similar cases of disappeared children have been reported.

In Bolivia, *los polillas* (street children) of Cochabamba is the name given to several thousand abandoned children between the ages of eight and 15. They steal, sell drugs, shine shoes and are often addicted to drugs themselves. Brazil has upwards of 10,000,000

street children out of a total of 50,000,000 aged 15 or under, according to a UNICEF worker. Similar numbers have been reported for El Salvador, Guatemala and Peru.

In Mexico City, many children die each year from working in a dump called Basurero de Santa Fe. Here, they sort trash, contracting parasites and skin and intestinal diseases.

In Honduras in 1987, there were allegations that trafficking in children existed for the purpose of selling body parts.

In Recife, Brazil, where brothels abound, there are numerous cases of younger teenage girls working as prostitutes.

Torture of children is known to be common in Chile, Guatemala and Honduras, where violence resulting from clashes between left-wing and right-wing forces is the result of political turmoil. Electric shocks, beatings, kickings, slashings, psychological torture and sexual abuse are among the practices used against children as young as 10 years of age. It is not uncommon also for children to be forced to witness the torture of parents and other adults.

In Brazil, children as young as seven work on sugar plantations; in Chile, many children work as street vendors after being forced out of their homes for economic reasons; Mexican children between eight and 14 work on sugar plantations cutting sugar cane.

least detrimental alternative   *See* BEST INTERESTS OF THE CHILD.

legal immunity   *See* IMMUNITY, LEGAL.

legal rights of persons identified in reports
In the United States persons criminally accused of child abuse have a right to be represented by a lawyer. In juvenile or family court proceedings the right to counsel varies from state to state. Approximately one half of all states grant the right to counsel in civil as well as criminal proceedings.

Some critics of present child abuse laws argue that persons accused of child abuse should be entitled to counsel in all proceedings. Civil proceedings can establish the basis for removal of a child from the home and for further criminal charges. Even when a civil proceeding does not result in criminal charges or removal of the child, some believe that the investigation itself and subsequent supervision by a child protection agency is likely to infringe on the parent's legal rights.

lesion   A term frequently used to describe injuries resulting from abuse, lesion can refer to an injury of any type to any part of the body.

liability of reporters   The fear of being sued could prevent some people from reporting suspected abuse or neglect to child protection authorities. This is especially true when abuse is suspected but cannot be proven without further investigation. In an effort to remove this barrier to reporting, all MANDATED REPORTERS in the United States are granted immunity from civil and criminal prosecution when reports are made in good faith. Further, in at least 40 states voluntary (nonmandatory) reporters are exempt.

Communications between doctor and patient, psychologist or social worker and client, and clergy and parishioner often receive special legal protection under the law. Although some jurisdictions require these professionals to report confessions of dangerous crimes, most states classify information passed between these parties as privileged communication. However, reports of suspected abuse or neglect are not afforded this protection. In fact, these professionals are usually classified as mandated reporters and are therefore required to report all cases of suspected maltreatment. A majority of states in the United States impose criminal and/or civil penalties on mandated reporters for failure to report such cases. In at least one case (*LANDEROS V. FLOOD*) a physician has been found legally liable for failing to report suspected abuse.

lice   Head lice are not uncommon in children. These small parasitic insects attach themselves to the scalp and survive by sucking blood through the skin. Children frequently acquire them from casual contact while playing or at school.

Treatment of an infested child involves repeated application of medicated shampoo and careful inspection of the hair for the insects or their eggs. This process requires persistence and usually takes place at home under a physician's instructions. If untreated, lice can cause significant discomfort to the child and may result in infection. Neglected children are sometimes found to have severe infestations of head or body lice that have gone untreated for a lengthy period of time.

Pubic lice are found in the groin area and sometimes produce bluish spots on the skin that disappear when the lice are treated. The presence of pubic lice on a child who has not reached sexual maturity is a strong indicator of possible SEXUAL ABUSE. When pubic lice are discovered on a child of any age, a careful examination should be conducted to determine how the insects were transmitted and whether there is other evidence of sexual abuse.

Liverpool Society for the Prevention of Cruelty to Children   Founded in Britain in 1883, this society was a project of a Liverpool banker, Thomas Agnew. After visiting the United States in 1881 and learning of the New York Society for the Prevention of Cruelty to Children, Agnew took steps to establish a similar welfare organization in his home city. He was subsequently involved in helping to found the London Society in July 1884. This organization merged in 1889 with many other child welfare groups and was then renamed the National Society for the Prevention of Cruelty to Children. (*See also* NATIONAL SOCIETY FOR THE PREVENTION OF CRUELTY TO CHILDREN [BRITAIN].)

local authorities   In the United States the child protection agency designated by the mandated state agency to serve a particular area is known as the local authority. A local authority may be a branch of the state agency, a private agency under government contract or a county department of social services. The term may also be applied to a COMMUNITY COUNCIL (FOR CHILD ABUSE AND NEGLECT).

Local authorities have primary responsibility for child protection in BRITAIN. Specifically, local authorities include councils of nonmetropolitan counties and metropolitan districts, the London boroughs and the common council of the City of London. Local social service authorities are under the general supervision of the secretary of state for social services or the secretary of state for Wales. Policy-making for management of child abuse cases is the responsibility of an Area Review Committee appointed by the local authority. In addition to child protection, local authorities have responsibility for child care, delinquency prevention, foster care, legal advocacy for children and adoption. (*See also* PROTECTIVE SERVICES.)

loss of childhood   *See*   PARENTIFIED CHILD.

low birth weight   Premature birth, inadequate prenatal care or SUBSTANCE ABUSE by the mother during pregnancy can cause infants to be significantly below normal weight at birth. Low birth weight may require an extended hospital stay until infants are healthy enough to be cared for at home. Premature infants often spend the first days of their lives in an incubator.

Many experts believe treatment for low birth weight and other medical problems can interfere with the natural mother-infant bonding process, placing the child at increased risk of abuse (BONDING FAILURE). Many hospitals are now taking steps to increase contact between mothers and infants who require intensive medical attention.

M

malabsorption syndrome   Any of a number of specific conditions, often inherited, that interfere with the absorption of nutrients in the intestines. Malabsorption can be caused by a number of childhood diseases, many of them fatal. It is a frequent cause of organically based FAILURE TO THRIVE SYNDROME.

malpractice   Failure to diagnose and report child abuse or neglect may leave physicians and other professionals open to malpractice suits. In *LANDEROS V. FLOOD* the California Supreme Court held a physician and hospital liable for failure to diagnose abuse in an infant who showed clear signs of BATTERED CHILD SYNDROME.

mandated agency   Under the CHILD ABUSE TREATMENT AND PREVENTION ACT OF 1974 each state is required to designate an agency responsible for receiving and investigating reports of child abuse and neglect. Most states designate their social services departments. See APPENDIX 2 for a list of each state's mandated agency and its address.

mandated reporter   Many people, by virtue of their professional or occupational status, are specifically required by state or federal law to report all cases of suspected child abuse or neglect to the mandated agency. Legal penalties are imposed for failure to report and some mandated reporters have been sued successfully for failing to report cases.

The occupational and professional categories whose practitioners are mandated reporters vary slightly according to different state laws but usually include: physician, psychologist, social worker, counselor, teacher, law enforcement officer and child care personnel. In approximately half of the states all citizens are considered mandated reporters. (*See also* DOCTRINE OF SOVEREIGN IMMUNITY; see APPENDIX 6 for state listings of mandated reporters.)

Mann Act   In response to concern over what was termed white slavery, in 1910 the U.S. Congress passed the Mann Act. This legislation made interstate transportation of females for prostitution or enticement for immoral purposes a federal offense. If found guilty under the terms of the Mann Act an individual can be fined up to $5,000, receive five years in prison, or both. In some circumstances, cases involving SEXUAL ABUSE of children can incur judicial action under the terms of the Mann Act. (*See also* CHILD SLAVERY.)

marasmus, nutritional   A lack of sufficient protein in the diet causes a condition known as nutritional marasmus. Characterized by emaciation, an apparently enlarged head, wide, staring eyes, shrunken buttocks and loose skin folds, it is the product of prolonged and severe dietary inadequacy. Nutritional marasmus may occur when breast feeding is reduced or ended and not replaced by an adequate source of nutrition. Repeated severe infection can also cause symptoms similar to those of marasmus.

masked deprivation   *See* EMOTIONAL NEGLECT.

masturbation   Masturbation refers to the manipulation of one's own or another's genitals for sexual gratification. Exhibitionists may seek to obtain sexual gratification by masturbating in the presence of a child. Other CHILD MOLESTERs may force or encourage children to masturbate in their presence or may participate in the masturbation. Nurses, babysitters and parents have been reported, on occasion, to masturbate infants and young children as a way of quieting them.

Though self masturbation by children is not considered a damaging behavior, frequent or open masturbation may be an indicator that the child is a victim of sexual abuse. This is especially true in the case of young children.

Masturbation also plays an important role in the practice of PEDOPHILIA. Pedophiles are strongly aroused by children and often maintain large collections of CHILD PORNOGRAPHY as a fantasy aid to masturbation.

maternal drug dependence Use of drugs, including alcohol, during pregnancy can cause severe and lasting damage to the fetus. Facial malformation, growth retardation and damage to the central nervous system are all present in children suffering from FETAL ALCOHOL SYNDROME. Infants born to mothers addicted to opiates may also become addicted, and they experience painful withdrawal symptoms at birth.

Many states now require that pregnant women who are drug or alcohol dependent be reported to a mandated agency for investigation of child abuse or neglect. Instances in which an infant is removed from the mother's care at birth are, however, rare. (*See also* SUBSTANCE ABUSE and ADDICTION, INFANTILE.)

maternal rejection syndrome *See* FAILURE TO THRIVE SYNDROME.

matricide This term refers to the murder of one's mother. Matricide is relatively rare; Federal Bureau of Investigation crime statistics list 152 matricides out of a total of 18,996 murders in the United States during 1985. Statistics show that most matricides are committed by sons. Though little is known about the motivation of children who kill their mothers, information from case studies suggests a strong link between matricide and child abuse. Most such murders occur during or shortly after an episode of child abuse.

Psychiatric profiles of mothers murdered by a son show a pattern of overly restrictive and harsh treatment of the son. Close examination of these profiles often indicates a strong sadistic component of the relationship. Also, mothers in these studies often behaved seductively toward the son yet quickly followed such behavior with brutal treatment. Despite the strong erotic component of these relationships INCEST was rarely consummated. Further, in most of these cases fathers were typically absent or extremely passive. (*See also* PARRICIDE, REACTIVE and PATRICIDE.)

media coverage of child abuse It has long been true in the United States that there is widespread public response to media coverage of child abuse and neglect. Newspapers and magazines in the 19th century and, more recently, radio and television coverage of child maltreatment issues, have been useful and effective means of publicizing needs in this area.

As early as the 1870s, when the now-famous MARY ELLEN WILSON case was written about in the *New York Times*, reporters and editors recognized the public's interest in child abuse. Some observers have drawn a correlation between the increase in media coverage of abuse and neglect and the response via private organizations and public agencies that seek to protect children and prevent child maltreatment. Whether or not there is a cause-and-effect relationship and despite some critics' charges that sensational reporting often does little more than titillate its audience, it is clear that, beginning in the late 19th century, the media in all its forms has promoted greater public awareness of child abuse and neglect.

Following C. Henry Kempe's report of "The Battered-Child Syndrome," in the July 7, 1962, issue of the *Journal of the American Medical Association*, many professional journals, popular magazines and newspapers increased their coverage of a wide range of child maltreatment issues. Numerous articles detailed the problem, focusing particularly on the psychopathology of abusing parents and varieties of physical abuse cases, but also reported on other facets such as sexual abuse and corporal punishment.

According to one source, over the last three decades there have been over 1,700 articles published in professional journals alone, pieces that focus on child abuse and attendant issues. Likewise, newspaper coverage of the topic has grown enormously. In the 30-year period between 1950 and 1980, the *New York Times Index* lists 652 articles on child abuse. And popular magazine coverage of abuse and neglect increased as well. For the 10 years following publication of Kempe's article in the AMA journal, 28 articles about child abuse were printed in magazines read by the general public, a figure contrasting sharply with the previous decade during which only three stories on abuse were published.

It is apparent to many experts that, in the 1970s and 1980s, changes in public policy regarding child abuse and neglect were precipitated to some degree by greater coverage of the subject. In this respect, the 20th century is similar to the previous century, when public and private agencies were established in apparent response to news coverage of child protection issues. In this sense, the media has positively influenced the heightened public awareness of and interest in child abuse and neglect.

George Gerbner, Catherine J. Ross and Edward Zigler, eds., *Child Abuse: An Agenda for Action* (New York: Oxford University Press, 1980).

Medicaid   Title XIX of the Social Security Act—known as Medicaid—was signed into law by President Lyndon B. Johnson on July 30, 1965. Medicaid is jointly funded by the federal government and the states. It provides a range of medical services to low-income individuals who meet state criteria for that category. Of particular relevance to child abuse is the inclusion of families who participate in the Aid to Families with Dependent Children Program (AFDC). Children in those eligible families receive a number of medical services under Medicaid. Among those services are early and periodic screening and diagnosis (EPSD). EPSD provides medical screening to children on a regular basis, beginning in infancy. Medicaid and AFDC are credited with making a strong contribution toward eliminating or reducing SITUATIONAL ABUSE AND NEGLECT associated with POVERTY and poor health care. (*See also* SOCIAL SECURITY ACT.)

medical evaluation   A thorough medical evaluation is important in the identification of abuse or neglect as well as the treatment of injuries resulting from maltreatment. The physician conducting the evaluation should be trained in recognition of medical conditions associated with abuse. Serious injury may be overlooked due to a lack of visual evidence or because the examiner fails to recognize subtle signs of trauma.

Thorough assessment requires the involvement of several different disciplines, including psychiatry, pediatrics, social work and nursing. In many cases a specialist in pediatric neurology, radiology, ophthalmology, dentistry or other area is necessary to evaluate the existence and the extent of injury fully. When abuse or neglect is suspected as the cause of death, an AUTOPSY by a pathologist trained in FORENSIC MEDICINE is appropriate.

In many cases evidence of trauma is easily recognizable. Since one purpose of the medical evaluation is to gather evidence for the existence of nonaccidental injury, the physician must be skilled in determining the possible causes of a particular injury as well as the approximate time it was inflicted. While it is not often possible to say with absolute assurance precisely how a child was injured, it is often possible to rule out certain causes. Suspicion of abuse is often aroused when a caretaker's account of how a child was injured does not coincide with medical evidence.

More often a physician is called upon by parents to treat a sick or injured child when no suggestion of maltreatment is made. A physician must constantly be aware of suspicious explanations or behavior by caretakers as well as physical evidence of abuse.

A complete medical evaluation may involve a SKELETAL SURVEY to detect the FRACTURES and evidence of other internal injury. When SEXUAL ABUSE is a possibility a thorough examination of the genitalia, mouth and anus, with appropriate tests for VENEREAL DISEASE and, in adolescents, pregnancy, is conducted. Other tests may reveal inadequate nutrition or other evidence of NEGLECT.

Frequently, more than one form of maltreatment is observed in a child. Presence of PHYSICAL ABUSE will alert the medical specialist to look for other evidence of maltreatment such as neglect or PSYCHOLOGICAL MALTREATMENT.

The medical specialist must be skilled in differentiating abuse-related trauma from disease-related symptoms that mimic abuse. Various diseases, congenital conditions and even birthmarks can be confused with sequelae of abuse or neglect. Certain folk medicine remedies (see CAO GIO) also produce lesions that are frequently interpreted as evidence of abuse by examining physicians.

Despite the difficulty of confronting a parent with the information that the child could not have injured him or herself, the physician's first responsibility is to protect the child. This involves notifying the proper child protection authorities and, in some cases arranging for the child to be hospitalized for treatment, observation and/or protection. Honest and sensitive discussion of the problem with caretakers immediately following diagnosis may improve the likelihood that they will cooperate in efforts to prevent further maltreatment. The primary purpose of the medical evaluation is to identify evidence of abuse or neglect, not specifically to identify the abuser. Evidence obtained by the physician should be presented to the proper law enforcement or child protection authorities charged with the INVESTIGATION of child abuse.

medical model Since World War II, the medical model has greatly influenced public perceptions of child abuse and neglect. By presenting abuse as a form of psychopathological illness, the medical model held out hope that it, like other sicknesses, could be isolated and cured. Dominance of the medical approach to child abuse may stem in part from developments in pediatric radiology (see RADIOLOGY, PEDIATRIC) that allowed physicians to diagnose unusual patterns of bone trauma that appeared to be the result of battering.

Popularization of the term BATTERED CHILD SYNDROME by C. Henry Kempe and his associates further strengthened the perception of child abuse as illness. Subsequent attention by the popular media created the perception of all abused children as victims of sadistic PHYSICAL ABUSE. This vision of child abuse played an important role in mobilizing political action on behalf of abused children. Within five years of publication of an article entitled "The Battered Child Syndrome" in the *Journal of the American Medical Association*, each of the 50 states had adopted a law that required reporting of suspected child abuse and neglect. The medical image of child abuse continues to heavily influence approaches to treatment and prevention.

In spite of its usefulness in generating public action the medical model is frequently criticized for ignoring societal causes of abuse and neglect. Focusing attention on individual pathology, while useful and appropriate in many situations, may not be sufficient to eliminate underlying causes of child maltreatment. Some critics of the medical model argue that it amounts to BLAMING THE VICTIM and call for a more balanced approach to the problem. (*See also* DEFECT MODEL OF CHILD ABUSE, PSYCHOPATHOLOGY.)

medical neglect The issue of medical care neglect has been the subject of much heated debate and many legal battles. Failure of parents to provide for or permit necessary medical treatment may be based on religious belief, fear, ignorance, misunderstanding or lack of concern.

In cases of serious acute illness and life-threatening or disabling chronic disease it may be necessary to obtain a court order to allow treatment. When ongoing treatment is required, supervision of the court or foster placement may be necessary to ensure proper medical care. A distinction is usually made between situations in which medical intervention has a reasonable possibility of succeeding and fatal diseases such as cancer in which medical procedures are mostly palliative.

Parents are also expected to provide preventive or "well child" care. While standards may vary, most states and countries have laws requiring immunization against life-threatening communicable disease. In the United States many states will not allow unimmunized children to enroll in school. Most pediatricians recommend that children be fully immunized before age two.

It is also recommended that the nutritional status of an infant be monitored by a physician. An absolute minimum of two visits during the first year of life, with the first visit taking place before two months of age, is considered the least amount of care necessary for healthy development. Pediatricians differ in their minimum standards of well child care. Many believe that two visits during the first 12 months is insufficient. Other examples of inadequate preventive care are failure to treat recognized visual impairment and allowing a child to suffer painful tooth decay without dental treatment.

Barton Schmitt, a professor of pediatrics at the University of Colorado School of Medicine, recommends that physicians take a five-step approach when faced with a medically neglected child:

First, care should be taken to determine the existence of financial, transportation or similar barriers. Parents or caretakers should be helped to eliminate such barriers.

Second, the parents' questions about their child's condition should be answered as completely as possible. The risks associated with treatment and the expected outcome should be explained as should the risks of forgoing treatment.

Third, the physician should attempt to work through a third party such as a relative, friend or member of the clergy.

Fourth, if the family continues to refuse treatment the physician should inform them and the third party that he or she is obligated to refer the case to the courts.

Fifth, if the family fails to respond to the warning the physician should seek a court order.

Norman S. Ellerstein, ed., *Child Abuse and Neglect: A Medical Reference* (New York: John Wiley, 1981).

Alejandro Rodriguez, *Handbook of Child Abuse and Neglect* (Flushing, N.Y.: Medical Examination Publishing Co., 1977).

medicine, forensic *See* FORENSIC MEDICINE.

Menkes Kinky Hair Syndrome This rare inherited disease inhibits the absorption of copper into the system, resulting in brittle bones and possibly death. Due to the multiple fractures present in infants suffering from this disease it is often confused with the BATTERED CHILD SYNDROME. The name derives from characteristic changes in the hair of those with this disease. Hair is stubby, coarse and ivory in color.

mental cruelty Often used as grounds for divorce, mental cruelty may also form the basis for intervention in a family by child protection agencies. As a legal term, mental cruelty refers to a pattern of behavior by an individual that threatens the mental and physical health of another. Courts differ in the type and severity of actions they consider to be mental cruelty. In recent years the definition has generally expanded to include behavior that was not previously considered abusive. A child who is the target of mental cruelty by a parent or caretaker is a victim of PSYCHOLOGICAL MALTREATMENT

mental injury A term used in some child abuse laws, mental injury refers to intellectual or psychological damage. Determination of the existence and extent of mental injury is usually based on a comparison of a child's performance and behavior with that of other children of the same age and cultural background.

Legal definitions of mental injury usually depend upon evaluation by a qualified psychiatrist, psychologist or pediatrician. Further, the impairment must be attributable to an act or acts of omission or commission by an adult responsible for the child. Pennsylvania law (Act 124, 1975) defines mental injury as "a psychological condition . . . which: (1) renders the child chronically and severely anxious, agitated, depressed, socially withdrawn, psychotic, or in reasonable fear that his/her life and/or safety is threatened; (2) makes it extremely likely that the child will become chronically and severely anxious, agitated, depressed, socially withdrawn, psychotic, or be in reasonable fear that his/her life is threatened; or (3) seriously interferes with the child's ability to accomplish age-appropriate developmental milestones, or school, peer, and community tasks."

Mental injury may result from PSYCHOLOGICAL MALTREATMENT as well as PHYSICAL ABUSE, SEXUAL ABUSE and NEGLECT.

mental retardation Ironically, mental retardation is seen as both a cause and a result of child abuse.

Mental retardation can result from child battering, nutritional and medical neglect, drug or alcohol use during pregnancy, and other forms of maltreatment. SUBDURAL HEMATOMA due to battering is perhaps the major cause of traumatically induced mental retardation among children. Battered infants are especially susceptible to brain damage because the infant cranium is soft and does not afford the same protection provided by the fully developed adult bone structure.

Mentally retarded or developmentally delayed children are often singled out as targets for abuse by their caretakers. Parents may feel angry, frustrated and/or guilty as a result of having a retarded child. These feelings are sometimes directed toward the child in the form of abusive behavior. The child is also more likely to be the recipient of abuse connected with family stress, alcohol and drug abuse, and mental illness on the part of the parent or primary caretaker. Mentally retarded children and adults are more vulnerable to physical and sexual assaults from outside as well.

Because many children suffering from mental retardation are cared for in institutions or community-based programs, they are often the victims of INSTITUTIONAL ABUSE AND NEGLECT. For centuries these children and adults were subjected to imprisonment, beating, sexual misuse and starvation, and were sometimes put to death. Even now, vast differences exist in the quality of care provided for mentally retarded individuals in different communities and countries around the world.

Sharon R. Morgan, *Abuse and Neglect of Handicapped Children* (Boston: College-Hill Press, 1987).

A. Sandgrund, R. Gaines and A. Green, "Child Abuse and Mental Retardation: A Problem of Cause and Effect," *American Journal of Mental Deficiency*, 79:3(1975), pp. 327-330.

microcephaly A condition in which the cranial capacity is abnormally small, microcephaly may develop following a blow to the head. Damage caused by microcephaly is usually irreversable. (*See also* CENTRAL NERVOUS SYSTEM INJURIES.)

Minnesota Multiphasic Personality Inventory (MMPI) Psychometric tests are sometimes used to detect emotional disturbance in children who have been abused. Most such tests can be administered and interpreted only by trained psychologists. The Minnesota Multiphasic Personality Inventory (MMPI) is one of the most popular tests used in the assessment of older children.

The MMPI consists of over 500 items that must be answered true, false, or "cannot say." Originally developed as a means of classifying patients in mental hospitals, the test is divided into 10 basic scales that measure characteristics such as hypochondria, depression, hysteria, paranoia, hypomania and schizophrenia.

minor   *See* CHILD.

Miranda warnings   In cases of alleged child abuse and neglect, as in other alleged crimes, an accused person is protected against self-incrimination by the so-called Miranda warnings, based on the 1966 U.S. Supreme Court decision in *Miranda v. Arizona.* In that ruling, the court held that statements made by an individual who has been taken into custody cannot be used by the prosecution *against that individual* unless procedural safeguards against self-incrimination have been exercised. Briefly stated, the Miranda warnings cover the following points:

1. An individual has the right to remain silent.
2. Anything said by an individual can and will be used against that individual in a court of law.
3. An individual has the right to talk with a lawyer and to have the lawyer present during questioning.
4. If an individual cannot afford to hire a lawyer, one will be appointed to represent that individual prior to any questioning, if the individual so desires.

misdemeanor   In criminal court proceedings offenses are distinguished according to how serious they are perceived to be. FELONIES are considered most serious and are punishable by more severe penalties. Misdemeanors are treated less severely, traditionally receiving prison sentences no longer than one year. In some cases misdemeanors and

felonies are tried in different courts, with alleged felons receiving greater procedural safeguards. (*See also* COURT, DUE PROCESS.)

Model Protection Act   The NATIONAL CENTER ON CHILD ABUSE AND NEGLECT in Washington, D.C., has prepared a guide for states wishing to develop their own child abuse legislation. Known as the Model Protection Act, this document served as the basis of new child abuse laws in virtually all of the 50 states.

molestation   *See* CHILD MOLESTER.

Mongolian spots   Birthmarks are sometimes mistaken for bruises on young children and infants, arousing suspicion of child abuse. Mongolian spots appear on some children at birth. These are grayish blue in color and last from two to three years. These spots can appear on any part of the body, but are most commonly found on the back and buttocks. Though Mongolian spots are found on children of all races, they appear more frequently on dark-skinned infants.

moral neglect   Failure of parents to instill positive social values in their children is sometimes referred to as moral neglect. Early child protection efforts leaned heavily on inadequate moral training as justification for intervening in a family. Delinquency by children and family poverty were seen as evidence of parents' moral weakness and early societies for the protection of children often removed children from their homes for these reasons.

Today, moral neglect alone is usually not considered grounds for removing a child from home. Poverty is largely seen as a societal rather than a moral problem. Illegal acts of children are handled through the juvenile court system. Removal of a child from home due to delinquency takes place in the context of treatment or, in some cases, punishment. Parents who allow or encourage their children to engage in illegal activity may be subject to criminal charges for contributing to the delinquency of a minor.

Mothers Anonymous   Self-help groups for mothers who abuse their children are sometimes called Mothers Anonymous. Although these groups operate similarly to PARENTS ANONYMOUS, they are not affiliated with a national organization such as P.A.

mouth injuries   Injuries to the mouth and surrounding area are relatively common in children. Determination of whether trauma is due to accident or abuse often depends on the plausibility of the caretaker's explanation of the accident and on the age of the child. While some types of oral injuries are common in children learning to walk, such injuries are less likely to be accidental in pre-toddlers or children who have been walking for some time.

Mouth injuries include tearing of the frenum (the small, v-shaped muscle joining the lip to the gum at the front of the mouth); cuts, abrasions and contusions of the lips; loosening, intrusion (forcing back into the gum), avulsion (total removal) and fractures of the teeth; and laceration of the tongue or gums. Fracture of the mandible (lower jaw), and less frequently the maxillary bone (upper bone structure), may also result from a forceful blow to the mouth area.

Prompt attention to oral injuries by a physician or dentist is important. Avulsed teeth have a 90% chance of being saved if replaced in the socket within 15 minutes of removal. The success rate of reimplantation drops 15% after one hour. Tooth fractures should also receive prompt attention from a dentist to avoid loss of the tooth.

Neglect of proper oral hygiene can cause unnecessary pain and discomfort as well as permanent damage to a child's mouth. Though it is often difficult to determine whether neglect of dental needs is intentional, poor oral hygiene is often indicative of more general MEDICAL NEGLECT.

Dentists can be especially helpful in early identification of possible abuse or neglect involving oral damage and hygiene. Many areas require that dentists report suspected child maltreatment to local child protection or law enforcement authorities.

multidisciplinary team   Identification and treatment of child abuse and neglect often requires a variety of different skills and perspectives. Multidisciplinary teams have been found to be an effective way of helping professionals work together in diagnosing and treating child abuse. Such teams are used widely in many different countries. In the United States some states specifically require the use of multidisciplinary teams.

Composition of teams may vary but most teams include representatives from the fields of social service and medicine. Members of the mental health, nursing, education, legal and law enforcement professions are frequently included. Inclusion of a representative of the agency legally charged with investigation of reported abuse is recommended as a means of improving coordination of services and reducing conflict.

In addition to identification and treatment planning, multidisciplinary teams may also provide consultation, community education and prevention services. Many teams are based in hospitals. Other models include interagency programs and teams directly connected to a government agency.

Though some teams experience relatively high levels of disagreement between members and occasional disputes over turf, most experts agree that the advantages of the multidisciplinary approach outweigh the disadvantages. Use of multidisciplinary teams has been credited with improving the quality and coordination of treatment, lessening the need for out-of-home placement, strengthening families, reducing the chance of reinjury, and lowering the overall cost of treatment.

multiple maltreatment   Child abuse is rarely confined to a single incident or mode of abuse. Investigation of suspected abuse often reveals forms of maltreatment other than that reported. Physically abused children are often neglected. Victims of sexual abuse may also be subjected to psychological or physical abuse.

The combination of several forms of maltreatment often presents special problems for treatment of abused and neglected children. Failure to identify all forms of maltreatment may lead to inappropriate intervention. Unrecognized or untreated abuse may have lasting effects. Careful ASSESSMENT of each child's situation is essential to ensure proper treatment and protection.

Munchausen Syndrome by Proxy   Baron K.F.H. von Munchausen was an 18th-century German mercenary with a penchant for telling tall tales. Accounts of his adventures were further embellished in a pamphlet entitled "Baron Munchausen's Narrative of His Marvellous Travels and Campaigns in Russia." In the early 1950s an English physician used the term "Munchausen Syndrome" to describe a psychiatric disorder characterized by dramatic and untruthful medical histories and feigned symptoms. Munchausen Syndrome by Proxy refers to a rare form of abuse in which a medical disorder in the child is fabricated by a parent or caretaker. The perpetrator may present false medical his-

tories, inflict physical symptoms, alter lab specimens and directly induce disorders in the child. As a result of these fabrications, the child may be subjected to frequent unnecessary hospitalizations, painful tests, potentially harmful treatment and even death. The importance of taking a full social history and verifying the child's medical history is emphasized in the detection of Munchausen Syndrome by Proxy.

mutilation, genital   *See* CASTRATION, CLITORIDECTOMY and INFIBULATION.

mysopedic offender   This type of pedophile (*see* PEDOPHILIA) is the most sadistic of all sexual offenders. Mysopeds are sometimes referred to as "child haters" and are responsible for most brutal rapes and murders of children. Though quite uncommon, mysopeds have often been the focus of a great deal of media attention. Some of the more widely publicized cases involve mentally disordered men with long histories of molesting children, who commit a number of rape/murders before being apprehended.

One well-known case involved an Illinois man who worked as a clown entertaining children in hospitals and at home. When finally arrested for a sexual offense, he confessed to sexually assaulting and strangling 32 teenage boys and young men.

N

National Advisory Centre on the Battered Child   Located in London, the National Advisory Centre on the Battered Child was formed from the National Society for the Prevention of Cruelty to Children's battered child research department. The National Centre later became the NSPCC Haringey Special Unit, an interdisciplinary team providing treatment and consultation services.

National Center for Missing and Exploited Children   The National Center for Missing and Exploited Children began operations in 1984, a result of growing public concern over the problem of missing and sexually exploited children in the United States. A nonprofit organization, the center was created by an act of Congress and funded initially by the Office of Juvenile Justice and Delinquency Prevention, United States Department of Justice.

In addition to operating a toll-free hotline for reporting information leading to the location or recovery of a missing child (1-800-843-5678), the center serves as a clearinghouse for information concerning the problem of missing and exploited children. Technical assistance is available to individuals, groups, state and local agencies on the prevention of the exploitation and victimization of children. Training is also provided to law enforcement and child protection agencies on procedures to be followed in the investigation and prosecution of cases involving missing or exploited children. For more information, see APPENDIX 1.

National Center for the Prevention and Treatment of Child Abuse and Neglect   *See* KEMPE NATIONAL CENTER FOR THE PREVENTION AND TREATMENT OF CHILD ABUSE AND NEGLECT.

National Center for the Study of Corporal Punishment and Alternatives in the Schools (NCSCPAS)   Founded in 1976, as part of the Department of School Psychology at Temple University, this center provides information and opportunity to study the psychological and educational aspects of school discipline. One of several such organizations devoted to eliminating corporal punishment from the schools, the NCSCPAS established the Delaware Valley Discipline Clinic to provide diagnoses and counseling as well as consultation to schools.

The NCSCPAS runs workshops, nationally and internationally, arranges legal advocacy for protesting corporal punishment in schools and has an extensive collection of articles and news clippings that focus on discipline. The center publishes *Discipline Helpline*, a journal, several times annually as well as a bibliography of publications related to corporal punishment. It holds semiannual executive committee meetings and maintains a free telephone consultation service. (*See also* APPENDIX 1.)

National Center on Child Abuse and Neglect (NCCAN)   NCCAN is a government office administered by the Children's Bureau, Administration for Youth and Families, Office of Human Development Services, United States Department of Health and Human Services. The center was established in 1974 by the National Child Abuse Prevention and Treatment Act. The purpose of the center is to:

1. generate new knowledge and improve child protection, prevention and treatment programs;
2. collect, analyze and disseminate information related to child abuse and neglect;
3. help states and local communities implement programs; and
4. coordinate all federal initiatives related to child abuse and neglect.

Since its inception, NCCAN has awarded over 400 grants for projects directed toward the prevention, identification and treatment of child abuse and neglect. The center also funds an annual study of suspected maltreatment reports received by state protective service agencies.

NCCAN has also been responsible for helping states comply with the CHILD ABUSE PREVENTION AND TREATMENT ACT. The primary mechanism for encouraging compliance has been the awarding of federal grants to states for implementation of child abuse programs. To be eligible for funds states must have laws conforming to those outlined in federal legislation.

The dissemination of information is an important function of the center. Information on programs related to child abuse and neglect, state and territorial child protection laws, relevant judicial decisions, and descriptions of child protection programs operated by the various states are compiled by the center. This information is available to all citizens, and much of the material is disseminated through the Clearinghouse on Child Abuse and Neglect Information.

In addition to the national office in Washington, D.C., the center operates 10 National Child Welfare Resource Centers for the purpose of assisting in information transfer and stimulating the development of local support networks (see APPENDIX 12). Together with the U.S. Department of Defense, NCCAN operates the Military Family Resource Center. This program provides technical assistance to the military in establishing and improving support systems for military families stationed in all parts of the world.

NCCAN frequently sponsors meetings for the discussion of special topics as well as the more broadly focused National Conference on Child Abuse and Neglect. For more information, see APPENDIX 1.

National Child Abuse Hotline—1-800-4-A-CHILD or 1-800-422-4453 The National Child Abuse Hotline was established in 1982 to provide crisis counseling and referral assistance throughout the United States.

Trained counselors are available 24 hours a day, seven days a week to provide assistance to over 120,000 people who call each year. (See also HOTLINES.)

Hotline callers wishing to report abuse or neglect are encouraged to make such reports directly to the appropriate child protection agency in their areas. If the caller cannot afford the follow-up telephone call or if the counselor believes a follow-up call is unlikely to be made, the hotline can often connect the caller directly with an agency in their area. Calls from children and adolescents are routinely connected to the appropriate agency.

Approximately 30% of callers to the child abuse hotline ask for assistance in making a child abuse report. Forty percent of calls involve crisis counseling and referral to treatment providers or emergency shelters. The remaining calls are requests for information or professional consultation.

The National Child Abuse Hotline is located in Hollywood, California, and is operated by CHILDHELP USA, a nonprofit organization that focuses on prevention, treatment and research related to child abuse. For more information, see APPENDIX 1.

National Clearinghouse for Child Abuse and Neglect Information The clearinghouse, which maintains a large data base (File 64) available through DIALOG Information Services, Inc., was established as a resource center for individuals who want comprehensive information about child abuse and maltreatment. A variety of publications, made available at cost of reproduction, and special services to professionals, are provided by the clearinghouse, which is a component of the NATIONAL CENTER ON CHILD ABUSE AND NEGLECT (NCCAN).

National Committee for Prevention of Child Abuse Founded in 1972, this volunteer-based organization is concerned with preventing all forms of child abuse. It has 67 chapters located in all 50 states and the District of Columbia. The committee maintains an active network of child abuse prevention organizations and a national public awareness campaign. It helps provide prevention services and acts as a facilitator for other, independent programs dealing with child abuse and neglect; it also publishes educational materials in all areas of child abuse, some of which are available in Spanish. For more information, see APPENDIX 1.

National Legal Resource Center for Child Advocacy and Protection Founded in 1978, this organization is sponsored by the Young Lawyers Division of the American Bar Association. Its staff provides services relating to issues about child abuse and neglect, missing and exploited children, adoption, learning disabilities, child support and foster care. It maintains a training and technical assistance program, the National Legal Resource Center for Child Welfare Programs, which addresses issues of interest to those dealing with child advocacy and protection. Its publications include the *ABA Juvenile and Child Welfare Law Reporter*, a monthly publication, as well as various books and pamphlets. For more information, see APPENDIX 1.

national register The idea of a nationwide repository of child abuse reports has often been advanced as a way to monitor trends, conduct research and track offenders who move from place to place to avoid apprehension. It has not been possible to establish such a register in the United States because differences in state laws, definitions of abuse, and rules regarding confidentiality have made this information difficult to collect and compare. Similar impediments to a national register of child abuse reports exist in Canada and in Great Britain, which consist of separate territories, provinces and/or countries.

National Society for the Prevention of Cruelty to Children This British organization was originally named the London Society for the Prevention of Cruelty to Children and

was founded by clergyman Benjamin Waugh in 1884. In 1889 it merged with 31 other child welfare groups that had been established throughout Britain, taking the name by which it is known today. Queen Victoria was a patron of the NSPCC, which received a royal charter in May 1895. Its official mission as "to prevent the public and private wrongs of children."

The NSPCC was instrumental in securing passage of the landmark Prevention of Cruelty to and Protection of Children Act of 1889. The society operated branches in Dublin, Belfast and Cork until 1956, when the Irish Society assumed jurisdiction. The Scottish National Society, formed in 1899, received a royal charter as the Royal Scottish Society for the Prevention of Cruelty to Children.

Today, NSPCC inspectors make home visits and rely also on a network of community playgroups to help prevent abuse of children. In some areas of Britain, the NSPCC provides 24-hour support.

National Study on Child Neglect and Abuse Reporting Lack of adequate information concerning the incidence of abuse and neglect and the characteristics of both victims and perpetrators has long been a problem. In 1973, the Children's Bureau of the United States Department of Health, Education and Welfare contracted with the AMERICAN HUMANE ASSOCIATION to investigate the feasibility of developing a national clearinghouse on child abuse and neglect. The first study was conducted in 1974 with 23 states and other governmental jurisdictions participating.

Objectives of the national study include the following:

- enumeration and description of families, perpetrators and children involved in official reports of maltreatment
- determination and description of referral sources; geographic distribution and responses of the protective services system
- identification and description of trends in reported maltreatment of children

Participation in the study is voluntary. Since the first study, data collection and analysis have been modified to allow for greater participation. Thirty-six jurisdictions submitted a total of 458,000 individual case reports in 1982.

In addition to publishing an annual statistical report the national study now provides technical support to the National Center for Child Abuse and Neglect, state and local child protection agencies, researchers and the general public. In recent years the project's emphasis has shifted from design and implementation of reporting systems to analysis of data for purposes of policy development.

Native Americans   *See* INDIAN CHILD WELFARE ACT OF 1978.

natural dolls   A young victim of SEXUAL ABUSE may not have developed the verbal skills to communicate accurately her/his experience, or may simply find it very difficult or threatening to tell anyone about the episode. Hence, gathering information from the child is a difficult and sensitive task.

Natural dolls have proven to be a useful tool in the diagnosis and treatment of young victims of sexual abuse. The dolls are constructed with genitalia, body cavities, and pubic hair. Children frequently find it less difficult to act out the abuse using the dolls, or to point to the doll's sexual organs when discussing the abuse. Family life educators and programs focusing on the prevention of sexual abuse have also found natural dolls to be a useful educational device. Police, protective service workers and lawyers use the dolls to investigate allegations of abuse and to present court testimony.

NCCAN   *See* NATIONAL CENTER ON CHILD ABUSE AND NEGLECT.

NCSCPAS   *See* NATIONAL CENTER FOR THE STUDY OF CORPORAL PUNISHMENT AND ALTERNATIVES IN THE SCHOOLS.

neglect   Repeated failure to meet minimal standards for a child's nutritional, clothing, medical, educational, safety and/or emotional needs constitutes neglect. Neglect is the most frequent form of maltreatment, occurring twice as often as all other forms of abuse combined. Deaths and serious injury of children are more likely to result from neglect than abuse. Some longitudinal research indicates that neglected children may suffer more lasting emotional damage than physically abused children.

Neglect may be willful, as when a parent refuses to send a child to school, or unintended, as in the case of a caretaker suffering from severe mental illness who is incapable of providing adequate care.

Parents who neglect a child's needs because they lack adequate knowledge of parenting usually respond to teaching when it is given sensitively. Ignorance of proper child care can often be corrected by arranging for instruction from a visiting nurse or PARENT AIDE.

Poor judgment may be exercised by caretakers who are immature or who were themselves neglected. Safety neglect is a significant cause of death among young children. Children under the age of three years have not developed a safety consciousness and are especially susceptible to accidents. While all children are likely to suffer preventable accidents on occasion, repeated serious accidents indicate that a child's caretaker is unable or unwilling to take the necessary steps to protect him or her.

Parents who repeatedly refuse to change behaviors that are grossly neglectful pose a serious threat to a child's welfare. In such cases, court intervention and possible removal from the home may be necessary to protect the child's well-being.

POVERTY may affect parents' ability to provide the physical necessities for their children. By itself poverty does not provide a sufficient reason for labeling parents as neglectful. Studies show that the majority of children living in poor families are not neglected.

Often conditions that are unhealthy for children can be corrected by the provision of adequate support for food, clothing and housing. Failure by a society to provide an adequate minimum level of support for all children is sometimes called SOCIAL ABUSE.

Various forms of mental illness or emotional disturbances can play a role in parental neglect. Psychotic parents are unable to care for children and may become abusive. More often, depression contributes to parents' inability to provide for their children. Norman Polansky, author of several studies on child neglect, has described a condition known as the APATHY-FUTILITY SYNDROME, similar to psychological depression, which may be observed in severely and chronically neglectful mothers. This syndrome is characterized by emotional numbness, limited intellectual ability and other factors that are often related to the mother's own deprivation during childhood.

Gross neglect resulting in serious physical harm to a child is not difficult to identify. In other situations the identification of neglect may depend on the awareness of day care, school or medical professionals and their own individual standards of child care. Statutory definitions of neglect are often vague and may differ according to geographical location and cultural values.

In an effort to standardize the concept of neglect Polansky and others developed the CHILDHOOD LEVEL OF LIVING SCALE. This checklist is completed by a protective service worker or other child care professional and yields a numerical rating of the quality of the child's care. Scores are then compared to predetermined standards to determine the adequacy of care.

Investigation of suspected neglect must take into account each child's unique situation as well as the cultural and familial context in which he or she lives. A thorough evaluation includes a medical examination; a review of medical records for evidence of immunization status, number of accidental injuries and frequency of medical checkups; a report from day care or school officials concerning attendance, academic performance, behavior and diet; and a family assessment conducted by a trained social worker, including a home visit to assess the child's environment.

neglect, community *See* COMMUNITY NEGLECT.

neglect, emotional *See* EMOTIONAL NEGLECT.

neglect, indicators *See* INDICATORS OF CHILD ABUSE AND NEGLECT.

neglect, institutional *See* INSTITUTIONAL ABUSE AND NEGLECT.

neglect, medical *See* MEDICAL NEGLECT.

neglect, moral *See* MORAL NEGLECT.

neglect, neurological manifestations *See* NEUROLOGIC MANIFESTATIONS OF ABUSE AND NEGLECT.

neglect, prediction of *See* PREDICTION OF ABUSE AND NEGLECT.

neglect, situational *See* SITUATIONAL ABUSE AND NEGLECT.

C. Henry Kempe and Ray E. Helfer, eds., *The Battered Child*, 3rd ed. (Chicago: University of Chicago Press, 1980).

Norman A. Polansky, Mary Ann Chalmers, Elizabeth Buttenwieser and David P. Williams, *Damaged Parents* (Chicago: University of Chicago Press, 1981).

neglectful parents *See* CHARACTERISTICS OF ABUSING AND NEGLECTFUL PARENTS.

neonaticide The killing of an infant immediately following birth is known as neonaticide. In some cultures neonaticide has been considered an acceptable form of limiting family size or eliminating malformed infants. Historically, some societies drew a

Table 6   123

Table 6
Reports of Neglect for 34 States
Providing Complete Information, 1984–1985

State	1984	1985
Arizona	3,905	5,121
California	115,870	143,500
Connecticut	6,044	6,328
Delaware	1,550	1,755
Florida	23,891	25,072
Georgia	15,489	16,540
Hawaii	854	815
Idaho	3,725	4,275
Illinois	75,846	59,734
Indiana	17,704	20,127
Iowa	12,202	11,584
Kentucky	22,826	26,367
Louisiana	24,904	30,538
Maine	602	1,052
Massachusetts	3,157	3,290
Michigan	17,959	17,264
Mississippi	1,377	2,032
Missouri	32,302	33,537
Nevada	5,354	6,288
New Hampshire	617	529
New Jersey	8,241	7,241
New Mexico	7,314	9,295
New York	68,614	68,287
North Dakota	1,186	1,238
Oregon	6,103	4,476
Pennsylvania	564	516
South Dakota	1,908	3,033
Tennessee	20,565	22,172
Texas	43,405	40,638
Utah	3,404	3,422
Vermont	483	491
Washington	16,767	16,414
Wisconsin	8,436	9,948
Wyoming	3,233	2,084
Total	576,401	605,003

Figures represent substantiated reports.
No figures available (for 1981–1982).
Figures represent fiscal years, not calendar years.

sharp distinction between neonaticide and INFANTICIDE. These groups often developed rituals by which a child was accepted or rejected by the mother's husband. Until ritually accepted, an infant was not considered human and could therefore be murdered or abandoned with impunity.

Today neonaticide is relatively rare; however, reports of murdered or abandoned newborns are still heard from time to time in most countries.

Netherlands In 1970, the Society for the Prevention of Child Abuse and Neglect was founded in the Netherlands. Through this agency and via the Child Welfare Counselling Centres, cases of child abuse and neglect are reported. There is an emphasis on supportive programs and treatment for victims of child abuse and neglect, in particular toward victims of sexual abuse and incest. The Dutch government is actively involved in prevention and education programs to combat child abuse and neglect, and the Health and Welfare Ministry has sole responsibility for administering these services.

As a result of international pressure, the Dutch government curtailed the sale of child pornography after the Netherlands was identified as a center of its production and distribution.

neurologic manifestations of abuse and neglect Over half of all abused or neglected children show signs of impaired cognitive, language, learning, motor or psychological development. Physical abuse of children is a significant cause of mental retardation and cerebral palsy. Studies have shown that even in the absence of retardation, abused children tend to score lower than nonabused children on intelligence tests.

Neurologic impairment may be caused by obvious damage to the CENTRAL NERVOUS SYSTEM, such as MACROCEPHALY or spinal cord injury; however, neurologic injury is often the result of more subtle trauma. Nerve damage caused by shaking may not be readily apparent to an examining physician but may be reflected later in developmental delays.

Neglect also plays an important role in the production of neurological and developmental impairment. Poor nutrition and lack of social and sensory stimulation is associated with retarded intellectual, motor and emotional development. These forms of neglect are typical in battered children but are also found when no evidence of physical abuse is apparent. Infants who do not receive adequate TACTILE STIMULATION may exhibit signs of motor and intellectual impairment and later may have difficulty forming emotional attachments. Failure to provide adequate medical treatment for illness or injury may also cause neurological damage.

Because of the high rate of neurological problems associated with abuse and neglect, all child victims should be screened for neurodevelopmental deficits. A careful neurologic examination includes assessment of cranial nerve and cerebellar functioning, reflexes and focal damage, as well as evaluation of gross and fine motor skills, sensory-motor abilities, activity level and attention span.

Developmental screening can involve compiling a careful history of the child's development from a caretaker, observation by a medical practitioner trained in the identification of neurologic impairment, use of developmental checklists, and formal developmental screening tests. Using screening tests, such as the Denver Developmental Screening Test (DDST), is the preferred method of assessment.

Neurologic impairment can be both the cause and the result of abuse. Developmentally delayed children require additional time and patience from parents. Frustrated parents, especially those with unrealistically high expectations for their child's behavior, are more likely to abuse their children. Abuse increases the likelihood of neurological impairment, which, in turn, increases the probability of abuse.

Norman S. Ellerstein, *Child and Neglect: A Medical Reference* (New York: John Wiley and Sons, 1981).

Alejandro Rodriguez, *Handbook of Child Abuse and Neglect* (Flushing, N.Y.: Medical Examination Publishing Co., 1977).

New York House of Refuge   The New York House of Refuge, the first reform school in the United States, was opened by the Society for the Reformation of Juvenile Delinquents in 1825. As its name suggests, the facility also housed children who had been abused or neglected along with children who had committed delinquent acts.

Norway   As in other Scandinavian nations, Norway has a highly refined social welfare system that seems to preclude perception of widespread violence against children. Extensive child care provisions for all workers, maternity leave and education classes for new parents, as well as readily available contraception and abortion foster an atmosphere that appears to alleviate some tensions and preconditions associated with abuse or neglect.

Although some incidents of child abuse do occur and family violence is recognized as a problem, the focus in Norway is weighted heavily toward diagnosis and treatment rather than prevention, since abuse appears to take place relatively seldom. Some programs have been established in Norway to find ways of assisting violence-prone families. In 1972, Norway passed legislation that prohibited use of violent disciplinary actions against children.

nutritional deficiency   *See* MARASMUS, NUTRITIONAL; RICKETS; SCURVY.

nutritional marasmus   *See* MARASMUS, NUTRITIONAL.

O

offender, fixated   *See* FIXATED OFFENDER.

opinion evidence   *See* EVIDENCE.

***opu hule* (turned stomach)**   Originating among Native Hawaiian islanders, this culturally based belief stipulates that tossing or jiggling a young child up and down will result in *opu hule*, or a "turned stomach." This term means that the stomach has been twisted or displaced. Children who suffer from symptoms of indigestion, fussiness or general discomfort are often thought to be suffering from *opu hule*. Tossing or bouncing a child is considered to be a form of child abuse and is frowned upon in the Native Hawaiian culture.

order of protection   In the United States, the legal basis for court intervention in the family of an abused or neglected child is an order of protection. The order is typically issued by a juvenile court and places the child under the supervision of an authority, usually the designated child protection agency. Typically, children are allowed to remain at home while under an order of protection, provided the family meets specific conditions spelled out in the order. Failure to comply with these terms may result in the parents being held in contempt of court, fined and/or imprisoned. Violation of such orders is also likely to prompt the court to take custody of the child.

The NATIONAL CENTER ON CHILD ABUSE AND NEGLECT lists the following conditions that are usually included in an order of protection:

- Refrain from any conduct that is detrimental to the child(ren).
- Refrain from any conduct that would make the home an improper place for the child.
- Give adequate attention to the care of the home.
- Comply with visitation terms if the child has been removed from the home.
- Comply with the treatment plan.

ossification   Formation of new bone, known as ossification, is visible on X rays and can be an important clue in the detection of child battering. A trained physician can determine if there is a history of multiple fractures by examining a series of X rays for evidence of ossification, which indicates the healing of old fractures, as well as searching the X rays for more recent trauma. (*See also* FRACTURES.)

osteogenesis imperfecta   Sometimes mistaken for BATTERED CHILD SYNDROME, osteogenesis imperfecta is an inherited condition that causes bones to be very brittle and easily fractured.

overlaying   Overlaying refers to the suffocation of an infant by an adult lying on top of it. Prior to the 20th century many infants were thought to have died as a result of overlaying (also known as stifling). Deaths that are now attributed to SUDDEN INFANT DEATH SYNDROME were frequently thought to be the result of the mother intentionally or accidentally overlaying the infant during the night. Overlaying was considered a negligent act by a mother and was punished in the Roman Catholic and Anglican churches. Fear of accidental suffocation led to the custom of mothers and infants sleeping in separate beds, an uncommon practice in earlier times.

A special device was developed in 17th-century Europe to prevent accidental overlaying. This device, called an *arcuccio*, consisted of a metal and wood arch. The infant, protected underneath the *arcuccio*, could sleep in the same bed with the mother without the possibility of accidental suffocation. Some countries made failure to use the *arcuccio* a punishable offense References to the use of the *arcuccio* can be found as late as 1890. (*See also* CULTURAL FACTORS, SUDDEN INFANT DEATH SYNDROME.)

P

PA buddy   PARENTS ANONYMOUS groups, much like Alcoholics Anonymous, assign sponsors, or buddies, to members. The buddy, usually a more experienced member of the group, serves a function similar to a PARENT AIDE. A PA member may contact her/his buddy for advice and support at any time. Use of the buddy system serves an important function in preventing child abuse by providing a nonthreatening source of support in a crisis. The buddy receives the benefit of an increased sense of confidence and self-control by helping another person improve his/her parenting skills.

paddling   One of many forms of CORPORAL PUNISHMENT, paddling is a variation of CANING in which school officials (teachers or administrators) sometimes strike students with the flat side of a wooden paddle to promote discipline. Although the practice is a time-honored one, it has numerous detractors and several international children's rights organizations work to prohibit paddling and other forms of corporal punishment.

In the United States, the practice of paddling was challenged in a case brought before the United States Supreme Court by three junior high school students in Dade City, Florida. The case, *INGRAHAM V. WRIGHT*, exposed the potential and real injuries accruing from the practice of paddling. Ultimately, the Supreme Court found that public schools had the constitutional right to exercise paddling or any other form of "reasonable" corporal punishment. To date, there are only nine states in the United States in which paddling or any other means of corporal punishment is prohibited. In many other countries of the world corporal punishment in any form is illegal.

pancreatitus   This term refers to damage to the pancreatic ducts, usually caused by abdominal trauma. Laceration of the pancreas causes the enzymes amylase and lipase to be released into the peritoneal cavity causing a large buildup of fluid and inflammation of the peritoneum (the membrane enclosing the abdominal cavity).

Occasionally pancreatitus is contained within a smaller area, causing an abscess or a fibrous capsule called a pseudocyst to develop. These developments result in the appearance of a painful lump in the upper abdomen two to three weeks after the injury. Surgical intervention is required to correct such lesions.

Pancreatitus is rare in childhood. When it is present child abuse is strongly suspected. A radiographic study of long bones to detect other evidence of battering can be helpful in confirming this suspicion.

parens patriae   This legal doctrine provides the foundation for a court's entry into the realm of the family. When parents are determined to be unable or unfit to provide adequate and proper care for a child, the court can step in to safeguard the BEST INTERESTS OF THE CHILD. Parens patriae literally means "guardian of the community," and rests on the principle that the state is the ultimate and absolute protector of all citizens, especially children.

This doctrine was first established in the United States in 1838 in the case of Mary Ann Crouse. At that time, the court ruled that a child's parents, "when unequal to the task of education or unworthy of it, be supplanted by the parens patriae." The ruling was widely upheld in the courts throughout the 1800s. By the early 20th century it had become the legal basis on which the juvenile court was established. Its acceptance as a fundamental prerogative of a court means that in cases of suspected child abuse or neglect, the court is the best judge of a child's home environment and that environment's effect on a child's welfare.

In 1968, passage of the UNIFORM CHILD CUSTODY JURISDICTION ACT limited use of parens patriae in cases of CHILD STEALING. The exception occurs in cases where a child requires emergency protection. Under the UCCJA, an emergency condition can result in the court's instituting immediate measures to protect the child. In custody dispute cases that involved child stealing, the doctrine of parens patriae was found to contribute directly to multiple child custody adjudications. (*See EX PARTE CROUSE.*)

parent, surrogate   *See* SURROGATE PARENT.

parent aides   Many child abuse treatment programs provide special assistance to families in the form of paraprofessionals who serve as role models to parents. These parent aides may be paid or may volunteer their time. Aides perform many different services, such as modelling appropriate parenting techniques, helping to identify problems, teaching specific skills, serving as advocates and giving emotional support and nurturance. Most of all, parent aides serve as friends of the family.

Parent aides are sometimes described as SURROGATE PARENTs. They provide emotional support for both parents and children. Some experts believe it is necessary for parents to go through a REPARENTING process in which they experience the warmth, acceptance and positive learning they did not receive from their parents. Parent aides are usually older adults or couples who, in addition to having been parents themselves, have had special training in working with abusive or neglectful parents.

This type of family support works best in combination with a comprehensive treatment program. Parent aides are often members of a MULTIDISCIPLINARY TEAM. Some hospitals in the United States use parent aides to perform a role similar to that of the HEALTH VISITOR in Britain. Aides are assigned to parents within a few days of the child's birth and continue assisting the parents as long as necessary, usually six to 18 months.

parent education   Special programs designed to teach parenting skills are used to treat and prevent child abuse and neglect. Specific parenting skills taught in these programs vary. Many courses for young or neglectful parents focus on basic skills such as proper hygiene and feeding. Abusive parents often expect children to perform beyond their developmental capabilities. Learning about normal developmental patterns helps create more realistic expectations and may help reduce frustration. Programs for parents of older children often focus on improving communication skills. Parent Effectiveness Training, developed by Thomas Gordon, PhD, is an example of such a program.

During the past decade many public schools have begun to offer family life education classes as part of the regular school curriculum. These programs are designed to help adolescents make informed choices about marriage and childrearing.

Many child protection experts believe parent education programs are ineffective for unmotivated parents. Further, some abusive parents have sufficient knowledge but need assistance of other kinds. However, when used as part of a comprehensive treatment and prevention effort, parent education is an important resource for many families.

Thomas Gordon, *Parent Effectiveness Training* (New York: Peter H. Wyden, 1970).

Parental Kidnapping Prevention Act of 1980 (P.L. 96-611)   In order to address more effectively issues related to child stealing in custody disputes, this federal law requires that each state honor other states' custody determinations.

parenthood, psychological   *See* PSYCHOLOGICAL PARENTHOOD.

parentified child   Children inappropriately placed in the role of parent are said to be parentified. A parentified child may be expected to behave as an adult or be given primary responsibility for care of younger siblings. In some cases children are expected to take care of a parent's emotional or physical needs. Forcing children into adult roles too soon may lead to impaired emotional development sometimes referred to as loss of childhood. (*See also* PSEUDOMATURITY and ROLE REVERSAL.)

Parent-Infant Traumatic Syndrome (PITS)
The combination of subdural hematomas and specific types of bone lesions was labeled the Parent-Infant Traumatic Syndrome by radiologist John Caffey in 1946. Using improved X-ray techniques, Caffey and his associates were able to detect a pattern of trauma that they believed to be of suspicious origin.

Specifically the PITS, also called the battered baby syndrome, involves multiple fractures and other lesions of bone and cartilage in various states of healing. Bone damage typically occurs at joints and often appears to be the result of twisting or vigorous shaking. The combination of bone lesions and head trauma suggests a specific type of injury that is unlikely to be accidental.

The ability to detect unusual patterns of bone injury was an important advance in recognition and treatment of physical child abuse. Physicians who suspected nonaccidental injury could examine full skeletal X rays for additional evidence of abuse. Radiologic evidence is still an important tool in the diagnosis of battered children and is often presented in court as physical evidence of abuse. (*See also* BATTERED CHILD SYNDROME, RADIOLOGY, PEDIATRIC).

parents, abusive   *See* CHARACTERISTICS OF ABUSING AND NEGLECTFUL PARENTS.

parents, neglectful   *See* CHARACTERISTICS OF ABUSING AND NEGLECTFUL PARENTS.

Parents Anonymous   Begun as a parent group in Redondo Beach, California, Parents Anonymous is now the largest child abuse treatment program in the United States. With 1,000 chapters in 42 states, PA serves approximately 60,000 families per year. Parent groups have also been formed in Canada, Australia, West Germany and England. In addition to these groups for parents, PA offers over 250 groups for abused children.

Membership includes parents who have abused their children, and others interested in preventing child abuse. Members are not required to admit to parenting problems though many find it helpful to share such problems. First names are used at weekly meetings to protect the anonymity of group members.

Informal support provided by members serves an important purpose in preventing future abuse. Members share telephone numbers and are encouraged to call one another when a crisis arises. The national office of Parents Anonymous also operates a toll-free hotline (800-421-0353/800-356-0386 in California) providing telephone crisis counseling and referral information.

Seventy-five percent of PA members are self-referred; 25% are ordered by courts to attend Parents Anonymous meetings.

Though sometimes described as a self-help program, Parents Anonymous is actually a blend of peer support and professional treatment. Parent groups are led by a parent and facilitated by a mental health professional. All professional facilitators volunteer their time to help the group function effectively. Leadership responsibility rests with a member selected by the group to serve as chapter chairperson.

Evaluations have demonstrated the success of Parents Anonymous in reducing both frequency and severity of physical, verbal and emotional abuse. The longer parents participate in the program the more lasting the improvement.

Because it relies heavily on volunteers PA is considered to be one of the most cost-effective means of preventing child abuse. In 1987 the average cost of serving a family was approximately $200 per year. All services are provided without charge. Costs of operating national and regional offices, the hotline and other services are funded through grants and donations.

Parents Anonymous was founded in 1971 as a private, not-for-profit corporation "dedicated to the identification, treatment and prevention of child abuse." The group works with families through "peer led professionally facilitated self help groups" in the interest of preventing child abuse and avoiding placement of children. According to recent information published by PA, over 1,000 parent groups now provide free service to more than 60,000 families per year. PA also operates toll-free crisis hotlines and referral telephones in 19 states, offering telephone counseling and referral to adults and children. The national office publishes a monthly newsletter, *The Insider*. For more information, see APPENDIX 1.

Parents Anonymous buddy   *See* PA BUDDY.

parents' rights   Legal rights of parents often come into conflict with those of children and the state during the course of INVESTIGATION or treatment of child abuse or neglect. Parents have the right to custody and supervision of children and to make decisions on behalf of a child under the legally established age of majority.

In the United States, the balance between rights of parents and those of the state has been defined in several court cases. *PRINCE V. MASSACHUSETTS* limited a parent's discretion in requiring or allowing a child to work. *Wisconsin v. Yoder* confirmed the right of Amish parents to educate children at home rather than send them to secondary school. Other decisions have allowed parents to withhold permission for nonessential medical treatment for religious reasons; established parents' right to use reasonable physical force in disciplining children; and have denied parents the right to prevent school officials from using CORPORAL PUNISHMENT on their child.

Parents' rights are frequently at issue when a government agency seeks to remove a child from parental custody. Most states require an agency to provide clear and convincing evidence that a child is at risk before parental custody can be terminated. Concern over the legal rights of parents has led many child protection agencies to seek alternatives to removal of children from parental custody.

In the United States a group of parents and professionals calling themselves Victims of Child Abuse Laws (VOCAL) has formed to promote parents' rights and to combat what they believe are overzealous attempts to protect children.

While some countries do not operate according to a concept of individual rights, most have laws pertaining to a parent's role. In SWEDEN, for example, parents are not allowed to use physical force in disciplining their children. (*See also* TERMINATION OF PARENTAL RIGHTS.)

parents' rights, termination of   *See* TERMINATION OF PARENTAL RIGHTS.

Parents and Teachers Against Violence in Education (PTAVE)   Founded in Australia in 1978, this group is primarily concerned with eliminating CORPORAL PUNISHMENT from schools and institutions. It condemns the cruel and humiliating treatment of children who are under the care of teachers or other professional caregivers and seeks to legislate against such behavior toward children.

It maintains a speakers' bureau and archives, and works with other advocacy groups on behalf of children's welfare.

In 1983, PTAVE became a nonprofit organization in the United States and has worked to increase awareness of school administrators, educators and the general public concerning the negative effects of corporal punishment of children. In the United States and in Australia, PTAVE has been effective in eliminating corporal punishment in some, but not all, public schools. For more information, see APPENDIX 1.

Parents United   A self-help group for families of sexually abused children, Parents United began in Santa Clara, California, in 1972. The organization now has over 140 chapters in the United States and Canada. Parents United also promotes Daughters and Sons United (DSU), a self-help group for sexually abused children, and Adults Molested As Children (AMACU), a self-help organization for men and women who were victims of child sexual abuse.

Parents United groups meet weekly but members may contact their sponsor, an experienced group member assigned to them, at any time. The groups were designed to function as a part of a Child Sexual Abuse Treatment Program (CSATP). The CSATP model, developed by Henry and Anna Giarretto, combines professional counseling with the crisis intervention and long-term support provided by PU members.

Parents United also sponsors educational conferences for members and professionals and publishes a bimonthly newsletter, the *PUN*.

For more information on Parents United, Daughters and Sons United, and Adults Molested as Children, see APPENDIX 1.

parricide, reactive   A rare and extreme reaction to child abuse is murder of the abusive parent by the victim. Parricide accounts for approximately 1% of all murders.

Most children maintain a strong, albeit conflicted, attachment to the parent even in the face of repeated abuse. Profiles of children who murder an abusive parent or parents generally show that these children have no significant history of violent behavior. In most cases there is a long history of abuse. Murders usually occur shortly after, or during, an abusive episode. Handguns or rifles are the most frequent murder weapons.

Little is known about the reasons for reactive parricide. Theorists disagree as to the motivation of children who kill their parents. Some attribute the phenomenon to a preference for violent behavior learned from the parents themselves. Others believe these murders to be the desperate reaction of extreme rage committed by a child who feels powerless.

Eli Newberger and Richard Bourne, eds., *Unhappy Families* (Flushing, N.Y: PSG Publishing Co., 1985).

passive abuser   Child abuse can include other perpetrators, in addition to the person who actually beats or otherwise abuses the victim. It also includes the parent or caretaker who stands by and fails to take action to protect the child from abuse. Termed a passive abuser, this person is also responsible for the abuse and may face legal charges.

patria potestas   According to the terms of this early Roman law, a father had full and absolute power over his children. Historically, this legal power originally included INFANTICIDE, but that was gradually eliminated from the law.

patricide   The murder of one's father. In 1985, 209 fathers in the United States were murdered by one of their children. Patricide accounted for about three-fourths of 1% of all homicides. Case studies suggest a strong connection between child abuse and patricide.

Fathers who are murdered by a son tend to be cruel, dominant, critical and competitive with them. Mothers are often passive, sometimes dependent, sometimes overprotective of the son. Fathers frequently display jealousy of the son's attachment to the mother. In many cases the father is physically abusive to the mother in the presence of the son. The son, unable to gain the father's approval, becomes the mother's protector. Patricide usually occurs during or shortly following an episode in which the father abused a family member. Murder of a parent by a daughter is rare.

Paul and Lisa, Inc.   A private, nonprofit organization in Westbrook, Connecticut, founded by Frank Barnaba in 1980, Paul and Lisa, Inc., fights sexual abuse and exploitation of children. The organization is named for St. Paul's Church in Westbrook, Connecticut, and for Lisa, an adolescent victim of the sex industry. It has four goals: education, prevention, counseling/referral and rehabilitation. The organization seeks to educate the general public about the growing problem of sexual abuse of children, and works with local, state and federal officials to review the effectiveness of laws pertaining to sexual abuse. The organization's long-term goal is to establish a treatment center to train health care professionals and treat victimized children.

pederasty Anal intercourse between an adult male and a boy (usually between the ages of 12 and 16 years) is known as pederasty. Men who engage in this practice are known pederasts. Though others may lable the pederast as homosexual this may be a misnomer. Many pederasts also have sexual relations with women and are often repelled by the thought of intercourse with other adult males. Likewise it is improper to assume that homosexuals are pederasts. Most homosexuals are not pederasts and strongly disavow the practice.

The term pederasty is derived from the Greek roots *ped*, meaning boy, and *erastes*, meaning lover. Originally the word had much the same meaning as pedophile and the two words are sometimes used interchangeably. (*See also* PEDOPHILIA.)

pedophilia Pedophilia refers to a sexual preference for children. Specifically, the pedophile is an adult who is sexually attracted to children who have not yet reached the age of puberty. Sexual attraction of an adult for an adolescent is known as HEBEPHILIA. Definitions notwithstanding, the term pedophile is often used to refer to any adult who is sexually attracted to someone below the legal age of consent.

True pedophiles are exclusively attracted to sexually immature children and have little to do with adolescents who are more sexually developed. Most pedophiles are not violent toward children and may go to great lengths to gain the child's confidence before attempting a sexual act. In some cases a pedophile's desires may be confined to fantasy and not manifested in overt sexual molestation of children.

Not all sexual molestation of children is perpetrated by pedophiles. Children are often victims of sexual assaults simply because they are less able to defend themselves.

Pedophiles frequently develop a great deal of skill in meeting children and developing their trust. Formal and informal networks of child molesters are often used to share information on individual children or sites where it is easy to meet children. Some organizations such as the North American Man/Boy Love Association in the United States and the British Pedofile Information Exchange claim large memberships and actively support the practice of pedophilia. Some pedophiles choose a job such as teaching or managing a video arcade that will bring them into contact with children. Others may volunteer to coach a children's team, serve as a scout leader, babysitter or in a similar capacity. The pedophile is often known to the parents and may seek to gain their trust as well as the child's.

Pornography and prostitution also play an important role in pedophilia. Pedophiles are, of course, the primary purchasers of child pornography. They are also frequently the suppliers of such material, often exchanging material among themselves. Children are in great demand as prostitutes. Though many countries impose strict penalties for engaging in sex with a minor, some travel agencies have organized sex tours to countries where laws are less stringent and child prostitutes more plentiful. (*See also* FIXATED OFFENDERS.)

People's Republic of China Although there has been little, if any, formal investigation into child abuse and neglect in China, existing evidence suggests that there is very little abusive behavior toward children there. Western observers have remarked on child rearing practices that follow a much different pattern than in most other nations of the world. Some of these practices reflect prevailing beliefs about the state's responsibility toward providing for children's needs. Other behaviors and attitudes are tied closely to the notion that the individual is less important than society as a group.

Physical punishment of children in China is not condoned, although it does occur; it is not permitted in schools. Because of extensive government-sponsored health care that begins during the preschool years (before age seven), it is considered unlikely that a child could be physically abused and have it go undetected.

As in some other cultures, China is a nation that values children and places responsibility for a child on all adults in a community. Parents therefore are under some scrutiny at all times, albeit more or less benign scrutiny. Any infractions of what the Chinese consider acceptable parental behavior are investigated by neighbors. Parents who abuse children are considered in need of help; abuse is deviant behavior and therefore the subject of group discussion and consideration. In the event that an abused child is discovered, the neighborhood group to which the parent belongs (nearly all adult Chinese belong to these groups) would question the parent and would try to find some remedy for the situation that caused the abuse.

Historically, China was known to cherish certain practices considered abusive, including foot-binding, INFANTICIDE, extreme neglect, child slavery, concubinage and child marriage. In addition, in pre-communist China there were many reports of children who begged in the streets, who were malnourished, who had been abandoned. Culturally, girls were considered an economic drain and many female infants were killed immediately after birth or in times of famine. Similarly, girl children were more likely to be sold as slaves, especially during difficult financial times.

Until 1950, when the Marriage Law was passed, women and children virtually were property and could be treated as such by husbands and fathers. To many experts who have visited China and who are familiar with pre-communist social conditions, it is clear that after the revolution in 1949, conditions for women and children improved. One way this was achieved was to provide each individual with a role in building society. Because of this, older people are found providing child care in homes where their children work and their grandchildren need looking after. Many experts on child maltreatment cite this extended family system as a main reason for low incidence of child abuse and neglect. Unlike other societies where mothers are often somewhat isolated and are responsible for several young children day in and day out, in China the extended-family household forestalls this from occurring.

Cases of abuse and neglect that are reported in China are said to be the result of frustration and rage. Often, it appears, the abuse is perpetrated by fathers. The Chinese view women as inherently better equipped to provide child care, although men are expected to participate as equals in domestic tasks and in child rearing. (*See also* CHILD SLAVERY.)

Jill E. Korbin, ed., *Child Abuse and Neglect: Cross Cultural Perspectives* (Berkeley: University of California Press, 1981).

periostitis Inflammation of the periosteum (the fibrous membrane covering bones). Presence of periostitis in a child is evidence of physical trauma. Twisting of a limb or a blow directly to the bone can tear the periosteum away from the bone, causing blood to collect in the newly created cavity. Periostitis is not immediately detectable on an X ray but begins to appear as new bone forms in the affected area. (*See also* RADIOLOGY, PEDIATRIC and BATTERED CHILD SYNDROME.)

perjury False testimony under oath, given with the knowledge that it is untrue, constitutes the crime of perjury. In child abuse trials perjury is most often a concern with the testimony given by adults. Groups representing divorced parents express concern that false accusations of SEXUAL ABUSE are increasingly used as a tactic in bitter custody disputes. Proving sexual abuse of young children often depends on the testimony of adults close to the alleged victim. Even when no corroborating evidence is found, it is often difficult to prove that a witness intended to deceive the court.

Young children may become confused and may be more susceptible to coercion than adult witnesses. However, many experts believe that perjury is rarely an issue when children testify concerning their own abuse. Controversy over the reliability of young children's testimony continues to build as more and more courts allow children to testify. (*See also* TESTIMONY.)

petechiae A very small bruise, caused by broken capillaries. (*See also* BRUISES.)

petition A petition filed in juvenile or family court serves a purpose similar to that of an INDICTMENT in a criminal court. Sometimes referred to as a COMPLAINT, the petition spells out specific conditions that give rise to charges of abuse or neglect as well as the time, date and place where each event was observed. Filing a written petition is the first step in initiating court action. The petition serves as a formal notice of charges to the alleged abuser.

In most jurisdictions the petitioner is the child protection worker; however, law enforcement officers and physicians may file a petition. A few states allow anyone to file a child abuse or neglect petition.

Child protection workers usually do not file a petition until after an initial INVESTIGATION has been conducted and the report is considered to be founded. FOUNDED REPORTS do not necessarily result in a petition. If the child protection worker believes parents will comply voluntarily with recommendations, or that the conditions that precipitated maltreatment no longer exist, it is unlikely that a petition will be filed. Civil court intervention is usually initiated for the purpose of ensuring compliance with recommendations and/or removing a child from home.

Before filing a petition the child protection agency, usually in consultation with an attorney, may attempt to determine whether: (1) there is sufficient admissible evidence to obtain a favorable judgment; (2) whether the complainants, witnesses and victim are available for trial; (3) whether witnesses are credible; and (4) whether there is physical evidence to support the charges. Child protection workers must also consider the probable effects of a trial on the victim and his or her family.

physical abuse The NATIONAL CENTER ON CHILD ABUSE AND NEGLECT defines physical abuse as "an act of commission by a parent or caretaker which is not accidental and . . . which results in physical injury, including fractures, burns, bruises, welts, cuts and/or internal injuries."

Throughout history children have been subject to all types of physical abuse, from beatings to INFANTICIDE. The maxim "spare the rod and spoil the child" continues to serve as a guide to childrearing for many parents. With the exception of some Scandinavian countries physical punishment is a legal and accepted form of parental discipline around the world.

Despite its widespread acceptance, most countries attempt to place limits on physical punishment. Some experts think of abuse as a continuum beginning with mild forms of physical discipline such as light spanking and ranging all the way to severe beating and murder. The definition above implies physical punishment is permissible as long as no permanent or observable injury results. In Denmark all forms of corporal punishment are outlawed.

There are some indications that parental violence toward children is decreasing in the United States. In a national survey of families conducted in 1975 and again in 1985, Murray Straus of the University of New Hampshire and Richard Gelles found the incidence of severe violence (kicking, biting, hitting with a fist, hitting with an object, beating, attacking or threatening with a gun or a knife) declined from 36 per 1,000 to 19 per 1,000 children. The study's authors suggest that the decrease may be due to prevention and treatment efforts and to improved economic conditions.

Reports of suspected physical abuse comprise just over one-fourth of all reported maltreatment in the United States. While reports of suspected physical abuse continue to grow they are doing so at a slower rate than reports of other forms of abuse. Still, if the rate of abuse found in the Straus and Gelles study is accurate (they believe it underestimates abuse in both years), only one-half of all severe physical abuse was reported during 1985.

Recognition of physical abuse has increased substantially since the early 1960s. C. Henry Kempe's efforts called the attention of physicians and others to the BATTERED CHILD SYNDROME. Advances in pediatric radiology made it possible to detect patterns of bone trauma that tended to conflict with caretakers' explanations of accidental injury. Child abuse reporting laws now require a wide range of professionals to report all forms of suspected abuse. In at least one case, *LANDEROS V. FLOOD*, physicians have been held liable for civil penalties for failure to report abuse. Still, cases of physical abuse are sometimes overlooked.

When a child is brought for medical treatment, the caretaker's account of the injury can alert the examining physician to the possibility of abuse. An unexplained injury, e.g., "I just found him this way," is sometimes an attempt to deny abuse. Explanations that do not seem plausible also merit further investigation. Allegedly self-inflicted injuries of young children may be suspicious in origin.

Often children will readily state that an adult caused the injury. Experts believe children rarely lie about such matters.

Most parents bring their children to a physician or hospital immediately after an injury. Abusive parents often delay seeking medical attention for their child, hoping the child will not need treatment. Often the person who brings the child for treatment is not the person who was with the child at the time of injury.

Pediatrician Barton Schmitt recommends the following steps be followed by physicians in evaluating possible child abuse.

1. Take a complete history of the injury.
2. Perform a complete physical examination, including mouth, eardrums and genitals, noting signs of physical trauma and the approximate age of bruises and other injuries.
3. Order a SKELETAL SURVEY.
4. Order LABORATORY TESTS to determine clotting time.
5. Take color photographs of injuries for later documentation.
6. Examine siblings for signs of possible abuse.
7. Write a complete medical report.
8. Observe and record the child's behavior.
9. Conduct a developmental screening.

Physical abuse can take many different forms and can result in a number of different injuries. Internal trauma such as SUBDURAL HEMATOMA or ABDOMINAL INJURIES, though serious, are not immediately apparent. For a more detailed description of injuries resulting from physical abuse, see: ALOPECIA, TRAUMATIC; BATTERED CHILD SYNDROME; BITING; BRUISES; BURNS; CENTRAL NERVOUS SYSTEM INJURIES; CORD INJURIES; EYE INJURIES; FRACTURES; MOUTH INJURIES; POISONING; and WHIPLASH SHAKEN INFANT SYNDROME.

Barton D. Schmitt, in C. Henry Kempe and Ray E. Helfer, eds., *The Battered Child*, 3rd ed. (Chicago: University of Chicago Press, 1980).

Table 7
Reports of Physical Injury to Children
for 34 States Providing Complete Information, 1984–1985

State	1984	1985
Arizona	4,313	4,572
California	72,025	86,694
Connecticut	3,916	4,254
Delaware	1,090	974
Florida	14,400	12,796
Georgia	6,003	8,553
Hawaii	1,245	1,424
Idaho	1,800	1,877
Illinois	16,507	14,716
Indiana	8,843	10,423
Iowa	6,323	6,355
Kentucky	7,931	9,081
Louisiana	8,426	8,647
Maine	811	836
Massachusetts	4,830	5,097
Michigan	5,354	5,594
Mississippi	527	1,168
Missouri	6,979	7,044
Nevada	672	826
New Hampshire	454	478
New Jersey	4,105	5,869
New Mexico	3,556	4,808
New York	50,332	47,106
North Dakota	757	867
Oregon	3,177	3,060
Pennsylvania	5,510	4,880
South Dakota	652	856
Tennessee	7,699	9,071
Texas	17,015	17,013
Utah	964	1,082
Vermont	393	473
Washington	13,850	11,733
Wisconsin	5,150	6,678
Wyoming	1,050	653
Total	286,659	305,558

Figures represent substantiated reports.
No figures available (for 1981–1982).
Figures represent fiscal years, not calendar years.

David G. Gil, *Violence Against Children*
(Cambridge, Mass.: Harvard University Press,
1973).
C. Henry Kempe and Ray E. Helfer, eds., *The
Battered Child*, 3rd ed. (Chicago: University of
Chicago Press, 1980).

place of safety order   Under provisions of
the Children and Young Persons Act of 1969,
anyone in BRITAIN can apply for an order to
remove a child from a dangerous place. The
emergency order, known as a place of safety
order, may be issued by a magistrate at any
time. Magistrates can authorize applicants to
take custody of the child for a period not to
exceed 28 days.

Applicants for such an order do not have to
prove abuse or neglect; however, the
magistrate must have reasonable cause to
believe that: (1) the child's proper development is being avoidably prevented or
neglected; (2) his or her health is being
avoidably impaired or neglected; or (3) the
child is being ill-treated.

A place of safety order may also be used to
prevent removal of a child from a safe place.
Siblings of the identified child are also
covered by the order. Children may be taken
without parents' knowledge, but applicants
are expected to inform them as soon as possible after removal. Parents have little opportunity to appeal a place of safety order.

Place of safety orders are typically used in
emergencies where a child is in immediate
danger. Concern has been expressed by some
experts that these orders are too easy to obtain,
increasing the possibility of unnecessary
removal.

placement of abused children   Removal of
maltreated children from their parents may be
necessary to ensure proper treatment and to
prevent further abuse. Governments base their
authority to assume custody of a child on the
doctrine of PARENS PATRIAE. Under this
doctrine the state assumes a vital interest in
ensuring the safety and welfare of children.
However, many critics charge that the govern-

ments have overstepped this responsibility by
removing children unnecessarily.

Today, over 500,000 children are in FOSTER
CARE in the United States. Though most placements of children are considered a temporary
measure while parents and/or children receive
treatment, many child care experts express
concern over the tendency of these arrangements to continue over a period of years. Often
children are moved from one temporary placement to another, creating added instability in
their already turbulent lives. Some argue that
removing a child from home for any but the
most dangerous of situations may be more
harmful than allowing the child to remain at
home with supervision from an outside agency.

The United States' ADOPTION ASSISTANCE
AND CHILD WELFARE REFORM ACT attempts to
eliminate unnecessary removal of children
from home and to reduce the length of time
children spend in temporary placement. Except in EMERGENCIES, child protection agencies must demonstrate that a serious attempt
has been made to treat families at home. Use
of PARENT AIDES, HOMEMAKER SERVICES, outpatient treatment and other services are encouraged as a way of maintaining the child at
home. When children are removed, the law
requires that placement decisions be reviewed
by a judge and that CASE PLANS be reassessed
every six months.

When a child is in immediate danger, law
enforcement officials and, in most states,
protective service agencies have authority to
take EMERGENCY CUSTODY of the child. Prior
approval of a court is not necessary in most
areas; however, emergency placement
decisions must be reviewed by a judge within
48 to 72 hours after the child is removed.

In BRITAIN, children can be removed from
home for up to 28 days under a PLACE OF
SAFETY ORDER. The order can be obtained by
anyone but must be approved by a magistrate.

Placement decisions are difficult. Child
protection authorities must balance possible
benefits of removal against the inevitable
trauma that will be experienced by both

children and parents. The AMERICAN HUMANE ASSOCIATION in its manual, *Helping in Child Protective Services*, suggests the following criteria be considered:

- likelihood that the child has or will suffer permanent physical or mental injury if left at home
- whether parents refuse to obtain needed medical or psychiatric treatment for the child
- whether a special environment is necessary for the child's treatment
- whether the child's age, physical condition or other characteristics render him or her incapable of self-protection
- evidence suggests that parents frequently resort to inappropriate and extreme methods of punishment
- parents cannot or will not guarantee the child's safety at home
- the home itself represents an immediate danger; e.g., inadequate heat, extremely unsanitary conditions, lack of food
- whether the emotional impact of the ASSESSMENT increases the likelihood that the child will be abused
- the child's caretaker cannot be located

Other specific criteria may include evidence that the parents are severely impaired due to SUBSTANCE ABUSE or mental illness.

poisoning Abuse-related poisoning of children is relatively rare; however, a significant number of accidental poisonings are a result of parental NEGLECT of normal safety precautions.

Deliberate poisoning of children may be due to a disturbed parent's impulsive act or desire to get revenge. More frequently, intentional poisoning involves a drug overdose, ostensibly for the purpose of quieting an upset child.

Failure of caretakers to exercise adequate safety precautions is more often a cause of child poisoning than deliberate acts. Specifically, improper storage of chemicals and

medications significantly increases the likelihood of accidental poisoning. Multiple accidental poisonings occur most often in households characterized by high levels of stress, including illness, recent death of a family member, marital discord and parental drug or alcohol abuse. Children whose caretakers abuse alcohol or drugs are particularly at risk. The easy accessibility of these substances increases the risk of accidental ingestion. Substance abusers also have a diminished capacity to provide adequate care and are frequently neglectful.

Poison centers offer immediate telephone consultation in the event of poisoning. There are over 650 such centers in the United States. Telephone numbers of nearby centers are usually listed under emergency numbers at the front of most telephone directories. In addition to providing lifesaving emergency advice these centers can be especially helpful in identifying victims of repetitive poisoning (approximately one-fourth of all poisonings).

Poland *See* SOCIALIST EASTERN EUROPE.

polymorphic perverse offender Sexual offenders are sometimes classified according to the type of victim and/or sexual acts they prefer. PEDOPHILES, for example, direct their sexual feelings and actions primarily (in many cases exclusively) toward children. Most rapists attack only female victims. However, some sexual offenders appear to be indiscriminate in their choice of victims or sexual acts. They may be described as polymorphic perverse offenders.

This description follows a classification used by Sigmund Freud to describe indiscriminate sexuality. Freud coined the term polymorphous perversity to describe the behavior of individuals who had been seduced as children.

As currently used, the term refers to sex offenders who engage in many different forms of sexual assault (i.e., vaginal rape, sodomy, exhibitionism) and who may attack people of any age. This type of offender accounts for a very small percentage of all child SEXUAL ABUSE.

Polynesia As a cultural area, Polynesia comprises numerous islands scattered throughout a portion of the Pacific Ocean. Although their urban areas and most towns are now considered in large part Western in culture and practice, Hawaii, Samoa and New Zealand are among those islands that were traditionally included in Polynesian culture.

Over the last five decades, research conducted into child-rearing practices in both traditional and transitional Polynesian society has enabled observers to make some assessments concerning the incidence of child abuse. Insofar as it has been possible to judge, traditional Polynesian culture does not support abusive behavior toward children; in fact, Polynesian kinship structure, with its concept of collective family, promotes a degree of affection and warmth among all adults for all children seldom found elsewhere. According to informed observers, it is fairly clear that there has never been the tendency toward aggressive or neglectful child-rearing behaviors on any level of the traditional Polynesian culture. Although INFANTICIDE had been acceptable (and encouraged) during earlier times, studies indicate that it was practiced only as a way of maintaining optimum population levels and preserving existing life.

All adults in Polynesian villages are viewed as parents by all children. Living arrangements encourage a casual, relaxed attitude toward small children, who are not expected to maintain any particular standards of behavior until they are about two years old. At that time they are considered ready to join the circle of children somewhat older than they are, to learn appropriate social behavior from peers and siblings, as well as from adults. At this time, children begin to be disciplined, to learn independence (which is a highly valued trait) and to mature to the point that they will be able to join the circle of adults when they reach maturity. The latter occurs when girls begin menstruation and when boys

are ritually circumcised, usually at about age 15.

Studies show that when individuals from traditional Polynesian villages move to urban and suburban settings, the strong cultural patterns that have served to prevent child abuse are no longer maintained in the same way. Statistics also show that Polynesians living in cities in New Zealand and in the Hawaiian Islands exhibit high rates of child abuse. Researchers theorize that this is due most likely to the breakdown in traditional cultural practices surrounding child rearing. Further, the parenting styles functional for small village life in rural Polynesia—which included collective family situations and a casual attitude about disciplining younger children—have generally led to charges, when judged by Western standards, that traditional Polynesian parents are neglectful and derelict in their duties.

pornography, child *See* CHILD PORNOGRAPHY.

post-traumatic hypopituitarism *See* DWARFISM.

poverty Child abuse and neglect has been described as a classless phenomenon by numerous writers, researchers and clinicians. While it is true that abuse and neglect can be found in every socioeconomic stratem, statistics show that a disproportionate number of reported cases of abuse and neglect involve low-income families. Studies have shown that poverty status is strongly related to neglect. Poor children are also highly represented among victims of more serious forms of abuse.

It has been argued that low-income families are more likely to be investigated and reported on than middle- and upper-income families. Suggestions have been made that, if higher income families were subjected to the same scrutiny, an equal amount of abuse would be found. To date no significant evidence has been presented to support this position.

Cross-cultural evidence from Western and Eastern societies also supports the assertion that poverty and child abuse are related. Anthropological studies from New Guinea, Africa, Turkey and South America all have documented the increased risks to children raised in poverty.

The mere existence of poverty has been labeled as a form of societal abuse. Poor children who are denied the basic elements necessary for healthy development suffer many of the same consequences as those from whom these elements are intentionally withheld. Social policy researchers David Gil, Leroy Pelton and others have argued that attributing abuse and neglect to individual or family pathology masks true societal causes of the phenomenon. Further, the individual, as opposed to societal, view of child abuse is seen as a means of promoting certain professional and political interests at the expense of a more lasting solution.

Increased stress is often given as the reason for the association between poverty and abuse. Families with severely restricted incomes are constantly faced with difficult choices and may suffer from inadequate housing, poor health care and malnourishment. Such conditions are seen as neglectful and may contribute to physical, emotional or sexual abuse.

Despite its obvious contributions to increased stress and poor living conditions, poverty is by no means synonymous with abuse or neglect as statutorily defined. Only a relatively small proportion of children living in impoverished families are reported to child protection agencies. Parents of such children, through skill, determination and luck, are frequently able to overcome the burdens of poverty. It is clear, however, that poverty places children at significant risk.

Michael B. Katz, *Poverty and Policy in American History* (New York: Academic Press, 1983).

————, *In the Shadow of the Poorhouse* (New York: Basic Books, 1986).
Leroy H. Pelton, *The Social Context of Child Abuse and Neglect* (New York: Human Sciences Press, 1981).
————, "Child Abuse and Neglect: The Myth of Classlessness," *American Journal of Orthopsychiatry*, 48(October 1978), pp. 607-617.

prediction of abuse and neglect   Several researchers have attempted to develop screening tests that will predict the likelihood of abuse. Various methods used include pencil and paper questionnaires, standardized interviews and direct observation of parent-child interaction. Presently, all screening is voluntary. High-risk groups such as teenaged parents are most often targeted for screening; however, some hospital programs have attempted to screen all parents of newborns.

Many tests focus on parental characteristics such as emotional deprivation, history of abuse as a child and intelligence. Others examine characteristics of the child. Studies indicate that developmental disabilities, irritability and other traits increase the likelihood that a child will be abused. Several screening devices attempt to measure stress factors, such as POVERTY and SOCIAL ISOLATION. Some researchers attempt to measure the quality of interaction between parent and child. Finally, various attempts have been made to combine these approaches.

To date no completely accurate screening method has been developed. Experts caution that, although screening may be useful in targeting prevention efforts, it should not be considered a diagnostic tool. Identification of a person as potentially abusive does not mean they are in fact abusing a child. Parents cannot be forced to submit to screening tests nor can potentially abusive parents be required to accept help. Concern over PARENTS' RIGHTS has caused many practitioners to be very cautious in use and interpretation of various screening methods.

preponderance of the evidence *See* EVI-
DENTIARY STANDARDS.

presentment In some situations, usually an
emergency, a grand jury may issue a written
accusation of a crime without having received
a COMPLAINT from a prosecutor. This document is the equivalent of an INDICTMENT.

prevention Efforts to prevent child abuse
and neglect are often classified as either
primary or secondary. Primary prevention
seeks to protect children from maltreatment
before it occurs. This approach may be
directed at the general public or at specially
targeted high-risk families. Secondary
prevention attempts to prevent the recurrence
of maltreatment or to keep a potentially
abusive situation from getting worse. Subjects
of secondary prevention are usually identified
through reports of suspected abuse or neglect.

Prevention can take many different forms.
Methods frequently used in *primary prevention* include hospital-based neonatal programs
that promote mother-infant bonding, home
visitors (also called home HEALTH VISITORS or
PARENT AIDES), parent education, and counseling programs. Most such programs are
directed at parents and operate from the
premise that by learning more about childrearing they will be less likely to abuse or neglect
their children. SEXUAL ABUSE prevention
usually directed at children often takes the
form of school-based programs that use
books, films, plays and puppetry to inform
children about the dangers of sexual abuse and
ways in which they might protect themselves.

Secondary prevention often involves the
entire family in some form of counseling,
behavior modification or treatment. Intervention is usually targeted to specific family
problems, such as a parent's ways of disciplining children or stress management, that are
thought to underly the abuse.

Michael Wald and Sophia Cohen, in a
review of prevention efforts published in the
Family Law Quarterly, identified four
problems that must be addressed in develop-

ing successful prevention programs. First,
abuse must be clearly defined. There is much
disagreement as to what sorts of situations
constitute abuse or neglect. Programs must
have a clear definition of the type(s) of behavior they wish to prevent if they are to be
successful. Secondly, some understanding of
the causes of abuse and neglect is necessary.
Causes are often complex and poorly understood. Third, prevention strategies should be
directed where they will do the most good.
Most primary prevention efforts are too costly
to allow inefficient use. Fourth, there is little
accurate information about the effectiveness
of various prevention techniques. Prevention
of child abuse and neglect is a relatively new
field. Adequate evaluation of programs would
require large, carefully designed studies.

Treatment after confirmation of child
abuse or neglect is sometimes referred to as
tertiary prevention.

Michael S. Wald and Sophia Cohen, "Preventing
Child Abuse—What Will It Take," *Family Law
Quarterly*, 20:2(Summer 1986), pp. 281-302.

prevention, primary *See* PREVENTION.

prevention, secondary *See* PREVENTION.

prevention, tertiary *See* PREVENTION.

**Prevention of Cruelty to and Protection of
Children Act of 1889 (Britain)** As a direct
result of actions taken by the National Society
for the Prevention of Cruelty to Children
(NSPCC), in 1889 the British Parliament
enacted a law that established penalties for the
ill-treatment and neglect of children. The act
was amended in 1894 and again in 1904. In
cases where neglect or abuse of a child meant
the parent or guardian could benefit financial-
ly from a child's life insurance policy, legal
penalties were increased.

prima facie Literally, "at first sight." Prima
facie evidence is that which is sufficiently
strong to prove the allegations in a case of

suspected child abuse or neglect. It is considered proof of the suspected charges; however, this evidence is only considered proof in the absence of contradictory or rebutting evidence.

In virtually all states, admissible evidence in a child abuse or neglect case must fall within one of the two following standards of proof. Either clear and convincing evidence must be presented or a preponderance of the evidence must fall in favor of either the plaintiff or the defendant. Prima facie evidence could come under either of these two standards. (*See also* EVIDENTIARY STANDARDS.)

primary prevention   *See* PREVENTION.

Prince v. Massachusetts   In 1944, a landmark United States Supreme Court case determined that "the custody, care, and nurture of the child resides first in the parents, whose primary function and freedom include preparation for obligations that the state can neither supply nor hinder." However, the court went on to say that, in some cases, the state has an overriding interest in protecting children.

This decision involved a child whose aunt permitted her to sell religious literature on the streetcorner. At legal issue in the case was the charge that parents, guardians or custodians are not free to make martyrs of their children. Sarah Prince, a Jehovah's Witness, was charged with violating Massachusetts's child labor laws by having her nine-year-old niece, of whom she had custody, sell copies of *Watchtower* and *Consolation* on the street. The court affirmed Prince's conviction by a lower court. Its assertion that "the power of the state to control the conduct of children reaches beyond the scope of its authority over adults" affirmed the state's right to intervene against the wishes of parents and children when necessary for a child's protection.

The findings in *Prince v. Massachusetts* provided the basis for subsequent judicial rulings in which the rights of other individuals (i.e., parents) or groups (i.e., schools) take precedence over those of children. (*See also* WISCONSIN V. YODER; TINKER V. DES MOINES.)

Robert H. Mnookin, *Child, Family and State: Problems and Materials on Children and the Law* (Boston: Little, Brown and Company, 1978).

private zone   Private zone is a term used in teaching young children how to identify and avoid sexual advances. Breasts, buttocks and genitalia (areas covered by a bathing suit) are all considered to be part of the private zone, which should not be touched by anyone other than the child. Obvious exceptions are made for situations such as examination by a physician or bathing by a parent or appropriate caretaker. In such instances, the quality of the touching is emphasized and the child is encouraged to use various means to avoid contact that makes them feel uncomfortable. Among other options, children are taught to call for help loudly and to run to a safe place nearby, such as a neighbor's house or a police station, for help. *Private Zone* is also the title of a read-aloud book for children written by Frances S. Dayee (New York: Warner Books, 1984).

privileged communications   In many countries the patient or client may refuse to allow information revealed in a personal conference with his or her physician, psychotherapist or lawyer to be presented in court. This legal protection is sometimes called the doctor-patient privilege. Child abuse reporting laws often override privileged communications in situations where the reporting of abuse or prosecution of an abuser might be inhibited. Most jurisdictions, however, continue to protect communications between lawyer and client. (*See also* CONFIDENTIALITY.)

probate court   *See* COURT.

procedural due process   *See* DUE PROCESS.

proceeding, civil   *See* CIVIL PROCEEDING.

projection Psychodynamic explanations of abuse emphasize the abusing parent's reliance on projection as a mechanism for coping with stress. Projection can be described as a process whereby an individual ascribes his or her own feelings to another person. A parent may project feelings of self-hatred onto a child. The child then becomes a scapegoat for the parent's anger and low self-esteem.

Often a particular child becomes unconsciously associated with painful earlier events in the parent's life. The TARGET CHILD may be described as a monster or a demon, suggesting a symbolic association between the child and the parent's own uncontrollable rage. Externalizing feelings of self-hatred is a form of denial that prevents the parent from acknowledging and confronting these feelings. The parent's unconscious need to avoid confronting internal rage may be so strong that when the target child is removed from home another child becomes the object of projection.

Psychodynamic treatment of abusers often centers on helping them acknowledge and understand their own feelings. If treatment is successful the abuser learns to differentiate between his or her own feelings and the child's behavior.

proof, burden *See* BURDEN OF PROOF.

proof, standards of *See* EVIDENTIARY STANDARDS.

property, children as *See* CHILDREN AS PROPERTY.

prosecution, criminal *See* CRIMINAL PROSECUTION.

prostitution, child *See* CHILD PROSTITUTION.

protection, order of *See* ORDER OF PROTECTION.

Protection of Children Against Sexual Exploitation Act of 1977 (P.L. 95-225) Enacted into law in February of 1978, this was the first piece of federal legislation in the United States to deal directly with CHILD PORNOGRAPHY. Prosecutors found it difficult to obtain convictions due to a provision that limited the law's application to pornographic material produced for commercial purposes. Most child pornographers were able to avoid prosecution by trading material rather than selling it.

Table 8

Indictments/Convictions for Child Pornography
Before and After the Child Protection Act of 1984

Year	Indictments	Convictions
1978	13	13
1979	1	1
1980	11	10
1981	14	15
1982	19	7
1983	6	15
1984 (pre-Act)	5	3
1984 (post-Act)	55	35
1985	123	102
1986 (first 5 months)	24	27

Source: *Child Pornography and Pedophilia.* Report by the Permanent Subcommittee on Investigations, Committee on Governmental Affairs, United States Senate, 1986.

In 1984 Congress deleted the commerciality requirement as well as a provision that required the material to be legally obscene. This amendment, known as the Child Protection Act of 1984, greatly increased the number of convictions for production and distribution of child pornography. In the two years following enactment of the Child Protection Act, 164 child pornographers were convicted compared to 64 convictions in the five-plus years preceding the amendment.

protective custody Physicians, social workers and certain other professionals often have the power to detain a child until a DETENTION request can be filed with the court. In some cases oral permission of a judge must be obtained before a child is held in protective custody. (*See also* EMERGENCIES, EMERGENCY CUSTODY.)

protective services Vincent DeFrancis, a prominent figure in the United States' child protection movement and former director of the Children's Division of the American Humane Association (now the American Association for Protecting Children), defines protective services as:

> a specialized casework service to neglected, abused or exploited children. The focus of the services is preventive and non-punitive and is geared toward a rehabilitation of the home and a treatment of the motivating factors.

In the United States every state has a legally designated child protection agency. Each Canadian province provides for child protection services. In Britain child protection is the responsibility of LOCAL AUTHORITIES.

Child protective services are distinguished from other social services by their involuntary nature. Abused and neglected children are often too young or do not know how to ask for help. Few abusive parents request intervention from a protective services agency. Typically, clients are resistant and hostile toward protective service workers.

Protective service workers have legal authority to intervene against parents' wishes in order to determine whether a child is being abused or neglected. If evidence of abuse or neglect is found, the protective service agency may petition a court for additional powers to act on behalf of the child. When a child is in immediate danger of serious injury the child protective worker may be granted EMERGENCY CUSTODY powers.

Despite their legal authority, child protection services focus on rehabilitation rather than punishment. Though most parents initially resist help, protective service workers attempt to engage them in a cooperative effort to eliminate conditions that contributed to maltreatment of their children. If at all possible, protective service agencies try to keep children at home with their natural families.

Tasks of protective service workers can be divided into five categories: INVESTIGATION of complaints, diagnosis or ASSESSMENT of service needs, case planning, TREATMENT and case monitoring. Agencies often have separate units that perform investigatory and treatment-related functions respectively. In practice, the investigation phase often comprises a large proportion of protective services. Increased reporting of suspected abuse and neglect in the United States coupled with relatively stable funding have forced protective service agencies to shift resources away from treatment and prevention to investigation.

Vincent DeFrancis, *The Fundamentals of Child Protection* (Denver: American Humane Association, 1978).

Wayne M. Holder and Cynthia Mohr, eds., *Helping in Child Protective Services* (Denver: American Humane Association, 1980).

U.S. Department of Health, Education and Welfare, Office of Human Development Services, Administration for Children, Youth and Families, Children's Bureau, National Center on Child Abuse and Neglect. *Child Protective Services: A Guide for Workers* (Washington, D.C.: 1979; [OHDS] 79-30203).

pseudocyst of the pancreas A fibrous capsule indicative of acute pancreatitis. Development of a pseudocyst may become apparent as a painful mass in the upper abdomen two to three weeks following injury of the pancreas. Surgical intervention is required. (*See also* PANCREATITIS.)

pseudomaturity Neglected children sometimes appear to be much more mature than other children of their age. This pseudomaturity is usually the result of ROLE REVERSAL in which an immature parent looks to the child for care and nurturance. Immature parents may have unrealistic expectations of their children, which place them in the role of caretaker to younger siblings, protector of the parent or even the parent's romantic partner.

Pseudomaturity exacts a high price from children. Forced to forgo their own emotional development in order to care for parents they typically grow into adults lacking the emotional resources to form healthy, close relationships. They may be extremely dependent on others for emotional support and as parents may follow a pattern similar to that of their own upbringing.

psychological maltreatment Psychological, or emotional, maltreatment encompasses acts of abuse as well as acts of neglect. The NATIONAL CENTER ON CHILD ABUSE AND NEGLECT defines emotional abuse as verbal or emotional assault, close confinement and/or threatened harm. Emotional neglect includes lack of adequate nurturing, withholding affection, knowingly allowing a child to engage in maladaptive behavior and/or refusal to provide other essential care. Using these definitions, a study conducted with funding from the United States Department of Health, Education and Welfare found that approximately one child in every 1,000 suffers emotional neglect while 2.2 in every 1,000 children are emotionally abused.

Cultural norms for child rearing play an important role in determining what kinds of behavior are viewed as injurious to a child's psychological well-being. In practice, definitions of psychological maltreatment may vary widely within a particular culture. Though all 50 states in the United States have laws dealing with child abuse and neglect some states do not specifically mention psychological maltreatment. Many states refer to mental injury as a form of maltreatment but fail to specify the legal criteria for determining the existence of such injury. Others refer only to emotional damage as a result of a physical injury. Few states have enacted statutes that specifically define emotional abuse or neglect as separate forms of maltreatment.

In general, legal definitions of psychological maltreatment tend to be more restricted than those employed by non-governmental child welfare and mental health agencies. In the absence of a clear definition the determination of psychological abuse or neglect is usually based on both community standards and professional opinion.

Despite the ambiguity of child protection laws, some children have been removed from their parents due to the parents' emotional instability or after being allowed to witness acts of cruelty inflicted on another family member.

Most experts agree that psychological maltreatment involves a pattern of destructive behavior on the part of an adult— not a single incident. Though virtually all children will be exposed to some form of emotional abuse or neglect at times, those who are repeatedly subjected to such treatment may suffer permanent psychological or intellectual damage.

In an attempt to create a better understanding of the types of behavior that constitute psychological maltreatment, Dr. James Garbarino, president of the Erikson Institute for Advanced Study in Child Development, Chicago, Illinois, and his colleagues have identified five categories of abuse/neglect: rejecting, isolating, terrorizing, ignoring and corrupting.

Rejecting refers to an attitude of hostility toward the child or a total indifference to the child's needs. Cross-cultural studies have shown that this type of behavior exists in many different cultures and is frequently associated with high levels of social and economic stress.

Preventing a child from normal social experiences, i.e., SOCIAL ISOLATION, may also constitute abuse. An example of isolation is the parent who consistently denies a child the opportunity to associate with his or her peers.

Terrorizing involves repeated verbal assaults on a child, causing the child to live in constant fear. Threats of abandonment, severe punishment or death fall into this category.

Ignoring a child can inhibit normal emotional and intellectual development. This type of maltreatment may be especially damaging to infants who need emotional, tactile and intellectual stimulation for healthy development.

Finally, corrupting refers to the parent or caregiver who encourages a child to engage in behavior that is destructive, antisocial or damaging. Two obvious examples of corrupting are encouraging a child to engage in prostitution or stealing. Both activities place the child at significant risk of harm and deny him or her a normal social experience.

James Garbarino, Edna Guttmann and Janis Wilson Seeley, *The Psychologically Battered Child* (San Francisco: Jossey-Bass, 1986).

psychological parenthood Psychological parenthood plays an important role in decisions concerning removal of an abused child from the home. The concept is based upon the idea that a child may establish close psychological bonds with an adult other than a biological parent. An adult becomes a psychological parent through daily interaction and sharing with a child. A parent who is absent, rejecting or inactive is unlikely to fulfill a child's need for a psychological parent.

In their influential book, *Beyond the Best Interests of the Child*, Joseph Goldstein, Anna Freud and Albert Solnit argue that such a close relationship is crucial for healthy development of a child. They advocate restraint in removing children from psychological parents. Since the book's publication, many courts have given greater consideration to the quality of the relationship between a child and his or her primary caretaker.

Separation from a psychological parent is usually painful and upsetting to a child. Child protection workers and courts usually avoid interrupting ties between a child and his or her psychological parent unless separation is absolutely necessary for the protection of the child.

Joseph Goldstein, Anna Freud and Albert Solnit, *Beyond the Best Interests of the Child* new ed. (New York: The Free Press, 1979).

psychological tests A variety of psychological tests are used to evaluate emotional and adjustment problems in children who have been abused. The four most commonly used tests are the Minnesota Multiphasic Personality Test (MMPI), Rorschach, Thematic Apperception Test (TAT) and Draw a Person Test (DAP).

The MMPI presents a number of statements to the subject, who is asked to respond "true," "false" or "cannot say." In the Rorschach children are asked to interpret a series of inkblots. These interpretations are used as an aid in understanding the child's perceptions of reality and social interaction patterns. The TAT consists of a series of pictures suggesting some type of social interaction. Respondents are required to describe what they think is happening in the picture. Children taking the DAP are directed to draw a picture of themselves, a family member, friend or group of people. Interpretation of the drawings is based on the details included (or excluded), the relationships among the figures and the story the child tells about the drawing. All of these tests may be used in the assessment of a variety of emotional problems and are designed to be administered by persons specifically trained in psychometry.

In addition to these tests, several tests have been designed especially for the assessment of PSYCHOLOGICAL MALTREATMENT or related problems. Many of these tests were originally developed as research instruments. While most focus on maltreatment in the home some were specifically designed for out-of-home settings. Table 9 contains a list of some of these tests.

psychopathological abuse *See*   PSYCHO-PATHOLOGY.

psychopathology The importance of mental illness and emotional disturbance as factors contributing to child abuse and neglect is the subject of an ongoing debate among experts. While virtually all scholars and practitioners admit that mental illness may cause parents to neglect or abuse their children there is widespread disagreement as to the prevalence of psychopathological abuse.

Table 9

Tests Used in Detecting and Assessing
Psychological Abuse/Neglect

Test	Developer
Adult-Adolescent Parenting Inventory	Family Development Associates
Bayley Scales of Infant Development	N. Bayley
Bronfenbrenner's Parental Behavior Questionnaire	Urie Bronfenbrenner
Child Assessment Schedule	Kay Kline Hodges
Child Behavior Checklist	T.M. Achenback
Children's Reports of Parental Behavior Inventory	Earl S. Schaefer
Family Environmental Scale	Rudolf H. Moos
Family Adaptability and Cohesion Evaluation Scale	David H. Olson et al.
Interparental Conflict and Influence Scales	J.C. Schwartz and D.C. Zuroff
Maternal Characteristics Scale and Childhood Level of Living Scale	Norman A. Polansky
Michigan Screening Profile of Parenting	Ray E. Helfer
Parental Acceptance-Rejection Questionnaire	Ronald P. Rohner
Personality Assessment Questionnaire	Ronald P. Rohner
Quality of Supervision and Burnout Questionnaire	Calton Munson
State-Trait Anxiety Inventory	C.D. Spielberger et al.
Tennessee Self-Concept Scale	W.H. Fitts
Ward Atmosphere Scale and Work Environment Scale	Rudolf H. Moos

Adapted from: James Garbarino, Edna Guttmann and Janis Wilson Seeley, *The Psychologically Battered Child* (San Francisco: Jossey-Bass, 1986).

A rather extreme view holds that all child abuse is, by definition, psychopathological. Labeling child abuse as a specific form of illness ignores the complex interplay between intrapsychic factors and external forces that may lead to abuse in some situations but not in others. Further, traditional ways of treating mental illness, such as psychotherapy or drug therapy, are not always effective in changing abusive behavior.

Several psychologists and psychiatrists have attempted to isolate a diagnostic category similar to the medical classification, BATTERED CHILD SYNDROME. Though some have been successful in identifying relationships between various diagnostic categories, for example depression (or schizophrenia) and child abuse, the specific role of psychopathology continues to be elusive. Though it is relatively easy to understand how severe depression may lead to parental neglect, it is more difficult to explain why many parents who suffer from this and other forms of mental illness do not neglect or abuse their children.

Many researchers argue that psychopathology is secondary to cultural and environmental factors as a contributor to child maltreatment. Indeed, a great number of abusers do not appear to suffer from any serious mental disorder as defined by currently accepted diagnostic categories. Some experts have argued that preoccupation with the notion that abuse reflects psychopathology has diverted attention from underlying problems of poverty and family stress. Critics charge that, by identifying the individual rather than society as the root of child maltreatment, efforts to combat abuse and neglect have been misdirected. Current approaches to treatment and prevention seem to take a middle ground in this debate, combining psychotherapeutic approaches with education, public awareness programs and support services.

In individual cases, severe mental illness of a caretaker may form the basis for temporary removal of a child from home. Parents who are prone to frequent psychotic breaks or deep depression may be unable to care for their children during these episodes. However, most forms of mental illness are cyclical, and parents are usually quite capable during periods of remission.

psychosocial deprivation   *See* EMOTIONAL NEGLECT.

psychosocial dwarfism   *See* DWARFISM.

PTAVE   *See*   PARENTS AND TEACHERS AGAINST VIOLENCE IN EDUCATION.

puberty rites   *See* INITIATION RITES.

punishment, corporal   *See*   CORPORAL PUNISHMENT.

purpura   A purplish collection of petechiae less than one centimeter in diameter. (*See also* BRUISES.)

Purtsher retinopathy   This term refers to retinal hemorrhaging as a result of sudden compression of a child's chest. Pressure applied to the chest by hitting, grasping or shaking can produce Purtsher retinopathy without the additional intracranial bleeding that normally occurs in conjunction with ocular hemorrhaging. (*See also* EYE INJURIES.)

R

radiology, pediatric Documentation and development of the BATTERED CHILD SYNDROME owes a great deal to advances in pediatric radiology. As early as 1906 physicians began to study X rays of infants. The first X-ray department in a children's hospital was established in 1926. Twenty years later John Caffey, a pediatric radiologist, published an article describing the joint occurrence of SUBDURAL HEMATOMAS and FRACTURES of the long bones in infants. Though he lacked confirming evidence, Caffey suggested that the injuries might have been the result of unreported child abuse. Subsequent findings by Caffey, Frederick Silverman (Stanford University) and others established a strong link between certain types of infant fracture and abuse. This phenomenon of multiple fractures in various stages of healing, accompanied by subdural hematomas, was subsequently called the PARENT-INFANT TRAUMATIC SYNDROME, the battered baby syndrome and the CAFFEY-KEMPE SYNDROME.

Skeletal fractures resulting from child battering are unlikely to be mistaken for accidents; however, certain conditions such as SCURVY, congenital SYPHILIS, osteogenesis imperfecta (an inherited trait), INFANTILE CORTICAL HYPEROSTOSIS, MENKES KINKY HAIR SYNDROME and congenital indifference to pain can produce similar bone lesions. A standard skeletal evaluation for child abuse includes X rays of the skull, chest, spine, upper and lower limbs.

Bone lesions in infants often involve displacement of the periosteum, small chip fractures and damage to cartilaginous tissue near the joints. Injury may not be detectable until formation of new bone tissue (OSSIFICATION) begins.

Radiologists' increasing ability to differentiate abuse-related patterns of fractures, coupled with other medical and social information, made it possible for physicians to diagnose child battering with much greater confidence and accuracy. A full radiological survey is now standard in cases where abuse of an infant or child is suspected. X rays can be used as a case management tool to detect ongoing abuse and also as an aid in diagnosis.

Though pediatric radiologists were instrumental in bringing back into the public eye the problem of child abuse, it soon became apparent that a relatively small percentage of abused children suffered fractures. By reintroducing the plight of battered children, pediatric radiologists laid important groundwork for identification and treatment of other forms of abuse.

rape Though some writers refer to any unwanted sexual contact as rape, the term is most often understood to mean sexual attack involving penile penetration. Laws often distinguish two different types of rape: forcible and statutory. Forcible rape is defined by the combination of penetration, use of force or threat, and nonconsent of the victim. Statutory rape involves sexual assault on a child under the age of consent. Since a child is not considered capable of giving informed consent to sexual relations prior to a specific, legally defined age, the use of force and the child's agreement are irrelevant in cases of statutory rape. The actual age at which a child may legally consent to sexual relations varies. In most locations children may give legal consent at age 14 or 16.

Emergency assessment and treatment of child rape victims focuses on three separate areas: (1) treatment of physical and psychological trauma; (2) collection of evidence for legal prosecution; and (3) prevention of pregnancy and venereal disease. A thorough medical examination is standard procedure for rape victims. It is preferable that the physician be of the same sex as the victim. A trained counselor and/or supportive relative may also help put the child at ease. Virtually all rape victims can benefit from counseling or psychiatric services.

For subsequent legal prosecution it is important that physical evidence be collected by a trained examiner as soon after the assault as possible. Many hospital emergency rooms have rape kits available for gathering legal evidence. Specimens are collected, labeled and sealed in the kit, usually a manila envelope or box. The sealed container is then given to the investigating police officer.

Specimens are taken from the vagina, mouth and anus and tested for evidence of sperm and/or gonorrhea. Serological tests for syphilis are also ordered. When the victim is of child-bearing age a pregnancy test is also performed.

Rape is a criminal act and, as such, should be reported to law enforcement officials immediately. Reports to a child protection agency are necessary if the perpetrator is a family member or when there is reason to believe the child will not receive adequate treatment or protection.

Because of differing legal definitions of rape it is difficult to determine the number of children who are victimized. Reports of child sexual abuse often involve acts other than penetration. Further, some jurisdictions do not include male victims in their statistics. Incestuous rapes often go unreported.

Though some laws make a distinction between penetration and other acts of sexual assault, the psychological effects of such abuse may not be that different. Studies show that factors such as the level of violence involved, the relationship of the perpetrator to the victim and the period of time over which the abuse took place are more significant than the specific type of sexual act. (*See also* INCEST, SEXUAL ABUSE.)

reactive parricide *See* PARRICIDE, REACTIVE.

real evidence *See* EVIDENCE.

reasonable doubt *See* BEYOND A REASONABLE DOUBT.

receiving home When a temporary PLACEMENT OF AN ABUSE CHILD is needed, a receiving home may be used. The home may be a family, a group home or shelter. Receiving homes are intended to provide temporary housing while more permanent plans are being made.

records, sealing of *See* SEALING OF RECORDS.

regional resource centers Under the CHILD ABUSE PREVENTION AND TREATMENT ACT OF 1974, 10 regional centers were established. These centers serve as extensions of the NATIONAL CENTER ON CHILD ABUSE AND NEGLECT, providing information and technical assistance to local residents. Regional centers have since been replaced by 10 National Child Welfare Resource Centers, which focus on specific topics related to abuse and neglect.

See APPENDIX 2 for a listing of National Child Welfare Resource Centers.

regressed offender The regressed offender represents one of two categories commonly used to describe male perpetrators of child SEXUAL ABUSE. Unlike the FIXATED OFFENDER, who has a long-standing preference for children, the regressed offender is primarily attracted to adults as sexual partners. And he may continue to have relations with adults after he becomes sexually involved with children.

The psychosexual development of the regressed offender usually gives few indications of later sexual deviance. However, it appears that he may harbor strong doubts about his sexual adequacy. A particularly stressful situation or series of events, such as marital difficulty, a physical ailment or financial strain, may cause these doubts to resurface. As a way of coping with what he experiences as an overwhelming situation, the regressed offender engages in sexual activity with children, hoping to regain control. Sexual assault on children may be temporary or it may become a permanent regression to deviant behavior.

Though they usually express regret for their actions later, regressed offenders are often deeply depressed and may not think or care about the consequences of their behavior during the actual molestation.

religious aspects From time to time questions arise as to whether certain religious practices constitute child abuse. Religious beliefs concerning punishment, child labor, medicine and sexuality may conflict with social norms of childrearing and, sometimes, with the law. Such conflicts usually pit parents' rights to raise their children according to their own beliefs against the state's duty to protect children.

The question of when to intervene in religiously motivated childrearing practices is often decided on a case-by-case basis. In the United States, where freedom of religion is guaranteed by the First Amendment, the Supreme Court has traditionally been reluctant to interfere with parents' religious practices. *WISCONSIN V. YODER* established the right of Amish parents to remove their children from school after the eighth grade. In *PRINCE V. MASSACHUSETTS* the high court affirmed parents' right to require their children to engage in certain religious practices. Several medical neglect cases have affirmed the right of parents to withhold medical treatment on religious grounds in all but life-threatening circumstances.

Religious practices involving punishment or deprivation of children may constitute abuse. In such cases the actual and potential harm done to the child must be weighed against parents' rights and any possible benefits the child might derive from this type of religious training. Public agencies are most likely to intervene in situations where children are severely abused or neglected. Child protection workers are sometimes placed in

the position of having to distinguish legitimate religiously based childrearing practices from idiosyncratic abuse. Situations where parents are responding to religious delusions or are not members of any recognized religious group are not considered to constitute grounds for special consideration.

Internationally, differing religious and cultural beliefs pose a significant problem for comparing childrearing practices of different nations. Attempts to launch an international campaign against child abuse have been hampered by disagreement over certain practices that have religious significance yet are considered abusive by most standards. Nevertheless, some practices such as genital mutilation have been widely condemned.

removal of child *See* DISPOSITION.

reparenting Many parents who abuse or neglect their children did not receive adequate parenting during their own childhood. Reparenting is an attempt to intervene in the intergenerational cycle of abuse by providing parents with the nurturance and structure they missed in their early years. Parents are provided with a SURROGATE PARENT such as a PARENT AIDE who can provide the necessary emotional support while serving as a positive parenting role model. Through identification with surrogate parents, the abusive parents are able to become more effective in raising their own children.

reporting Most countries now require reporting of suspected child abuse and neglect to law enforcement authorities or a child protection agency. In the United States, the CHILD ABUSE PREVENTION AND TREATMENT ACT, a federal law enacted in 1974, encouraged states to strengthen laws specifically requiring reporting of child abuse and neglect.

Reporters of suspected abuse or neglect are usually asked to supply the name and address of the child, the parents' names and addresses, the type and extent of injuries suffered, any evidence of previous abuse, and information

Table 10

INFORMATION TO BE OBTAINED FROM THE REPORTER

- The name, age, sex, ethnic background and permanent address of the child
- Present location of the child and location where incidents occurred, if different from permanent address
- Name of person or institution responsible for the child's welfare (and address, if different from the permanent address of the child)
- Name and address of the person alleged to be responsible for the abuse and/or neglect
- The family composition (e.g., names, sex, ages of siblings and other adults normally present)
- The nature and extent of the suspected abuse or neglect, including any available information on prior injury to the child or siblings
- The action taken by the reporting source or others, including whether or not the child has been placed in protective custody
- The reporter's name, telephone number and address, if he/she is willing to provide this information
- The type of reporting source (e.g., mandatory, permissive, anonymous)
- The relationship of the reporter to the child and family
- The willingness of the reporter to share with the family his/her role in initiating the report; and his/her willingness to participate in the assessment process if appropriate
- The motives of the reporter, if possible to evaluate
- Possible witnesses to the incident that caused the child's condition
- The date and time the oral report is received

U.S. Department of Health, Education and Welfare, Office of Human Development Services, Administration for Children, Youth and Families, Children's Bureau, National Center on Child Abuse and Neglect. *Child Protective Services: A Guide for Workers* (Washington, D.C.: 1979; [OHDS] 79-30203).

that may lead to the identification of the perpetrator. In some areas reports can be filed anonymously. Others require that the reporter identify him/herself to the agency receiving the report but withhold the reporter's name from the accused perpetrator.

To facilitate prompt investigation of life-threatening situations most laws allow initial reports to be made verbally. Reporters are usually required to file a full written report within a certain period of time. Many jurisdictions have established toll-free 24-hour HOT-LINES to facilitate reporting. In addition to these local services there are two hotlines that serve the entire United States.

Reporting laws usually require or specifically permit certain professionals to report cases of suspected maltreatment to the agency charged with investigation. In some jurisdictions anyone who has reason to suspect that a child is being abused or neglected is legally obligated to report. About 50% of all reports of child abuse and neglect are made by friends, relatives or neighbors. MANDATED REPORTERS are usually granted immunity from civil or criminal prosecution for reports made in good faith. Penalties, ranging from a small fine to imprisonment, are often imposed on mandated reporters who fail to report suspected abuse or neglect.

While reporting laws are usually clear about who is required to report suspected maltreatment, they are often vague about exactly what kinds of injuries/behavior should be reported. Many local statutes define abuse and neglect in broad terms or not at all. Conditions specifically mentioned range from serious physical injuries to vaguely defined MENTAL INJURIES and NEGLECT.

In Canada, Britain and the United States lack of specificity in the types of injuries that should be reported has led to charges of frivolous reporting. Some critics believe that failure to define clearly abuse and neglect, overburdens child protection agencies and causes some families to be subjected to needless invasions of privacy. Proponents of present laws argue that a broad definition of abuse and neglect is necessary to cover all situations that might seriously harm a child. This view holds that it is better to tolerate some overreporting than to run the risk of failing to identify children in need of help.

American Association for Protecting Children, *Highlights of Official Child Neglect and Abuse Reporting, 1985* (Denver: American Humane Association, 1987).

U.S. Department of Health, Education and Welfare, Office of Human Development Services, Administration for Children, Youth and Families, Children's Bureau, National Center on Child

Table 11

BASIC ELEMENTS OF REPORTING LAWS

- Who is required to report
- What should be reported
- Where or to whom it should be reported
- How much evidence is necessary to trigger a report
- Penalties for failure to report
- Immunity from prosecution for "good faith" reports
- Suspension of privileged communication laws

Abuse and Neglect. *State Child Abuse and Neglect Laws: A Comparative Analysis, 1985* (Washington, D.C.: Clearinghouse on Child Abuse and Neglect Information, April 1987).

Margaret H. Meriwether, "Child Abuse Reporting Laws: Time for a Change," *Family Law Quarterly*, 20:2(Summer 1986), pp. 141-171.

res gestae   *See* EXCITED UTTERANCE.

Table 12

National Estimates of Child Abuse and Neglect Reports

Year	Number of Reports	Rate of Increase
1976	669,000	—
1977	838,000	25.3%
1978	836,000	-2.4%
1979	988,000	18.2%
1980	1,154,000	16.8%
1981	1,225,000	6.1%
1982	1,262,000	3.0%
1983	1,477,000	17.0%
1984	1,727,000	16.9%
1985	1,928,000	11.6%
1986	2,086,000	8.2%

Sources: *Abused Children in America.* Select Committee on Children, Youth, and Families (Washington, D.C.: U.S. Government Printing Office, 1987) and *Highlights of Official Child Neglect and Abuse Reporting, 1986* (Denver: American Humane Association, 1988).

res ipsa loquitur This legal doctrine is borrowed from the evidentiary law of negligence. It is invoked in child abuse or neglect cases and permits use of circumstantial evidence. This admissible evidence only infers that abuse or neglect has occurred, but as the term implies, "the thing speaks for itself." Evidence of this sort presented to the court includes, for example, medical reports or X rays detailing the condition of a suspected victim of abuse or neglect. (*See also* EVIDENTIARY STANDARDS.)

retardation *See* MENTAL RETARDATION.

retinal hemorrhage A blow to the body causes blood to rush out of the impacted area into surrounding vessels. This rapid increase in pressure causes capillaries to rupture. A blow to the head or chest causes small clots to form inside of or in front of the retina. Evidence of these hemorrhages remains present for up to two weeks.

Since retinal hemorrhages are often caused by head trauma, the child should also be examined for the presence of SUBDURAL HEMATOMA.

reversible growth failure   *See* DWARFISM.

reversible hyposomatotropic d w a r f i s m
See DWARFISM.

rickets Lack of sufficient quantities of vitamin D causes rickets, a condition that disturbs the normal development of bones. Rickets may occur as a result of nutritional neglect (*see* NEGLECT).

role reversal Parents who abuse or neglect their children often have unrealistically high expectations for their behavior. Sometimes these parents engage in a reversal of roles in which the child becomes the comforter and caretaker of the parent while the parent largely ignores his or her parental responsibilities. Evidence of role reversal may be seen in young children who demonstrate a kind of PSEUDOMATURITY, shouldering responsibilities normally assumed by much older children or adults. Parents, on the other hand, may be unable to give emotional support and direction.

Role reversal may also be seen in cases of INCEST. The child assumes the role of sexual partner to the parent and, frequently, takes on other responsibilities normally performed by the spouse. Being forced prematurely to act as an adult, the child is denied the opportunity to follow the normal pattern of maturation. The child's own developmental needs are suppressed, leading to what is often referred to as the loss of childhood (*see* PARENTIFIED CHILD).

Some mental health experts speculate that parents may be repeating their own childhood in which they assumed a parental role. An alternate explanation is that parents who, as children, were not required to accept responsibility and were protected from the consequences of their actions, are as adults unable to function maturely. It is likely that both types of childhood experience can contribute to role reversal; however, different treatment approaches might be taken depending upon the parent's specific developmental deficit.

runaways Studies of children and adolescents who run away from home show that many are running away from abuse. One study of runaway youths found that 73% of females and 38% of males reported having been abused. While female runaways are more likely to have been sexually abused, males are more often physically abused.

Ironically, some teenagers may actually increase their chances of abuse by leaving home. Runaways are often easy prey for adults seeking to lure them into prostitution. Unable to secure a job that pays enough to support them, both males and females are enticed by the promise of large sums of money in exchange for engaging in illicit activities. In addition to sexual exploitation, youths living on the streets are often robbed or assaulted. (*See also* ADOLESCENT ABUSE, SEXUAL ABUSE, THROWAWAY CHILDREN.)

Arlene McCormack, Mark-David Janus and Ann Wolbert Burgess, "Runaway Youths and Sexual Victimization: Gender Differences in an Adolescent Runaway Population," *Child Abuse and Neglect*, 10(1986), pp. 387-395.

S

sadism   Sadism is a relatively rare form of sexual perversion in which sexual gratification is derived by hurting or humiliating another person. Though assaults involving sadism comprise a very small proportion of all child SEXUAL ABUSE, highly publicized accounts of MYSOPEDIC OFFENDERS have led to a public misconception concerning their prevalence.

The overwhelming majority of sadistic sexual offenses are committed by men. When sadistic assaults occur they are likely to result in physical injury or, in extreme cases, death. Sexual pleasure is derived from the victim's visible suffering. The sadist usually exerts much greater force than would be necessary to overpower the child. Though usually described as a sexual offense, sadism actually combines physical, psychological and sexual abuse.

Some psychodynamically oriented therapists have explained sadism as a PROJECTION of the attacker's own self-hatred. By punishing the child the perpetrator symbolically punishes himself.

scalds   The most frequent type of abusive burns of children is a wet burn, or scald. Over one-fourth of all reported scalds can be likened to abuse. Most nonaccidental scalds are caused by overheated tap water. At 130 degrees F, a full thickness scald can occur on an adult in 30 seconds, at 150 degrees in two seconds. A child's thin skin burns even more quickly.

Abusive scalds often have different patterns than accidental scalds. Forcing a child to sit in a bath tub of hot water may result in a "donut burn," where the center of the buttocks is protected by the relative coolness of the tub while the surrounding area is burned. Glove or stocking burns are most likely to result from the hand or foot being forceably held in hot water. When scalds are caused by splashing careful observation of burn marks can reveal the direction from which the hot liquid came. This evidence should be compared to the caretaker's account for inconsistencies.

A study of scald victims revealed that 71% of the cases in which the child was brought to treatment by someone other than the primary caretaker were the result of abuse. Of children whose treatment was delayed two hours or more, 70% were found to be victims of abusive burns. (*See also* BURNS.)

SCAN team   SCAN stands for Suspected Child Abuse and Neglect. Usually attached to a hospital or outpatient mental health facility, the SCAN team is charged with assessing children and their families to determine whether abuse has occurred. If it is determined that the child has, in fact, been abused the team makes specific recommendations for treatment.

Teams are composed of professionals from different disciplines, all of whom have special training in diagnosis of child abuse and neglect. Typically, SCAN teams review only the most difficult cases, such as those involving SEXUAL ABUSE of a young child. More clear-cut decisions are handled by protective service staff. (*See also* ASSESSMENT and MULTIDISCIPLINARY TEAM.)

scapegoating   Often one child in a family is singled out as the recipient of the most abuse. Reasons for this type of selection are complex and varied. Usually scapegoating begins at a very early age, sometimes at birth. Infants who are irritable, colicky and who do not respond well to parental nurturing may become targets for abuse. Premature infants are more likely to become scapegoats than those carried to full term.

Scapegoating is frequently described as an interactive process in which the child's physical, social or psychological characteristics combine with those of the parent to increase the likelihood of abuse. Children perceived as difficult, unresponsive or hyperactive are at risk. Other traits can include psychological impairment, learning disabilities, physical defects or chronic illness.

Caretakers of scapegoated children range from normally capable persons under stress to those with severe PSYCHOPATHOLOGY. Parents may perceive a particular child as reflecting their own defects or inadequacies. In such situations the parent's self-hatred is misdirected toward the child. The child has become a symbol of all the parent dislikes in him or herself.

Maltreatment by caretakers is quickly internalized by children. Scapegoated children come to have low self-esteem and see themselves as bad and deserving of punishment. As they grow older many of these children actually seek punishment by acting out at home or in school. They may also invite abuse from peers by taunting and provoking them. Because the children see themselves as deserving of abuse they offer only token self-defense when they are subsequently attacked.

As they grow older, victims of severe scapegoating continue to have difficulty in establishing close relationships with peers, teachers and others. Prolonged treatment is often required to help these children develop a capacity for displaying warmth toward themselves and others.

Scotland In Scotland, child protective services fall under the general jurisdiction of the Scottish Development Department and the Scottish Home and Health Department. In 1968, the Social Work Act in Scotland reorganized the various services provided to children and families, and replaced juvenile courts with a system thought to be more responsive to the needs of children.

The judicial services change was made in 1971 from a court system dealing with juveniles to one that brings a youthful offender before a panel of individuals (generally three people) plus the reporter of the offense, a social worker, and one or both of the child's parents. Children who fall within the confines of this hearing system are under 16 years of age and there are a variety of statutory grounds under which a child may be required to appear. Options after a hearing are discharge of a case, placement on supervision, and residential supervision.

scurvy Scurvy, a result of vitamin C deficiency, increases susceptibility to bruising and is often mistaken for BATTERED CHILD SYNDROME. Conversely, many cases of child battering were misdiagnosed as scurvy during the late 19th and early 20th centuries by physicians who failed to consider the possibility of abuse or who wished to protect the parents.

sealing of records Many jurisdictions require a court order to examine criminal records of youthful offenders. Such records are considered "sealed."

Sealing of records is a controversial issue. Many youth advocates believe that by restricting access to court records adolescents will be protected from negative labeling and discrimination in school or in later employment. Others believe sealing makes it difficult to identify serious offenders who pose a threat to society. When the youthful offender has a history of abusing other children, sealing of criminal records may prevent parents, school officials and law enforcement officers from taking steps to protect younger children adequately.

Under certain circumstances records of adult offenders may be sealed or expunged. While sealing of adult records is less common, many of the same arguments, for and against, apply.

secondary prevention *See* PREVENTION.

secrecy SEXUAL ABUSE that continues for an extended period of time usually involves an element of secrecy. The abuser may bribe or coerce the victim not to tell about their encounters. Children themselves may maintain secrecy about abuse due to embarrassment, fear of being punished, fear of parental rejection or abandonment or, in the case of very young children, simply because they do not have sufficient verbal capacity to explain the problem. Some therapists speculate that enforced silence may be related to later development of nonverbal means of coping with stress, such as SUBSTANCE ABUSE, withdrawal or depression.

In cases of INCEST, secrecy may extend to other members of the family. Often the mother is accused of being a PASSIVE ABUSER, silently condoning sexual activity between the father and a child. Reasons for this phenomenon are complex and not fully understood. The mother may tacitly encourage the child to act as a substitute in order to avoid sexual relations with the father. In other cases she may fear abandonment or reprisal.

Failure to report known abuse not only makes one a silent partner to maltreatment but also increases the harm to the child. Studies suggest that psychological damage from abuse is related to the length of time the child was abused.

seductive behavior   Seductive or inappropriate sexual behavior toward an adult may be a sign that a child has been sexually abused (*see* SEXUAL ABUSE). Sexually victimized children often learn that in order to gain the attention or affection of an adult they must appeal to them sexually. Such behavior, once learned, may be directed toward adults other than the abuser, increasing the risk of further abuse.

Seductive behavior may range from overly affectionate kissing, stroking, massaging etc., to overt sexual advances such as fondling the genitals or making sexual comments. Children who act seductively toward adults are often blamed for initiating sexual activity with them. Claims of seduction by a child have frequently been introduced in court as a defense against charges of child molestation. Others cite this apparent sexual aggressiveness as evidence that children enjoy sex with adults. Such claims notwithstanding, sexual relations between an adult and a child are considered to be an abusive act on the part of the adult and are outlawed in most countries around the world.

Experts in the treatment of child sexual abuse stress that seductive behavior on the part of children is learned from adults. The child who feels unloved may find that this is the only way to get the affection he or she craves. Starved for affection, the child may interpret sexual exploitation by an adult as genuine affection. As the child grows older, sexual submissiveness often gives way to intense anger toward the adult and/or self-loathing often manifesting itself in depression and SELF-DESTRUCTIVE BEHAVIOR.

self-destructive behavior   In the general population, self-destructive acts by children are rare. Among neglected, and especially abused, children the incidence of such behavior is much higher. Studies have shown that up to 40% of abused children exhibited self-destructive tendencies compared with 2% of children with no history of abuse or neglect.

Abused children are more likely to engage in a range of harmful activities, including provocative acts designed to elicit punishment, accident proneness and suicide attempts. Self-destructive acts usually follow parental beatings or separation from the parent—real or threatened.

Neglected children display two to three times the amount of self-harming behavior as their peers who have not experienced abuse or neglect. Physically and sexually abused victims are even more likely than neglected children to exhibit this behavior—eight to 10 times more. Though neglected children share many of the same negative environmental conditions suffered by abused children, they are less likely to be subjected to physical violence and SCAPEGOATING.

Children who are punished frequently and brutally will assume they are bad and deserving of punishment. They often cannot connect the punishment with any specific behavior and consequently develop a general sense of self-hatred, unworthiness and low SELF-ESTEEM.

These feelings form the basis of later aggressive and self-destructive behavior.

self esteem   Feelings of low self-worth are often cited as both cause and result of child abuse. Several psychiatric studies of abusive parents have found them to have unusually negative images of themselves. Many clinicians and researchers believe parents' low self-esteem can be attributed to abusive or neglectful treatment they received as children. These parents may project their feelings onto children by constantly punishing or degrading them (*see* PROJECTION). In turn their children may grow up to be abusive parents.

Building self-esteem is often one of the most important goals in the treatment of abusers. In some cases treatment may involve a process known as REPARENTING, in which parents receive instruction and nurturance from a trained older adult. In a sense, the parent takes on another parent who can give the positive feedback and modeling they did not receive as children.

Abused children often develop a distorted view of themselves, seeing virtually everything they do as bad. Parental abuse and neglect is interpreted by the child as confirmation of perceived badness. Many children become so invested in this negative self-image that they stubbornly resist the efforts of therapists, foster parents and others to change this false view. For this reason, long-term psychotherapeutic treatment of abused children is sometimes necessary to eliminate this distorted sense of self.

self-help groups   The number of people involved in self-help groups has grown dramatically since the 1950s. Alcoholics Anonymous, perhaps the most famous self-help organization, has thousands of groups around the world. Many mutual aid groups have patterned themselves after AA's 12-step program. Others are less structured, simply providing a forum for people with similar concerns to share experiences and emotional support.

The characteristic that distinguishes self-help from other treatment of educational groups is the degree of responsibility exercised by members. Self-help groups are totally controlled by their members.

PARENTS ANONYMOUS is the largest organization of groups for parents who abuse their children. Several groups for victims of sexual abuse have formed since the late 1970s.

Self-help has proven effective in helping parents who want to control abusive impulses. Members often make themselves available to one another in times of crisis, serving as a safety valve for explosive emotions. A desire to change is essential for members of self-help groups. Though child abuse agencies often refer parents to such groups, membership is voluntary.

Groups also serve an important educational function. Parents learn coping skills from others with similar experiences. Victims of sexual abuse often learn they are not alone in their feelings of low self-esteem, guilt or similar reactions.

Though self-help groups can be very effective they are not for everyone. Abusers who are not motivated to change may need more structured assistance. In some cases specialized treatment is necessary in addition to participation in a self-help group.

self-incrimination   *See* MIRANDA WARNINGS.

Senate Subcommittee on Children and Youth   In February 1971, the U.S. Senate Subcommittee on Children and Youth was established after Senator Walter F. Mondale promoted further action on proposals made at the 1970 White House Conference on Children. As part of its research, the subcommittee published *Rights of Children, Part I*, a document that indicated the direction this subcommittee would take. As a result of subcommittee action over the course of several years, Public Law 93-247 was signed on December 20, 1973, and was in force as the

CHILD ABUSE PREVENTION AND TREATMENT ACT OF 1974 on January 31.

sentencing   The final phase of a criminal trial is pronouncement of the judge's order of punishment for a convicted defendant. Persons convicted of criminal charges related to child abuse or neglect may be imprisoned, fined or placed on probation. Actual sentences vary widely and depend on several factors, including local statutes, whether the crime is classed as a FELONY or MISDEMEANOR and the severity of the act. Sentencing occurs only in criminal trials and does not directly involve victims of maltreatment. The corresponding phase of civil court proceedings is the DISPOSITION.

sequelae   Children suffer many consequences of abuse and neglect. Aftereffects of maltreatment are sometimes referred to collectively as *sequelae*. The most obvious effects of abuse are physical trauma such as cuts, bruises or broken bones. Less apparent results of abuse include psychological harm, internal physical injuries such as brain damage, or impaired growth. Victims of sexual abuse may experience extreme feelings of low self-worth, sexual dysfunction in adulthood, an inability to trust others and similar sequelae of exploitation.

Aftereffects of abuse may appear as a delayed reaction many years after the traumatic incident or may be attributed to other causes. While some pedophiles (*see* PEDOPHILIA) argue that sex with children is not harmful, reports of adults who were sexually victimized as children indicate that the experience can have severe and long-lasting consequences.

Protection of children from further abuse, while essential, does not address the consequences of previous abuse. Treatment of psychological damage is often a time-consuming and expensive process. If left untreated, victims of abuse may continue to suffer from the aftereffects of abuse and may grow up to become abusers themselves. (*See also* CYCLE OF ABUSE, PSYCHOLOGICAL MALTREATMENT, PHYSICAL ABUSE, SEXUAL ABUSE, NEGLECT.)

Margaret A. Lynch and Jacqueline Roberts, *Consequences of Child Abuse* (London: Academic Press, 1982).

service plan   After completion of an ASSESSMENT the child protection worker develops a plan for addressing specific problems and creating a safe environment for the abused child. The service plan (sometimes called a case plan) is often developed with the assistance of a MULTIDISCIPLINARY TEAM. If feasible, the abused child and his or her family is also involved in the planning process.

The first step in developing a service plan is setting realistic goals for the child and family. Treatment or service goals correspond directly to specific problems identified in the assessment. Goals may be described as proposed solutions to these problems. Some service plans make a distinction between short- and long-term goals.

Next in the planning process is the creation of measurable, time-limited objectives. Objectives are the standards by which progress toward identified goals can be monitored. Another way of viewing objectives is as a set of specific actions that must be taken to achieve a particular goal.

The final phase of service planning involves identifying and selecting the kinds of help the child and family will need in order to achieve the service goals. A wide range of services may be required to achieve the desired goals. Some examples of assistance that can be included in the service plan are: CATEGORICAL AID; HOMEMAKER SERVICES or PARENT AIDES; individual, family or marital counseling; temporary FOSTER CARE; and legal aid.

Service plans that set reasonable goals and have the family's support are the most likely to succeed. Families who are actively involved in the planning process usually have more confidence in the plan and tend to cooperate more fully in its implementation.

sexual abuse Reports of sexual abuse are growing faster than any other type of child maltreatment in the United States. Despite increasing public interest in its prevention and treatment, sexual abuse remains one of the least understood forms of abuse.

Many popular myths exist concerning the child molester and the victimized child. The common image of the sexual offender as a dirty old man in a trenchcoat is refuted by statistics showing that most offenders are under 30 years of age and are known (and very often related) to the victim.

Another area of confusion centers on the nature of child sexual abuse. While most people acknowledge that sexual relations between an adult and a child are harmful, there is disagreement over the age at which a person is able to give informed consent to sexual relations. A nationwide minimum of 18 has been suggested in the United States, where the age of consent varies from state to state. Small groups have even banded together in the United States and Britain to advocate total repeal of laws that prevent adult-child sex.

History

Though sexual misuse of children has recently been "rediscovered" in Western society, historical accounts show that the problem has a long and saddening history. Many times, in many different cultures, sexual victimization of children has actually been institutionalized and permitted by law. Even more frequently sexual abuse has flourished in spite of laws and mores that nominally prohibit such behavior. Sale and prostitution of children remains a well-documented way of life in many parts of the world.

In ancient Greek and Roman society CASTRATION was practiced as a way of making boys more sexually attractive to adult males. Young girls and boys were present in ap-

proximately equal numbers in brothels of the period.

Child marriage has been widely practiced throughout history and is still common in some countries. Until the third century A.D. Talmudic law permitted the betrothal of girls beginning at the age of three years and one day. Subject to the father's permission, sexual intercourse was the method of sealing marital intentions with such a young girl.

For most of recorded history children—girls in particular—have been afforded the legal status of parental property. Rape of a young girl was often treated as a property offense against the father. Because the rapist had reduced the child's ability to bring a large dowry, he was required to reimburse the father for the lost income. In some cases the man was forced to marry his victim.

Victimization of children continued in medieval Europe. In 15th-century France the legal age of consent (the age at which the child was deemed competent to marry or engage in sexual relations) was six.

Widespread abuse also was alleged to have occurred at the hands of clergy in convents and during confession. Many young girls were cruelly executed for alleged fornication with the devil. Historians speculate that these girls may actually have been sexually assaulted by the same men who put them to death.

The lust for sexual relations with children appears to have been a major preoccupation with Victorian men. Prostitution flourished in 19th-century London, and the practice of deflowering young virgins was described as obsessional. London brothels were remarkable for their large numbers of young girls. An estimated 58% of the illegal prostitutes in Vienna during this period were minors. Child pornography also became a popular item in the Victorian era, a phenomenon that shows no signs of diminution even today.

During the 19th century in the United States, Chinese girls were bought and sold at prices ranging from $1,500 to $3,500. Prior to the abolition of slavery, black children were treated as sexual property and frequently brutalized by their white owners.

Many American, British, French and German children were lured or sold into white slavery during the late 19th century. These children, most of them around the ages of 12 and 13, were often exported to Hong Kong, Thailand, India and various South American countries.

Despite laws prohibiting such practices, sexual misuse of children continues to flourish in modern society. Undeterred by public outcry against it, the demand for child pornography still provides a stimulus for exploitation. A significant proportion of prostitution around the world involves minors. And child marriage continues to be commonplace in India and some other countries.

Sexual Abuse Today

Definitions of sexual abuse vary from culture to culture and even within societal groups. Some groups engage in permissive practices or sexual rituals that would be viewed with alarm in other cultures. Others consider western sexual norms overly harsh and conducive to victimization. Despite this variation, all groups have rules governing sexual contact between children and adults. The incest taboo prohibiting intrafamilial sexual relations is almost universal.

Of the many definitions of sexual abuse that have been offered, the one proposed by the NATIONAL CENTER ON CHILD ABUSE AND NEGLECT (NCCAN) is perhaps the most comprehensive:

Table 13

TYPES OF CHILD SEXUAL ABUSE

RAPE—forceful genital intercourse
GENITAL INTERCOURSE—without force
ANAL INTERCOURSE
FELLATIO—oral contact with the male genitals
CUNNILINGUS—oral contact with the female genitals
ANALINGUS—oral contact with the anus
CASTRATION—removal of the testicles
CLITORIDECTOMY—removal of the clitoris
GENITAL TOUCHING—including clothed and unclothed touching, fondling of the male or
    female genitals
INTENTIONAL SEXUAL TOUCHING—of the breasts, buttocks or thigh, clothed or
    unclothed
SEXUAL INTERCOURSE BETWEEN ADULTS IN THE PRESENCE OF A CHILD
TAKING SEXUALLY EXPLICIT PHOTOGRAPHS OF A CHILD
FORCING OR ENCOURAGING A CHILD TO TOUCH AN ADULT'S GENITALS
ENCOURAGING A CHILD TO ENGAGE IN SEXUAL ACTIVITY WITH OTHER
    CHILDREN FOR THE BENEFIT OF AN ADULT
EXHIBITIONISM—deliberate display of the genitals to a child, usually for the sexual
    gratification of the perpetrator
SEXUAL KISSING
CHILD'S CARETAKER IS INVOLVED IN PROSTITUTION

contacts or interactions between a child and an adult when the child is being used for the sexual stimulation of the perpetrator or another person. Sexual abuse may also be committed by a person under the age of eighteen when that person is either significantly older than the victim or when the perpetrator is in a position of power or control over another child.

This definition includes a variety of sexual behavior ranging from EXHIBITIONISM to RAPE. Another significant feature is its inclusion of children as potential abusers as well as victims.

In the United States estimates of the prevalence of child sexual abuse vary widely. Most experts believe that only a small proportion of this abuse is reported to law enforcement or child protection agencies. Confirmation of this belief is found in numerous studies of adults who describe unreported sexual abuse during their own childhood or adolescence. Such studies have estimated that anywhere from 6% to 62% of all females experience some form of sexual molestation as children or teens. Rates for boys fall between 3% and 31%. A 1985 *Los Angeles Times* poll conducted throughout the United States found that 27% of all women and 16% of men reported being molested as children.

Reasons for the wide variation in estimated occurrence include the use of different research methods, different upper age limits and definitions.

Approximately 132,000 reports of sexual abuse were received by state agencies in the United States during 1986. The American Humane Association estimates that almost twice as many new assaults actually take place every year. The National Committee for the Prevention of Child Abuse estimates that one million U.S. children are sexually abused each year. Recent surveys conducted in Britain and Sweden suggest percentages of sexual abuse similar to those in the United States. Official reports of abuse are, however, lower in these countries than in the United States.

One important aspect of sexual abuse that sets it apart from other forms of maltreatment is its lack of association with class or race. Unlike PHYSICAL ABUSE, it occurs with approximately equal frequency in all social classes. White and non-white children experience equivalent amounts of sexual abuse.

Victims

Statistically, girls are two and one-half times more likely to be sexually abused than boys. Seventy-one percent of all victims are girls.

Studies have identified several factors that may place some girls at greater risk than others. Marital conflict, separation and divorce were found to be more prevalent in the families of sexually abused girls. Specifically, these girls were more likely to have lived *without* their natural father and more likely to have lived *with* a stepfather. Mothers of victimized girls were more likely to be employed outside the home or to be ill or disabled.

Like girls, boys are most often the victims of men. Victimized boys are more likely than their female counterparts to come from an impoverished environment, to be physically abused and to suffer their abuse at the hands of someone outside the family. Some experts believe sexual abuse of boys is less likely to be reported than that involving girls.

Another factor associated with sexual abuse is SOCIAL ISOLATION. These children have fewer friends than their peers and may be isolated in other ways as well. It is not clear, however, whether this phenomenon is a contributing factor or a result of abuse. Clinical evidence indicates that abuse victims are often depressed and withdrawn.

Sexually victimized children also tend to report, more often than their peers, a poor relationship with their parents. Mothers are most frequently reported as the parent with whom the relationship is most strained.

Absence of the mother greatly increases the risk to girls. Those living without their mothers are three times more likely to suffer sexual abuse than those whose mothers are present.

In an effort to avoid further sexual abuse many adolescents run away from home. Ironically these teens may actually increase their likelihood of being abused. A recent study of runaways in a Canadian shelter found that 71% of female and 38% of male runaways had been sexually victimized. The authors speculated that much of the abuse occurred after leaving home. Adolescents living on the streets are particularly vulnerable to sexual assault and may in desperation, turn to prostitution as a means of financial support.

Perpetrators of Sexual Abuse

Sexual abuse is predominantly a male crime. Ninety percent of all child sexual molestation is committed by men. Ninety-five percent of female victims are victimized by men. Men are responsible for approximately 80% of all sexual abuse of boys.

About 70% of sexual abusers are known to children before the abuse takes place. The most frequent offenders are fathers and stepfathers. A child's relationship to the offender is an important predictor of the duration of abuse. When the offender is previously unknown to the child the abuse is likely to be limited to one incident per child, such as an exhibitionistic episode. This type of offender is likely to have a large number of victims. Incestuous abuse often involves repeated molestations of the same child over a period of three to four years.

Most sexual abuse of children is perpetrated by young heterosexual men who are considered quite normal by others. Eighty percent of all these offenders engage in their first sexual abuse before the age of 30. Though alcohol or drug intoxication is often blamed, less than one-third of these offenders are drug or alcohol dependent. Only 5% show evidence of serious mental illness. And, of all adults,

homosexual men are the least likely to commit a sexual offense against a child.

Perpetrators are more likely than others to have been sexually victimized as children. While FIXATED OFFENDERS are aroused exclusively by children and seek them as sexual partners, a more frequent motive of abusers may be a need for intimacy, power or control. This is especially true of INCEST. Many report difficulty in relating to adult sexual partners and feel inadequate. Ironically, many offenders have rigid and repressive ideas about sex.

Though research on recidivism is fragmentary and inconclusive, many experts view the child sexual offender as particularly resistant to treatment. Fixated offenders who have assaulted a large number of children are thought to be less likely to benefit from treatment than REGRESSED OFFENDERS who have a less extensive history of abuse.

Effects of Sexual Abuse

Children differ in their reactions to sexual abuse. Clinical and empirical studies indicate that sexually victimized children are more likely to be: fearful, anxious, depressed, angry and hostile. Twenty percent to 40% of these children show signs of significant emotional disturbance following the abuse. Child victims sometimes exhibit inappropriate sexual behavior as a result of the abuse. Excessive sexual curiosity, open masturbation and exposure of the genitals are frequently observed in young victims. Older children and adolescents may become promiscuous or display inappropriately seductive behavior toward adults and are at greater risk of delinquency. Young girls and older boys seem to be most seriously affected by this type of abuse.

Children often feel extremely guilty about their involvement in sexual abuse. Even in cases where there has been a brutal assault, a child may feel that she or he was in some way responsible for or deserving of the abuse. Guilt feelings are almost universal among in-

Table 14

**ESTIMATED NUMBER OF SEXUAL ABUSE CASES REPORTED
TO STATE AGENCIES IN THE UNITED STATES, 1976-1985**

Year	Number of Reports	Rate of Increase
1976	7,559	—
1977	11,617	53.7%
1978	12,257	5.5%
1979	27,247	122.3%
1980	27,366	37.1%
1981	37,441	.2%
1982	56,607	51.2%
1983	71,961	27.1%
1984	113,267	54.4%
1985	139,998	23.6%

Source: American Humane Association, 1976-83; 1984-85 estimated from data in *Abused Children in America*, Select Committee on Children, Youth and Families (Washington, D.C.: U.S. Government Printing Office, 1987).

cest victims who may feel responsible for the breakup of their parents' marriage.

Conversely, some incest victims see themselves as holding the family together by preventing a divorce. In such cases the daughter may become, in effect, a surrogate wife filling a role the mother is unable or unwilling to play (*see* ROLE REVERSAL). Guilt can also appear as a byproduct of the confusing and often contradictory feelings about incest. Though sexual contact is frequently painful and frightening for a child, there is sometimes an element of pleasure in such contact. A child may enjoy the exclusive and deceptively warm attention of an adult when he or she feels unloved. Taking any enjoyment in such an obviously bad act can be a source of intense guilt that continues long after the abuse has stopped.

Physical effects of sexual abuse can include vaginal and anal tearing as well as a variety of abrasions and/or lacerations to other parts of the body. Children who have been forcibly abused may suffer hematomas, frac-

tures and similar injuries associated with battering.

A number of sexually transmitted diseases (STDs) may be contracted by victimized children. The presence of SYPHILIS or GONORRHEA in a child is strong evidence of sexual abuse. With the exception of congenital transmission, these diseases are spread almost exclusively through sexual contact.

Impregnation is a factor to be considered when postpubertal females are the victims. Pregnancy poses serious physical and psychological health risks to the young adolescent. Children born to young mothers have higher mortality rates and are more susceptible to a number of physical problems.

Sexually molested children may exhibit somatic symptoms that appear to be unrelated to physical aspects of the abuse. Secondary complaints may include sleep disturbance, abdominal pain, ENURESIS, ENCOPRESIS, vomiting and loss of appetite.

Sexual abuse during childhood often continues to affect the lives of victims long after the abuse has ended. Women with a history of

Table 15
Reports of Sexual Maltreatment
for 34 States Providing Complete Information, 1984–1985

State	1984	1985
Arizona	2,528	3,500
California	43,056	54,121
Connecticut	1,019	1,512
Delaware	350	513
Florida	5,799	5,353
Georgia	1,992	3,872
Hawaii	279	277
Idaho	1,277	1,453
Illinois	7,134	10,597
Indiana	2,411	3,318
Iowa	2,864	3,052
Kentucky	2,172	3,456
Louisiana	3,190	3,660
Maine	865	990
Massachusetts	2,826	3,484
Michigan	2,928	3,518
Mississippi	377	571
Missouri	2,663	2,844
Nevada	412	438
New Hampshire	327	359
New Jersey	1,155	1,842
New Mexico	1,705	2,436
New York	8,132	8,345
North Dakota	307	351
Oregon	3,947	4,364
Pennsylvania	4,285	5,481
South Dakota	487	674
Tennessee	5,387	8,092
Texas	8,732	9,454
Utah	941	1,065
Vermont	436	607
Washington	9,491	9,691
Wisconsin	5,063	6,609
Wyoming	495	461
Total	135,032	166,360

Figures represent substantiated reports.
No figures available (for 1981–1982).
Figures represent fiscal years, not calendar years.

childhood sexual victimization have higher levels of depression, anxiety, SUBSTANCE ABUSE and SELF-DESTRUCTIVE BEHAVIOR. They are also more likely to feel isolated and stigmatized, experience some type of SEXUAL DYSFUNCTION or avoidance, or have difficulty trusting others.

Abuse at the hands of adult males appears to be more disturbing than that perpetrated by females or adolescents. Fathers and step-fathers are reported to have the most psychologically damaging effects.

The use of force is related to the serious-ness and duration of the trauma experienced. Not surprisingly, abuse over a long period of time is associated with more traumatic and longer lasting SEQUELAE.

Prevention

Systematic efforts to prevent sexual abuse of children are relatively new. Current preven-tion programs are directed primarily toward school-age children. These programs employ a variety of approaches, including structured school curricula, children's books, films, pup-pet shows, theater performances and talks by well-known sports or media celebrities.

Most programs attempt to familiarize children with the concept of sexual abuse by defining "bad" behaviors or situations. Children are taught to recognize, for example, inappropriate touching, and are alerted to simple actions they can take to prevent such abuse. Frequently they are encouraged to tell another trusted adult about the abuse. They may also be taught various methods of resis-tance, including: verbal refusal (saying no), running away and even martial arts tech-niques.

Other prevention efforts focus on parents and professionals. Parents are taught how to educate their children about sexual abuse. In-struction often includes suggestions for the detection of abuse and what to do when abuse is discovered. Professional training of teachers, physicians, police and mental health workers has followed similar lines, often em-phasizing detection.

Lindsay G. Arthur, "Child Sexual Abuse: Improv-ing the System's Response," *Juvenile and Family Court Journal*, 37:2(1986).

A.W. Burgess, A.N. Groth, L.L. Holstrom and S.M. Sgroi, *Sexual Assault of Children and Adoles-cents* (Lexington, Mass.: Lexington Books, 1978).

David Finkelhor, *A Sourcebook on Child Sexual Abuse* (Beverly Hills, Calif.: Sage Publications, 1986).

———, *Child Sexual Abuse* (New York: Free Press, 1984).

Adele Mayer, *Sexual Abuse* (Holmes Beach, Fla.: Learning Publications, 1985).

Florence Rush, *The Best Kept Secret: Sexual Abuse of Children* (Englewood Cliffs, N.J.: Prentice-Hall, 1980).

Holly Smith with Edie Israel, "Sibling Incest: A Study of the Dynamics of 25 Cases," *Child Abuse and Neglect*, 11(1987), pp. 101-108.

sexual abuse, adolescent perpetrators of *See* ADOLESCENT PERPETRATORS OF SEXUAL ABUSE.

sexual dysfunction Victims of child SEXUAL ABUSE often experience sexual dif-ficulties in later life. Adult survivors of sexual abuse may report difficulty becoming aroused, pain during intercourse, inability to achieve orgasm or extreme physical revulsion during sex. Because some of their first sexual experiences involved force, coercion or ex-ploitation many survivors come to associate these dynamics with all sexual encounters. Some adults experience flashbacks during which the sexual abuse is vividly recalled.

Subsequent reactions to sexual abuse range from total avoidance of all intimate relation-ships to frenetic, promiscuous sexual activity. In an effort to avoid painful memories or future exploitation some victims of sexual molestation close themselves off from any relationship that may lead to intimacy. Others, seeking to prove that they are in control of their sexuality or perhaps reacting to feelings of worthlessness and guilt, develop a pattern of compulsive sexual behavior. Some experts believe female survivors may see their sexuality as a way of gaining power over men and thereby regaining control of themselves. Though they are often extremely active sexually, survivors who exhibit this reaction usually achieve little pleasure from sex and have difficulty experiencing true intimacy with their sexual partner.

Males who are sexually victimized by a man often display hypermasculine behavior in an effort to prove to themselves and others that they are heterosexual. Abuse by an adult of the same sex is often accompanied by intense self-doubt concerning the victim's sexual orientation. Victims commonly feel responsible in some way for the abuse. When the assailant is of the same sex the child often believes that, since the adult was attracted to him, he must be homosexual. If the child has internalized negative attitudes toward homosexuality the fear of homosexuality may intensify guilt feelings leading to even greater distress over sexuality.

Survivors of child sexual abuse often lack knowledge of how intimate relations develop. Children who are forced into sexual behavior prematurely may learn how to relate only sexually. These children may have difficulty relating to peers on a level appropriate to their age. Incest survivors often complain of being robbed of their childhood because they were prevented from developing the kind of family and peer relationships considered an important part of healthy development. The inability to develop intimacy often leads to later marital and/or sexual dysfunction.

Expert help and a supportive environment is usually necessary to help the survivor overcome problems related to sexual abuse. A number of self-help and formal therapy groups are available for the adult survivor (*see* APPENDIX 1). As awareness of the lasting effects of such victimization grows, more adults are seeking help in overcoming problems related to child sexual abuse.

sexual exploitation Child sexual exploitation involves the use of children as prostitutes, models for pornographic purposes, or objects of sexual molestation. Exploitation is usually, but not exclusively, undertaken for the economic gain of an adult. No reliable estimates of the incidence of sexual exploitation are available. Recent estimates of sexual abuse often fail to include victims of pornography or prostitution. Law enforcement officials believe sexual exploitation of children to be one of the most underreported crimes. (*See also* CHILD PORNOGRAPHY, CHILD PROSTITUTION and SEXUAL ABUSE.)

Seth L. Goldstein, *The Sexual Exploitation of Children* (New York: Elsevier, 1987).

sexual trafficking Illegal trade in women and children for sexual purposes has been practiced since ancient times. In the late 19th and early 20th centuries child prostitution and white slavery was a source of great public concern in Europe and in North America, where newspapers estimated that 60,000 children per year were kidnapped or lured into prostitution. Though accurate information on the extent of sexual trafficking was unavailable, sensational, sometimes racist accounts in the media spurred the enactment of laws specifically prohibiting the sexual exploitation of children.

The extent of sexual trafficking in children is still unknown. Though large numbers of children are thought to be victims of kidnapping and sexual exploitation, estimates of the extent of such activities are controversial and largely based on anecdotal data. Youthful prostitutes are in great demand and often command higher prices than adults. Significant numbers of runaway children and adolescents are known to be lured or coerced into prostitution.

Existence of international trade in children and adolescents is also hard to document. Children in developing countries may be enticed or sold into illicit activity in hopes of economic gain. Reports of children being sold by parents surface from time to time but it is not known if the practice is widespread. (*See also* CHILD SLAVERY and PROSTITUTION.)

sexually transmitted disease (STD) Presence of a sexually transmitted disease in a child under the age of puberty is a strong indicator of SEXUAL ABUSE. It is extremely rare for such diseases to be contracted in any way other than by sexual contact. A thorough physical examination for possible sexual abuse should include taking cultures from genitals, mouth and anus. A blood test is necessary to detect syphilis. (*See also* GONORRHEA; SYPHILIS; VENEREAL DISEASE; and WARTS, VENEREAL.)

A.W. Burgess, A.N. Groth, L.L. Holstrom and S.M. Sgroi, *Sexual Assault of Children and Adolescents* (Lexington, Mass.: Lexington Books, 1978).

shaken baby syndrome   *See* WHIPLASH SHAKEN INFANT SYNDROME.

Sheppard-Towner Infancy and Maternity Act   This legislation, passed in 1921, established the first United States program to provide major funding to alleviate a wide range of problems suffered by infants and young children as a result of nutritional deficiency, generally poor health and lack of adequate care. The act was sponsored by the CHILDREN'S BUREAU, an agency established in 1912 during an era of social reform.

sibling abuse   Violence between siblings is widespread in Western culture. Interestingly, such assaults constitute a relatively small proportion of all child abuse cases reported to investigatory authorities. This fact in part reflects a belief that sibling violence is a normal part of family life that should be handled without outside interference. Underreporting may also be due to a tendency to cite parents for failing to protect the victimized sibling rather than labeling the child as the abuser.

Studies show that young children are more likely than their older siblings to hit, push or throw objects at a brother or sister. Brother-sister violence is most commonly observed. Less frequently observed is fighting between brothers. Violence between sisters ranks a distant third.

Though sibling abuse has been estimated to be the most frequent manifestation of family violence, it is the least likely to result in death. Sibling murders constituted less than 1.5% of all homicides reported in the United States during 1985. Male siblings were the most frequent perpetrators. Brothers were also six times more likely to be killed than sisters.

Sexual contact between siblings, though legally defined as INCEST, often does not result in a report of child abuse. Exploratory sexual contact between young children is usually seen as a normal part of sexual development. When one or both siblings are adolescents or when contact results in trauma, infection or pregnancy the situation is viewed with greater alarm.

Denial is an important factor in parents' failure to protect a child adequately from sibling attacks. Parents are often embarrassed or afraid of abusive behavior in their children. Once convinced that a child is at risk of serious harm, most parents are able to intervene effectively.

Reasons for sibling attacks range from simple jealousy to family dysfunction to severe PSYCHOPATHOLOGY. It is generally believed that children who have been abused by a caregiver are more likely to behave aggressively toward their peers.

SIDS   *See*   SUDDEN INFANT DEATH SYNDROME.

situational abuse and neglect   Situational abuse and neglect refers to circumstances over which the parents or caretakers have little control. POVERTY and discrimination are such conditions and often are associated with abuse or neglect. Though programs such as Aid to Families with Dependent Children and HEAD

START have helped reduce the effects of such circumstances, many children throughout the world still suffer from the effects of discrimination and poverty.

skeletal survey When child battering is suspected a skeletal survey is often conducted to search for signs of previous battering. Physicians look for signs of multiple FRACTURES of the types most likely to result from abusive treatment. Careful examination of these X rays can reveal OSSIFICATION resulting from previous fractures.

SLAM *See* SOCIETY'S LEAGUE AGAINST MOLESTERS.

slavery, child *See* CHILD SLAVERY.

sleep deprivation Children who are severely abused, physically or psychologically, often do not get adequate sleep. In some cases a noisy, disruptive household or insufficient nutrition may interfere with sleep. Sleep deprivation often impairs intellectual functioning and makes children irritable and distractable. Negative behaviors resulting from a lack of sleep may make children more susceptible to abuse by his or her caretaker.

In severe cases of sleep deprivation secretion of the growth hormone somatotropin is inhibited, causing psychosocial DWARFISM. Cases of abuse-related dwarfism are rare. Once normal sleep patterns are reestablished, children usually experience a period of rapid growth, which in most cases reverses growth inhibition.

slick but sick syndrome The term slick but sick was coined by psychologist Logan Wright and describes the capacity of some abusive parents to hide underlying PSYCHOPATHOLOGY. By comparing convicted child batterers with a carefully matched control group of nonabusing parents, Wright was able to distinguish personality differences between the two groups. On certain psychological tests, batterers gave responses very similar to nonbatterers when the socially desirable answer to a question was logical or apparent. However, answers to the Minnesota Multiphasic Personality Inventory (MMPI), a less-apparent, empirically devised measure of psychopathology, showed that battering parents were actually much more disturbed than they appeared initially. The ability of abusive parents to present themselves as more healthy than they may actually be has been used to explain the often confusing evidence obtained in clinical studies of child abusers. Other researchers have emphasized the importance of societal pressures and stresses over the individual psychopathology of the abuser. The latter hypothesize that almost any parent or caregiver under certain stressful conditions will resort to child abuse. Proponents of the belief that child abusers are emotionally disturbed point to phenomena like the slick but sick syndrome to explain abusive behavior by adults who appear healthy.

social abuse Children often suffer as victims of poverty and discrimination. Most child advocates believe societies, and the governments that represent them, have a responsibility to provide for the safety and well-being of children and families. These responsibilities may include protecting children from all forms of physical, sexual and psychological maltreatment (including racial discrimination), making sure children are well-nourished, have adequate housing and receive necessary medical care. Failure by society to provide for children's basic needs is sometimes referred to as social abuse. Though social abuse is not addressed by child abuse laws, many experts believe it is an indirect cause of much child abuse and neglect.

social isolation Abusive or neglectful parents tend to be isolated from helping networks. Social isolation may be externally imposed in the case of a parent who is ostracized by neighbors and relatives or internally imposed by the parent's choice.

Frequent changes of residence may contribute to social isolation. Abused children may also engage in social WITHDRAWAL, turning inward and isolating themselves from peers, family members and others.

Neglectful parents are significantly less likely to belong to an organization such as a church or parent teacher association. They also have fewer close friends and tend to socialize less often.

One explanation for social isolation is that neglectful parents may be suffering from depression, which renders them incapable of normal social functioning. Another is that parents use detachment from others as a defense. Fearing rejection, they avoid forming close relationships. This may also explain their difficulty in forming a strong attachment to their own children.

A number of methods are used to reduce social isolation and encourage the formation of a network of supporting friends. Individual, group and family therapy may help reduce psychological blocks to developing reciprocal relationships. Groups such as PARENTS ANONYMOUS serve as helping networks and encourage members to be available to one another whenever help is needed. (*See also* WITHDRAWAL.)

social learning model of child abuse
Some theorists explain child abuse as a result of a learned pattern of relating to others. As children, parents may learn violent ways of expressing anger or frustration. Later these maladaptive coping mechanisms may be reflected in a range of aggressive behavior, including child abuse. Social learning theorists often look to parental models as the source of much, but not all, social learning. In contrast to a psychoanalytic approach, which postulates that early experiences leave largely unchangeable emotional imprints, social learning theory holds open the possibility of learning new ways of parenting.

Social Security Act   This federal legislation was initially passed in 1935 and has been amended several times to provide for establishment of various social programs, many of which directly relate to child and family welfare.

Title IV of the act supports state welfare services, i.e., day care, foster care and varied preventive and protective programs. Provisions of Title IV also ensure that child support is paid by absent parents, and provide for establishment of paternity. Originally, Title IV also encompassed funding for states' Aid to Families with Dependent Children programs, but this is now provided under Title XX services to children.

Title V designates monies in support of Maternal and Child Health and other health care services for children from low-income families. Title XIX funds MEDICAID, a medical assistance program for low-income people. Part of this assistance includes psychotherapy services for families and individuals. Title XX establishes state grants for service programs such as prevention of child abuse and neglect; preserving, rehabilitating and reuniting families; and referring individuals to institutions where appropriate.

Mandated protective service agencies serving children receive most of their funding via Title IV and Title XX. In December 1980, passage of an amendment to Title XVIII of the Social Security Act included provisions entitled the Parental Kidnapping Prevention Act of 1980. This altered federal criminal law regarding abduction and transportation of a child across state lines by a parent. It specifically addressed needs of victims of child stealing by parents. The amendment also authorized establishment of a Parent Locator Service to help find children who were abducted by parents.

Socialist Eastern Europe   There are varying degrees of awareness of child abuse and neglect in the Eastern European countries of Bulgaria, Poland, Rumania, Yugoslavia, Hungary and the German Democratic Republic. Despite the impression that these nations ignore the realities of child maltreatment, there is evidence that governments address the issue, at least to some degree. One of the more aggressive actions has been taken by the German Democratic Republic, which has mandatory reporting laws.

According to the United Nations International Year of the Child Secretariat, there have been some studies of children's rights in Hungary and Poland. Further, Poland has been involved since 1978 in helping to codify children's rights worldwide. As part of Poland's contribution to the International Year of the Child, it proposed to the United Nations General Assembly a Draft Convention on the Rights of the Child and is currently part of a committee to make amendments to that draft proposal.

In Hungary, diagnosis of physical abuse has recently been given attention by researchers. Poland has no definitions of child abuse, as it does not recognize abuse as an important social problem and reporting is limited. However, the government has passed legislation dealing with the issues related to child protection in instances of neglect. There are indications that Polish child protection services are viewed as inadequate. Some research suggests that institutional neglect and abuse may exist in Poland, and that social norms provide a setting in which abusive behavior toward children is sustained.

Researchers in Bulgaria note that corporal punishment is denied in some families but that Bulgarian children may be subject to harsh treatment in the form of emotional coldness, hostility, verbal aggression and disapproval.

In Yugoslavia, another country in which some limited studies have been done, intentional child abuse is not a perceived problem, but pre-delinquency is defined as a social issue of some proportion.

Society for the Prevention of Cruelty to Children (United States) Founded in 1875 in New York City, this organization was based on the premise that, "The child is an animal ... If there is no justice for it as a human being, it shall at least have the rights of the stray cur in the street. It shall not be abused." It was among the earliest of the child protective services in the United States.

These words, by one of the founders of the SPCC, Henry Bergh, reveal the need that existed in the United States at a time when cities were growing and child abuse and neglect was being identified by Progressive Era reformers. After five years had passed, the SPCC saw similar groups founded in nearly a dozen other cities.

SPCC efforts focused on court action, gaining custody of children from abusive or neglectful parents and placing them in institutions where they received a modicum of better care.

The SPCC also worked to end child prostitution and child labor. In particular, SPCC workers in New York City were successful in combating the *padrone* system, whereby poor Italian families would pay to send their children to America under the protection of a padrone. The padrone, however, would not send the child's wages back to the parents in Italy, but merely force the child to work for no pay at all.

Society for the Protection of Women and Children from Aggravated Assaults (Britain) This British organization was founded in London, England, in 1857. This early group's activities focused principally on women, although it published *Compassionate Justice*, which was a study of cruelty to children. The latter was part of an attempt to heighten awareness of child abuse and neglect, which several decades later became the subject of well-publicized charitable reform efforts. When this happened, the society worked on behalf of legal changes to benefit abused children.

Society's League Against Molestation (SLAM) A California-based organization that seeks to combat sexual molestation of children. SLAM was formed by the grandmother of a two and one half-year-old girl who was raped and murdered by a mentally disordered sexual offender who had just been released from a treatment program.

sodomy Though the term can refer to any form of sexual intercourse considered to be unnatural according to societal standards, sodomy is most commonly used to refer to anal intercourse between two males. In the context of child SEXUAL ABUSE sodomy is used to describe anal intercourse between an adult male and a child of either sex.

In addition to the emotional trauma caused by sexual abuse, sodomy can also result in physical harm to children. Sodomy is especially painful for young children who are likely to suffer anal tears or enlargement. Diseases such as gonorrhea and syphilis can also be conveyed through anal intercourse. Presence of a SEXUALLY TRANSMITTED DISEASE in a child is strong, but all too frequently overlooked, evidence of sexual abuse.

Children who have been subjected to sodomy may be reluctant to reveal their victimization but may complain of anal discomfort, and may soil undergarments or exhibit other somatic and behavioral signs of trauma. (*See also* ENCOPRESIS.)

soiling *See* ENCOPRESIS.

Sovereign Immunity, Doctrine of   *See* DOCTRINE OF SOVEREIGN IMMUNITY.

Soviet Union *See* USSR.

spanking *See* AVERSIVE CONDITIONING.

special child *See* TARGET CHILD.

spinal cord injury *See* CENTRAL NERVOUS SYSTEM INJURY.

splitting Splitting refers to an intrapsychic process often employed by children who have been abused. Unable to understand how a parent can be both good and bad, children split positive and negative attributes and see others and themselves as either good or bad. This process may lead to the creation of scapegoats or a PARENTIFIED CHILD.

In the case of a child who sees the parent as only good and therefore incapable of doing wrong, the child interprets the parent's abusive behavior as a reflection of his or her own badness. The child may then become a willing scapegoat, actually seeking out punishment.

The parentified child, identifying with the good parent, seeks to fill the role of the neglectful or abusive parent. Parentification is reflected in a kind of pseudo-maturity that exceeds the child's years. Often taking on extra household responsibilities and working hard in school, this child cannot do enough to please. When abused or neglected by the parent the child redoubles efforts to please.

spouse abuse Spouse abuse includes physical and mental injury of a wife or husband by their marital partner. Though spouse abuse refers to the victimization of either partner, the overwhelming majority of such abuse involves battering of wives by their husbands.

Wife-battering appears to be closely associated with child abuse. One study of mothers and their children in battered women's shelters found that 70% of children had been abused or neglected. In most cases the husband was responsible for the child abuse. About one-fourth of the children were abused by both mother and father. A very small number were abused by the mother only. (*See also* FAMILY VIOLENCE and YO-YO SYNDROME.)

staff flight Maintaining qualified, well-trained and experienced protective service workers is a constant struggle in agencies charged with investigating and treating child abuse. Turnover rate among staff in these agencies has been estimated at 85% per year. While efforts to improve working conditions, provide additional training and ensure higher salaries have helped, the stressful nature of protective service work continues to contribute to early staff burnout. Social workers and investigators often find themselves working alone in highly charged emotional situations. Abusive parents or caretakers, frightened and angry when confronted, often direct their anger toward the protective service employee. Working with children who have been abused can also prove to be frustrating and heart-wrenching work for the human service professional who is sometimes powerless to reverse the effects of abuse. Over a period of time even the most highly motivated and best trained protective services worker may become discouraged and alienated from his or her work.

standard of proof   *See*   EVIDENTIARY STANDARDS.

Stanley v. Illinois   This case, decided by the United States Supreme Court in 1971, involved an unwed father who, upon the death of his children's mother, was not allowed custody of his three children. The state of Illinois invoked a law automatically making children of unmarried fathers wards of the state upon death of the mother. The father, Peter Stanley, petitioned the court for custody of his children, arguing that he had been denied equal protection under the law as granted in the Fourteenth Amendment to the U.S. Constitution.

The Supreme Court reversed the Illinois decision and granted custody to the father. *Stanley v. Illinois* is often cited as establishing the principle that prevents a state from separating children from their parents unless, by due process, the parent is proven to be unfit.

Robert H. Mnookin, *Child, Family and State: Problems and Materials on Children and the Law* (Boston: Little, Brown, 1978).

starvation   One of the most extreme results of child neglect is death from starvation. Though rare in the most Western countries, cases of starvation continue to surface every year. In some African countries where drought and war have severely restricted food supply, starving infants and children are a common sight. Starvation in third world countries is often described as a form of societal neglect. However, many experts are reluctant to characterize poverty-induced starvation as abuse or neglect.

In contrast to deaths from inadequate nutrition in developing countries, child starvation in developed countries is generally thought to be intentional. The most frequent victims are infants who appear to have been totally neglected. A high percentage tend to be born prematurely to mothers of low intelligence who already have large families. Though undernourished children usually respond quickly to proper care and nutrition in a hospital, they rarely receive such attention. Autopsies of starved infants usually show other evidence of gross neglect.

status offense   The term status offense refers to an action that is considered to be a criminal or delinquent act when engaged in by a person under a certain age, usually 16 years. A status offense may involve repeatedly defying parents' wishes, running away from home or being truant from school. In the United States many states have eliminated legal sanctions for status offenses, opting instead for categories such as CHINS (Child In Need of Services) or FWSN (Families With Service Needs). These new categories allow for court intervention in difficult cases; however, the court's role is often to provide an ASSESSMENT, make recommendations and monitor compliance with those recommendations.

stifling   *See* OVERLAYING.

stimulation, tactile   *See* TACTILE STIMULATION.

stipulation   At the beginning of a trial lawyers for both parties may enter into an oral or written agreement concerning certain facts of the case that are uncontested. These facts may include names and addresses of persons involved, relationships among the parties, ages etc. The stipulation serves as a basis for introduction of EVIDENCE and limits debate to those areas about which there is clear disagreement.

stomach, turned   *See* OPU HULE.

stress   Stress of various kinds is frequently associated with child abuse and neglect. Factors such as marital difficulty, POVERTY, work-related problems and SOCIAL ISOLATION have all been found to be related to increased levels of child abuse. Despite the association between stress and abuse it may not be correct to say that stress causes abuse. Many parents under a great deal of stress do not abuse or neglect their children.

Murray Straus, a noted researcher of FAMILY VIOLENCE, emphasizes the importance of mediating factors in establishing the link between stress and child maltreatment. Parents who were abused by their parents, in particular by the father, or who witnessed violence between their parents were more likely to abuse their own children. Straus suggests that violent responses to stress are learned, not innate.

Parents under stress are usually not uncontrollably driven to abuse their children. Parents who are abusive are more likely to approve of physical violence as a means of settling disputes. Marital violence is a strong predictor of child abuse. Both of these findings support the idea that parents who approve of or who regularly use physical force as a way of coping also abuse their children more often. Stress may increase the likelihood that parents who approve of violence will abuse their children but does not, by itself, produce violence.

Though stress may not directly cause child abuse, increases in family and societal stress may result in higher levels of abuse. Periods of high unemployment are frequently accompanied by increased family violence. Extreme poverty appears to increase the likelihood of abuse. Interestingly, however, occupational status and level of education do not appear to be related to abuse.

Learning how to cope with stress effectively is an important part of the treatment for perpetrators of child abuse. In many cases, parents are taught specific alternatives to physical punishment as a method of discipline or releasing frustrations. Groups such as PARENTS ANONYMOUS place a great deal of importance on establishing support networks for parents under stress. Parents who have a number of contacts outside the family are usually better able to cope with stress than those who are relatively isolated.

subdural hematoma   Battering or shaking may result in intracranial hemorrhaging, causing blood to collect immediately beneath the skull. This collection of blood, known as subdural hematoma, is usually caused by the tearing of veins running from the cerebral cortex to the dural sinuses.

Subdural hematoma may occur on only one side of the brain (lateral) or on both sides of the brain (bilateral). Eighty percent of all subdural hematomas in children are bilateral.

Almost all subdural hematoma are caused by trauma induced by the head striking or being struck by a heavy object, or by the rapid jerking motion of the head when an infant is shaken.

Although the most frequent cause of death in battered infants, it may also be one of the most frequently overlooked injuries. The absence of external signs, even in the presence of massive internal bleeding, make diagnosis difficult. Subdural hematoma can be detected through the presence of blood in the subdural and cerebrospinal fluid and through the use of cranial computed tomography (CT).

subgaleal hematoma   A collection of blood immediately underneath the scalp, called subgaleal hematoma, can be the result of HAIRPULLING. Blood accumulation is caused by the rupture of blood vessels attached to the outside of the cranium.

subpoena Witnesses and accused perpetrators of child abuse may be subpoenaed to testify in court. The most common type of subpoena is sometimes referred to by its Latin name, *subpoena ad testificandum*. This type of subpoena is a written document, issued by a court or authorized agency, that requires the recipient to appear in a specified court at a certain day and time. Subpoena is literally translated as "under penalty." Failure to comply with a subpoena can result in a fine or imprisonment.

A *subpoena duces tecum*, literally, under penalty take with you, requires the recipient to bring certain relevant documents to court. In child abuse or neglect cases this type of subpoena may be issued to a physician or mental health professional, requiring them to submit treatment records of the victim or alleged abuser. Normally such information is considered PRIVILEGED COMMUNICATIONS; however, in many jurisdictions child abuse reporting laws specifically abrogate such privileges when abuse or neglect is suspected.

substance abuse Parental abuse of alcohol and other drugs can affect the child in two ways. Substance abuse during pregnancy can result in neonatal addiction and birth defects (*see* ADDICTION, INFANTILE). After birth, substance abuse by parents greatly increases the likelihood that a child will be abused or neglected.

It has been estimated that one-third of all child abuse is alcohol-related. One study found that 41% of families with an addicted parent abused or neglected at least one child. The same study found that 42% of drug- or alcohol-addicted parents had been physically or sexually abused as children.

Research also shows that heavy use of marijuana during pregnancy can produce exaggerated tremors, vision problems and startle reflexes in newborns. Heroin and other opiates contribute to low birth weight and increase the risk of stillbirth and infant mortality. Phencyclidine (PCP), also known as "angel dust," can remain in the system for over a year and may be transported through breast milk and amniotic fluid. This is particularly dangerous since very low amounts of PCP can produce psychosis, teratogenesis (embryonic tumors) or developmental delay.

Infants born to addicted women sometimes display tremors, irritability, prolonged shrill crying, fever, vomiting, watery stools and other withdrawal symptoms. Severity of withdrawal seems to be in proportion to the amount of drug consumed by the mother on a daily basis

Heavy drinking during pregnancy can produce a number of birth defects and abnormalities, including those associated with FETAL ALCOHOL SYNDROME.

Drugs also play a large role in the sexual exploitation of children. One-third of all sexual assaults on children take place while the perpetrator is under the influence of alcohol.

Looking for excitement and sometimes running from abuse at home, young girls and boys are often lured into drug usage by pimps. PROSTITUTION becomes a means of obtaining drugs that, in turn, offer escape from the experience of emotional pain and lowered self-esteem associated with this lifestyle.

substantiation The accuracy of suspected abuse or neglect reports is determined through a process known as substantiation. Confirmed reports are referred to as FOUNDED or substantiated. Substantiation of suspected abuse or neglect is a prerequisite for further action by a child protection agency. In EMERGENCIES the substantiation decision may be made immediately by the authorized protective service worker. Nonemergency decisions are usually made after all results of an investigation are available. In such situations the substantiation decision may be made in consultation with a supervisor or MULTIDISCIPLINARY TEAM. Standards applied to investigation of reports vary according to local definitions of abuse and protective service agency policies.

Table 16
Substantiation Rates by State, 1981–1985*

	1981	1982	1983	1984	1985
Arkansas	34.0	38.0	37.0	36.0	37.0
Colorado[a]	60.0	59.0	57.0	63.0	65.0
Florida	47.0	49.0	49.0	53.3	57.3
Hawaii	53.0	54.0	48.0	51.0	57.0
Illinois	43.1	46.6	44.1	45.6	49.2
Iowa	20.2	17.5	23.2	25.9	24.6
Kansas[b]	34.0	34.0	33.0	33.0	28.0
Kentucky	49.0	47.0	44.0	44.0	44.0
Louisiana[b,c]	33.0	34.0	36.0	37.0	37.0
Maine	56.0	61.0	49.0	52.0	51.0
Michigan[b,c]	43.0	41.0	41.0	40.0	39.0
Mississippi	55.0	44.0	48.0	50.0	51.0
Nebraska	50.2	43.6	45.9	53.3	60.6
Nevada	52.0	51.0	56.0	55.0	52.0
New York[b]	37.8	37.9	34.4	36.0	37.0
North Carolina	41.5	40.6	40.8	39.0	39.0
North Dakota	49.9	49.5	54.1	60.1	58.7
Oklahoma[c]	37.0	39.0	40.0	36.0	35.0
Oregon	75.3	88.6	89.4	60.5	66.7
Pennsylvania	34.2	32.9	35.4	37.0	36.8
South Carolina[c]	36.0	33.0	31.0	32.0	30.0
South Dakota	78.0[d]	72.0[d]	52.0	46.0	44.0
Texas	60.8	61.8	60.4	57.4	55.6
Utah	33.7[c]	29.1	31.7	35.5	32.8
Vermont	45.0	52.0	50.0	50.0	52.0
Virginia[c]	39.0	31.9	28.8	28.2	24.6
West Virginia[e]	40.0	40.0	40.0	40.0	40.0
Wisconsin	18.0	19.9	24.6	33.3	30.3
Wyoming[b]	34.0	45.0	44.0	45.0	64.0
Average substantiation rate for 29 states	44.5%	44.6%	43.7%	44.0%	44.8%

*Twenty-nine states provided substantiation data for all years requested, 1981–1985.
[a]Percent of substantiated reports may be higher for Colorado than other states because counts of substantiated reports going into state registry were screened by counties before submission.
[b]State provided totals representing family reports and child reports, but did not indicate whether percent substantiated reports represented either or both types of reports.
[c]State totals and percents are state fiscal year counts, not calendar year totals.
[d]South Dakota reported "it is felt that there were procedural reporting issues that caused such a high substantiation rate [for 1981–1982]."
[e]West Virginia percents "are estimates. The substantiation rate varies from geographic location to geographic location . . ."

Table 17
Substantiation Rates by State, 1985†

State	Percent	State	Percent
Alabama[a]	39.0	Nevada	52.0
Arkansas	37.0	New Jersey	38.3
Colorado[b]	65.0	New Mexico	57.0
Connecticut	70.0	New York[e]	37.0
Delaware[c]	55.6	North Carolina	39.0
Florida	57.3	North Dakota	58.7
Hawaii	57.0	Ohio	23.2
Idaho	46.7	Oklahoma[f]	35.0
Illinois	49.2	Oregon	66.7
Indiana[d]	52.3	Pennsylvania	36.8
Iowa	24.6	Rhode Island	45.6
Kansas[e]	28.0	South Carolina[f]	30.0
Kentucky	44.0	South Dakota	44.0
Louisiana[e,f]	37.0	Texas	55.6
Maine	51.0	Utah	32.8
Massachusetts	38.0	Vermont	52.0
Michigan[e,f]	39.0	Virginia[f]	24.6
Mississippi	51.0	West Virginia[g]	40.0
Missouri[e]	44.1	Wisconsin	30.3
Montana	50.0	Wyoming[e]	64.0
Nebraska	60.6		
Average substantiation rate for 41 states:	45.3%		

†Forty-one states provided substantiation data for 1985.
[a] Alabama estimated substantiation through telephone survey.
[b] Percent of substantiated reports may be higher for Colorado than other states because counts of substantiated reports going into state registry were screened by counties before submission.
[c] Delaware totals reported are duplicated and may involve one or several children; reports are incident based.
[d] Indiana provided percent of 1985 reports substantiated for two types of reports: neglect reports—48.8%, and abuse reports—52.3%.
[e] State provided totals representing family reports and child reports, but did not indicate whether percent of reports substantiated was based on either or both types of reports.
[f] State totals and percents are state fiscal year counts, not calendar year totals.
[g] West Virginia percents "are estimates. The substantiation rate varies from geographic location to geographic location . . ."

In the United States, the percentage of substantiated child abuse and neglect reports declined during the 1970s. Since 1981 this percentage has remained at approximately 44%. However, as the tables indicate, substantiation rates vary widely from state to state.

Research suggests that reports filed by professionals are more likely to be substantiated than those filed by others. Reasons for this phenomenon are not clear. Some writers speculate that professionals may be more familiar with diagnostic procedures and legal definitions of abuse and therefore are better able to judge when a report should be filed. Professionals may also be more cooperative with investigators and more likely to follow up on their reports. In one study of reported abuse and neglect in New York (Eckenrode et al.), researchers found substantiation rates for professionals' reports to be 26% higher for neglect, 23% higher for physical abuse and 11% higher for sexual abuse.

Anonymous reports tend to have the lowest substantiation rates of all sources. This has led some policy analysts to suggest that agencies refuse to accept referrals from unidentified sources. Most agencies continue to accept such reports though many use telephone screening to eliminate those that are obviously frivolous.

Recently, concern over the investigation and substantiation process has increased. Some parent groups have argued that parents are often subjected to stressful and unnecessary investigation.

Increased pressure from groups such as VOCAL (Victims of Child Abuse Laws) has made the difficult decision of substantiation even harder. Though most people agree on such decisions when the situation is obviously life-threatening, the majority of cases involve less clear-cut circumstances. Often the decision boils down to a combination of skill, experience and intuition on the part of protective service personnel. (*See also* FOUNDED REPORT, INVESTIGATION and UNFOUNDED REPORT.)

substantive due process   *See* DUE PROCESS.

sudden infant death syndrome (SIDS)
The sudden unexpected death of an infant in which there is no recognized lethal condition. Also known as crib death and cot death, sudden infant death syndrome (SIDS) has been the subject of wide speculation and heated debate within the medical community. Though child abuse and neglect are generally acknowledged as possible causes of SIDS, much disagreement exists as to the percentages of deaths attributable to these factors.

One of the first recorded mentions of SIDS can be found in the well-known biblical account of King Solomon. Solomon was asked to settle a dispute between two women who claimed to be the mother of the same infant. One mother's infant had died previously as a result of OVERLAYING. This dispute over the existing infant was, of course, settled when Solomon proposed that the child be cut in two. The woman who relinquished her claim in order to save the child was determined to be the true mother.

Until the 19th century, overlaying was considered the primary cause of SIDS. Death was attributed to the mother inadvertently rolling on top of the infant, thereby suffocating it.

Overlaying was thought to be preventable and was punished by the early Roman Catholic and Anglican churches. In the 17th century the *arcuccio* was invented to prevent overlaying. This arch made of wood and steel was placed over the baby to prevent suffocation or stifling, as it was called. Failure to use this device was a punishable offense in some countries. References to use of the *arcuccio* can be found as late as 1890.

Physicians, baffled by a lack of identifiable symptoms, have suspected many different causes for SIDS. The belief that death was related to an enlarged thymus gland led to the practice of preventative irradiation of the thymus during the 1930s and 1940s. This safety measure was later found to cause cancer. A large thymus gland is now considered a common characteristic of most infants.

SIDS has also been attributed to hypersensitivity to milk, viral infections, dietary deficiencies, respiratory infection, a reaction to the household dust mite, botulism and sleep apnea. The possibility of INFANTICIDE has been suggested by many physicians.

Epidemiologic studies in the United States have established the rate of SIDS at about 2.3 per thousand live births. Most deaths occur between the ages of one and six months. SIDS is most likely to occur during the winter months and is more common in poor and nonwhite populations. Infant victims are more likely to have been born prematurely and to have had a low birth weight and a minor respiratory infection.

Mothers of infants who die from SIDS tend to be younger than average and are less likely to seek medical treatment for their children. Drug addicted mothers have been found to be five to nine times more likely to have infants die of SIDS.

Though some parents of SIDS infants are described as unintentionally neglectful, many may have provided excellent emotional and physical care.

Sudden infant death syndrome is a distressing and puzzling phenomenon. Its cause cannot be attributed to any one factor. Conditions such as sleep apnea are strongly suspected in some cases. Though the number of SIDS deaths in which abuse or neglect are a major cause is thought to be small, it is difficult to determine the number of maltreatment-related deaths with any acceptable degree of accuracy.

Warren G. Guntheroth, *Crib Death: The Sudden Infant Death Syndrome* (Mount Kisco, N.Y.: Futura, 1982).

supervision   The term supervision is used in three different ways when speaking of child abuse and neglect. First, supervision may refer to the responsibility for protecting and guiding a child, usually a parental responsibility.

When a child protection agency invested with authority to intervene determines that a child's caretakers are not giving adequate supervision it may assume responsibility for the child.

Supervision also refers to oversight of a case by the child protection worker. Under this meaning of the word the entire family is the subject of supervision. Such intervention is usually guided by a SERVICE PLAN that outlines specific tasks and objectives for the family. The primary function of the child protection worker is to ensure that the family is taking steps necessary for protection of the child.

Finally, the process by which cases are reviewed is also referred to as supervision. Case review usually involves a meeting between the child protection worker and his or her superior to discuss both the family's progress and the worker's management of the case. This type of supervision helps make sure proper procedures are followed and may delay or prevent BURNOUT. Ongoing support and instruction are particularly important for counteracting job-related stress and maintaining the morale of child protection workers.

supporting services   Abusive and neglectful parents are often subject to social, emotional and economic stress. Prevention of further maltreatment of children may require addressing the underlying causes of family stress as well as direct treatment of the abuse.

Support services include a wide variety of human services that help families function more effectively. Impoverished families will benefit from economic assistance, possibly in the form of CATEGORICAL AID. Other services include vocational training, educational assistance, child care and recreation. In some cases, support services alone may be sufficient to reduce family stress to a manageable level.

surrogate parent   Children who are abused or neglected by their parents may benefit from a surrogate parent. The surrogate may be a relative, family member or a trained PARENT AIDE. Children benefit from additional nurturance and direction given by a surrogate parent, and biological parents can learn child care skills by the surrogate's example. In some cases the surrogate actually acts as a parent to abusive or neglectful parents, giving them emotional support and direction. Surrogate parents may be especially helpful to young or emotionally immature parents.

suspected child abuse and neglect team
See SCAN TEAM.

suspended judgment   *See* DISPOSITION.

swaddling The ancient custom of tightly wrapping infants in a long strip of cloth is still practiced in some cultures. Swaddling restricts the child's movements and is said by critics to be physically, socially and emotionally damaging. In Turkey some mothers swaddle their infants and strap them to their backs while working or traveling. Though held to be abusive in most Western countries, swaddling is considered simply a convenient way of carrying an infant in other cultures.

Sweden As with other Scandinavian countries, Sweden recognizes the existence of child abuse and neglect; but as a social problem of large proportion it seems not to exist. In 1957, the Swedish National Board of Health drew up regulations to address the issue of child abuse and a research institute was established to study the problem. Swedish society comprises many welfare components, among them extensive state-funded child care facilities. It appears that some tensions and frustrations contributing to child maltreatment in other cultures may not develop as quickly or easily in Sweden.

In general, physical punishment of children has long been recognized in Sweden as a less-than-desirable disciplinary procedure. In 1966, the Parenthood and Guardianship Code removed the previously sanctioned parental right to beat a child without fear of legal prosecution under the Criminal Code. In July 1979, a law that forbade all physical punishment of children was enacted. (*See also* COMMISSION ON CHILDREN'S RIGHTS, 1978.)

Richard J. Gelles and Ake W. Edfeldt, "Violence Towards Children in the United States and Sweden," *Child Abuse and Neglect*, 10(1986), pp. 501-510.

syphilis The most damaging of the VENEREAL DISEASES, syphilis attacks the heart, blood vessels, spinal cord, brain and bones as well as the genitals. It can be fatal. Sexual intercourse is the primary method by which spirochetes, the common name of the syphilis bacterium, are transmitted. Syphilis can also be contracted through kissing and through contact with open sores.

Chancres (pimples, blisters or open sores) appear about three weeks after infection. Early treatment with penicillin is usually effective; however, some penicillin-resistant strains have developed. Treatment can stop the disease but cannot reverse physiological damage done to the brain and spinal cord.

Congenital syphilis passed to an infant from an infected mother can weaken bones, causing lesions in the joints and periosteum. These lesions are sometimes mistaken for battering-induced wounds. Blood tests and the presence of other symptoms can aid in accurate diagnosis.

The appearance of syphilis in a child is a strong indicator of SEXUAL ABUSE. A blood test for syphilis is an important part of a comprehensive medical examination for children who have been sexually assaulted.

T

tactile stimulation Touching and holding infants appears to be important for their healthy sensory and emotional development. Early studies of HOSPITALISM led researchers to conclude that, in addition to adequate food and shelter, close physical and emotional contact with a nurturing adult is essential for normal development. Infants who did not receive such contact appeared dull and listless. Several eventually died despite availability of sufficient food, shelter and medical care.

Some experts speculate that FAILURE TO THRIVE SYNDROME is due not only to inadequate nutrition but to a lack of tactile stimulation as well. Parents who fail to develop an attachment to their infant may be cold and physically rejecting. Deprived infants can often be recognized by their eagerness to be held by strangers at a time when others their age demonstrate a normal fear of strangers.

Parents who were neglected as children often have a difficult time learning how to hold and touch their babies. Often they must be taught how to touch, rock and soothe their infants. Those who were physically or sexually abused must often overcome negative associations with physical contact. Some early intervention programs focus on teaching high-risk parents how to touch, hold and care for their infants in a positive and mutually enjoyable way. (*See also* EMOTIONAL NEGLECT, BONDING FAILURE.)

Taiwan There is little or no official recognition, either by health care professionals or the government, of child abuse and neglect in Taiwan. Traditional Chinese family structure in Taiwan is built along lines similar to those found in the cultures of some other developing nations, that is, there is a strong emphasis on respect and obedience to adults. In Taiwan, filial piety has its roots in ancient Chinese teachings, and variations on this theme of complete obedience to parents by children are still stressed today.

Some actions toward children that would be considered marginally or explicitly abusive in the West—twisting the ear or pinching the face, kicking and beating, hitting the head—are in fact disciplinary behaviors in Taiwan. Similarly, the parent-child bond in Taiwan, influenced by strong notions of filial piety, might be considered emotionally unhealthy or even abusive by some Western standards.

Jill E. Korbin, ed. *Child Abuse and Neglect: Cross-Cultural Perspectives* (Berkeley: University of California Press, 1981).

Tardieu, Ambroise A 19th-century professor of legal medicine who lived in Paris, Ambroise Tardieu is credited with being the first person to note and describe the group of symptoms that would later be called the BATTERED CHILD SYNDROME. He also wrote descriptions of parents who abused their children and of the sociocultural conditions that give rise to child abuse. Much of what he reported is consistent with modern research findings.

target child Typically, one child in a family is singled out as the target of abuse. Reasons for selection of a particular child are not fully understood. In some cases the child may be considered difficult or frustrating, for example, an infant who cries frequently; in other cases the child may have a physical deformity or simply be considered unattractive by the parent. Through a process known as SCAPEGOATING the child becomes identified to the parent(s) as a "problem child." Because the target child may, indeed, be difficult to care for, he or she may be accused of causing the abuse. Attempts to rationalize abuse of a target child often result in BLAMING THE VICTIM. Focusing on the abused child's negative behavior may divert attention from the parent's inappropriate or brutal handling of the situation.

Treatment of the abuser seeks to change negative attitudes toward the target child. Often, peer support groups such as PARENTS ANONYMOUS and parent training are helpful in presenting different ways in which parents can respond to frustrating situations.

team, community *See* COMMUNITY TEAM.

termination of parental rights A court may determine that it is in the best interest of an abused or neglected child legally to end all ties between the child and his or her biological parent. Once parental rights have been terminated the child is free for adoption by another family. Exact criteria for termination vary according to location; however, the following are examples of grounds that are considered sufficient in many areas.

- Abandonment
- Severe alcohol or drug abuse by the parent(s)
- Parent is mentally retarded or seriously mentally ill
- Repeated abuse or neglect of the child
- Child has been in foster care for a significant period of time and the parents either have not made a serious attempt to improve the conditions that led to the child's removal or have not cooperated with plans for the child to return home.

In most locations juvenile or family courts have jurisdiction over parental rights. Though EVIDENTIARY STANDARDS differ, most states require CLEAR AND CONVINCING EVIDENCE that parents are unfit or that the BEST INTERESTS OF THE CHILD will be served by terminating parental rights.

Child advocates differ in their ideas about the process for termination of parental rights. Some believe children should remain with the natural parents in all but clearly life-threatening or permanently and severely damaging situations. Supporters of this view emphasize the need for more and better interventions to help maintain the child at home and oppose efforts to make it easier to terminate parental

rights. Another point of view focuses on the potential danger to the child of remaining in an abusive situation and the damaging effects of frequent or prolonged foster placement. This group believes the decision of whether to terminate parents' rights should be made relatively quickly to avoid long periods of uncertainty and to free the child for adoption at an earlier age. (*See also* PARENTS' RIGHTS.)

tertiary prevention *See* PREVENTION.

testimony Most EVIDENCE produced in trials related to child abuse and neglect takes the form of testimony. This type of evidence includes any written or spoken statement made under oath to establish a fact. Testimony is usually given in court in the presence of both the plaintiff and defendant. WITNESSES presenting testimony on behalf of one party are subject to questioning, or cross-examination, by the opposing party.

Usually, only testimony concerning facts directly observed or otherwise perceived by the witness are admissible in court. Hearsay testimony, involving observations made by persons other than the witness, is allowed only under certain circumstances. Some courts allow introduction of hearsay testimony in preliminary hearings. In such cases an adult, usually the person who conducted the initial INVESTIGATION, is allowed to testify concerning the nature of alleged abuse. Judges usually allow this type of testimony in an effort to protect children from trauma associated with repeated court appearances.

Under the rules of *res gestae* statements made during the excitement of an event may also be admitted as evidence. This rule is often referred to as the EXCITED UTTERANCE exception to the hearsay rule. Remarks made by a child to a teacher, parent, caseworker or similar party in a state of excitement following an abusive incident are allowed as testimony even though they are technically hearsay. Excited utterances are allowed under the theory that the urgency of the circumstances eliminates the element of self-interest, there-

Table 18

HINTS FOR TESTIFYING

- Dress appropriately.
- Prepare ahead of time.
- Don't memorize your testimony.
- Expect to feel anxious.
- Speak a little louder and slower than you feel is necessary.
- Be sincere and dignified.
- Speak clearly and distinctly.
- Use appropriate language.
- Answer the question that was asked.
- Let the attorney develop your testimony.
- If you don't know the answer to a question, say so. Don't guess.
- Don't make your testimony conform to other testimony you may have heard.
- When answering questions, look at the person asking the questions or at the judge or jury.
- Tell the truth.

How to survive cross-examination:

- Be careful about what you say and how you say it.
- Listen carefully to the question; don't answer it unless you understand it.
- If a question has two parts requiring different answers, answer it in two parts.
- Keep calm.
- Answer positively rather than doubtfully.
- If you are testifying as an expert, be prepared to reconcile or distinguish your opinion from opposing schools of thought.
- Don't close yourself off from supplying additional details.
- Don't allow yourself to be rushed.
- Don't get caught by a trick question.

Source: U.S. Department of Health and Human Services, Office of Human Development Services, Administration for Children, Youth and Families, Children's Bureau, National Center on Child Abuse and Neglect, *Child Protection: The Role of the Courts* (Washington, D.C.: Government Printing Office: 1980; [OHDS] 80-30256), 1980; p. 59.

fore increasing the likelihood that the statement is true. Timeliness is important in determining the admissibility of a res gestae statement. Statements made after a significant passage of time are not likely to be admitted as testimony. However, the precise amount of time allowed between the alleged abuse and the child's excited utterance is unclear. In at least one case, *State of Rhode Island v. Creighton*, the court accepted as evidence a statement made 14 hours after the event. The Rhode Island court reasoned that there was sufficient evidence in the record to establish that the victim was still under stress at the time of the statement.

Testifying in court can be a frightening experience for an adult. The experience may be terrifying for a child. Victims of SEXUAL ABUSE are frequently asked to describe embarrassing and traumatic experiences in a large, formal courtroom in the presence of the alleged assailant. Some experts characterize the formal process of testifying in court as equally traumatic as the abuse itself.

Recently, steps have been taken to make the process of testifying less traumatic to the child. Some courts attempt to reduce the number of court appearances required of a child. Provisions for separate waiting rooms prevent children from having to share a room with defense witnesses. Increasingly, courts allow children to testify IN CAMERA, on videotape or through closed-circuit television. These methods of testifying may eliminate some of the trauma of a court appearance. Measures that interfere with the defendant's right to cross-examine a witness are not permitted.

In sexual abuse trials NATURAL DOLLS may be used as aids to testimony. Children are often embarrassed to talk about genitalia and may use idiosyncratic terminology. Use of anatomically correct dolls can both reduce embarrassment and allow for clearer testimony.

Others who may testify in child abuse hearings include anyone who may have observed the abuse, police or child protection workers who conducted the initial investigation, character witnesses and relevant experts.

testimony, videotaped *See* VIDEOTAPED TESTIMONY.

therapeutic day care centers Specialized day care centers that provide both supervision and treatment of abused children are a valuable resource for child protection. Structured treatment usually focuses on behavioral and educational problems of children who have been abused. Therapeutic day care may be used by children in FOSTER CARE or while children remain at home. Usually, families of children in therapeutic day care are simultaneously receiving treatment at the center or from an outside provider.

throwaway children A significant proportion of children labeled as runaways are actually throwaways. The term throwaway refers to a child who is forced or encouraged to leave home by parents or caretakers. This form of extreme NEGLECT affects adolescents as well as younger children. An estimated 10% to 20% of children housed in runaway shelters are throwaways. Though the throwaway is often labeled a problem child, the parent's inability or unwillingness to care for him or her is a significant factor in the child's behavioral difficulty.

Tinker v. Des Moines Independent School District In 1965, a group of school children was prohibited by the Des Moines, Iowa, School District from wearing black armbands to protest hostilities in Vietnam. Students who wore the armbands were suspended from school. The children, through their parents, filed a petition in U.S. District Court to prohibit the school system from disciplining them for expression of their political beliefs. After a hearing, the court found in favor of the school district, citing their right to take reasonable actions to prevent a disturbance. This decision was appealed to the U.S. Supreme Court, which in 1969 reversed the lower court's decision, holding that children as well as adults have a right to freedom of speech under the First Amendment to the Constitution of the United States.

The Supreme Court's ruling in *Tinker v. Des Moines* established an important legal precedent for children's rights. By ruling that children are entitled to specific rights the court recognized them as independent individuals with their own interests. Though subsequent decisions have modified the scope of children's rights, the principles confirmed in this case have afforded children much greater legal protection than they had previously enjoyed.

tithingman In 17th-century Massachusetts, most communities, divided into church parishes, relied on a tithingman to determine whether families met responsibilities toward their members and toward society in general. A tithingman (whose presence was based on English tradition) could arrest individuals for legal infractions and could intervene in family disputes. A tithingman was responsible for judging whether parents were fulfilling their duties toward their children. The concept was devised as a way of ensuring social order rather than as a means of protecting children. Parents who did not act responsibly were seen as threats to community welfare.

toe tourniquet syndrome   Emotionally disturbed parents have been known to strangle their children's appendages, such as toes or fingers, by tying hair or thread around the base. Restricted blood flow can cause severe pain and may result in loss of the appendage.

This relatively rare practice is apparently related to a superstitious belief of unknown origin. Most frequent victims of this form of abuse are infants from six weeks to 10 months of age. When toe tourniquet syndrome is suspected, evidence may be found in the form of loose threads or hairs in bedclothing or garments. Thorough examination by a physician may also help determine the cause of injury.

trafficking, sexual   *See* SEXUAL TRAFFICKING.

trauma   The term trauma is most often used to describe an injury, wound or shock, of any kind, to the body. PHYSICAL ABUSE often leaves visible signs of trauma on a child's body.

Trauma can also refer to a painful or damaging emotional experience. This kind of trauma is present in virtually all types of child abuse. Emotional trauma is usually concomitant with physical trauma but may endure long after all signs of physical injury have disappeared. Victims of child abuse often report nightmares, flashbacks or panic attacks long after the danger of abuse is gone

Support and therapy groups are available in many areas to help both child and adult survivors of abuse overcome the effects of emotional trauma associated with abuse. For more information on such groups, see APPENDIX 1.

trauma X   Another name for child abuse, most frequently used in medical facilities. Some hospitals use the term trauma X to refer to a child abuse and neglect program. For instance, the Trauma X Team at Boston Children's Hospital was an early example of a MULTIDISCIPLINARY TEAM.

treatment   Abuse and neglect victims usually require specialized treatment to restore their physical and emotional well-being. When parents or other family members are responsible for maltreatment, family therapy is often recommended to prevent further danger to the child. Perpetrators of abuse outside the family usually receive individual psychiatric treatment.

Diagnosis and planning for treatment of abuse and neglect is often carried out by a MULTIDISCIPLINARY TEAM, which includes professionals with specialized training in pediatrics, psychiatry, psychology, social work and child protection. In some cases a child protection worker is responsible for providing all treatment directly. More often, treatment takes many different forms and is given by professionals with different skills. When indirect methods are used, the child protection caseworker is responsible for coordinating treatment and monitoring the client's progress. Specific methods employed in treatment of child abuse and neglect include: individual counseling, group counseling, marital or family counseling, educational treatment (such as parent education), a friendly visitor (usually a peer who can provide emotional support), psychotherapy, therapeutic day care or day treatment, FOSTER CARE, HOMEMAKER SERVICES, SELF-HELP GROUPS and medical care.

The decision of which methods to use is based on a psychosocial ASSESSMENT of the situation. Although treatment usually includes other members of the family, the child's safety and well-being is the ultimate goal of all treatment for abuse or neglect. In addition to protecting the child, a series of specific treatment goals are included in a SERVICE PLAN. Progress toward goals is monitored by the caseworker and forms the basis for decisions to terminate the protective service agency's involvement.

Treatment of certain types of abusers may be highly specialized. Some sexual offenders have proven to be resistant to traditional methods of psychiatric treatment. Recently several innovative approaches to treatment of sexual offenders have been employed by forensic mental health specialists. These methods usually involve a combination of behavioral and group therapy.

Victims of SEXUAL ABUSE may also require special treatment. Sexually abused children must be helped to overcome the tendency to blame themselves for their abuse and to learn new ways of relating to adults. Sexual abuse victims are forced to assume inappropriate adult roles, such as surrogate spouse, lover or prostitute. Treatment may focus on helping children learn to be children again. Overcoming feelings of low self-esteem and fear of emotional attachment are also important tasks.

Until recently, sexual abuse was shrouded in secrecy. Many adults who were molested as children did not receive treatment and still bear emotional scars from their abuse. Adults abused as children often suffer SEXUAL DYSFUNCTION, depression, debilitating anxiety and difficulty forming emotional attachments. Recently, several organizations have formed that offer self-help groups or referral to treatment services. Some of these groups are ADULTS MOLESTED AS CHILDREN UNITED, INCEST SURVIVORS ANONYMOUS and INCEST SURVIVORS RESOURCE NETWORK INTERNATIONAL.

In the United States many state and local government agencies have sponsored specialized treatment services for victims of abuse. Child abuse treatment units are often attached to hospitals, community mental health centers or child welfare agencies. In addition, PARENTS ANONYMOUS provides self-help groups for abusers in most states and in many locations in Canada.

Jeffrey A. Kelly, *Treating Child-Abusive Families* (New York: Plenum Press, 1983).
Arthur H. Green, *Child Maltreatment* (New York: Jason Aronson, 1980).

trust funds   See CHILDREN'S TRUST FUNDS.

Tunbridge Wells Study Group   The Tunbridge Wells Study Group, composed of representatives from a variety of disciplines, was an outgrowth of a conference held at Tunbridge Wells, England, shortly after the death of MARIA COLWELL. The group sought ways to improve the coordination and management of child abuse services and was influential in the development and passage of the Children Act of 1975. (*See also* CHILDREN AND YOUNG PERSONS ACTS [BRITAIN].)

turned stomach   See OPU HULE.

U

underground networks In the United States several informal networks of safe homes shelter parents and children fleeing court orders that give custody to an allegedly abusive ex-spouse. Typically, these networks serve children and their mothers who have been unsuccessful in convincing a court that the father sexually abused the child. Lacking proof of the father's unfitness, courts have awarded visitation rights or in some cases, sole custody of the child to the father. An unknown number of mothers have chosen to hide their child rather than subject the child to what they believe would be further abuse.

Underground networks appear to be loosely organized. Though little is known about them, an estimated five to 10 such organizations are now operating in the United States. Families who provide shelter for fugitive children and their parents often do so at great legal, personal and financial risk. Sometimes called "key masters," sheltering families must maintain strict secrecy to avoid arrest and to protect their guests.

Many experts in the field of child protection have criticized underground networks for encouraging illegal behavior and subjecting children to additional disruption. Groups representing divorced fathers maintain that many mothers simply do not want to share custody of the child and have leveled false accusations of sexual abuse in an effort to deny access to the father.

Supporters of underground networks argue that they are made necessary by a failure of the legal system. Sexual abuse of young children is often difficult to prove. In some cases judges may not fully understand the nature of child sexual abuse, in others prosecutors simply lack sufficient EVIDENCE. Convinced that the child was indeed molested by the father some mothers decide to risk imprisonment to protect their child

unfounded report Child abuse reporting laws generally require designated persons to report *suspected* abuse or neglect to an investigatory agency. If, upon investigation of a report, the reported conditions are determined not to be neglectful or abusive as defined by law, a report may be designated "unfounded." Reports may also be judged unfounded when there is a lack of sufficient evidence to establish the occurrence or extent of a potentially harmful condition.

The terms unfounded and unsubstantiated report are frequently used interchangeably. Criteria for substantiation of a report vary according to how maltreatment is defined by local laws, EVIDENTIARY STANDARDS and the investigator's ASSESSMENT of the potential for harm.

Recent United States government statistics show that slightly more than one-half of all reported cases of abuse and neglect are designated unfounded. Statistics from individual states vary widely, suggesting the importance of local laws and investigatory practices in determining SUBSTANTIATION.

In most cases child protection authorities cannot intervene further on behalf of a child once a case is determined to be unfounded. In some jurisdictions intervention may proceed with parents' permission.

UNICEF Founded in 1946, following World War II, the United Nations International Children's Emergency Relief Fund (UNICEF) addresses issues of child malnutrition, disease and illiteracy worldwide. In 1953, the United Nations gave UNICEF a virtually perpetual mandate. It now has committees in 33 countries and seeks to inform the public about conditions in developing countries that affect children. In 1984, UNICEF gave approximately $1.4 billion in aid to children in developing nations. Workers at the local level provide health and nutrition services, education, and training in parenting skills for women and girls.

Uniform Child Custody Jurisdiction Act (UCCJA)   Approved in 1968 by the National Conference of Commissioners on Uniform State Laws, the UCCJA was designed to protect children from child stealing by resolving issues of jurisdiction in child CUSTODY cases. The act attempts to ensure that the best interests of the child are met. In custody disputes involving the UCCJA, best interest is most often interpreted as the child's primary need for stability.

As late as 1981, 46 states had adopted the UCCJA, which provides for only one state— generally the state in which the custody was originally decreed—to assume jurisdiction .over a child custody case. By so doing, the UCCJA attempts to prevent a subsequent state court from modifying an original custody decree issued by another state. The act emphasizes interstate cooperation, although it does not make such cooperation mandatory; but passage of the PARENTAL KIDNAPPING PREVENTION ACT OF 1980 strengthened the jurisdictional criteria established in the UCCJA.

Union of Soviet Socialist Republics   *See* USSR.

United Nations Declaration of the Rights of the Child, 1959   On November 20, 1959, the United Nations General Assembly unanimously adopted this declaration, which asserts rights and freedoms for the world's children. It is probably the best known of all international statements concerning adult responsibilities and obligations toward children. The declaration was conceived as a way in which to make a positive statement concerning certain principles to which children are by right entitled. The preamble to the declaration establishes that, due to physical and mental immaturity, children need special safeguards both before and after birth.

In 10 principles, the declaration states that all children have the following rights: to develop in a normal and healthy manner; to have a name and a nationality from birth; to enjoy adequate housing, nutrition, recreation and medical services, including special services for the handicapped; to enjoy, if possible, the care and nurturance of their parents; to have an education; to be protected against cruelty, neglect and abuse, racism, discrimination, exploitation and religious persecution. The declaration states further that children are to be raised "in a spirit of understanding, tolerance, friendship among all peoples, peace and universal brotherhood and in full consciousness" that their talents should be dedicated to serving fellow human beings.

The declaration is similar to the Universal Declaration of Human Rights, a previous world-body statement that did not specifically address the needs of children. In adopting the Declaration of the Rights of the Child, the United Nations General Assembly placed the groundwork for a more comprehensive document, the DRAFT CONVENTION ON THE RIGHTS OF THE CHILD, submitted to the world body in 1978. See APPENDIX 12 and APPENDIX 13 for texts of the 1959 declaration and the 1978 draft.

United Nations International Children's Emergency Relief Fund   *See* UNICEF.

United States Children's Bureau   *See* CHILDREN'S BUREAU.

USSR   According to available reports by experts, child abuse and neglect in the Soviet Union is rare or nonexistent. One possible reason given for this is that children are highly valued in Soviet society. Further, the cross-cultural nature of defining child abuse automatically excludes certain types of behavior from Soviet definitions of abuse or neglect. It is generally considered that all individuals in the Soviet Union—including children—in almost all arenas of life have fewer personal freedoms and a less extensive range of personal choices open to them. For children in Soviet society, this limited range of options could be considered psychological abuse according to some standards, although within the context of local norms it would not generally be termed abuse. Much of this debate focuses on human rights issues, which transcend discussions of child abuse and neglect.

CORPORAL PUNISHMENT is not generally acceptable in Soviet education, according to most accounts. However, lack of concrete evidence makes conclusive statements impossible.

utterance, excited *See* EXCITED UTTERANCE.

V

venereal disease   Many myths abound concerning the methods by which venereal diseases can be transmitted to children. Toilet seats, bathwater and towels have all been blamed. All of these media are extremely unlikely transmission sources. The primary method of infection of children, and adults, is through sexual intercourse. Discovery of venereal disease in a child strongly suggests that the child has had sexual contact with someone infected by the disease.

Examination of the throat, rectum and genitals for the presence of gonorrhea, and blood tests for syphilis, are essential parts of a thorough medical evaluation for SEXUAL ABUSE. Genital herpes and VENEREAL WARTS also suggest sexual activity.

GONORRHEA, the most common of the venereal diseases, causes the mucous membranes to become inflamed and can cause blindness in infants. SYPHILIS, a more serious bacterial infection, can cause fatal damage to the central nervous system and circulatory system. Most states allow medical treatment without parental consent for children who have venereal disease. Some states require that all cases of pre-adolescents infected with venereal disease be reported to the mandated protective service agency. (*See also* SEXUALLY TRANSMITTED DISEASE.)

ventricular septal defect   The partition that separates the left and right ventricles of the heart is occasionally damaged by battering. Though both the heart and lungs are normally protected by the rib cage, rapid compression caused by a blow to the thoracic region can cause serious injury. Damage to the septum of the heart inhibits proper functioning and can cause death.

verbal abuse   PSYCHOLOGICAL MALTREATMENT includes verbal abuse as well as other forms of restrictive and punitive behavior. Verbal abuse covers a range of spoken messages that can usually be grouped into the categories of rejecting, terrorizing or corrupting. This type of abuse often occurs in combination with other forms of maltreatment.

Studies show that consistent verbal abuse can have serious and lasting effects on children. Low self-esteem resulting from verbal harassment may promote a wide range of destructive and defeating behavior. Verbal and psychological abuse has been associated with poor school performance, antisocial and self-destructive behavior.

While most child abuse laws do not specifically identify verbal abuse many make provisions for psychological/emotional abuse or MENTAL INJURY. Substantiation of verbal abuse usually depends upon psychiatric and/or psychological evaluation of the child, coupled with documentation of the abuse itself.

verification   Reports of suspected abuse and neglect must be investigated to determine whether there is sufficient cause to believe that a child has been abused or neglected. Verified reports of maltreatment are often referred to as FOUNDED REPORTS or substantiated abuse. (*See also* INVESTIGATION.)

victim, blaming   *See* BLAMING THE VICTIM.

victim, identification with   *S e e*   IDENTIFICATION WITH THE VICTIM.

Victims of Child Abuse Laws   *See* VOCAL.

Victims of Crime Act (P.L. 98-473)
Beginning in 1985, the U.S. Congress created a victims' compensation and assistance fund. The fund, made up of fines levied against persons convicted of certain federal offenses, makes grants to victim assistance and compensation programs. These programs compensate victims of crime or their survivors for medical expenses, loss of income and funeral

expenses. Victim assistance programs also offer services such as crisis intervention, HOTLINES, temporary shelter, counseling and other services. Funding priority is given to programs that serve victims of sexual assault, spouse abuse or child abuse.

videotaped testimony   A number of states and local authorities now allow child victims of SEXUAL ABUSE to provide legal testimony via videotape. If a child's testimony is videotaped early in the process he or she may be spared the trauma of giving repeated accounts of the abusive incident. Videotaping can also eliminate the stress and possible intimidation of testifying in the presence of the alleged abuser (often a family member or friend).

Legal scholars disagree as to the fairness of allowing videotaped testimony. Many U.S. lawyers believe such testimony violates the accused's right to confront the witness, as set forth in the Sixth Amendment to the Constitution.

In an attempt to ensure procedural DUE PROCESS some courts require that the defendant, the defendant's lawyer, the trial judge and prosecutor be present at the videotaping. Others allow taping without the defendant if the child appears in court for cross-examination.

Videotaped testimony is sometimes criticized as being subject to manipulation by both parties. Since taping is usually done with one camera the jury does not have the opportunity to observe equally the actions of other people present at the time of the testimony (e.g., the defendant). Subtle clues such as body language and flushing of the skin may be difficult or impossible to observe on videotape.

Some states (e.g., Kansas) attempt to limit trauma to the child and reduce chances of intimidation by specifically requiring use of a one-way mirror or similar device that allows the defendant to see and hear the child but prevents the child from seeing the defendant. Questions on behalf of the defendant are sub-

mitted by his or her legal counsel. Many state statutes allowing videotaped testimony are new and have not been fully tested in court.

violence, family   *See* FAMILY VIOLENCE.

VOCAL (Victims of Child Abuse Laws) This self-help and referral organization was founded in 1984, and there are currently over 100 chapters in the United States. The group lobbies against abuses of justice in alleged cases of child abuse and neglect. In one Minnesota community, 24 individuals were charged at one time with abuse, although only one person was ultimately convicted and two were acquitted. Charges against the other 21 people were dropped. As a result, some of those involved in the allegations wished to protect others from unjust accusation of child abuse. They put this desire into action by founding VOCAL

Soon after establishment of the U.S. group, in British Columbia, Canada, a chapter of VOCAL was formed by a father falsely accused of abusing his daughter. In its indictment of the Canadian government's system of investigating abuse cases, VOCAL points out that British Columbia's 1980 Family and Child Service Act maintains anonymity of the accuser and presumes guilt during investigations of alleged abuse. Further, the act provides that child abuse complaints be kept on file for two years even if they are unfounded, a situation that places a stigma on innocent individuals.

In response to these criticisms, a committee to evaluate investigations of suspected child sexual abuse in the province was established by the human resources minister of British Columbia in April 1986. According to statistics, in FY1983-84, 30% of 2,474 reports of child abuse were unfounded.

Paul and Shirley Eberle, *The Politics of Child Abuse* (Secaucus, New Jersey: Lyle Stuart, 1987).

voir dire   Literally, "to speak the truth." This legal procedure permits attorneys to question prospective jurors in child abuse and neglect cases for possible bias. It also establishes grounds on which expert witnesses can be questioned to determine their qualifications prior to TESTIMONY.

voluntary intervention   Some abusive parents seek help voluntarily. Increased accessibility of HOTLINES and SELF-HELP GROUPS has made it easier and less threatening for parents to request help. In most areas child protection agencies actively encourage self-referral. Since many abusive and/or neglectful parents are never reported, self-help programs may reach many families that would not otherwise have received help.

Parents who seek help voluntarily tend to be more highly motivated to change their behavior. When parents are reported by someone else, fear of prosecution or removal of their children often leads them to cover up problems rather than face them openly. Denying or minimizing abusive behavior often prevents perpetrators of abuse from benefiting from treatment.

Following an INVESTIGATION in which abuse or neglect is substantiated parents may be given the opportunity to seek help voluntarily. In such cases the child protection agency agrees not to seek court intervention if parents follow a mutually agreed upon plan of treatment.

W

wanton The term wanton is used in court proceedings to denote extremely reckless or malicious behavior. Perpetrators of abuse or neglect are often accused of willful and wanton acts against a child. Wanton acts are considered to be more serious than simple carelessness.

WAR *See* WORLD OF ABNORMAL REARING.

warrant A warrant is a document, issued by a judge, that authorizes arrest or detention of a person. Search of a particular place and seizure of specified items may also be authorized.

When particularly serious acts of maltreatment are committed or perpetrators fail to cooperate with child protection authorities a warrant may be sought from the court. In order to issue such a document the judge must be satisfied that there is reasonable cause to believe that a crime has been committed. United States law does not require that a hearing be held or that the subject of the warrant be notified prior to its issuance.

warts, venereal Condyloma acuminata, commonly known as venereal warts, is sometimes found in children who have been sexually abused. The warts are small, appear in clusters and may be found in any area involved in direct sexual contact. Appearance of condyloma acuminata in children is strong evidence of SEXUAL ABUSE. There is no reason to believe that this condition is acquired in any way other than by sexual contact.

whiplash shaken infant syndrome Parents and caretakers sometimes express their frustration toward a crying, irritable or otherwise uncooperative infant by shaking the baby. Since even vigorous shaking rarely

leaves easily observable external signs it is often thought to have no serious health consequences. Clinical evidence, however, has proven that even playful shaking of infants can have serious—sometimes permanent—effects. Shaking and the resultant SEQUELAE were first differentiated from the BATTERED CHILD SYNDROME by radiologist John Caffey in the early 1970s. Caffey cited cases in which infants and children, who showed no external signs of battering or abuse, had suffered serious head and spinal cord injury and, in several instances, death, from shaking.

Closer examination showed that many of these infants suffered SUBDURAL HEMATOMA, RETINAL HEMORRHAGING and damage to the periosteum of long bones. Further study showed connections among the practice of shaking and permanent brain damage, mental retardation, blindness, visual loss, motor deficits, seizures and hypopituitarism.

The injury most frequently associated with the shaking of infants is subdural hematoma. Shaking is also suspected as a major factor in unexplained SUDDEN INFANT DEATH SYNDROME.

Infants in their first six months of life are the most likely victims of whiplash shaken infant syndrome. During infancy the head is heavier in proportion to total body weight than at any other time. This fact, coupled with relatively weak supporting neck muscles, makes this age group very sensitive to the sudden backward-forward motions associated with whiplash.

The absence of external signs make this syndrome difficult to diagnose. Adding to the diagnostic difficulty is the reluctance of parents and caretakers to give the physician an accurate medical and social history. Victims of shaking may show symptoms of respiratory difficulty, fever, irritability, lethargy, decreased appetite or vomiting, along with a number of other somewhat vague symptoms, none of which are sufficient to confirm a diagnosis of whiplash shaken infant syndrome

A thorough medical/social history and a complete physical examination by a physician familiar with the syndrome and with the subtle signs of head injury increases the likelihood of an accurate diagnosis. Careful fundiscopic examination is an important tool for detecting retinal hemorrhages. In recent years, the use of cranial computed tomography (CT) has greatly increased the ability to detect the presence of subdural hematoma.

A great deal remains to be learned about the long-term effects of the whiplash injuries to infants.

Lucinda J. Dykes, "The Whiplash Shaken Infant Syndrome: What Has Been Learned?" *Child Abuse and Neglect*, 10:2(1986), pp. 211-221.

White House Conferences on Children

As a result of early-20th-century legislative and policy reforms, the first White House Conference on Children was held in 1909. President Theodore Roosevelt, an avid reformer, strongly supported the conference, which was attended by over 200 delegates. Until this time there had been little legislative acknowledgment at the federal level of the abuse or neglect suffered by young children in the United States. The White House Conference brought together concerned men and women who worked to recommend a variety of federal policies acknowledging children's need of protection from abuse or neglect. These policies were aimed at alleviating some of the negative conditions affecting children and families.

The 1909 conference was the first of the White House-sponsored meetings held each decade in the United States. Attendees at the initial gathering in 1909 acknowledged the role of the home in prevention or development of problems. They also suggested ways in which these problems might be approached, suggestions often informed by contemporary views on childrearing. Due to resolutions passed at the first White House Conference on Children, a federal CHILDREN'S BUREAU was established in 1912 to oversee these initial

federal efforts on behalf of children and to ensure continuity of their implementation. Subsequent White House Conferences on children have focused on issues considered most pressing and timely for their period.

Joseph M. Hawes and N. Ray Hiner, *American Childhood, A Research Guide and Historical Handbook* (Westport: Greenwood Press, 1985).

willful   The term willful is often used in legal proceedings related to child abuse or neglect. It implies knowledge and understanding of an act as well as the intention that any consequences normally associated with that particular act should occur. In some cases, the acts must be proven to be willful before they are considered illegal or negligent.

Wilson, Mary Ellen   In 1873, a well-publicized case of child abuse involving an eight-year-old New York girl named Mary Ellen Wilson became a rallying issue of reformers. Because of the notoriety surrounding the Mary Ellen Wilson case, reformers established the New York Society for the Prevention of Cruelty to Children (NYSPCC) in 1874.

Mary Ellen was an illegitimate daughter of Thomas McCormack and had been boarded out until she was nearly two years old. She then was placed under the care of the Superintendent of the Out-Door Poor in New York. Her natural father and stepmother were given charge of Mary Ellen on the stipulation that they report annually to the city's Commissioners of Charities and Corrections. After her father's death, Mary Ellen's stepmother remarried. She was then abused and neglected by these stepparents, Francis and Mary Connolly.

Among the reports of her abuse were those that described her being kept chained to a bed and beaten with a rawhide cord by her stepmother. When neighbors heard her screams, they approached the police department but were unsuccessful in getting help for Mary Ellen. They then went to the local chapter of the American Society for the Prevention of Cruelty to Animals, and the group petitioned the court on her behalf. When the *New York Times* received information about the girl's mistreatment it began newspaper coverage of the case, of the subsequent formation of the New York SPCC, and of the many other child abuse, abandonment and neglect cases that flourished in New York City and surrounding areas.

Mary Ellen's stepmother, Mrs. Connolly, was convicted and sent to jail for one year as a result of her actions. Mary Ellen was sent to live at the Sheltering Arms children's home and was later indentured to a farmer.

The Guide to American Law Yearbook, 1987 (St. Paul, Minn.: West Publishing Co., 1987).
Barbara J. Nelson, *Making an Issue of Child Abuse* (Chicago: University of Chicago Press, 1984).

Wisconsin v. Yoder   This 1972 ruling by the U.S. Supreme Court affirmed parents' rights to raise children according to their own religious beliefs. The case actually involved three respondents: Jonas Yoder, Adin Yutzy and Wallace Miller. All were followers of the Amish religious sect. At issue was the state's ability to prevent Amish families from removing children from public schools after completing the eighth grade. Though they received vocational training at home, the children were not enrolled in any public or private school. The respondents and other members of this sect believed formal high school education interfered with the religious development, and therefore the religious freedom, of their children. The Supreme Court agreed with them and overturned their convictions for violating Wisconsin's compulsory school attendance law.

Wisconsin v. Yoder is often seen as limiting the rather broad powers granted to the state in *PRINCE V. MASSACHUSETTS.* (*See also* PARENTS' RIGHTS and RELIGIOUS ASPECTS.)

Robert H. Mnookin, *Child, Family and State: Problems and Materials on Children and the Law* (Boston: Little, Brown and Company, 1978).

withdrawal   Children subjected to severe abuse may withdraw from social contact, appearing dull and listless. Typically, they avoid doing anything that might attract attention or arouse the anger of their parents. Withdrawn children often exhibit a robot-like compliance with parental demands, demonstrating their desire to do virtually anything to avoid further abuse.

Withdrawal and HYPERVIGILANCE are usually observed in children who have been victims of the most severe forms of physical abuse from an early age. These children may appear visibly anxious or afraid in the presence of their parents. In a hospital emergency room these symptoms are a signal to physicians and nurses to look for other signs of nonaccidental injury.

When removed from home children may continue to appear withdrawn. It may take several years in a safe and therapeutic setting before they are able to develop a close, trusting relationship with anyone.

witness   Trials related to child abuse or neglect may include testimony from lay witnesses and EXPERT WITNESSES. The kind of testimony allowed by the court depends upon the type of witness.

Lay witnesses are required to have first-hand knowledge of facts to which they testify. Inferences or conclusions may not be drawn by such witnesses. Hearsay evidence, facts not directly observed or experienced by the witness, is usually not permitted. An exception to the rule against hearsay testimony is sometimes made in preliminary hearings to spare a child from trauma related to repeated court appearances. In such cases a third party may present testimony based upon the child's account of the alleged abuse.

When the reputation or character of the defendant or respondent is in question a lay witness may be called to testify. In a dependency hearing such testimony may center on the parents' fitness to adequately care for the child. Character witnesses are usually asked to state their own qualifications to give testimony, their relationship with the party in question and their knowledge of that party's reputation in the community. Rumors and witnesses' personal opinions about the party are not admissible.

An expert witness is anyone who, in the judge's opinion, possesses special knowledge or skills beyond those of the judge or jury. Expert witnesses may be called by either party in a case or may be appointed by the court. Unlike lay witnesses, expert witnesses are allowed to make inferences and express opinions. Inferences or opinions must be within the witness's area of expertise. For example, a psychologist may testify about the psychological effects of abuse but is not allowed to give an opinion concerning the extent of physical injuries.

The allegedly abused child may be called as a witness by either party. The judge is responsible for determining whether the child's testimony is admissible as evidence. A child's competence to testify is based on age, maturity and level of understanding. In some areas the minimum age of witnesses is specified by law.

Child witnesses may be allowed to testify in judge's chambers, on videotape or closed circuit television rather than in the courtroom. Alternative ways of testifying can help reduce trauma to the child caused by reliving abuse in a threatening setting before a large group of strangers. Attempts to reduce trauma to the child must be balanced with the defendant's right to cross-examine witnesses.

The petitioner (usually the state) is the first to call witnesses in a hearing. Questioning of witnesses takes the form of: (1) direct examination by the attorney calling the witness; (2) cross-examination by the opposing attorney; (3) rebuttal or redirect examination by the first attorney concerning issues raised in the cross-examination; and (4) recross-examination by the opposing attorney on issues raised in the rebuttal examination. After a party has

called all its witnesses it rests its case. Under ordinary circumstances, once a party has rested its case it is not allowed to call additional witnesses. (*See also* ADJUDICATORY HEARING, COURT, CIVIL PROCEEDING, CRIMINAL PROSECUTION and EVIDENCE.)

witness, expert   *See* EXPERT WITNESS.

World of Abnormal Rearing (WAR)   The concept of the world of abnormal rearing, known by the acronym WAR, was developed by pediatrician Ray E. Helfer, a professor of medicine at Michigan State University. WAR describes a cyclical process in which children fail to learn basic interpersonal skills and later, as parents, are unable to teach such skills to their children. This dysfunctional pattern of development is not limited to children who are physically or sexually abused but includes those who suffer various kinds of emotional abuse and neglect. Dr. Helfer stresses the importance of parents breaking the cycle by learning principles of interpersonal behavior not learned in childhood.

The basic skills necessary to healthy development are, according to Helfer: learning how to meet one's needs appropriately, the ability to delay gratification, learning that one is responsible for one's own actions but not those of others, the ability to make decisions and solve problems, learning how to trust others, and developing the ability to separate feelings and actions.

Abused children often learn inappropriate or malfunctional ways of meeting their needs. Children who are ignored or neglected may learn that abuse is the only form of attention available from parents. Because their needs are so frequently frustrated some children do not learn to delay immediate gratification in hopes of obtaining a greater reward later. Such children enter adulthood lacking this important work and parenting skill.

Children must also learn to be responsible for their behavior. Most learn this principle from parental teaching and discipline. When discipline is sporadic or abusive children become confused about the consequences of their actions. In many abusive families a ROLE REVERSAL takes place in which the child assumes the role of a parent's caretaker. The parent may be unable or unwilling to reciprocate. Forced to direct their attention to meeting a parent's needs children are prevented from mastering tasks important to their own development.

Abuse further complicates the process of learning to differentiate between one's self and others. Because they are often punished or abandoned the children may come to feel responsible for causing the maltreatment. If beaten or molested, the child assumes that he or she did something to deserve it. This inappropriate sense of guilt contributes to future self-destructive and abusive behavior.

Maltreated children usually have few choices. Feeling trapped they develop a sense of helplessness that prevents them from learning constructive approaches to problem-solving. As adults they may find themselves unable to make decisions and may feel they have little control over their lives.

The ability to trust is perhaps most difficult for maltreated children to develop. Exploited, battered or neglected they learn to fear rather than trust. Inability to trust not only prevents children from developing loving relationships, but makes it difficult for them to seek protection from abuse as well. Children may look with suspicion on a concerned adult's attempts to help. Carried into adulthood the inability to trust may contribute to marital and child rearing difficulties.

Finally, the ability to distinguish feelings from actions is an important developmental task. Children often lash out at others because they are angry. As they grow older they learn that being angry does not justify or compel such behavior. They learn other ways of expressing anger.

Abused children are frequent targets of adults who have not learned to separate feelings and actions (*see* TARGET CHILD). As adults these victims are likely to direct their own anger, frustration or sexual feelings at children without stopping to consider the wisdom of their actions.

Each of these abilities, if not mastered, can contribute to inadequate or abusive parenting. Parents cannot teach such developmental tasks if they have not learned them. Left unchecked, developmental deficits are passed from generation to generation, contributing to a cycle of abuse and neglect.

Helfer believes the WAR is best interrupted in childhood before severe damage is done. Various treatment and parent education programs have demonstrated that much can be done to break the cycle during adulthood as well.

X

X rays X rays are nonluminous electromagnetic rays of very short wavelength. Discovered by the German physicist Wilhelm Roentgen, the X ray achieved its name because of its then unknown properties. Because of its ability to penetrate opaque or solid substances, the X ray is used in combination with photographic film for the study of internal body structures not normally visible. The study of the body through X rays is known as radiology.

Brief exposure to X rays produces a photograph of the bones often called an X ray, but more specifically known as a roentgenogram. The typical roentgenographic procedure transmits a small amount of radiation that has no harmful effects. Prolonged exposure to X rays can, however, destroy body tissue.

Advances in pediatric radiology (*see* RADIOLOGY, PEDIATRIC) from the 1930s through the 1950s made it possible to determine both the type of force that caused a bone fracture and the approximate age of the injury. This information, along with other medical evidence, allowed physicians to check the validity of a caretaker's explanations of particular injuries. An especially important finding first reported by John Caffey was the combination of multiple FRACTURES of the long bones and SUBDURAL HEMATOMA. Caffey was one of the first to propose battering as the most likely cause for this combination of injuries. This observation was later expanded upon and publicized by C. Henry Kempe and others as the BATTERED CHILD SYNDROME

Today a SKELETAL SURVEY is standard practice when child battering is suspected. Using barium sulfate (a tasteless compound that, when swallowed, appears as an opaque substance on a roentgenogram) physicians are also able to detect GASTROINTESTINAL INJURIES.

Other more recent medical advances such as computed tomography (CT scans) and magnetic resonance imaging (MRI) are also used in the identification of abuse related trauma.

Y

yo-yo syndrome   Violent marital disputes can seriously affect the emotional, intellectual and physical well-being of children. A study of the effects of marital violence on children conducted by Britain's NATIONAL SOCIETY FOR THE PREVENTION OF CRUELTY TO CHILDREN likened children to a yo-yo moving up and down in a pattern of restlessness and violence.

The name yo-yo syndrome has come to describe the situation of many children in violent households. Often shuttled back and forth between parents, these children suffer a range of problems directly related to their volatile environment. They are frequently blamed by parents for their marital problems and may be used as pawns in their parents' bitter disputes. If a child possesses traits similar to one parent he or she may become the victim of SCAPEGOATING by the other parent.

Though yo-yo children may also be physically abused or neglected, the psychological scars caused by the turbulence around them can be just as damaging. Yo-yo children usually feel responsible for family violence, engaging in self-destructive acts or attempting to serve as a buffer between parents.

Parents are often quite resistant to treatment, making it difficult to ensure a safe home environment for the child. It may be necessary to remove the child from home to prevent further trauma.

Jean G. Moore, "Yo-Yo Children—Victims of Matrimonial Violence." *Child Welfare*, 54(8):1975, pp. 557-566.

Yugoslavia   *See*   SOCIALIST EASTERN EUROPE.

APPENDIXES

1. ORGANIZATIONS
2. NATIONAL CHILD WELFARE RESOURCE CENTERS
3. STATE CHILD PROTECTION AGENCIES AND REPORTING PROCEDURES
4. CHILD ABUSE PREVENTION AND TREATMENT ACT
5. STATE CHILD ABUSE STATUTES
6. STATE MANDATED REPORTERS
7. TYPES OF IMMUNITY GRANTED BY STATES
8. ABROGATION OF PRIVILEGED COMMUNICATIONS
9. SELECTED STATE CHILD ABUSE AND NEGLECT REPORTS—FAMILIES AND CHILDREN
10. NATIONAL ESTIMATES OF CHILD ABUSE AND NEGLECT REPORTS
11. TRENDS IN CHILD ABUSE FUNDING
12. UNITED NATIONS DECLARATION OF THE RIGHTS OF THE CHILD, 1959
13. DRAFT UNITED NATIONS CONVENTION ON THE RIGHTS OF THE CHILD
14. CHILD WELFARE STATUTES—CANADA
15. PROVINCIAL DEFINITIONS OF CHILD IN NEED OF PROTECTION—CANADA

1. ORGANIZATIONS

Adolescent Perpetrator Network
Kempe National Center
125 Oneida Street
Denver, CO 80220

Located at the Kempe National Center at the University of Colorado School of Medicine, this group provides support for professionals working with adolescent offenders. It serves over 300 individuals and publishes a newsletter, the *Interchange*, as well as an annotated bibliography containing material on treatment of adolescent sex offenders.

Adults Molested as Children United (AMACU)
c/o Parents United
P.O. Box 952
San Jose, CA 95108
(408) 280-5055

Self-help groups for adults who were sexually abused as children. Affiliated with Parents United.

American Association for Protecting Children (AAPC)
American Humane Association
Children's Division
9725 E. Hampden Ave
Denver, CO 80231
(303) 695-0811

A division of the American Humane Association, which was founded in 1877, the AAPC provides training, evaluation and assistance to community and state agencies in the area of child maltreatment. The AAPC publishes materials detailing various aspects of child protection, including *Protecting Children*, a quarterly newsletter. The AAPC acts as an advocate for child protection legislation and maintains a data base of reports on abuse and neglect.

Center for the Study of Parental Acceptance and Rejection
Box U-158
Storrs, CT 06268
(203) 486-4513

Based at the University of Connecticut, this nonprofit center was founded in 1981. Staff and visiting scholars study causes, correlates, and consequences of acceptance/rejection of children by parents—e.g., child abuse and neglect. Provides locus for independent research projects concerning families and children, of both a national and international nature

Children's Defense Fund
122 C St., N.W.
Washington, DC 20001
(202) 628-8787

The Children's Defense Fund is a privately supported, nonprofit organization founded in 1969. It gathers data and provides information about programs and policies affecting children. The CDF has offices in Ohio, Mississippi, Texas, Minnesota and Virginia, and has national headquarters in Washington, D.C. Among its major interests are· adolescent pregnancy prevention, early screening and diagnosis to prevent medical problems, support for federal projects such as Headstart, and other health care, job training, foster care and child support programs. The CDF publishes several newsletters and other advocacy tools

Child Find
P.O. Box 277
New Paltz, NY 12561
(914) 255-1848
(800) I-AM-LOST
(800) A-WAY-OUT

Maintains a toll-free telephone number for missing children—800-I-AM-LOST—and publishes a quarterly newsletter as well as a directory of missing children.

CHILDHELP USA
6463 Independence Avenue
Woodland Hills, CA 91367
(818) 347-7280

Established in 1983, CHILDHELP USA is a nonprofit organization that serves the needs of neglected and abused children. It operates the National Child Abuse Hotline (1-800-4-A-CHILD), disseminates literature, posters etc., related to prevention of child abuse, provides treatment and evaluation services, operates a residential treatment center for children between the ages of two and 12, and funds research related to child abuse and neglect

Child Keyppers' International
P.O. Box 6292
Lake Worth, FL 33466
(800) 448-7676

Founded in 1982, this group exists to help recover missing children, prevent child abuse and educate people concerning the dangers of child abduction. Supports identification of children through fingerprinting and other methods, advocates legislation addressing children's issues, publishes teaching manuals and varied materials aimed at promoting child safety, prevention of child abuse education etc. Maintains a missing children's databank, publishes a quarterly and a missing child directory.

Child Welfare League of America
440 First St., N.W.
Washington, DC 20001
(202) 638-2952

A privately supported, not-for-profit organization incorporated in 1920, the CWLA described itself in a recent annual report as "devoting its efforts to helping deprived, neglected and abused children and their families." The CWLA provides information, conducts research and develops standards for children's services. Its membership comprises 450 children's agencies, with 125,000 staff members, and 1,000 affiliates throughout the United States and Canada. The organization currently serves 2,000,000 children annually. The CWLA publishes a bibliography of its numerous publications, including articles from *Child Welfare*, a bimonthly journal of the CWLA.

Daughters and Sons United (DSU)
c/o Parents United
Box 952
San Jose, CA 95108
(408) 280-5055

Daughters and Sons United is a self-help group for victims of intra-familial child sexual abuse. DSU is affiliated with PARENTS UNITED, a self-help organization for families of sexually abused children. At weekly meetings, children are given emotional support and helped to cope with the initial crisis. Group meetings are designed to help victims understand their feelings about the abuse, improve communication skills and learn how to prevent future sexual assaults. Children between the ages of five and 18 are accepted as members.

Defense for Children International/Defense des Enfants-International
Case Postale 88
CH-1211 Geneva, Switzerland
22-340558

Defense for Children International-U.S.A. (DCI-USA)
210 Forsyth Street
New York, NY 10002
(212) 353-0951

Part of Defense for Children International (see above), DCI-USA is a national advocacy organization that aims to protect children from exploitation, abuse and neglect. It publishes *The Children's Tribune* and maintains a computer data base on international child abuse, provides court representation on behalf of children and investigates child abuse and neglect. DCI-USA holds consultative status with UNICEF and at the United Nations.

End Violence Against the Next Generation (EVAN-G)
977 Keeler Ave.
Berkeley, CA 94708
(415) 527-0454

Founded in 1971, EVAN-G works to eliminate the use of corporal punishment in schools and institutions. Membership consists of psychologists, teachers, lawyers, parents etc., all of whom are concerned with educating the public about corporal punishment and with promoting alternative methods of childrearing and education. The group publishes a quarterly, *The Last Resort*.

Incest Survivors Anonymous (ISA)
P.O. Box 5613
Long Beach, CA 90805-0613
(213) 422-1632 tape of meetings
(213) 428-5599 messages

According to its informational literature, this self-help group was founded in 1980 with the "sole purpose . . . to help the incest survivor who wants to stop negative behavior (get out of the victim role)." The organization, which is a private, nonprofit group, is patterned (with permission) after Alcoholics Anonymous. Members of ISA provide peer support at meetings nationally. The group runs a speakers' bureau and disseminates ISA-published information on incest written and donated by incest survivors and pro-survivors.

Incest Survivors Resource Network, International
P.O. Box 911
Hicksville, NY 11802
(516) 935-3031

An educational resource service of the Task Group on Family Trauma, New York Yearly Meeting of the Religious Society of Friends (Quakers). Members help promote education, professional therapeutic intervention and self-help to help incest survivors resolve trauma.

International Society for Prevention of Child Abuse and Neglect

Based at the C. Henry Kempe National Center for Child Abuse and Neglect (see below), the International Society provides a worldwide forum for disseminating information on child abuse and neglect. The society holds international congresses on a biennial basis and publishes *Child Abuse and Neglect: The International Journal.*

C. Henry Kempe National Center for the Prevention and Treatment of Child Abuse
1205 Oneida Street
Denver, CO 80220
(303) 321-3963

Established in 1972, according to its program guide, the center provides "training, consultation, program development and evaluation and research in all forms of child abuse and neglect." Affiliated organizations include Hope for the Children, a diagnostic and treatment center; the KEEPSAFE project; the National Child Abuse and Neglect Clinical Resource Center (NCCAN); the National Association of Counsel for Children; the International Society for Prevention of Child Abuse and Neglect; and the Colorado Child Protection Council.

National Center for the Study of Corporal Punishment and Alternatives in the Schools (NCSCPAS)
253 Ritter Hall
Temple University
Philadelphia, PA 19122
(215) 787-6091

Founded in 1976 as part of the Department of School Psychology at Temple University, the center is a nonprofit organization that provides information about the effects of corporal punishment on children. The center conducts research, provides legal advocacy and maintains a collection of material on discipline and corporal punishment. Provides training, presents workshops, and periodically publishes a journal, *Discipline*, and a bibliography of publications related to corporal punishment. Maintains a free telephone consultation service and sponsors the Delaware Valley Discipline Clinic, which provides diagnosis and remediation of discipline problems.

National Center for Missing and Exploited Children
1835 K Street, N.W., Suite 700
Washington, DC 20006
(202) 634-9821

Provides information on missing and abused children. Operates a hotline for reports concerning missing children, publishes a number of pamphlets, brochures etc. Advocates on behalf of child protection legislation.

National Center on Child Abuse and Neglect (NCCAN)
Children's Bureau, Office of Human Development Services
Administration for Children, Youth and Families
U.S. Department of Health and Human Services
P.O. Box 1182
Washington, DC 20013

Established in 1974 as part of the Child Abuse Prevention and Treatment Act (P.L. 93-247), NCCAN aids professionals in providing help to children and families in need of support services. It is part of the Children's Bureau, an arm of the Department of Health and Human Services. NCCAN conducts research related to child abuse and neglect, develops programs addressing these issues and has established a system for disseminating information to the public and private sectors. NCCAN maintains the Clearinghouse on Child Abuse and Neglect Information and provides a catalog of publications available for purchase

National Child Abuse Hotline
1345 El Centro Avenue
P.O. Box 630
Hollywood, CA 90028
(800) 422-4453
(800) 4-A-CHILD

Operated by the Los Angeles, California, CHILDHELP USA center, since 1982, the hotline has provided telephone crisis counseling, referral and information on a 24-hour-a-day, seven-day-a-week basis.

National Committee for Prevention of Child Abuse
332 South Michigan Ave., Suite 950
Chicago, IL 60604-4357
(312) 663-3520

Founded in 1972 this volunteer-based organization is concerned with preventing all forms of child abuse. It has 67 chapters located in all 50 states and the District of Columbia. The committee maintains an active network of child abuse prevention organizations and a national public awareness campaign. It helps provide prevention services and acts as a facilitator for other, independent programs dealing with child abuse and neglect, and publishes educational materials, some of which are available in Spanish, in all areas of child abuse.

National Legal Resource Center for Child Advocacy and Protection
American Bar Association/Young Lawyers Division
1800 M Street, N.W., Suite 200
Washington, DC 20036
(202) 331-2250

Founded in 1978, this organization is sponsored by the Young Lawyers Division of the American Bar Association. Its staff provides services relating to issues about child abuse and neglect, missing and exploited children, adoption, learning disabilities, child support and foster care. It maintains a training and technical assistance program, the National Legal Resource Center for Child Welfare Programs, which addresses issues of interest to those dealing with child advocacy and protection. Its publications include the *ABA Juvenile and Child Welfare Law Reporter*, a monthly publication, as well as various books and pamphlets.

Parents and Teachers Against Violence in Education (PTAVE)
560 S. Hartz Ave., Suite 408
Danville, CA 94526
(415) 831-1661

Founded in Australia in 1978, this group is primarily concerned with eliminating corporal punishment from schools and institutions. Maintains a speakers' bureau and data base. Publishes several leaflets and pamphlets.

Parents Anonymous National Office
6733 S. Sepulveda Blvd., Suite 270
Los Angeles, CA 90045
(800) 421-0353
In California, (800) 356-0386

Parents Anonymous was founded in 1971 as a private, not-for-profit corporation "dedicated to the identification, treatment and prevention of child abuse." The group works with families through "peer led professionally facilitated self help groups" in the interest of preventing child abuse and avoiding placement of children. According to recent information published by PA, over 1,000 parent groups no provide free service to more than 60,000 families per year. PA also operates toll-free crisis hotlines and referral telephones in 19 states, offering telephone counseling and referral to adults and children. The national office publishes a monthly newsletter, *The Insider*.

Parents United
P.O. Box 952
San Jose, CA 95108
(408) 280-5055

Self-help groups for families of sexually abused children. Publishes a bimonthly newsletter, *The PUN*, distributes tapes and printed material on child sexual abuse and holds an annual convention.

Paul and Lisa, Inc.
P.O. Box 348
Westbrook, CT 06498
also:

Paul and Lisa, Inc.
315-317 West 47th Street
New York, NY 10036
(212) 247-3460

A private, nonprofit organization in Westbrook, Connecticut, founded in 1980, Paul and Lisa, Inc., fights sexual abuse and exploitation of children and seeks to educate the general public about the growing problem of sexual abuse of children. It works with local, state, and federal officials to review the effectiveness of laws pertaining to sexual abuse.

Society's League Against Molestation (SLAM)
c/o Women Against Rape/Childwatch
P.O. Box 346
Collingswood, NJ 08108
(609) 858-7800

Seeks to prevent sexual abuse and exploitation of children. Publishes a newsletter. Provides public education and assistance to victims and their families; advocates for stricter legislation.

UNICEF (United Nations International Children's Emergency Relief Fund)
United Nations
New York, NY

Founded in 1946, following World War II, the United Nations International Children's Emergen-cy Relief Fund addresses issues of child malnutri-tion, disease and illiteracy worldwide. Locally, UNICEF workers in developing nations provide health and nutrition services, education, and training in parenting skills for women and girls.

Victims of Child Abuse Laws (VOCAL)
P.O. Box 11335
Minneapolis, MN 55412
(612) 521-9714

A self-help and referral group, founded in 1984 by adults who had been charged (but who were never convicted) of child abuse. The organization lobbies against abuses of justice in alleged cases of child maltreatment.

VOICES in Action
P.O. Box 148309
Chicago, IL 60614
(312) 327-1500

VOICES, an acronym for Victims Of Incest Can Emerge Survivors, publishes a bimonthly newslet-ter for incest survivors and pro-survivors. It offers publications, including a "survival kit" concerning sexual abuse. VOICES holds an annual conference and provides free referral services to members. The group also works to prevent child sexual abuse.

2. NATIONAL CHILD WELFARE RESOURCE CENTERS

National Child Abuse and Neglect Clinical
   Resource Center
Kempe National Center
University of Colorado Health Sciences Center
1205 Oneida Street
Denver, CO 80220
(303)321-3963

National Child Welfare Resource Center for
   Management and Administration
University of Southern Maine
96 Falmouth Street
Portland, ME 04103
(207)780-4430
(800)HELP-KID

National Legal Resource Center for Child Welfare
American Bar Association
1800 M Street, N.W
Suite S-200
Washington, DC 20036
(202)331-2250

National Resource Center for Foster and Residential Care
Child Welfare Institute
1430 N. Peachtree St.
Suite 510
Atlanta, GA 30309
(404)876-1934

National Resource Center for Special Needs
   Adoption
A Division of Spaulding for Children
3660 Waltrous Road
P.O. Box 337
Chelsea, MI 48118
(313)475-8693

National Resource Center for Youth Services
The University of Oklahoma
125 North Greenwood Ave.
Tulsa, OK 74120
(918)585-2986

National Resource Center on Child Abuse and
   Neglect
American Association for Protecting Children
American Humane Association
9725 East Hampden Avenue
Denver, CO 80231
(303)695-0811

National Resource Center on Child Sexual Abuse
11141 Georgia Avenue
Suite 310
Wheaton, MD 20902
(301)949-5000 (Maryland)
(205)533-KIDS (Alabama)
(800)KIDS-006

National Resource Center on Family Based Ser-
   vices
The University of Iowa School of Social Work
Oakdale Campus, N240 OH
Oakdale, IA 52319
(319)335-4123

National Resource Institute on Children and Youth
   with Handicaps
Child Development and Mental Retardation Center
University of Washington
Mailstop WJ-10
Seattle, WA 98195
(206)543-2213

3. STATE CHILD PROTECTION AGENCIES AND REPORTING PROCEDURES

Source: U.S. Department of Health, and Human Services, Office of Human Development Services, Administration for Children, Youth and Families, Children's Bureau, National Center on Child Abuse and Neglect, *Child Abuse and Neglect: An Informed Approach to a Shared Concern*. Washington, D.C.: 1986.

Because the responsibility for investigating reports of suspected child abuse and neglect rests at the state level, each state has established a child protective services reporting system. Listed below are the names and addresses of the child protective services agency in each state, followed by the procedures for reporting suspected child maltreatment. A number of states have toll-free (800) telephone numbers that can be used for reporting.

Alabama
Alabama Department of Human
   Resources
Division of Family and
   Children's Services
Office of Protective Services
64 North Union Street
Montgomery, AL 36130-1801

During business hours, make reports to the County Department of Human Resources, Child Protective Services Unit. After business hours, make reports to local police.

Alaska
Department of Health and Social
   Services
Division of Family and Youth
   Services
Box H-05
Juneau, AK 99811

To make reports in-state, ask the operator for Zenith 4444. Out-of-state, add area code 907. This telephone number is toll-free.

American Samoa
Government of American Samoa
Office of the Attorney General
Pago Pago, American Samoa
   96799

Make reports to the Department of Human Resources at (684) 633-4485.

Arizona
Department of Economic Security
Administration for Children,
   Youth and Families
P.O. Box 6123
Site COE 940A
Phoenix, AZ 85005

Make reports to Department of Economic Security local offices.

Arkansas
Arkansas Department of Human
   Services
Division of Children and Family
   Services
P.O. Box 1437
Little Rock, AR 72203

Make reports in-state to (800) 482-5964.

California
Office of Child Abuse
   Prevention
Department of Social Services
714-744 P Street, Room 950
Sacramento, CA 95814

Make reports to County Department of Welfare and the Central Registry of Child Abuse (916) 445-7546, maintained by the Department of Justice.

Colorado
Department of Social Services
Central Registry
P.O. Box 181000
Denver, CO 80218-0899
Make reports to County Departments of Social Services.

Connecticut
Connecticut Department of
   Children and Youth Services
Division of Children's and
   Protective Services
170 Sigourney Street
Hartford, CT 06105

Make reports in-state to (800) 842-2288 or out-of-state to (203) 344-2599.

Delaware

Delaware Department of Services
for Children, Youth and Their
Families
Division of Child Protective
Services
330 East 30th Street
Wilmington, DE 19802

Make reports in-state to (800) 292-9582.

District of Columbia

District of Columbia Department
of Human Services
Commission on Social Services
Family Services Administration
Child and Family Services
Division
500 First Street, N.W.
Washington, DC 20001

Make reports to (202) 727-0995.

Florida

Florida Child Abuse Registry
1317 Winewood Boulevard
Tallahassee, FL 32301

Make reports in-state to (800) 342-9152 or
out-of-state to (904) 487-2625.

Georgia

Georgia Department of Human
Resources
Division of Family and Children
Services
878 Peachtree Street, N.W.
Atlanta, GA 30309

Make reports to County Departments of Family
and Children Services.

Guam

Department of Public Health and
Social Services
Child Welfare Services
Child Protective Services
P.O. Box 2816
Agana, GU 96910

Reports made to the State Child Protective
Services Agency at (671) 646-8417.

Hawaii

Department of Social Services
and Housing
Public Welfare Division
Family and Children's Services
P.O. Box 339
Honolulu, HI 96809

Make reports to each island's Department of
Social Services and Housing Child Protective
Services Reporting hotline.

Idaho

Department of Health and
Welfare
Field Operations Bureau of
Social Services Child
Protection
450 West State, 10th Floor
Boise, ID 83720

Make reports to Department of Health and
Welfare Regional Offices.

Illinois

Illinois Department of Children
and Family Services
Station 75
State Administrative Offices
406 East Monroe Street
Springfield, IL 62701

Make reports in-state to (800) 25-ABUSE or
out-of-state to (217) 785-4010.

Indiana

Indiana Department of Public
Welfare-Child Abuse and
Neglect
Division of Child Welfare-
Social Services
141 South Meridian Street
Sixth Floor
Indianapolis, IN 46225

Make reports to County Departments of Public
Welfare

Iowa

Iowa Department of Human
Services
Division of Social Services
Central Child Abuse Registry
Hoover State Office Building

Fifth Floor
Des Moines, IA 50319

Make reports in-state to (800) 362-2178 or out-of-state (during business hours) to (515) 281-5581.

Kansas

Kansas Department of Social and
　Rehabilitation Services
Division of Social Services
Child Protection and Family
　Services Section
Smith-Wilson Building
2700 West Sixth Street
Topeka, KS 66606

Make reports to Department of Social and Rehabilitation Service Area Offices.

Kentucky

Kentucky Cabinet of Human
　Resources
Division of Family Services
Children and Youth Services
　Branch
275 East Main Street
Frankfort, KY 40621

Make reports to County Offices in 14 state districts.

Louisiana

Louisiana Department of Health
　and Human Resources
Office of Human Development
Division of Children, Youth,
　and Family Services
P.O. Box 3318
Baton Rouge, LA 70821

Make reports to parish Protective Service Units.

Maine

Maine Department of Human
　Services
Child Protective Services
State House, Station 11
Augusta, ME 04333

Make reports to Regional Office of Human Services; in-state to (800) 452-1999 or out-of-state to (207) 289-2983. Both operate 24 hours a day.

Maryland

Maryland Department of Human
　Resources
Social Services Administration
Saratoga State Center
311 West Saratoga Street
Baltimore, MD 21201

Make reports to County Departments of Social Services or to local law enforcement agencies.

Massachusetts

Massachusetts Department of
　Social Services
Protective Services
150 Causeway Street, 11th Floor
Boston, MA 02114

Make reports to Area Offices or Protective Screening Unit or in-state to (800) 792-5200.

Michigan

Michigan Department of Social
　Services
Office of Children and Youth
　Services
Protective Services Division
300 South Capitol Avenue, Ninth Floor
Lansing, MI 48926

Make reports to County Departments of Social Services.

Minnesota

Minnesota Department of Human
　Services
Protective Services Division
Centennial Office Building
St. Paul, MN 55155

Make reports to County Departments of Social Services.

Mississippi

Mississippi Department of
　Public Welfare
Bureau of Family and Children's
　Services
Protection Department
P.O. Box 352
Jackson, MS 39205

Make reports in-state to (800) 222-8000 or out-of-state (during business hours) to (601) 354-0341.

Missouri
Missouri Child Abuse and
    Neglect Hotline
Department of Social Services
Division of Family Services
DFS, P.O. Box 88
Broadway Building
Jefferson City, MO 65103

Make reports in-state to (800) 392-3738 or
out-of-state to (314) 751-3448. Both operate 24
hours a day.

Montana
Department of Family Services
Child Protective Services
P.O. Box 8005
Helena, MT 59604

Make reports to County Departments of Family
Services.

Nebraska
Nebraska Department of Social
    Services
Human Services Division
301 Centennial Mall South,
    P.O. Box 95026
Lincoln, NE 68509

Make reports to local law enforcement agencies
or to local social services offices or in-state to
(800) 652-1999.

Nevada
Department of Human Resources
Welfare Division
2527 North Carson Street
Carson City, NV 89710

Make reports to Division of Welfare local
offices.

New Hampshire
New Hampshire Department of
    Health and Welfare
Division for Children and Youth
    Services
6 Hazen Drive
Concord, NH 03301-6522

Make reports to Division for Children and
Youth Services District Offices or in-state to
(800) 852-3345, Ext. 4455.

New Jersey
New Jersey Division of Youth
    and Family Services
P.O. Box CN717
One South Montgomery Street
Trenton, NJ 08625

Make reports in-state to (800) 792-8610. District offices also provide 24-hour telephone
services.

New Mexico
New Mexico Department of Human
    Services
Social Services Division
P.O. Box 2348
Santa Fe, NM 87504

Make reports to County Social Services offices
or in-state to (800) 432-6217.

New York
New York State Department of
    Social Services
Division of Family and Children
    Services
State Central Register of Child
    Abuse and Maltreatment
40 North Pearl Street
Albany, NY 12243

Make reports in-state to (800) 342-3720 or
out-of-state to (518) 474-9448.

North Carolina
North Carolina Department of
    Human Resources
Division of Social Services
Child Protective Services
325 North Salisbury Street
Raleigh, NC 27611

Make reports in-state to (800) 662-7030.

North Dakota
North Dakota Department of
    Human Services
Division of Children and Family
    Services
Child Abuse and Neglect Program
State Capitol
Bismarck, ND 58505

Make reports to County Social Services Offices.

Ohio

Ohio Department of Human
Services
Bureau of Children's Protective
Services
30 East Broad Street
Columbus, OH 43266-0423

Make reports to County Departments of Human
Services.

Oklahoma

Oklahoma Department of Human
Services
Division of Children and Youth
Services Child Abuse/Neglect
Section
P.O. Box 25352
Oklahoma City, OK 73125

Make reports in-state to (800) 522-3511.

Oregon

Department of Human Resources
Children's Services Division
Child Protective Services
198 Commercial Street, S.E.
Salem, OR 97310

Make reports to local Children's Services
Division Offices and to (503) 378-4722.

Pennsylvania

Pennsylvania Department of
Public Welfare.
Office of Children, Youth and
Families
Child Line and Abuse Registry
Lanco Lodge, P.O. Box 2675
Harrisburg, PA 17105

Make reports in-state to CHILDLINE (800)
932-0313 or out-of-state to (713) 783-8744.

Puerto Rico

Puerto Rico Department of Social Services
Services to Family With
Children
P.O. Box 11398
Fernandez Juncos Station
Santurez, PR 00910

Make reports to (809) 724-1333.

Rhode Island

Rhode Island Department for
Children and Their Families
Division of Child Protective
Services
610 Mt. Pleasant Avenue,
Bldg. #9
Providence, RI 02908

Make reports in-state to (800) RI-CHILD or
742-4453 or out-of-state to (401) 457-4996.

South Carolina

South Carolina Department of
Social Services
1535 Confederate Avenue
P.O. Box 1520
Columbia, SC 29202-1520

Make reports to County Departments of Social
Services.

South Dakota

Department of Social Services
Child Protection Services
Richard F. Kneip Building
700 Governors Drive
Pierre, SD 57501

Make reports to local social services offices.

Tennessee

Tennessee Department of Human
Services
Child Protective Services
Citizen Bank Plaza
400 Deadrick Street
Nashville, TN 37219

Make reports to County Departments of Human
Services

Texas

Texas Department of Human
Services
Protective Services for
Families and Children Branch
P.O. Box 2960, MC 537-W
Austin, TX 78769

Make reports in-state to (800) 252-5400 or
out-of-state to (512) 450-3360.

Utah
Department of Social Services
Division of Family Services
P.O. Box 45500
Salt Lake City, UT 84110

Make reports to Division of Family Services District Offices.

Vermont
Vermont Department of Social
   and Rehabilitative Services
Division of Social Services
103 South Main Street
Waterbury, VT 05676

Make reports to District Offices or to (802) 241-2131.

Virgin Islands
Virgin Islands Department of
   Human Services
Division of Social Services
P.O. Box 550
Charlotte Amalie
St. Thomas, VI 00801

Make reports to Division of Social Services (809) 774-9030.

Virginia
Commonwealth of Virginia
   Department of Social Services
Bureau of Child Protective
   Services
Blair Building
8007 Discovery Drive
Richmond, VA 23229-8699

Make reports in-state to (800) 552-7096 or out-of-state to (804) 281-9081.

Washington
Department of Social and Health Services
Division of Children and Family Services
Child Protective Services
Mail Stop OB 41-D
Olympia, WA 98504

Make reports in-state to (800) 562-5624 or local Social and Health Services offices.

West Virginia
West Virginia Department of
   Human Services
Division of Social Services
Child Protective Services
State Office Building
1900 Washington Street East
Charleston, WV 25305

Make reports in-state to (800) 352-6513.

Wisconsin
Wisconsin Department of Health
   and Social Services
Division of Community Services
Bureau for Children, Youth, and
   Families
1 West Wilson Street
Madison, WI 53707

Make reports to County Social Services Offices.

Wyoming
Department of Health and Social
   Services
Division of Public Assistance
   and Social Services
Hathaway Building
Cheyenne, WY 82002

Make reports to County Departments of Public Assistance and Social Services

4. CHILD ABUSE PREVENTION AND TREATMENT ACT

TITLE I—CHILD ABUSE PREVENTION AND TREATMENT ACT

SEC. 101. AMENDMENT TO THE CHILD ABUSE PREVENTION AND TREATMENT ACT.

The Child Abuse Prevention and Treatment Act (42 U.S.C. 5101 et seq.) is amended to read as follows:

"SECTION 1. SHORT TITLE AND TABLE OF CONTENTS.

"(a) SHORT TITLE.—This Act may be cited as the 'Child Abuse Prevention and Treatment Act'.

"(b) TABLE OF CONTENTS.—The table of contents is as follows:

"TABLE OF CONTENTS

"SEC. 2. NATIONAL CENTER ON CHILD ABUSE AND NEGLECT.

"(a) ESTABLISHMENT.—The Secretary of Health and Human Services shall establish an office to be known as the National Center on Child Abuse and Neglect.

"(b) APPOINTMENT OF DIRECTOR.—

"(1) APPOINTMENT.—The Secretary shall appoint a Director of the Center. Except as otherwise provided in this Act, the Director shall be responsible only for administration and operation of the Center and for carrying out the functions of the Center under this Act. The Director shall have experience in the field of child abuse and neglect.

"(2) COMPENSATION.—The Director shall be compensated at the annual rate provided for a level GS-15 employee under section 5332 of title 5, United States Code.

"(c) OTHER STAFF AND RESOURCES.—The Secretary shall make available to the Center such staff and resources as are necessary for the Center to carry out effectively its functions under this Act. The Secretary shall require that professional staff have experience relating to child abuse and neglect. The Secretary is required to justify, based on the priorities and needs of the Center, the hiring of any professional staff member who does not have experience relating to child abuse and neglect

"SEC. 3. ADVISORY BOARD ON CHILD ABUSE AND NEGLECT.

"(a) APPOINTMENT.—The secretary shall appoint an advisory board to be known as the Advisory Board on Child Abuse and Neglect.

"(b) SOLICITATION OF NOMINATIONS.—The Secretary shall publish a notice in the Federal Register soliciting nominations for the appointments required by subsection (a).

"(c) COMPOSITION OF BOARD —

(1) NUMBER OF MEMBERS.—The board shall consist of 15 members, each of which shall be a person who is recognized for expertise in an aspect of the area of child abuse, of which—

"(A) 2 shall be members of the task force established under section 4; and

"(B) 13 shall be members of the general public and may not be Federal employees.

"(2) REPRESENTATION.—The Secretary shall appoint members from the general public under paragraph (1)(B) who are individuals knowledgeable in child abuse and neglect prevention, intervention, treatment, or research, and with due consideration to representation of ethnic or racial minorities and diverse geographic areas, and who represent—

"(A) law (including the judiciary);

"(B) psychology (including child development);

"(C) social services (including child protective services);

"(D) medicine (including pediatrics);

"(E) State and local government;

"(F) organizations providing services to disabled persons;

"(G) organizations providing services to adolescents;

"(H) teachers;

"(I) parent self-help organizations;

"(J) parents' groups; and

"(K) voluntary groups

"(3) TERMS OF OFFICE.—(A) Except as otherwise provided in this subsection, members shall be appointed for terms of office of 4 years.

"(B) Of the members of the board from the general public first appointed under subsection (a)—

"(i) 4 shall be appointed for terms of office of 2 years;

"(ii) 4 shall be appointed for terms of office of 3 years; and

"(iii) 5 shall be appointed for terms of office of 4 years,

as determined by the members from the general public during the first meeting of the board.

"(C) No member of the board appointed under subsection (a) shall be eligible to serve in excess of two consecutive terms, but may continue to serve until such member's successor is appointed.

"(4) VACANCIES.—Any member of the board appointed under subsection (a) to fill a vacancy occurring before the expiration of the term to which such member's predecessor was appointed shall be appointed for the remainder of such term. If the vacancy occurs prior to the expiration of the term of a member of the board appointed under subsection (a), a replacement shall be appointed in the same manner in which the original appointment was made.

"(5) REMOVAL.—No member of the board may be removed during the term of office of such member except for just and sufficient cause.

"(d) ELECTION OF OFFICERS.—The board shall elect a chairperson and vice-chairperson at its first meeting from among the members from the general public.

"(e) MEETINGS.—The board shall meet not less than twice a year at the call of the chairperson. The chairperson, to the maximum extent practicable, shall coordinate meetings of the board with receipt of reports from the task force under section 4(f).

"(f) DUTIES.—The board shall—

"(1) annually submit to the Secretary and the appropriate committees of Congress a report containing—

"(A) recommendations on coordinating Federal child abuse and neglect activities to prevent duplication and ensure efficient allocations of resources and program effectiveness; and

"(B) recommendations as to carrying out the purposes of this Act;

"(2) annually submit to the Secretary and the Director a report containing long-term and short-term recommendations on—

"(A) programs;

"(B) research;

"(C) grant and contract needs;

"(D) areas of unmet needs; and

"(E) areas to which the Secretary should provide grant and contract priorities under sections 6 and 7; and

"(3) annually review the budget of the Center and submit to the Director a report concerning such review.

"(g) COMPENSATION.—

"(1) IN GENERAL.—Except as provided in paragraph (3), members of the board, other than those regularly employed by the Federal Government, while serving on business of the board may receive compensation at a rate not in excess of the daily equivalent payable to a GS-18 employee under section 5332 of title 5, United States Code, including traveltime.

"(2) TRAVEL.—Except as provided in paragraph (3), members of the board, while serving on business of the board away from their homes or regular places of business, may be allowed travel expenses (including per diem in lieu of subsistence) as authorized by section 5703 of title 5, United States Code, for persons in the Government service employed intermittently.

"(3) RESTRICTION.—The Director may not compensate a member of the board under this section if the member is receiving compensation or travel expenses from another source while serving on business of the board.

"SEC. 4. INTER-AGENCY TASK FORCE ON CHILD ABUSE AND NEGLECT.

"(a) ESTABLISHMENT.—The Secretary shall establish a task force to be known as the Inter-Agency Task Force on Child Abuse and Neglect.

"(b) COMPOSITION.—The Secretary shall request representation for the task force from Federal agencies with responsibility for programs and activities related to child abuse and neglect.

"(c) CHAIRPERSON.—The task force shall be chaired by the Director.

"(d) DUTIES.—The task force shall—

"(1) coordinate Federal efforts with respect to child abuse prevention and treatment programs;

"(2) encourage the development by other Federal agencies of activities relating to child abuse prevention and treatment;

"(3) coordinate the use of grants received under this Act with the use of grants received under other programs;

"(4) prepare a comprehensive plan for coordinating the goals, objectives, and activities of all Federal agencies and organizations which have responsibilities for programs and activities related to child abuse and neglect, and submit such plan to such Advisory Board not later than 12 months after the date of enactment of the Child Abuse Prevention, Adoption, and Family Services Act of 1988; and

"(5) coordinate adoption related activities, develop Federal standards with respect to adoption activities under this Act, and prevent duplication with respect to the allocation of resources to adoption activities.

"(e) MEETINGS.—The task force shall meet not less than three times annually at the call of the chairperson.

"(f) REPORTS.—The task force shall report not less than twice annually to the Center and the Board.

"SEC. 5. NATIONAL CLEARINGHOUSE FOR INFORMATION RELATING TO CHILD ABUSE.

"(a) ESTABLISHMENT.—Before the end of the 2-year period beginning on the date of the enactment of the Child Abuse Prevention, Adoption, and Family Services Act of 1988, the Secretary shall through the Center, or by contract of no less than 3 years duration let through a competition, establish a national clearinghouse for information relating to child abuse.

"(b) FUNCTIONS.—The Director shall, through the clearinghouse established by subsection (a)—

"(1) maintain, coordinate and disseminate information on all programs, including private programs, that show promise of success with respect to the prevention, identification, and treatment of child abuse and neglect, including the information provided by the National Center for Child Abuse and Neglect under section 6(b); and

"(2)maintain and disseminate information relating to—

"(A) the incidence of cases of child abuse and neglect in the general population;

"(B) the incidence of such cases in populations determined by the Secretary under section 105(a)(1);

"(C) the incidence of any such cases related to alcohol or drug abuse; and

"(D) State and local recordkeeping with respect to such cases.

"(c) COORDINATION WITH AVAILABLE RESOURCES.—In establishing a national clearinghouse as required by subsection (a), the Director shall—

"(1) consult with other Federal agencies that operate similar clearinghouses;

"(2) consult with the head of each agency that is represented on the task force on the development of the components for information collection and management of such clearinghouse;

"(3) develop a Federal data system involving the elements under subsection (b) which, to the extent practicable, coordinates existing State, regional, and local data systems; and

"(4) solicit public comment on the components of such clearinghouse.

"SEC. 6. RESEARCH AND ASSISTANCE ACTIVITIES OF THE NATIONAL CENTER ON CHILD ABUSE AND NEGLECT

"(a) RESEARCH.—

"(1) TOPICS.—The Secretary shall, through the Center, conduct research on—

"(A) the causes, prevention, identification, and treatment of child abuse and neglect; ·

"(B) appropriate and effective investigative, administrative, and judicial procedures with respect to cases of child abuse; and

"(C) the national incidence of child abuse and neglect, including—

"(i) the extent to which incidents of child abuse are increasing or decreasing in number and severity;

"(ii) the relationship of child abuse and neglect to nonpayment of child support, handicaps, and various other factors; and

"(iii) the incidence of substantiated reported child abuse cases that result in civil child protection proceedings or criminal proceedings, including the number of such cases with respect to which the court makes a finding that abuse or neglect exists and the disposition of such cases.

"(2) PRIORITIES.—(A) The secretary shall establish research and demonstration priorities for making grants or contracts for purposes of carrying out paragraph (1)(A) and activities under section 7.

"(B) In establishing research and demonstration priorities as required by subparagraph (A), the Secretary shall—

"(i) publish proposed priorities in the Federal Register for public comment; and

"(ii) allow not less than 60 days for public comment on such proposed priorities.

"(b) PUBLICATION AND DISSEMINATION OF INFORMATION.—The Secretary shall, through the Center—

"(1) as part of research activities establish a national data collection and analysis program, which, to the extent practical, coordinates existing State child abuse and neglect reports and which shall include—

"(A) standardized data on false, unfounded, or unsubstantiated reports; and

"(B) information on the number of deaths due to child abuse and neglect;

"(2) annually compile and analyze research on child abuse and neglect and publish a summary of such research;

"(3) compile, evaluate, publish, and disseminate to the States and to the clearinghouse, established under section 5, materials and information designed to assist the States in developing, establishing, and operating the programs described in section 10, including an evaluation of—

"(A) various methods and procedures for the investigation and prosecution of child physical and sexual abuse cases; and

"(B) resultant psychological trauma to the child victim;

"(4) compile, publish, and disseminate training materials—

"(A) for persons who are engaged in or intend to engage in prevention, identification, and treatment of child abuse and neglect; and

"(B) to appropriate State and local officials to assist in training law enforcement, legal, judicial, medical, mental health, and child welfare personnel in appropriate methods of interacting during investigative, administrative, and judicial proceedings with children who have been subjected to abuse; and

"(5) establish model information collection systems, in consultation with appropriate State and local agencies and professionals.

"(c) PROVISION OF TECHNICAL ASSISTANCE.—The Secretary shall, through the Center, provide technical assistance to public and nonprofit private agencies and organizations, including disability organizations and persons who work with children with handicaps, to assist such agencies and organizations in planning, improving, developing, and carrying out programs and activities relating to the prevention, identification, and treatment of child abuse and neglect.

"(d) AUTHORITY TO MAKE GRANTS OR ENTER INTO CONTRACTS.—

"(1) IN GENERAL.—The functions of the Secretary under this section may be carried out either directly or through grant or contract.

"(2) DURATION.—Grants under this section shall be made for periods of not more than 5 years. The Secretary shall review each such grant at least annually, utilizing peer review mechanisms to assure the quality and progress of research conducted under such grant.

"(3) PREFERENCE FOR LONG-TERM STUDIES.—In making grants for purposes of conducting research under subsection (a), the Secretary shall give special consideration to applications for long-term projects.

"(e) PEER REVIEW FOR GRANTS.—

"(1) ESTABLISHMENT OF PEER REVIEW PROCESS.—(A) The Secretary shall establish a formal peer review process for purposes of evaluating applications for grants and contracts under this section and determining the relative merits of the projects for which such assistance is requested.

"(B) Members of peer review panels shall be appointed by the Secretary from among individuals who are not officers or employees of the Office of Human Development Services. In making appointments to such panels, the Secretary shall include only experts in the field of child abuse and neglect.

"(2) REVIEW OF APPLICATIONS FOR ASSISTANCE.—Each peer review panel established under paragraph (1)(A) that reviews any application for a grant, contract, or other financial assistance shall—

"(A) determine the merit of each project described in such application; and

"(B) rank such application with respect to all other applications it reviews in the same priority area for the fiscal year involved, according to the relative merit of all of the projects that are described in such application and for which financial assistance is requested.

"(3) NOTICE OF APPROVAL.—(A) At the end of each application process, the Secretary shall make available upon request, no later than 14 days after the request, to the Committee on Education and Labor of the House of Representatives and the Committee on Labor and Human Resources of the Senate the list which identifies all applications reviewed by such panel and arranges such applications according to rank determined under paragraph (2) and a list of all applications funded.

"(B) In the instance in which the Secretary approves an application for a program without having approved all applications ranked above such application (as determined under subsection (e)(2)(B)), the Secretary shall append to the approved application a detailed explanation of the reasons relied on for approving the application and for failing to approve each pending application that is superior in merit, as indicated on the list under subsection (e)(2)(B)

"SEC. 7. GRANTS TO PUBLIC AGENCIES AND NONPROFIT PRIVATE ORGANIZATIONS FOR DEMONSTRATION OR SERVICE PROGRAMS AND PROJECTS.

"(a) GENERAL AUTHORITY.—The Secretary, through the Center, shall, in accordance with subsections (b) and (c), make grants to, and enter into contracts with, public agencies or nonprofit private organizations (or combinations of such agencies or organizations) for demonstration or service programs and projects designed to prevent, identify, and treat child abuse and neglect.

"(b) GRANTS FOR RESOURCE CENTERS.—The Secretary shall, directly or through grants or contracts with public or private nonprofit organizations under this section, provide for the establishment of resource centers—

"(1) serving defined geographic areas;

"(2) staffed by multidisciplinary teams of personnel trained in the prevention, identification, and treatment of child abuse and neglect; and

"(3) providing advice and consultation to individuals, agencies, and organizations which request such services

"(c) DISCRETIONARY GRANTS.—In addition to grants or contracts made under subsection (b), grants or contracts under this section may be used for the following:

"(1) Training programs—

"(A) for professional and paraprofessional personnel in the fields of medicine, law, education, social work, and other relevant fields who are engaged in, or intend to work in, the field of prevention, identification, and treatment of child abuse and neglect; or

"(B) to provide instruction in methods of protecting children from child abuse and neglect to children and to persons responsible for the welfare of children, including parents of and persons who work with children with handicaps.

"(2) Such other innovative programs and projects as the Secretary may approve, including programs and projects for parent self-help, for prevention and treatment of alcohol and drug-related child abuse and neglect, and for home health visitor programs designed to reach parents of children in populations in child risk is high, that show promise of successfully preventing and treating cases of child abuse and neglect, and for a parent self-help program of demonstrated effectiveness which is national in scope.

"(3) Projects which provide educational identification, prevention, and treatment services in cooperation with preschool and elementary and secondary schools.

"(4) Respite and crisis nursery programs provided by community-based organizations under the direction and supervision of hospitals.

"(5) Respite and crisis nursery programs provided by community-based organizations.

"(6)(A) Providing hospital-based information and referral services to—

"(i) parents of children with handicaps; and

"(ii) children who have been neglected or abused and their parents.

"(B) Except as provided in subparagraph (C)(iii), services provided under a grant received under this paragraph shall be provided as the hospital involved—

"(i) upon the birth or admission of a handicapped child; and

"(ii) upon the treatment of a child for abuse or neglect.

"(C) Services, as determined as appropriate by the grantee, provided under a grant received under this paragraph shall be hospital-based and shall consist of—

"(i) the provision of notice to parents that information relating to community services is available;

"(ii) the provision of appropriate information to parents of a child with handicaps regarding resources in the community, particularly parent training resources, that will assist such parents in caring for their child;

"(iii) the provision of appropriate information to parents of a child who has been neglected or abused regarding resources in the community, particularly parent training resources, that will assist such parents in caring for their child and reduce the possibility of abuse or neglect;

"(iv) the provision of appropriate follow-up services to parents of a child described in subparagraph (B) after the child has left the hospital; and

"(v) where necessary, assistance in coordination of community services available to parents of children described in subparagraph (B).

The grantee shall assure that parental involvement described in this subparagraphs is voluntary.

"(D) For purposes of this paragraph, a qualified grantee is a nonprofit acute care hospital that—

"(i) is in a combination with—

"(I) a health-care provider organization;

"(II) a child welfare organization;

"(III) a disability organization; and

"(IV) a State child protection agency;

"(ii) submits an application for a grant under this paragraph that is approved by the Secretary;

"(iii) maintains an office in the hospital involved for purposes of providing services under such grant;

"(iv) provides assurances to the Secretary that in the conduct of the project the confidentiality of medical, social, and personal information concerning any person described in subparagraph (A) or (B) shall be maintained, and shall be disclosed only to qualified persons providing required services described in subparagraph (C) for purposes relating to conduct of the project; and

"(v) assumes legal responsibility for carrying out the terms and conditions of the grant.

"(E) In awarding grants under this paragraph, the Secretary shall—

"(i) give priority under this section for two grants under this paragraph, provided that one grant shall be made to provide services in an urban setting and one grant shall be made to provide services in rural setting; and

"(ii) encourage qualified grantees to combine the amounts received under the grant with other funds available to such grantees.

"(7) Such other innovative programs and projects that show promise of preventing and treating cases of child abuse and neglect as the Secretary may approve.

"SEC. 8. GRANTS TO STATES FOR CHILD ABUSE AND NEGLECT PREVENTION AND TREATMENT PROGRAMS.

"(a) DEVELOPMENT AND OPERATION GRANTS.—The Secretary, through the Center, is authorized to make grants to the States for purposes of assisting the States in developing, strengthening, and carrying out child abuse and neglect prevention and treatment programs.

"(b) ELIGIBILITY REQUIREMENTS.—In order for a State to qualify for a grant under subsection (a), such State shall—

"(1) have in effect a State law relating to child abuse and neglect, including—

"(A) provisions for the reporting of known and suspected instances of child abuse and neglect; and

"(B) provisions for immunity from prosecution under State and local laws for persons who report instances of child abuse or neglect for circumstances arising from such reporting;

"(2) provide that upon receipt of a report of known or suspected instances of child abuse or neglect an investigation shall be initiated promptly to substantiate the accuracy of the report, and, upon a finding of abuse or neglect, immediate steps shall be taken to protect the health and welfare of the abused or neglected child and of any other child under the same care who may be in danger of abuse or neglect;

"(3) demonstrate that there are in effect throughout the State, in connection with the enforcement of child abuse and neglect laws and with the reporting of suspected instances of child abuse and neglect, such—

"(A) administrative procedures;

"(B) personnel trained in child abuse and neglect prevention and treatment;

"(C) training procedures;

"(D) institutional and other facilities (public and private); and

"(E) such related multidisciplinary programs and services,

as may be necessary or appropriate to ensure that the State will deal effectively with child abuse and neglect cases in the State;

"(4) provide for methods to preserve the confidentiality of all records in order to protect the rights of the child and of the child's parents or guardians;

"(5) provide for the cooperation of law enforcement officials, courts of competent jurisdiction, and appropriate State agencies providing human services;

"(6) provide that in every case involving an abused or neglected child which results in a judicial proceeding a guardian ad litem shall be appointed to represent the child in such proceedings;

"(7) provide that the aggregate of support for programs or projects related to child abuse and neglect assisted by State funds shall not be reduced below the level provided during fiscal year 1973, and set forth policies and procedures designed to ensure that Federal funds made available under this Act for any fiscal year shall be so used as to supplement and, to the extent practicable, increase the level of State funds which would, in the absence of Federal funds, be available for such programs and projects;

"(8) provide for dissemination of information, including efforts to encourage more accurate reporting, to the general public with respect to the problem of child abuse and neglect and the facilities and prevention and treatment methods available to combat instances of child abuse and neglect;

"(9) to the extent feasible, ensure that parental organizations combating child abuse and neglect receive preferential treatment; and

"(10) have in place for the purpose of responding to the reporting of medical neglect (including instances of withholding of medically indicated treatment from disabled infants with life-threatening conditions), procedures or programs, or both (within the State child protective services system), to provide for—

"(A) coordination and consultation with individuals designated by and within appropriate health-care facilities;

"(B) prompt notification by individuals designated by and within appropriate health-care facilities of cases of suspected medical neglect (including instances of withholding of medically indicated treatment from disabled infants with life-threatening conditions); and

"(C) authority, under State law, for the State child protective service system to pursue any legal remedies, including the authority to initiate legal proceedings in a court of competent jurisdiction, as may be necessary to prevent the withholding of medically indicated treatment from disabled infants with life-threatening conditions.

"(c) WAIVERS.—

"(1) GENERAL RULE.—Subject to paragraph (3) of this subsection, any State which does not qualify for assistance under this subsection may be granted a waiver of any requirement under paragraph (2) of this subsection—

"(A) for a period of not more than one year, if the Secretary makes a finding that such State is making a good faith effort to comply with any such requirement, and for a second one-year period if the Secretary makes a finding that such State is making substantial progress to achieve such compliance; or

"(B) for a nonrenewable period of not more than two years in the case of a State the legislature of which meets only biennially, if the Secretary makes a finding that such State is making a good faith effort to comply with such requirement.

"(2) EXTENSION.—(A) Subject to paragraph (3) of this subsection, any State whose waiver under paragraph (1) expired as of the end of fiscal year 1986 may be granted an extension of such waiver, if the Secretary makes a finding that such State is making a good faith effort to comply with the requirements under subsection (b) of this section—

"(i) through the end of fiscal year 1988; or

"(ii) in the case of a State the legislature of which meets biennially, through the end of fiscal year 1989 or the end of the next regularly scheduled session of such legislature, whichever is earlier.

"(B) This provision shall be effective retroactively to October 1, 1986.

"(3) REQUIREMENTS UNDER SUBSECTION (b)(10).—No waiver under paragraph (1) or (2) may apply to any requirement under subsection (b)(10) of this section.

"(d) REDUCTION OF FUNDS IN CASE OF FAILURE TO OBLIGATE.—If a State fails to obligate funds awarded under subsection (a) before the expiration of the 18-month period beginning on the date of such award, the next award made to such State under this section after the expiration of such period shall be reduced by an amount equal of the amount of such unobligated funds unless the Secretary determines that extraordinary reasons justify the failure to so obligate.

"(e) RESTRICTIONS RELATING TO CHILD WELFARE SERVICES.—Programs or projects relating to child abuse and neglect assisted under part B of title IV of the Social Security Act shall comply with the requirements set forth in paragraphs (1)(A), (2), (4), (5), and (10) of subsection (b).

"(f) COMPLIANCE AND EDUCATION GRANTS.—The Secretary is authorized to make grants to the States for the purposes of developing, implementing, or operating—

"(1) the procedures or programs required under subsection (b)(10);

"(2) information and education programs or training programs designed to improve the provision of services to disabled infants with life-threatening conditions for—

"(A) professional and paraprofessional personnel concerned with the welfare of disabled infants with life-threatening conditions, including personnel employed in child protective services programs and health-care facilities; and

"(B)the parents of such infants; and

"(3) programs to assist in obtaining or coordinating necessary services for families of disabled infants with life-threatening conditions, including—

"(A) existing social and health services;

"(B) financial assistance; and

"(C) services necessary to facilitate adoptive placement of any such infants who have been relinquished for adoption.

"SEC. 9. TECHNICAL ASSISTANCE TO STATES FOR CHILD ABUSE PREVENTION AND TREATMENT PROGRAMS.

"(a) TRAINING AND TECHNICAL ASSISTANCE.—The Secretary shall provide, directly or through grants or contracts with public or private nonprofit organizations for—

"(1) training and technical assistance programs to assist States in developing, implementing, or operating programs and procedures meeting the requirements of section 8(b)(10); and

"(2) the establishment and operation of national and regional information and resource clearing-houses for the purpose of providing the most current and complete information regarding medical treatment procedures and resources and community resources for the provision of services and treatment to disabled infants with life-threatening conditions, including—

"(A) compiling, maintaining, updating, and disseminating regional directories of community services and resources (including the names and phone numbers of State and local medical organizations) to assist parents, families, and physicians; and

"(B) attempting to coordinate the availability of appropriate regional education resources for health-care personnel.

"(b) LIMITATION ON FUNDING.—Not more than $1,000,000 of the funds appropriated for any fiscal year for purposes of carrying out this Act may be used to carry out this section.

"SEC. 10. GRANTS TO STATES FOR PROGRAMS RELATING TO THE INVESTIGATION AND PROSECUTION OF CHILD ABUSE CASES.

"(a) GRANTS TO STATES.—The Secretary, acting through the Center and in consultation with the Attorney General, is authorized to make grants to the States for the purpose of assisting States in developing, establishing, and operating programs designed to improve—

"(1) the handling of child abuse cases, particularly cases of child sexual abuse, in a manner which limits additional trauma to the child victim; and

"(2) the investigation and prosecution of cases of child abuse, particularly child sexual abuse.

"(b) ELIGIBILITY REQUIREMENTS.—In order for a State to qualify for assistance under this section, such State shall—

"(1) fulfill the requirements of sections 8(b) and 8(e) or receive a waiver under section 8(c);

"(2) establish a task force as provided in subsection (c);

"(3) fulfill the requirements of subsection (d); and

"(4) submit an application to the Secretary at such time and containing such information and assurances as the Secretary considers necessary, including an assurance that the State will—

"(A) make such reports to the Secretary as may reasonably be required; and

"(B) maintain and provide access to records relating to activities under subsections (a) and (b).

"(c) STATE TASK FORCES.—

"(1) GENERAL RULE.—Except as provided in paragraph (2), a State requesting assistance under this section shall establish or designate a State multidisciplinary task force on children's justice (hereinafter referred to as 'State task force') composed of professionals with knowledge and experience relating to the criminal justice system and issues of child abuse. The State task force shall include—

"(A) individuals representing the law enforcement community;

"(B) judicial and legal officers (including individuals involved with the defense as well as the prosecution of such cases);

"(C) child advocates;

"(D) health and mental health professionals;

"(E) individuals representing child protective service agencies;

"(F) individuals experienced in working with children with handicaps;

"(G) parents; and

"(H) representatives of parents' groups.

"(2) EXISTING TASK FORCE.—As determined by the Secretary, a State commission or task force established after January 1, 1983, with substantially comparable membership and functions, may be considered the State task force for purposes of this subsection.

"(d) STATE TASK FORCE STUDY.—Before a State receives assistance under this section, the State task force shall—

"(1) review and evaluate State investigative, administrative and judicial handling of cases of child abuse, particularly child sexual abuse; and

"(2) make recommendations in each of the categories described in subsection (e).
The task force may make such other comments and recommendations as are considered relevant and useful.

"(e) ADOPTION OF STATE TASK FORCE RECOMMENDATIONS.—

"(1) GENERAL RULE.—Subject to the provisions of paragraph (2), before a State receives assistance under this section, a State shall adopt recommendations of the State task force in each of the following categories—

"(A) investigative, administrative, and judicial handling of cases of child abuse, particularly child sexual abuse cases, in a manner which reduces the additional trauma to the child victim and which also ensures procedural fairness to the accused;

"(B) experimental, model and demonstration programs for testing innovative approaches and techniques which may improve the rate of successful prosecution or enhance the effectiveness of judicial and administrative action in child abuse cases, particularly child sexual abuse cases and which also ensure procedural fairness to the accused; and

"(C) reform of State laws, ordinances, regulations and procedures to provide comprehensive protection for children from abuse, particularly child sexual abuse, while ensuring fairness to all affected persons.

"(2) EXEMPTION.—As determined by the Secretary, a State shall be considered to be in fulfillment of the requirements of this subsection if—

"(A) the State adopts an alternative to the recommendations of the State task force, which carries out the purpose of this section, in each of the categories under paragraph (1) for which the State task force's recommendations are not adopted; or

"(B) the State is making substantial progress toward adopting recommendations of the State task force or a comparable alternative to such recommendations.

"(f) FUNDS AVAILABLE.—For grants under this section, the Secretary shall use the amount authorized by section 1404A of the Victims of Crime Act of 1984

"SEC. 11. MISCELLANEOUS REQUIREMENTS RELATING TO ASSISTANCE.

"(a) CONSTRUCTION OF FACILITIES.—

"(1) RESTRICTION ON USE OF FUNDS.—Assistance provided under this Act may not be used for construction of facilities.

"(2) LEASE, RENTAL, OR REPAIR.—The Secretary may authorize the use of funds received under this Act—

"(A) where adequate facilities are not otherwise available, for the lease or rental of facilities; or

"(B) for the repair or minor remodeling or alteration of existing facilities.

"(b) GEOGRAPHICAL DISTRIBUTION.—The Secretary shall establish criteria designed to achieve equitable distribution of assistance under this Act among the States, among geographic areas of the Nation, and among rural and urban areas of the Nation. To the extent possible, the Secretary shall ensure that the citizens of each State receive assistance from at least one project under this Act.

"(c) PREVENTION ACTIVITIES.—The Secretary, in consultation with the task force and the board, shall ensure that a majority share of assistance under this Act is available for discretionary research and demonstration grants.

"(d) LIMITATIONS.—No funds appropriated for any grant or contract pursuant to authorizations made in this Act may be used for any purpose other than that for which such funds were authorized to be appropriated.

"SEC. 12. COORDINATION OF CHILD ABUSE AND NEGLECT PROGRAMS.

"The Secretary shall prescribe regulations and make such arrangements as may be necessary or appropriate to ensure that there is effective coordination among programs related to child abuse and neglect under this Act and other such programs which are assisted by Federal funds.

"SEC. 13. REPORTS.

"(a) COORDINATION EFFORTS.—Not later than March 1 of the second year following the date of enactment of Child Abuse Prevention, Adoption, and Family Services Act of 1988 and every 2 years thereafter, the Secretary shall submit to the appropriate committees of Congress a report on efforts during the 2-year period preceding the date of the report to coordinate the objectives and activities of agencies and organizations which are responsible for programs and activities related to child abuse and neglect.

"(b) EFFECTIVENESS OF STATE PROGRAMS AND TECHNICAL ASSISTANCE.— Not later than two years after the first fiscal year for which funds are obligated under section 1404A of the Victims of Crime Act of 1984, the Secretary shall submit to the appropriate committees of Congress a report evaluating the effectiveness of—

"(1) assisted programs in achieving the objectives of section 10; and

"(2) the technical assistance provided under section 9

"SEC. 14. DEFINITIONS.

"For purposes of this Act—

"(1) the term 'board' means the Advisory Board on Child Abuse and Neglect established under section 3;

"(2) the term 'Center' means the National Center on Child Abuse and Neglect established under section 2;

"(3) the term 'child' means a person who has not attained the lesser of—

"(A) the age of 18; or

"(B) except in the case of sexual abuse, the age specified by the child protection law of the State in which the child resides;

"(4) the term 'child abuse and neglect' means the physical or mental injury, sexual abuse or exploitation, negligent treatment, or maltreatment of a child by a person who is responsible for the child's welfare, under circumstances which indicate that the child's health or welfare is harmed or threatened thereby, as determined in accordance with regulations prescribed by the Secretary;

"(5) the term 'person who is responsible for the child's welfare' includes—

"(A) any employee of a residential facility; and

"(B) any staff person providing out-of-home care;

"(6) the term 'Secretary' means the Secretary of Health and Human Services;

"(7) the term 'sexual abuse' includes—

"(A) the employment, use, persuasion, inducement, enticement, or coercion of any child to engage in, or assist any other person to engage in, any sexually explicit conduct or simulation of such conduct for the purpose of producing a visual depiction of such conduct; or

"(B) the rape, molestation, prostitution, or other form of sexual exploitation of children, or incest with children;

"(8) the term 'State' means each of the several States, the District of Columbia, the Commonwealth of Puerto Rico, the Virgin Islands, Guam, American Samoa, the Commonwealth of the Northern Mariana Islands, and the Trust Territory of the Pacific Islands;

"(9) the term 'task force' means the Inter-Agency Task Force on Child Abuse and Neglect established under section 4; and

"(10) the term 'withholding of medically indicated treatment' means the failure to respond to the infant's life-threatening conditions by providing treatment (including appropriate nutrition, hydration, and medication) which, in the treating physician's or physicians' reasonable medical judgment, will be most likely to be effective in ameliorating or correcting all such conditions, except that the term does not include the failure to provide treatment (other than appropriate nutrition, hydration, or medication) to an infant when in the treating physician's or physicians' reasonable medical judgment—

"(A) the infant is chronically and irreversibly comatose;

"(B) the provision of such treatment would—

"(i) merely prolong dying;

"(ii) not be effective in ameliorating or correcting all of the infant's life-threatening conditions; or

"(iii) otherwise be futile in terms of the survival of the infant; or

"(C) the provision of such treatment would be virtually futile in terms of the survival of the infant and the treatment itself under such circumstances would be inhumane

SEC. 15. AUTHORIZATION OF APPROPRIATIONS.

"(a) IN GENERAL.—There are authorized to be appropriated for purposes of carrying out this Act $48,000,000 for fiscal year 1988, and such sums as may be necessary for fiscal years 1989, 1990, and 1991. Of the funds appropriated for any fiscal year under this section, except as provided in the succeeding sentence (1)(A) $11,000,000 shall be available in each fiscal year for activities under sections 8(a) and 9 of this Act, giving special consideration to continued funding of child abuse and neglect programs or projects (previously funded by the Department of Health and Human Services) of national or regional scope and demonstrated effectiveness, (2) $5,000,000 shall be available in each such year for grants and contracts under section 7(a) of this Act, for identification, treatment, and prevention of sexual abuse, and (3) $5,000,000 shall be available in each such year for the purpose of making additional grants to the States to carry out the provisions of section 8(f) of this Act. With respect to any fiscal year in which the total amount appropriated under this section is less than $30,000,000, no less than $20,000,000 of the funds appropriated in such fiscal year shall be available as provided in clause (1) in the preceding sentence and of the remainder, one-half shall be available as provided for in clause (2) and one-half as provided for in clause (3) in the preceding sentence.

"(b) AVAILABILITY OF FUNDS WITHOUT FISCAL YEAR LIMITATION.—The Secretary shall ensure that funds appropriated pursuant to authorizations in this Act shall remain available until expended for the purposes for which they were appropriated "

SEC. 102 .CHILD ABUSE AND DISABILITY.

(a)STUDY.—The Director of the National Center on Child Abuse and Neglect shall conduct a study of—

(1) the incidence of child abuse among children with handicaps, including children in out-of-home placements, and the relationship between child abuse and children's handicapping conditions; and

(2) the incidence of children who have developed handicapping conditions as a result of child abuse or neglect.

(b) REPORT.—Not later than 2 years after the date of enactment of this Act, the Director shall report to the appropriate committees of Congress with respect to the study conducted pursuant to subsection (a). The report shall include—

(1) the information and data gathered;

(2) an analysis of such information and data; and

(3) recommendations on how to prevent abuse of disabled children.

SEC. 103. CHILD ABUSE AND ALCOHOLIC FAMILIES.

(a) STUDY—The Director of the National Center on Child Abuse and Neglect shall conduct a study of the incidence of child abuse in alcoholic families and the relationship between child abuse and familial alcoholism.

(b) REPORT.—Not later than 2 years after the date of enactment of this Act, the Director shall report to the appropriate committees of Congress with respect to the study conducted pursuant to subsection (a). The report shall include—

(1) the information and data gathered;

(2) an analysis of such information and data; and

(3) recommendations on how to prevent child abuse in alcoholic families.

SEC. 104. STUDY OF GUARDIAN-AD-LITEM.

(a) STUDY.—The Director of the National Center on Child Abuse and Neglect shall conduct a study of—

(1) how individual legal representation of children in cases of child abuse or neglect has been provided in each State; and

(2) the effectiveness of legal representation of children in cases of abuse or neglect through the use of guardian-ad-litem and court appointed special advocates.

(b) REPORT.—Not later than 2 years after the date of enactment of this Act, the Director shall report to the appropriate committees of Congress with respect to the study conducted pursuant to subsection (a). The report shall include—

(1) the information and data gathered;

(2) an analysis of such information and data; and

(3) recommendations on how to improve legal representation of children in cases of abuse or neglect.

SEC. 105. HIGH RISK STUDY.

(a) STUDY.—The Director of the National Center on Child Abuse and Neglect shall conduct a study—

(1) to identify groups which have been historically underserved or unserved by programs relating to child abuse and neglect; and

(2) to report the incidence of child abuse and neglect among children who are members of such groups.

(b) REPORT.—Not later than 2 years after the date of enactment of this Act, the Director shall report to the appropriate committees of Congress with respect to the study conducted pursuant to subsection (a). The report shall include—

(1) the information and data gathered;

(2) an analysis of such information and data; and

(3) recommendations on how to better meet the needs of underserved or unserved groups.

SEC. 106. PRESIDENTIAL COMMISSION ON CHILD AND YOUTH DEATHS.

(a) FINDINGS.—The Congress finds that—

(1) even by conservative estimates, during 1985 and 1986, child abuse fatalities in this country increased by 23 percent;

(2) the average age of children who die from abuse and neglect is two years old;

(3) child abuse fatalities are not inherently predictable but many are preventable;

(4) many accidental childhood injuries are likewise preventable;

(5) accidental childhood injuries remain the biggest killer and disabler of children between the ages of 1 and 14;

(6) in the face of stagnating infant mortality indicators, the United States is now tied for last place among 20 industrialized nations with respect to infant mortality;

(7) the teen suicide rate is starting to climb again, with deaths totaling over 5,000 in 1986; and

(8) homicide is the second leading cause of death in youths aged fourteen to twenty-four years.

(b) ESTABLISHMENT OF COMMISSION.—There is established a National Commission on Child and Youth Deaths (hereafter in this section referred to as the "Commission"). The Commission shall be composed of fifteen members as follows:

(1) Two members of the Senate, one to be selected by the Majority Leader of the Senate, the other to be selected by the Minority Leader of the Senate.

(2) Two members of the House, one to be selected by the Speaker of the House of Representatives, the other to be selected by the Minority Leader of the House.

(3) Four representatives of State government shall be selected by the President:

(A) The chief executive officer of a State.

(B) A chief State official responsible for administering child health and mental health programs.

(C) A chief State official responsible for administering children's social services programs.

(D) A chief State official responsible for administering law enforcement programs.

(4) The Secretary of Health and Human Services.

(5) Six at-large members, including representatives of community-based organizations with demonstrated expertise in the prevention and identification of child and youth deaths due to child abuse and neglect, infant mortality (including sudden infant death syndrome), suicide, homicide, and unintentional injuries, to be jointly selected by the Majority Leader of the Senate and Speaker of the House of Representatives.

(c) STUDY AND EVALUATION BY THE COMMISSION.—The Commission shall study and evaluate comprehensively Federal, State, and local public and private resources which affect child and youth deaths and shall—

(1) evaluate the adequacy and effectiveness of programs designed to prevent or identify child and youth deaths which are intentionally caused or which occur due to negligence, neglect, or a failure to exercise proper care, including child health and mental health services, child protective services, child welfare services, education, juvenile justice services, and law enforcement activities;

(2) evaluate the effectiveness of current Federal, State, and local policies and systems aimed at appropriately identifying and collecting accurate, uniform data on child and youth deaths in a coordinated fashion;

(3) evaluate the adequacy of current Federal, State, and local efforts to enable an appropriate distribution of properly trained child health, mental health, social services, protective services, education, juvenile justice, and law enforcement personnel to prevent and identify child and youth deaths; and

(4) identify current resource limitations on and intergovernmental and Federal interagency barriers to the care needed to prevent high child and youth death rates.

In order to conduct the study and evaluation required by this subsection, the Commission shall hold hearings in areas of the United States with high child and youth death rates.

(d) RECOMMENDATIONS AND REPORT OF THE COMMISSION.—(1) The Commission shall make recommendations with respect to—

(A) a national policy designed to reduce and prevent child and youth deaths, including recommendations for more accurate reporting systems and recommendations concerning appropriate roles for the Federal Government, States, and local governments and the private sector;

(B) specific changes needed in Federal laws and Federal programs to achieve an effective Federal role in preventing child and youth deaths, including the programs specified in subparagraph (A); and

(C) specific changes needed to improve national data collection with respect to child and youth deaths.

In making its recommendations, the Commission shall review recommendations made in recent regional and national conferences and reports on child and youth deaths.

(2) Within 12 months after the appointment of the Commission, the Commission shall prepare and transmit to the President and the appropriate committees of the Congress a report describing the activities of the Commission and containing information gathered and evaluations required by subsection (c) and recommendations required by paragraph (1) of this subsection.

(e) ADMINISTRATION PROVISIONS.—(1) A vacancy in the Commission shall be filled in the same manner as the original appointment was made. A vacancy in the Commission shall not affect its powers.

(2) Members shall be appointed for the life of the Commission.

(3) The members of the Commission shall elect a Chairman from among the members of the Commission.

(4) Eleven members of the Commission shall constitute a quorum, but a lesser number may hold hearings.

(5) The Commission shall hold its first meeting on a date specified by the President which is not later than 90 days after October 1, 1988. Thereafter, the Commission shall meet at the call of the Chairman or a majority of its members, but shall meet at least three times during the life of the Commission.

(f) COMPENSATION OF MEMBERS.—(1) Each member of the Commission who is not an officer or employee of the United States shall be compensated at a rate equal to the daily equivalent of the annual rate of basic pay prescribed for grade GS-18 of the General Schedule under section 5332 of title 5, United States Code, for each day (including traveltime) during which such member is engaged in the actual performance of duties as a member of the Commission. Each member of the Commission who is an officer or employee of the United States shall receive no additional compensation.

(2) While away from their homes or regular place of business in the performance of duties for the Commission, all members of the Commission shall be allowed travel expenses, including per diem in lieu of subsistence, at rates authorized for employees of agencies under sections 5702 and 5703 of title 5, United States Code.

(g) EXECUTIVE DIRECTOR OF COMMISSION.—(1) The Commission shall appoint an Executive Director who shall be compensated at a rate not to exceed the rate of basic pay prescribed for level V of the Executive Schedule under section 5316 of title 5, United States Code.

(2) With the approval of the Commission, the Executive Director may appoint and fix the compensation of such additional personnel as the Executive Director considers necessary to carry out the duties of the Commission.

(3) The Executive Director and the additional personnel of the Commission referred to in paragraph (2) may be appointed without regard to the provisions of chapter 51 and subchapter III of chapter 53 of such title relating to classification and General Schedule pay rates.

(4) Subject to such rules as may be prescribed by the Commission, the Executive Director may procure temporary or intermittent services under section 3109(b) of title 5, United States Code, at rates for individuals not to exceed $200 per day.

(5) Upon request of the Commission, the head of any Federal agency is authorized to detail, on a reimbursable basis, any of the personnel of such agency to the Commission to assist the Commission in carrying out its duties under this section.

(6) The Administrator of General Services shall provide to the Commission on a reimbursable basis such administrative and support services as the Commission may request.

(h) POWERS OF THE COMMISSION.—(1) For the purpose of carrying out this section, the Commission may hold such hearings, sit and act at such times and places, take such testimony, and receive such evidence, as the Commission considers appropriate. The Commission may administer oaths or affirmations to witnesses appearing before the Commission

(2) Any member or employee of the Commission may, if authorized by the Commission, take any action which the Commission is authorized to take by this subsection.

(3) The Commission may secure directly from any Federal agency such information as may be necessary to enable the Commission to carry out this section. Upon request of the Chairman of the Commission, the head of such agency shall furnish such information to the Commission.

(i) AUTHORIZATION OF APPROPRIATIONS.—For fiscal years beginning after September 30, 1987, there are authorized to be appropriated such sums as may be necessary to carry out this section.

(j) TERMINATION.—The Commission shall terminate 90 days after the date on which the Commission transmits the report required under subsection (d)(2) to the President and the appropriate committees of Congress.

TITLE II—CHILD ABUSE PREVENTION AND TREATMENT AND ADOPTION REFORM ACT OF 1978

SEC. 201. AUTHORIZATION FOR CHILD ABUSE PREVENTION AND TREATMENT AND ADOPTION REFORM ACT OF 1978.

Section 205 of the Child Abuse Prevention and Treatment and Adoption Reform Act of 1978 is amended to read as follows:

"AUTHORIZATION OF APPROPRIATIONS

"SEC. 205. (a) There are hereby authorized to be appropriated $6,000,000 for the fiscal year 1988, and such sums as may be necessary for each of the fiscal years 1989, 1990, and 1991 to carry out programs and activities under this Act except for programs and activities authorized under sections 203(b)(8) and 203(c)(1).

"(b) For any fiscal year in which appropriations under subsection (a) exceeds $5,000,000, there are authorized to be appropriated $3,000,000 for fiscal year 1988, and such sums as may be necessary for fiscal years 1989, 1990, and 1991 for the purpose of carrying out section 203(b)(8), and there are authorized to be appropriated $3,000,000 for fiscal year 1988, and such sums as may be necessary for fiscal years 1989, 1990, and 1991 for the purpose of carrying out section 203(c)(1).

"(c) The Secretary shall ensure that funds appropriated pursuant to authorizations in this Act shall remain available until expended for the purposes for which they were appropriated."

SEC. 202. AMENDMENTS TO CHILD ABUSE PREVENTION AND TREATMENT AND ADOPTION REFORM ACT OF 1978 RELATING TO ADOPTION ASSISTANCE AND SERVICES.

(a) MINORITY CHILDREN PLACEMENTS.—Section 203(b) of title II of the Child Abuse Prevention, Adoption, and Family Services Act of 1978 is amended by—

(1) striking the "and" at the end of paragraph (6);

(2) striking the period at the end of paragraph (7) and inserting "; and"; and

(3) adding the following new paragraph:

"(8) provide (directly or by grant to or contract with States, local government entities, public or private nonprofit licensed child welfare or adoption agencies or adoptive family groups and community-based organizations with experience in working with minority populations) for the provision of programs aimed at increasing the number of minority children (who are in foster care and have the goal of adoption) placed in adoptive families, with a special emphasis on recruitment of minority families—

"(A) which may include such activities as—

"(i) outreach, public education, or media campaigns to inform the public of the needs and numbers of such children;

"(ii) recruitment of prospective adoptive families for such children;

"(iii) expediting, where appropriate, the legal availablility of such children;

"(iv) expediting, where appropriate, the agency assessment of prospective adoptive families identified for such children;

"(v) formation of prospective adoptive family support groups;

"(vi) training of personnel of—

"(I) public agencies;

"(II) private nonprofit child welfare and adoption agencies that are licensed by the State and;

"(III) adoptive parents organizations and community-based organizations with experience in working with minority populations;

"(vii) use of volunteers and adoptive parent groups; and

"(viii) any other activities determined by the Secretary to further the purposes of this Act; and

"(B) shall be subject to the condition that such grants or contracts may be renewed if documentation is provided to the Secretary demonstrating that appropriate and sufficient placements of such children have occurred during the previous funding period."

(b) POST LEGAL ADOPTION SERVICES.—Section 203 is amended by adding the following new subsection:

"(c)(1) The Secretary shall provide (directly or by grant to or contract with States, local government entities, public or private nonprofit licensed child welfare or adoption agencies or adoptive family groups) for the provision of post legal adoption services for families who have adopted special needs children.

"(2) Services provided under grants made under this subsection shall supplement, not supplant, services from any other funds available for the same general purposes, including—

"(A) individual counseling;

"(B) group counseling;

"(C) family counseling;

"(D) case management;

"(E) training public agency adoption personnel, personnel of private, nonprofit child welfare and adoption agencies licensed by the State to provide adoption services, mental health services professionals, and other support personnel to provide services under this subsection;

"(F) assistance to adoptive parent organizations; and

"(G) assistance to support groups for adoptive parents, adopted children, and siblings of adopted children.

(c) PLACEMENT OF FOSTER CARE CHILDREN.—Section 203, as amended by subsection (b), is amended by adding the following new subsection:

"(d)(1) The Secretary shall make grants for improving State efforts to increase the placement of foster care children legally free for adoption, according to a pre-established plan and goals for improvement. Grants funded by this section must include a strong evaluation component which outlines the innovations used to improve the placement of special needs children who are legally free for adoption, and the successes and failures of the initiative. The evaluations will be submitted to the Secretary who will compile the results of projects funded by this section and submit a report to the appropriate committees of Congress. The emphasis of this program must focus on the improvement of the placement rate—not the aggregate number of special needs children placed in permanent homes. The Secretary, when reviewing grant applications shall give priority to grantees who propose improvements designed to continue in the absence of Federal funds.

"(2) Each State entering into an agreement under this subsection shall submit an application to the Secretary for each fiscal year in a form and manner determined to be appropriate by the Secretary. Each application shall include verification of the placements described in paragraph (1).

"(3)(A) Payments under this subsection shall begin during fiscal year 1989. Payments under this section during any fiscal year shall not exceed $1,000,000. No payment may be made under this subsection unless an amount in excess of $5,000,000 is appropriated for such fiscal year under section 205(a).

"(B) Any payment made to a State under this subsection which is not used by such State for the purpose provided in paragraph (1) during the fiscal year payment is made shall revert to the Secretary on October 1st of the next fiscal year and shall be used to carry out the purposes of this Act."

TITLE III—FAMILY VIOLENCE PREVENTION AND SERVICES ACT

SEC 301. AUTHORIZATION FOR FAMILY VIOLENCE PREVENTION AND SERVICES ACT.

(a) AUTHORIZATION.—Section 310(a) of the Family Violence Prevention and Services Act is amended by—

(1) striking "and" the first place it appears and inserting a comma; and

(2) by striking out the period at the end and inserting in lieu thereof the following: ", $26,000,000 for fiscal year 1988, and such sums as may be necessary for each of the fiscal years 1989, 1990, and 1991."

(b) LIMITATION ON FUNDS AVAILABLE.—Section 310 of such Act is amended by adding at the end thereof the following:

"(c) The Secretary shall ensure that funds appropriated pursuant to authorizations in this Act shall remain available until expended for the purposes for which they were appropriated."

SEC. 302. REMOVAL OF THREE-YEAR LIMIT ON GRANTS FOR SHELTERS.

Section 303(c) of the Family Violence Prevention and Services Act (42 U.S.C. 10402(c)) is amended by striking out the second sentence.

SEC. 303. AMENDMENTS TO FAMILY VIOLENCE PREVENTION AND SERVICES ACT.

(a) TECHNICAL AMENDMENT.—The Family Violence Prevention and Services Act is amended by striking out section 312 the first time such section appears in such Act (Public Law 98-457; 42 U.S.C. 10411).

(b) INFORMATION AND TRAINING GRANTS.—Section 311(b) of the Family Violence Prevention and Services Act is amended by inserting at the end thereof the following:

"(2)(A) The Secretary shall award grants or contracts to local law enforcement agencies, acting in coordination with domestic violence shelters, social service agencies and hospitals, for the purposes of—

"(i) the development of materials, to be provided to each abused family member at the time such spouse is identified by law enforcement officers, hospital personnel, social services personnel, education counseling personnel, and other appropriate personnel involved in the identification of family violence cases that include—

"(I) an explanation in basic terms of—

"(aa) the rights of the abused family member under the laws of the jurisdiction involved; and

"(bb) the services available to the abused family member, including intervention, treatment, and support services; and

"(II) phone numbers and addresses for the services described in subparagraph (A)(ii);

"(ii) the development of procedures whereby domestic violence shelter, hospital, social service, or law enforcement personnel provide to an abused family member a written report, relating to each incidence of physical abuse reported by the family member, that includes a description of physical injuries to the family member observed by such personnel; and

"(iii) the development of systems whereby domestic violence shelter or local social service personnel, with the consent of the abused family member involved, may obtain from local law enforcement personnel information relating to abuse of such family member, including a report describing the initial contact of such family member and the law enforcement agency.

"(B) The Secretary shall provide assurances that procedures will be developed under this paragraph to guarantee the confidentiality of the records maintained."

(c) FAMILY VIOLENCE PREVENTION PROJECT.—The Family Violence Prevention and Services Act is amended by adding at the end the following new section:

"FAMILY MEMBER ABUSE INFORMATION AND DOCUMENTATION PROJECT

"SEC. 313. The Secretary shall, directly or by grant or contract—

"(1) develop data on the individual characteristics relating to family violence;

"(2) provide for the objective documentation of data on the victims of family violence and their dependents based on injuries that are brought to the attention of domestic violence shelter, hospital, social service, or law enforcement personnel, whether or not formal civil or criminal action is taken; and

"(3) provide assurances that procedures will be developed to guarantee the confidentiality of records pertaining to any individual for whom data are compiled through this subsection."

TITLE IV—ADMINISTRATIVE PROVISIONS

SEC. 401. REGULATIONS.

(a) For any rule or regulation needed to implement this Act, the Secretary of Health and Human Services shall—

(1) publish proposed regulations for purposes of implementing the amendments made by this Act before the expiration of the 90-day period beginning on the date of the enactment of this Act;

(2) allow not less than 45 days for public comment on such proposed regulations; and

(3) publish final regulations for purposes of implementing the amendments made by this Act before the end of the 195-day period beginning on the date of the enactment of this Act.

Approved April 25, 1988.

5. STATE CHILD ABUSE STATUTES

Source: U.S. Department of Health, Education and Welfare, Office of Human Development Services, Administration for Children, Youth and Families, Children's Bureau, National Center on Child Abuse and Neglect. *Child Abuse & Neglect, State Reporting Laws*. Washington, D.C.: Government Printing Office, 1979; (OHDS) 80-30265.

STATE CHILD ABUSE REPORTING STATUTES

ALABAMA	§ 26-14-1 thru 13
ALASKA	§ 47.17.010 thru .070
ARKANSAS	ARK. STAT. ANN. § 42-807 thru 818
ARIZONA	§ 13-3619 thru 20, (Cum.Supp. 1985)
CALIFORNIA	CAL PENAL CODE § 1165-1174.5
COLORADO	COLO. REV STAT. § 19-10-102 thru 116
CONNECTICUT	§ 17-38a thru 38b, 46b-120
DELAWARE	16 § 901 thru 909
DISTRICT OF COLUMBIA	§ 2-1351 thru 1357 & 6-2101 thru 2107
FLORIDA	§ 8267.01 thru .07, 415.501 thru 507
GEORGIA	19-7-5
HAWAII	§ 350-1 thru 7
IDAHO	IDAHO CODE § 16-1601 thru 1625
ILLINOIS	23 § 2051 thru 2060
INDIANA	31-6-11-1 thru 20
IOWA	IOWA CODE ANN. § 232.67 thru .79
KANSAS	KAN. STAT. ANN. § 38-1501 thru 1554
KENTUCKY	199.335
LOUISIANA	14.403
MAINE	ME REV. STAT. ANN. tit. 22 § 4001 thru 4023
MARYLAND	MD CODE ANN. tit. § 5-901 thru 5-910
MASSACHUSETTS	MASS. GEN. LAWS ANN. Ch. 119 § 51A
MICHIGAN	MICH COMP LAWS ANN § 722.620
MINNESOTA	MINN. STAT § 626.556
MISSISSIPPI	§ 43-21-101
MISSOURI	MO. ANN STAT. § 210.110
MONTANA	MONT. CODE ANN. § 41-3-210 thru 208
NEBRASKA	28-710 thru 727 and 38-115 thru 117
NEVADA	NEV REV STAT. § 432B.220 thru .400
NEW HAMPSHIRE	N.H. REV. STAT. ANN. § 169-C:1 thru 39 and 169-D:17 (III) (Sep. Supp. 1986)
NEW JERSEY	N.J. STAT. ANN § 9:6-8.8 thru 8.20
NEW MEXICO	N.M. STAT. ANN. § 32-1-15 thru 32.1-25.1 (Cumm. Supp. 1985)
NEW YORK	N.Y. 411 thru 424 (Social Services)
NORTH CAROLINA	N.C. GEN. STAT. § 7A-572 (Supp. 1983)
NORTH DAKOTA	N.D. CENT. CODE § 50-25.1-02 thru 50.25.1-14 (Supp. 1985)
OHIO	2151.42.1, 2151.99, 2151.33 (Supp. 1984)
OKLAHOMA	OKLA. STAT. ANN. tit. 21, § 846 thru 9, 10 § 1104 thru 1107 (Supp. 1985)
OREGON	OR. REV. STAT. § 418.740 thru 755, 418.307 (Adv. Sheets 1985)
PENNSYLVANIA	PA. STAT. ANN. tit. 11 P.S. 2201 thru 2223 (Supp. 1985)
RHODE ISLAND	R.I. GEN. LAWS § 40-11-1 thru 16 (Supp. 1984)
SOUTH CAROLINA	S.C. CODE ANN. § 20-7-480 thru 690 (Supp. 1985)
SOUTH DAKOTA	26-10-10, 26-8-19.1, 26-8-43, 26-8-6 (Supp. 1985)
TENNESSEE	37-1-401 thru 411; 37-1-113, -116, -114; 37-1-128; 37-1-605,-606,-608
TEXAS	TEX. FAMILY CODE ANN. § 34.01 thru .07, 35.04,17.03
UTAH	UTAH CODE ANN. § 78-31-1 thru 14,78-36-3 (Supp. 1985)
VERMONT	VT. STAT. ANN. tit. 33 § 681 thru 689, 33 § 639 thru 642 (Supp. 1985)

VIRGINIA   VA. CODE § 63.144.010 thru .080, 26.12.1701 74.13.031
                            (Supp. 1986)
WASHINGTON   26.44.010 thru .080, 26.12.170, 74.13.031 (Supp. 1986)
WEST VIRGINIA   W. VA. CODE § 49-6A-1 thru -10, 49-1-2, 49-6-9 (Supp. 1985)
WISCONSIN   WIS. STAT. ANN § 48.981, 48.19 (Supp. 1985)
WYOMING   WY. STAT. ANN. § 14-3-201 thru 215 (Supp. 1985)

6. STATE MANDATED
REPORTERS

Source: U.S. Department of Health, Education and Welfare, Office of Human Development Services, Administration for Children, Youth and Families, Children's Bureau, National Center on Child Abuse and Neglect. *State Child Abuse and Neglect Laws: A Comparative Analysis, 1985*. Washington, D.C.: Clearing-house on Child Abuse and Neglect Information, April 1987

○ = Implied in Statute
● = Explicit in Statute

WHO MUST REPORT	Alabama	Alaska	American Samoa	Arizona	Arkansas	California	Colorado	Connecticut	Delaware	D.C.	Florida	Georgia	Guam	Hawaii
WHO HAS REPORTING RESPONSIBILITIES														
Any Person/Any Professional	●[1]			●[3]				●	●		●		●[6]	
All Medical Professionals/Personnel	○	●		○		●		○	●		○	●		●
Physicians/Medical Doctors	●	●	●	●	●	●	●	●	●	●	●	●	●	●
Dentists	●	●	●	●	●	●[4]	●	●	●	●	○	●	●	●
Nurses	●	●	●	●	●	●	●	●	●	●	●	●	●	●
Pharmacists	●	○		○		○		○	○		○	○	○	●
Medical Examiners/Coroners	●	○	●	●	●	●	●	●	○		●	○	●	●
Staff of Health Facilities	●		●	○	●		●	○	○		●	○	●	○
Medical Trainees	○	○	●	●	●	●	●	●	●	○	○	●	●	○
Other Medical Professionals*	●	●				●	●	●	●		●	●		○
"Mental Health Professionals"	●	○	●		●		●	●	○		●		●	○
All or Any Other Mental Health Professional	○				●			○	○					
Psychiatrists	○	●			○	●		○	○		○			
Psychologists	○	●		●	○	○		●	●		○	●		●
Therapists/Counselors	○	●		●	○	○		○	○		○			○
Crisis Intervention	○	●			○			○	○		○			
Educators														
Teachers/School Employees	●	●	●	●	●	●	●	●	●	●	●	●	●	●
School Administrators/Staff	●	●	●	●	●	●	●	●[10]	○	●	●	●[10]	●	●
"Out of Home Care Providers"		●		○	●	●		○[5]	○		○	●	○	○
Day Care Workers, Administrators, or Employees	●	○	●	○	●		●	●	○		●[17]	●	●	●[17]
Family Home	○	○	●	○	○		●	○	○		●[17]		○	
Preschool/Nursery School	○	○		○	○	●		○	○		●		○	●
Foster Parents				○	○	●		○	○		●[17]		●	●[17]
Residential/Institutional Care Staff				○	○	●		○	○		●[17]		○	●[17]
Social Workers	●	●	●	●	●	●	●	●	●	●	●	●	●	○[17]
State Employees-May Include Other Professional Categories						●		○	○		○			●[17]
"Law Enforcement or Legal"					●			○	○		○			●[17]
Law Enforcement Officers/Police/Peace Officers	●	●		●	●			●	○	●	●	●	●	●
Corrections/Probation/Parole Officers		●			○	●		○	○		○			●
Judges/Court Employees								○	○		○	○		●
Attorneys								○	○		○			
Miscellaneous Professional/Occupational Categories		●				●		○	○		○			
Clergy								●	○		○			
Religious Healing or Christian Science Practitioners		●	●			●	●	○	○		●		●	
Film or Photo Processors		●				●		○	○		○			
Friends, Neighbors, Relations								○	○		○			
Parents				●				○	○		○			
WHO MAY REPORT	●	●	●			●	●	●		●		●	●	●

(continued)

	WHO HAS REPORTING RESPONSIBILITIES													
WHO MUST REPORT	Idaho	Illinois	Indiana	Iowa	Kansas	Kentucky	Louisiana	Maine	Maryland	Massachusetts	Michigan	Minnesota	Mississippi	Missouri
Any Person/Any Professional	•		•	•[1]		•	•[3]		•[11]			13	•[14]	•[3]
All Medical Professionals/Personnel	○		○	•	•	•	○3		•			•	○	
Physicians/Medical Doctors	•	•	○	•	○	•	•	•	○	•	•	○	•	•
Dentists	○	•[4]	○	•	•	•	○	•[4]	○	•	•	○	•	•
Nurses	•	•	○	•	•	•	•	•	○	•	•	○	•	•
Pharmacists	○		○	○	○	○	○		○			○	○	○
Medical Examiners/Coroners	•	•	○	○	○	•	•	•	○	•	•	○	○	•
Staff of Health Facilities	○		○			•	○		○	•			○	○
Medical Trainees	•	•[9]	○	•	•	•	•	•	○	•	○	○	•	•
Other Medical Professionals*	○	•		•	•	○				•				
"Mental Health Professionals"	○		○	•		•		•					○	•
All or Any Other Mental Health Professional	○		○				○	○						
Psychiatrists	○	•	○	○		○						•	○	
Psychologists	○	•	○	•	•	○		•		•	•	•		
Therapists/Counselors	○		○	○		○			○	•	•		○14	
Crisis Intervention	○		○			○								
Educators														
Teachers/School Employees	•	•	○	•	•	•	•	•	•	•	•	•	•	•
School Administrators/Staff	○	•[8]	○	•	•	○	○	•[10]	○	•[10]	•[10]	•	•	•
"Out of Home Care Providers"	○	○	○	•[17]	•[17]	•	○	•	○		•[17]	•[17]	•	•
Day Care Workers, Administrators, or Employees	•	•	○	•[17]	•[17]	○	○	○	○	•				•
Family Home	○		○	•[17]		○	○							
Preschool/Nursery School	○	•	○	•		○	○		○					
Foster Parents	○	•	○	•		○	○		○					
Residential/Institutional Care Staff	○		○	•		○	○		○					
Social Workers	•	•	○	•	•	•	•	•	•	•	•	•	•	•
State Employees-May Include Other Professional Categories	○	•	○	○		○			•[12]					
"Law Enforcement or Legal"	○		○	○		○			•					
Law Enforcement Officers/Police/Peace Officers	○	•	○	•		•		•	•	•	•	•	•	•
Corrections/Probation/Parole Officers	○	•	○			○			•	•				•
Judges/Court Employees	○		○			○			•					
Attorneys	○		○		•	○							•	
Miscellaneous Professional/Occupational Categories	○		○			○			•					
Clergy	○		○	○		○							•	
Religious Healing or Christian Science Practitioners	○	•	○	○				•						•
File or Photo Processors	○		○			○								•
Friends, Neighbors, Relations	○		○			○								
Persons	○		○			○								
WHO MAY REPORT	·	•				•	•	•	•	•	•	•	•	•

(continued)

WHO MUST REPORT	Montana	Nebraska	Nevada	New Hampshire	New Jersey	New Mexico	New York	North Carolina	North Dakota	Ohio	Oklahoma	Oregon	Pennsylvania	Puerto Rico
WHO HAS REPORTING RESPONSIBILITIES														
Any Person/Any Professional		•		•	•	•		•				•	•5	
All Medical Professionals/Personnel		○		○	○	○		○		•		○		•
Physicians/Medical Doctors	•	•	•	•	○	•	•	○	•	•	•	•	•	○
Dentists	•	○	•4	•	○	○	•	○	•	○	•	•	•	○
Nurses	•	•	•	•	○	•	•	○	•	•	•	•	•	○
Pharmacists		○		○	○	○		○		○	○		○	○
Medical Examiners/Coroners	•	○	•	•	○	○	•	•	•		○	○	•	•
Staff of Health Facilities	•	•	•	•	○	○	•	○			○		•	•
Medical Trainees	•	○	•	•	○	•	•	○	○	•	•	•	•	○
Other Medical Professionals*	•	○	•	•	○	○	•	○			•			
"Mental Health Professionals"	○	○		○	○	○	•	○			○	○	•	
All or Any Other Mental Health Professional	•	○		○	○	○		○			○	•		
Psychiatrists	○	○	•	•	○	○		○			○	○		
Psychologists	○	○	•	•	○	○	•	○			•	○	•	
Therapists/Counselors	○	○	•	•	○	○		○			○	○		
Crisis Intervention		○	•	○	○	○		○				○		
Educators														
Teachers/School Employees	•	•	•	•	○	•	•	○	•	•	•	•	•	•
School Administrators/Staff	•	○	•	•10	○	○	•	○	•10	•	○	•	•	•
"Out of Home Care Providers"	•	○	•	•17	○	○	•	○	•	•	○		•	•
Day Care Workers, Administrators, or Employees	•17	○	•	•	○	○	•	○	•	•	○	•17	•	○
Family Home		○		○	○	○		○				•17	•	○
Preschool/Nursery School		○		○	○	○		○		•		○17	•	○17
Foster Parents	•	○	•	•	○	○	•	○				•17	•	○
Residential/Institutional Care Staff	•	○	•	○	○	○	•16	○				○	•	○
Social Workers	•	•	•	•	○	•	•	○	•	•	•	•	•	•
State Employees-May Include Other Professional Categories		○		○	○	○	•12	○			•	○		
"Law Enforcement or Legal"		○		○	○	○		○	•			○		•
Law Enforcement Officers/Police/Peace Officers	•	○	•	•	○	•	•	○	○			○	•	○
Corrections/Probation/Parole Officers		○		○	○	○		○				○		○
Judges/Court Employees		○		○	○	○		○				○		
Attorneys		○	•15	○	○	○		○			•	•	•	
Miscellaneous Professional/Occupational Categories		○	•	○	○	○		○				○		
Clergy		○	•15	○	○	○		○			•	○	•	
Religious Healing or Christian Science Practitioners	•	○	•	•	○	○	○	○		•	•	○	•	
Film or Photo Processors		○		○	○	○		○				•		
Friends, Neighbors, Relations		○		○	○	○		○				○		
Parents		○		○	○	○		○				○		
WHO MAY REPORT	•		•				•		•	•			•	•

(continued)

WHO MUST REPORT	Rhode Island	South Carolina	South Dakota	Tennessee	Texas	Utah	Vermont	Virgin Islands	Virginia	Washington	West Virginia	Wisconsin	Wyoming	TOTALS•	TOTALS°
WHO HAS REPORTING RESPONSIBILITIES															
Any Person/Any Professional	•			•	•	•							•	26	
All Medical Professionals/Personnel	○	•		•	○	•		•	•		•	•	○	19	17
Physicians/Medical Doctors	○	•	•	•	○	○	•	•	○	•	○	•	○	42	13
Dentists	○	•	•	○	○	○	•	•	○	•	•	•	○	37	18
Nurses	○	•	•	•	○	•	•	•	•	•	○	•	○	45	10
Pharmacists	○	○		○	○	○			○	•	○	○	○	3	37
Medical Examiners/Coroners	○	•	•	○	○	○	•	○	○	○	○	•	○	31	24
Staff of Health Facilities	○			•	○	○	•	•			○		○	22	19
Medical Trainees	○	○	•	○	○	○	•	○	•	○	○	○	○	31	24
Other Medical Professionals*	○			○	○	○	•					•	○	22	13
"Mental Health Professionals"	○	○	•	○	○	○	•	○	○		○	○	○	16	24
All or Any Other Mental Health Professional	○	•		•	○	○		•	•		•	•	○	9	18
Psychiatrists	○	○		○	○	○		○	○		○	○	○	6	28
Psychologists	○	○	•	○	○	○	•	○	○	•	○	○	○	25	22
Therapists/Counselors	○	○		○	○	○		○	○		○	○	○	7	29
Crisis Intervention	○			○	○	○						•	○	3	19
Educators															
Teachers/School Employees	○	•	•	•	○	○	•	•	•	•	•	•	○	48	7
School Administrators/Staff	○	•10	•10	•	○	○	•10	•	•	•10	•	•10	○	40	15
"Out of Home Care Providers"	○		•17	•17	○	○		•	•		•	•	○	26	20
Day Care Workers, Administrators, or Employees	○	•		•	○	○	•	•	•	•17		•	○	31	17
Family Home	○			•17	○	○			•			•	○	9	22
Preschool/Nursery School	○			•	○	○			•		•17	•	○	11	24
Foster Parents	○			•17	○	○		•	•		•		○	16	19
Residential/Institutional Care Staff	○	•		•17	○	○			•			•	○	13	21
Social Workers	○	•	•	•	○	○	•	•	•	•	•	•	○	46	9
State Employees-May Include Other Professional Categories	○			○	○	○							○	6	18
"Law Enforcement or Legal"	○			○	○	○							○	5	18
Law Enforcement Officers/Police/Peace Officers	○	•	•	•	○	○	•	•	•		•	•	○	36	13
Corrections/Probation/Parole Officers	○		•	○	○	○	•		•				○	10	19
Judges/Court Employees	○	•		•	○	○							○	4	16
Attorneys	○			○	○	○							○	4	17
Miscellaneous Professional/Occupational Categories	○			○	○	○							○	5	17
Clergy	○			○	○	○							○	5	16
Religious Healing or Christian Science Practitioners	○	•	•	•	•	○			•	•	•		○	22	15
Film or Photo Processors	○			○	○	○				•			○	5	16
Friends, Neighbors, Relations	○			•	○	○							○	1	16
Parents	○			○	○	○							○	1	17
WHO MAY REPORT		•	•				•	•	•	•	•	•		36	

NOTES:

1. Any person language qualified by "called upon to render aid or medical assistance" or "who examines, attends, or treats . . . "
2. Reporting law mandate does not apply if treatment is by spiritual means. See Religious Immunity or Exclusion, Chapter IV, infra.
3. Any person language qualified by "having responsibility for the care or treatment of children" or "care of children."
4. Mandated reporters includes dental hygienists.
5. Out-of-home care providers termed "child care personnel."
6. Within professional capacity only, as in "who in course of his employment occupation, or practice of his profession . . ."
7. Enumerated reporters not prohibited from reporting abuse or neglect that come to their attention in any private or nonprofessional capacity.
8. Mandated reporters includes truant officers.
9. Mandated reporters includes psychological assistants working under direct supervision.
10. Mandated reporters includes guidance counselors.
11. Any person language in that "a person other than [enumerated reporters] who has reason to believe that a child has been subjected to abuse shall report . . ." [MD. FAM. LAW CODE ANN. § 5-904 (1984)]
12. State employees are state's attorney or attorney general assistants.
13. Included in "a professional or his delegate who is engaged in the practice of the healing arts, social services, hospital administration, psychological or psychiatric treatment, child care, education, or law enforcement . . ." [MINN. STAT. ANN. § 626.556 (3) (a) (Supp. 1986)]
14. "Or any other person having cause to suspect that a child brought before him or coming before him for examination, care or treatment, or of whom he has knowledge through observation is a neglected child or an abused child . . ." [MISS. CODE ANN. § 43- 21-353 (Supp. 1985)]
15. Clergy or attorney not required to report if information obtained in confidential situation. See Waiver of Privileged Information, Chapter IV, infra.
16. Includes volunteers.
17. Reference only to licensed or otherwise certified child care providers.

7. TYPES OF IMMUNITY GRANTED BY STATES

Source: U.S. Department of Health, Education and Welfare, Office of Human Development Services, Administration for Children, Youth and Families, Children's Bureau, National Center on Child Abuse and Neglect. *State Child Abuse and Neglect Laws: A Comparative Analysis, 1985*. Washington, D.C.: Clearinghouse on Child Abuse and Neglect Information, April 1987

o = Implied in Statute
● = Explicit in Statute

*Mandated reporters have immunity for making reports in all jurisdictions

| | IMMUNITY PROVISIONS* | | | | | | |
| | Limitations | | Other Protected Actions | | | | |
	Good Faith Required	Good Faith Presumed	Cooperation with Investigation	Removal	Judicial Proceedings	"Any Other Action"	Child Protective Agency For Any Official Action
Alabama				●	●		
Alaska	●				●		
American Samoa	●	●		●	●		
Arizona	●[1]		o	o	●	●	o
Arkansas	●	●		●			
California	●[2]		●		●		
Colorado	●[7]	●		●	●		
Connecticut	●				●		
Delaware	●				●		
D.C.	●	●			●		
Florida	●	●			●[3]		●
Georgia	●				●	●[8]	
Guam	●	●		●	●		
Hawaii	●				●		
Idaho	●				●		
Illinois[4]	●	●		●			●
Indiana	●[1]	●			●		
Iowa	●		●		●		
Kansas	●		●	o	●		●
Kentucky	o[10]				●		
Louisiana	●[1]		●		●		
Maine	●	●	●		o		o
Maryland	●[1]		●		●		o
Massachusetts	●[1,2]						
Michigan	●[5]	●	o	o	o	●	o
Minnesota	●[1]		●				●
Mississippi	●	●			●		
Missouri	o[6]			●	●		

(continued)

	Limitations		Other Protected Actions				
	Good Faith Required	Good Faith Presumed	Cooperation with Investigation	Removal	Judicial Proceedings	"Any Other Action"	Child Protective Agency For Any Official Action
Montana	●		○[7]		●		●
Nebraska	●		●		●		
Nevada	●		●	●	●		●
New Hampshire	●		●		●		
New Jersey				●	●		
New Mexico	●	●	●		●		
New York	●	●		●			●
North Carolina	●	●	●	○	●	●	○
North Dakota	●[1]	●	●				●
Ohio					●		
Oklahoma	●				●		
Oregon	●				●		
Pennsylvania	●	●	●	●	●		
Puerto Rico	●		○	○	○	●	○
Rhode Island	●				●		
South Carolina	●	●			●		
South Dakota	●[1]		●	●	●		●
Tennessee	●	●	○	○	○	●	○
Texas	●				●		
Utah	●			●			
Vermont	●[1,9]						
Virgin Islands	●		○	○	○	●	○
Virginia	●			●	●		
Washington	●			●	●		
West Virginia	●		○	○	○	●	○
Wisconsin	●[1]	●					●
Wyoming	●	●				●	
TOTALS: (55 jurisdictions)	52	20	22	23	45	8	20

NOTES:

1. Includes an exemption from immunity for those suspected or charged with abuse or neglect.
2. Permitted reporters have immunity only if in good faith. See text.
3. Immunity in judicial proceedings limited: "A guardian ad litem shall be appointed by the court to represent the child in any child abuse or neglect civil or criminal judicial proceeding. Any person participating in a civil or criminal judicial proceeding *resulting from such appointment* shall be presumed prima facie to be acting in good faith and in so doing shall be immune from any liability, civil or criminal, that otherwise might be incurred or imposed." [FLA. STAT. ANN. § 415.508 (1) (Supp. 1985)]
4. Immunity extends to "any physician authorized and acting in good faith and in accordance with acceptable medical practice in the treatment of a child . . . for emergency treatment." [ILL. ANN. STAT. Ch. 23, § 2055 (Smith-Hurd Supp. 1985)]
5. Immunity does not extend "to a negligent act which causes personal injury or death or to the malpractice of a physician which results in personal injury or death." [MICH. COMP. LAWS ANN. § 722.625 (Supp. 1985)]
6. Immunity not provided to those who knowingly provide false or malicious reports.
7. Protected actions include furnishing hospital or medical records.
8. Protected actions include participation "in any judicial proceeding or any other proceeding resulting therefrom . . ." [GA. CODE ANN. § 19-7-7 (D) (Supp. 1985)] Immunity in the cooperation with the investigation, removal of the child, or in the CPS investigation not implied from this language.
9. Immunity extends only to mandated reporters.
10. Good faith requirement implied by language: "anyone acting *upon reasonable cause*" [KY. REV. STAT. § 199.335 (6) (Supp. 1984)].

8. ABROGATION OF PRIVILEGED COMMUNICATIONS

Source: U.S. Department of Health, Education and Welfare, Office of Human Development Services, Administration for Children, Youth and Families, Children's Bureau, National Center on Child Abuse and Neglect. *State Child Abuse and Neglect Laws: A Comparative Analysis, 1985*. Washington, D.C.: Clearinghouse on Child Abuse and Neglect Information, April 1987

○ = Implied in Statute
● = Explicit in Statute
◆ = No Excerpt Found

	WAIVER OF PRIVILEGED COMMUNICATIONS										
	In Judicial Proceedings			Must Report Despite Privilege							
	Abrogation of Physician-Patient Privilege	Waiver of All Professional Privileges Except Attorney-Client	Abrogation of Spousal Privileges	All	Clergy	Husband-Wife	Attorney-Client	Doctor-Patient	Social Worker-Client	Mental Health Prof.	Sexual Assault Counselors
Alabama		●									
Alaska	●		●								
American Samoa	●		●								
Arizona	●	●	●		●						
Arkansas	●	●	●								
California	●9										
Colorado	●10		●								
Connecticut			●								
Delaware	●	●	●								
D.C.	●9		●								
Florida	◆	◆	◆	◆							
Georgia			●								
Guam				●	●	●					
Hawaii	●		●								
Idaho		●	●								
Illinois		●					●				
Indiana	●		●			●		●			
Iowa	●		●								
Kansas	●9,12										
Kentucky		●4	●								
Louisiana		●	●								
Maine	●9		●					●	●	●	
Maryland				●							
Massachusetts									●	●	
Michigan		●		●							
Minnesota	3,5,●9,10		●								
Mississippi				●							
Missouri		●		●							

(continued)

	WAIVER OF PRIVILEGED COMMUNICATIONS										
	In Judicial Proceedings										
				Must Report Despite Privilege							
	Abrogation of Physician-Patient Privilege	Waiver of All Professional Privileges Except Attorney-Client	Abrogation of Spousal Privileges	All	Clergy	Husband-Wife	Attorney-Client	Doctor-Patient	Social Worker-Client	Mental Health Prof.	Sexual Assault Counselors
Montana		●									
Nebraska	●		●								
Nevada		●	●	●							
New Hampshire		●	●	●		●					
New Jersey◆											
New Mexico	●										
New York	10,●		●								
North Carolina	●		●								
North Dakota		●	●	●		●					
Ohio	●										
Oklahoma	●										
Oregon	7,9,●10,12		●						●		
Pennsylvania		●	●	●	●						
Puerto Rico◆											
Rhode Island		●	●	●		●					
South Carolina		●	●	●	●	●					
South Dakota	●		●								
Tennessee	●9	●	●								
Texas		●	●								
Utah			●								●
Vermont◆											
Virgin Islands		●	●	●		●					
Virginia			●								
Washington					●					●	
West Virginia		●	●								
Wisconsin	●3,10		●								
Wyoming		●4	●								
TOTALS: (55 Jurisdictions)	28	23	37	13	5	8	1	2	2	3	1

NOTES:

1. All mandatory reporters.
2. Includes attorney-client privilege.
3. Includes chiropractor.
4. Clergyman-penitent privilege.
5. Includes dentists.
6. Doctor-patient privilege.
7. Includes staff members of schools
8. Husband-wife, spousal privilege.
9. Mental health professionals, including psychotherapist.
10. Includes nurses
11. Special provision for sexual assault counselors
12. Includes social worker-client

9. SELECTED STATE CHILD ABUSE AND NEGLECT REPORTS— FAMILIES AND CHILDREN

Source: Select Committee on Children, Youth, and Families, U.S. House of Representatives, *Child Abuse and Neglect in America: The Problem and the Response*, hearing held in Washington, D.C, March 3, 1987. Washington, D.C.: U.S. Government Printing Office, 1987.

Table 9A

Child Abuse Reports by State for Families and Children, 1985

State	Family Reports	Child Reports
Alabama	18,141	31,385
Alaska	7,702	13,332
Arizona	24,866	43,043
Arkansas	12,592	20,081
California	146,724	272,953
Colorado	7,987	13,825
Connecticut	11,118	16,804
Delaware	4,651	8,051
Dist. of Columbia	3,416	6,073
Florida	75,328	130,393
Georgia	26,511	45,489
Hawaii	2,928	4,069
Idaho	7,880	13,640
Illinois	40,644	68,203
Indiana	19,576	33,868
Iowa	15,989	25,534
Kansas	14,375	23,592
Kentucky	20,073	34,839
Louisiana	19,938	35,802
Maine	5,847	10,121
Maryland	11,210	19,394
Massachusetts	30,167	47,060
Michigan	42,982	95,114
Minnesota	15,703	22,046
Mississippi	8,042	13,921
Missouri	41,150	75,953
Montana	3,188	5,516
Nebraska	7,952	13,765
Nevada	6,438	11,144
New Hampshire	3,765	6,517
New Jersey	27,239	47,126
New Mexico	6,971	12,061
New York	84,119	139,032
North Carolina	18,456	27,625
North Dakota	3,083	4,719

State	Family Reports	ChildReports
Ohio	38,128	65,965
Oklahoma	11,719	20,275
Oregon	9,646	12,765
Pennsylvania	12,126	20,980
Rhode Island	6,468	11,196
South Carolina	16,673	28,861
South Dakota	6,736	8,913
Tennessee	27,195	47,050
Texas	66,911	108,561
Utah	10,450	18,089
Vermont	2,572	4,452
Virginia	28,764	49,765
Washington	28,804	40,100
West Virginia	12,000	20,772
Wisconsin	14,110	24,411
Wyoming	1,916	2,319
Totals	1,090,969	1,876,564

10. NATIONAL ESTIMATES OF CHILD ABUSE AND NEGLECT REPORTS

Source: Select Committee on Children, Youth, and Families, U.S. House of Representatives, *Child Abuse and Neglect in America: The Problem and the Response*, hearing held in Washington, D.C, March 3, 1987. Washington, D.C.: U.S. Government Printing Office, 1987.

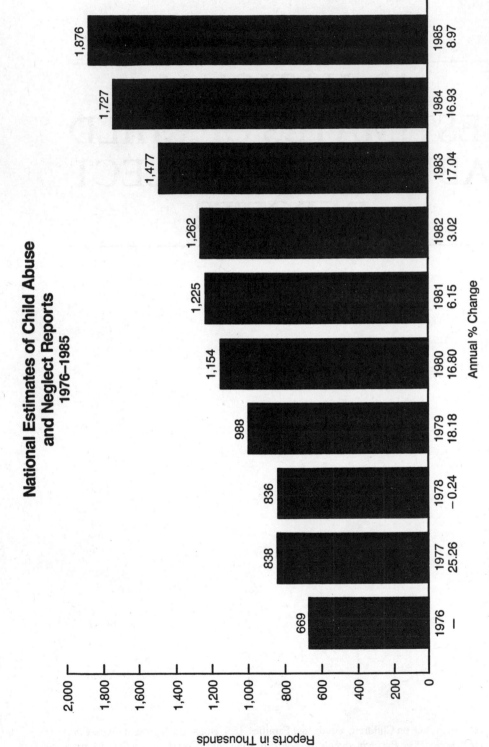

**National Estimates of Child Abuse
and Neglect Reports
1976–1985**

Reports in Thousands

	1976	1977	1978	1979	1980	1981	1982	1983	1984	1985
Reports	669	838	836	988	1,154	1,225	1,262	1,477	1,727	1,876
Annual % Change	—	25.26	−0.24	18.18	16.80	6.15	3.02	17.04	16.93	8.97

Annual % Change

Note: Child totals for 1976–1984 include the 50 states, District of Columbia, Puerto Rico, U.S. Virgin Islands, Guam and Marianas. The total for 1985 and the percent change
         1984–85, include the 50 states and the District of Columbia only.
Source: Data for 1976–1984 from American Association for Protecting Children, Inc., *Highlights of Official Child Neglect and Abuse Reporting, 1984.*
         Data for 1985 from Select Committee on Children, Youth, and Families survey.

11. TRENDS IN CHILD ABUSE FUNDING

Source: Select Committee on Children, Youth, and Families, U.S. House of Representatives, *Child Abuse and Neglect in America: The Problem and the Response*, hearing held in Washington, D.C, March 3, 1987. Washington, D.C.: U.S. Government Printing Office, 1987.

Table 11A (continued)
Trends in Child Abuse Reporting Compared to Trends in Total Funding to Address Child Abuse 1981–1985 by State

State	Percent Change in Child Abuse Reports			Percent Change in Total Funding (Constant Dollars)		
	1981	1985	Percent Change	1981	1985	Percent Change
Alabama	18,654	31,385	68.2%	47,192,707	49,469,963	+4.8%
Alaska	7,748	13,382	72.1%	·	·	·
Arizona	7,892	43,043	445.4%	31,108,673	30,420,142	−2.2%
Arkansas	14,393	20,081	39.5%	3,271,365	5,482,849	+67.6%
California	179,735	272,953	51.9%	385,147,404	480,603,448	+24.8%
Colorado	10,908	13,825	26.7%	·	·	·
Connecticut	10,180	16,804	65.1%	·	·	·
Delaware	4,741	8,051	69.8%	·	·	·
Dist. of Col.	5,113	6,073	18.8%	·	·	·
Florida	68,446	130,393	90.5%	102,551,899	129,952,127	+26.7%
Georgia	22,763	45,489	99.4%	11,324,069	40,217,404	+255.2%
Hawaii	2,635	4,069	54.4%	20,576,844	18,592,175	−9.6%
Idaho	9,578	13,640	42.4%	11,905,195	10,293,964	−13.5%
Illinois	47,586	68,203	43.3%	186,599,854	198,047,688	+6.1%
Indiana	21,929	33,868	54.4%	45,465,077	46,288,642	+1.8%
Iowa	24,349	25,534	4.9%	50,222,135	46,695,877	−7.0%
Kansas	19,492	23,592	21.0%	·	·	·
Kentucky	28,266	34,839	23.3%	28,597,431	34,880,171	+21.9%
Louisiana	29,406	35,802	21.8%	68,458,767	70,644,109	+3.2%
Maine	6,714	10,121	50.7%	23,446,467	27,624,999	+17.8%
Maryland	11,698	19,394	65.7%	89,122,266	59,557,428	−33.2%
Massachusetts	30,525	47,060	54.2%	·	·	·
Michigan	57,235	95,114	66.2%	126,264,136	143,273,017	+13.5%
Minnesota	13,205	22,046	67.0%	109,148,143	99,025,850	−9.3%
Mississippi	5,881	13,921	136.7%	28,057,952	23,593,667	−15.9%
Missouri	53,722	75,953	41.4%	100,437,497	62,073,991	−38.2%
Montana	5,243	5,516	5.2%	8,591,328	9,383,104	+9.2%

Table 11A
Trends in Child Abuse Reporting Compared to
Trends in Total Funding to Address Child Abuse
1981–1985 by State

State	Percent Change in Child Abuse Reports			Percent Change in Total Funding (Constant Dollars)		
	1981	1985	Percent Change	1981	1985	Percent Change
Nebraska	7,013	13,765	96.3%	•	•	•
Nevada	6,354	11,144	75.4%	10,209,400	9,618,703	-5.8%
New Hampshire	4,478	6,517	45.5%	•	•	•
New Jersey	23,758	47,126	98.4%	121,495,718	125,857,758	+3.6%
New Mexico	5,904	12,061	104.3%	16,883,508	18,493,118	+9.5%
New York	106,295	139,032	30.8%	•	•	•
North Carolina	27,017	27,625	2.2%	•	•	•
North Dakota	2,944	4,719	60.3%	11,413,224	8,726,035	-23.5%
Ohio	27,248	65,965	142.1%	•	•	•
Oklahoma	12,283	20,275	65.1%	•	•	•
Oregon	2,732	12,765	367.2%	•	•	•
Pennsylvania	13,703	20,980	53.1%	238,686,296	245,431,035	+2.8%
Rhode Island	3,784	11,196	195.9%	•	•	•
South Carolina	19,289	28,861	49.6%	35,199,143	32,940,517	-6.4%
South Dakota	4,890	8,913	82.3%	3,787,917	2,380,441	-37.2%
Tennessee	44,146	47,050	6.6%	69,422,070	70,592,044	+1.7%
Texas	81,819	108,561	32.7%	100,914,220	116,120,935	+15.1%
Utah	5,832	18,089	210.2%	•	•	•
Vermont	2,072	4,452	114.9%	•	•	•
Virginia	39,685	49,765	25.4%	37,057,163	26,309,239	-29.0%
Washington	33,832	40,100	18.5%	•	•	•
West Virginia	7,111	20,772	192.1%	22,692,720	29,090,517	+28.2%
Wisconsin	8,508	24,411	186.9%	•	•	•
Wyoming	2,589	2,319	-10.4%	•	•	•

Table 11B
Trends in Child Abuse Funding, by Program Source
FY 1981–1985 by State in Constant 1982 Dollars (Federal Sources)

State	Title XX	Title IVB	Title IVE	CAPTA	Other	Total Federal Funds	Total Federal Funds Less Title IVE
Alabama							
FY 1981	$28,697,879	$ 3,359,834	$ 1,677,868	$ 30,533	$ 99,158	$33,865,272	$32,187,404
FY 1985	33,286,059	3,581,782	2,160,734	136,930	273,078	39,438,583	37,277,849
% Change 81–85	+15.9%	+6.6%	+28.8%	+348.5%	+175.4%	+16.5%	+15.8%
Arizona							
FY 1981	$ 4,849,358	$ 978,373	$ 321,199	$ -0-	$ 915,203	$ 7,064,133	$ 6,742,934
FY 1985	3,904,569	245,862	2,008,103	126,866	300,259	6,585,659	4,577,556
% Change 81–85	−19.5%	−74.9%	+525.2%	+100%	−67.2%	−6.8%	−32.1%
Arkansas							
FY 1981	$ 1,116,192	$ 825,526	781,525	$176,058	• • •	$ 2,899,301	$ 2,117,776
FY 1985	1,849,154	2,130,172	747,262	159,274	• • •	4,885,862	4,138,600
% Change 81–85	+65.7%	+158%	−4.4%	−9.5%		+68.5%	+95.4%
California							
FY 1981	$80,513,919	$13,490,364	$56,638,116	$672,029	• • •	$151,314,428	$94,676,312
FY 1985	-0-	15,862,069	97,241,379	344,828	• • •	113,448,276	16,206,897
% Change 81–85	−100%	+17.6%	+71.7%	−48.7%		−25.0%	−82.9%
Florida							
FY 1981	$45,783,906	$ 1,673,358	-0-	$271,648	$4,207,673	$51,936,585	$51,936,585
FY 1985	56,098,802	6,615,098	$ 2,152,965	357,369	580,546	65,804,780	63,651,815
% Change 81–85	+22.5%	+295.3%	+100%	+31.6%	−86.2%	+26.7%	+22.6%
Georgia							
FY 1981	$ 848,656	$ 4,097,037	$ 2,231,958	$135,995	• • •	$ 7,313,646	$ 5,081,688
FY 1985	12,219,691	4,960,166	6,741,216	293,588	• • •	24,214,661	17,473,445
% Change 81–85	+1339.9%	+21.1%	+202.0%	+115.9%		+231.1%	+243.8%
Hawaii							
FY 1981	$14,453,961	$ 616,133	$ 20,465	$ 50,953	• • •	$15,141,512	$15,121,047
FY 1985	12,672,414	550,619	42,497	50,908	• • •	13,316,438	13,273,941
% Change 81–85	−12.3%	−10.6%	+107.7%	−.09%		−12.1%	−12.2%

State	Title XX	Title IVB	Title IVE	CAPTA	Other	Total Federal Funds	Total Federal Funds Less Title IVE
Idaho							
FY 1981	$ 6,927,195	$ 981,799	$ 319,542	-0-	...	$ 8,228,536	$ 7,908,994
FY 1985	5,266,379	1,293,103	287,931	$ 54,310	...	6,901,723	6,613,792
% Change 81–85	-23.9%	+31.7%	-9.9%	+100%	...	-16.1%	-16.4%
Illinois							
FY 1981	$ 76,510,649	$4,349,833	$ 4,280,380	$301,752	$2,434,251	$ 87,876,865	$ 83,596,485
FY 1985	107,434,405	6,550,130	18,132,555	360,069	10,135,370	142,612,529	124,479,974
% Change 81–85	+40.4%	+50.6%	+323.6%	+19.3%	+316.4%	+62.3%	+48.9%
Indiana							
FY 1981	$18,558,545	$3,772,032	$ 1,243,217	...	...	$23,573,794	$22,330,577
FY 1985	14,680,673	5,668,797	927,371	...	...	21,276,841	20,349,470
% Change 81–85	-20.9%	+50.3%	-25.4%	...	...	-9.7%	-8.9%
Iowa							
FY 1981	$17,995,611	$1,951,552	$11,186,046	$105,125	-0-	$31,238,334	$20,052,288
FY 1985	9,806,942	1,937,849	1,069,181	90,298	$5,767,672	18,671,942	17,602,761
% Change 81–85	-45.5%	-.7%	-90.4%	-14.1%	+100%	-40.2%	-12.2%
Kentucky							
FY 1981	$10,771,949	$3,988,223	$ 2,607,066	$177,730	...	$17,544,968	$14,937,902
FY 1985	11,903,448	3,364,655	3,554,310	130,172	...	18,952,585	15,398,275
% Change 81–85	+10.5%	-15.6%	+36.3%	-26.8%	...	+8.0%	+3.1%
Louisiana							
FY 1981	$41,427,149	$3,483,451	-0-	$174,740	$ 3,228,139	$48,313,479	$48,313,479
FY 1985	42,919,743	2,953,386	8,235,819	117,923	1,610,918	55,837,789	47,601,970
% Change 81–85	+3.6%	-15.2%	+100%	-32.5%	-50.1%	+15.6%	-1.5%
Maine							
FY 1981	$12,025,696	$ 370,450	$ 2,591,006	$ 80,300	...	$15,067,452	$12,476,446
FY 1985	8,702,586	865,517	3,056,034	62,069	...	12,686,206	9,630,172
% Change 81–85	-27.6%	+133.6%	+17.9%	-22.7%	...	-15.8%	-22.8%
Maryland							
FY 1981	$66,163,920	$1,682,260	$ 159,768	-0-	...	$68,005,948	$67,846,180
FY 1985	17,958,003	3,647,297	2,810,354	$ 46,379	...	24,462,033	21,651,679
% Change 81–85	-72.9%	+116.8%	+1659.0%	+100%	...	-64.0%	-68.1%
Michigan							
FY 1981	$21,937,901	$6,891,863	$18,840,471	$310,175	...	$47,980,410	$29,139,939
FY 1985	31,591,379	6,340,517	29,731,034	416,637	...	68,079,567	38,348,533
% Change 81–85	+44.0%	-8.0%	+57.8%	+34.3%	...	+41.9%	+31.6%

Table 11B (continued)

State	Title XX	Title IVB	Title IVE	CAPTA	Other	Total Federal Funds	Total Federal Funds Less Title IVE
Minnesota							
FY 1981	$52,352,891	$1,172,357	$ 3,156,340	$243,749	•	$56,925,337	$53,768,997
FY 1985	41,840,857	2,757,899	6,822,496	180,891	•	51,602,143	44,779,647
% Change 81-85	-20.1%	+135.2%	+116.2%	-25.8%	•	-9.4%	-16.7%
Mississippi							
FY 1981	$18,228,051	$1,387,580	$ 1,423,983	$120,051	•	$21,159,665	$19,735,682
FY 1985	14,536,207	2,240,517	1,137,931	150,564	•	18,065,219	16,927,288
% Change 81-85	-20.3%	+61.5%	-20.1%	+25.4%	•	-14.6%	-14.2%
Missouri							
FY 1981	$69,242,718	$5,456,187	$ 1,580,914	$ 38,543	•	$76,318,362	$74,737,448
FY 1985	27,864,952	3,762,366	11,453,218	129,603	•	43,210,139	31,756,921
% Change 81-85	-59.8%	-31.0%	+624.5%	+23.6%	•	-43.4%	-57.5%
Montana							
FY 1981	$ 2,450,535	$ 454,604	$ 1,686,938	$ 39,936	$ 179,015	$ 4,811,028	$ 3,124,090
FY 1985	2,711,638	492,500	1,063,793	44,828	90,776	4,403,535	3,339,742
% Change 81-85	+10.7%	+8.3%	-36.9%	+12.2%	-49.3%	-8.5%	-6.9%
Nevada							
FY 1981	$ 5,192,222	$ 400,882	$ 428,928	$ 45,956	•	$ 6,067,988	$ 5,639,060
FY 1985	5,856,357	517,241	330,557	48,209	•	6,752,364	6,421,807
% Change 81-85	+12.8%	+29.0%	-22.9%	+4.9%	•	+11.3%	+13.9%
New Jersey							
FY 1981	$33,623,126	$1,284,797	$ 2,141,328	$146,681	$4,923,983	$42,119,915	$39,978,587
FY 1985	26,125,862	2,603,448	4,487,069	211,207	3,294,828	36,722,414	32,235,345
% Change 81-85	-22.3%	+102.6%	+109.5%	+44.0%	-33.1%	-12.8%	-19.4%
New Mexico							
FY 1981	$ 8,271,211	$ 556,155	-0-	$181,214	•	$ 9,008,580	$ 9,008,580
FY 1985	8,812,184	1,301,011	$ 562,559	97,484	•	10,773,238	10,210,679
% Change 81-85	+6.5%	+133.9%	+100%	-46.2%	•	+19.6%	+13.3%

State	Title XX	Title IVB	Title IVE	CAPTA	Other	Total Federal Funds	Total Federal Funds Less Title IVE
North Dakota							
FY 1981	$ 9,283,521	$ 747,011	$ 679,344	$ 29,633	...	$10,739,509	$10,060,165
FY 1985	6,698,016	671,555	640,606	44,568	...	8,054,745	7,414,139
% Change 81–85	−27.9%	−10.1%	−5.7%	+50.4%		−24.9%	−26.3%
Pennsylvania							
FY 1981	$12,419,700	$ 8,847,966	$38,436,831	...	$ 749,465	$60,453,962	$22,017,131
FY 1985	9,870,690	15,086,207	30,172,414	...	1,465,517	56,594,828	26,422,414
% Change 81–85	−20.5%	+70.5%	−21.5%		+95.5%	−6.4%	+20.0%
South Carolina							
FY 1981	$21,180,942	$ 3,383,298	$ 595,289	$ 98,501	...	$25,258,030	$24,662,741
FY 1985	17,761,207	3,354,310	1,587,069	76,724	...	22,779,310	21,192,241
% Change 81–85	−16.2%	−.9%	+166.6%	−22.1%		−9.8%	−14.1%
South Dakota							
FY 1981	$ 792,594	$ 669,165	$ 953,638	$ 60,600	$ 331,050	$ 2,807,047	$ 1,853,409
FY 1985	764,409	478,093	698,644	65,351	84,976	2,091,473	1,392,829
% Change 81–85	−3.6%	−28.5%	−26.7%	+7.8%	−74.3%	−25.5%	−24.9%
Tennessee							
FY 1981	$51,014,676	$ 1,377,442	$ 2,149,848	$118,456	...	$54,660,422	$52,510,574
FY 1985	48,171,741	5,231,793	1,350,689	152,028	...	54,906,251	53,555,562
% Change 81–85	−5.6%	+279.8%	−37.2%	+28.3%		+.5%	+1.9%
Texas							
FY 1981	$67,868,140	$ 3,693,985	$ 5,583,827	$372,745	$ 184,115	$77,702,812	$72,118,985
FY 1985	56,710,484	7,987,865	9,740,584	324,345	-0-	74,763,278	65,022,694
% Change 81–85	−16.4%	+116.2%	+74.4%	−12.9%	−100%	−3.8%	−9.8%
Virginia							
FY 1981	$25,552,051	...	$ 2,802,933	$184,828	...	$28,539,812	$25,736,879
FY 1985	17,224,854	...	2,461,564	191,548	...	19,877,966	17,416,402
% Change 81–85	−32.6%		−12.18%	+3.6%		−30.4%	−32.3%
West Virginia							
FY 1981	$10,380,086	$ 551,392	$ 2,034,261	$ 53,533	...	$13,019,272	$10,985,011
FY 1985	10,758,621	1,702,586	3,879,310	68,966	...	16,409,483	12,530,173
% Change 81–85	+3.7%	+208.8%	+90.7%	+28.8%		+26.0%	+14.1%
Totals							
1981	$836,434,950	$ 82,494,909	$166,553,029	$4,221,464	$17,252,052	$1,106,956,404	$940,403,375
1985	666,002,326	114,754,410	255,287,248	4,533,936	23,603,940	1,064,181,860	808,894,612
% Change 81–85	−20.4%	+39.1%	+53.3%	+7.4%	+36.8%	−3.9%	−13.9%

Table 11C
Trends in Child Abuse Funding by Program Source
FY 1981–1985 by State in Constant 1982 Dollars (State Sources)

State	State General Funds	Other	Children's Trust Funds	Local Funds	Total State and Local Funding	Total Funding (Federal, State, and Local)	Total Funding Less Title IVE
Alabama							
FY 1981	$ 12,330,848	•	-0-	$ 996,587	$ 13,327,435	$ 47,192,707	$ 45,514,839
FY 1985	8,691,248	•	$215,517	1,124,615	10,031,380	49,469,963	47,309,229
% Change 81–85	−29.5%	•	+100%	12.8%	−24.7%	+4.8%	+3.9%
Arizona							
FY 1981	$ 24,044,540	-0-	-0-	•	$ 24,044,540	$ 31,108,673	$ 30,787,474
FY 1985	21,817,759	$1,803,707	$213,017	•	23,834,483	30,420,142	28,412,039
% Change 81–85	−9.3%	+100%	+100%	•	−.9%	−2.2%	−7.7%
Arkansas							
FY 1981	$ 353,319	•	•	$ 18,745	$ 372,064	$ 3,271,365	$ 2,489,840
FY 1985	571,125	•	•	25,862	596,987	5,482,849	4,735,587
% Change 81–85	+61.5%	•	•	+37.9%	+60.5%	+67.6%	+90.2%
California							
FY 1981	$233,832,976	-0-	•	•	$233,832,976	$385,147,404	$328,509,288
FY 1985	358,189,655	$8,965,517	•	•	367,155,172	480,603,448	383,362,069
% Change 81–85	+53.2%	+100%	•	•	+57.0%	+24.8%	+16.7%
Florida							
FY 1981	$ 50,615,314	•	•	•	$ 50,615,314	$102,551,899	$102,551,899
FY 1985	64,147,347	•	•	•	64,147,347	129,952,127	127,799,162
% Change 81–85	+26.7%	•	•	•	+26.7%	+26.7%	+24.6%
Georgia							
FY 1981	$ 4,010,423	•	•	•	$ 4,010,423	$ 11,324,069	$ 9,092,111
FY 1985	16,002,743	•	•	•	16,002,743	40,217,404	33,476,188
% Change 81–85	+299%	•	•	•	+299.0%	+255.2%	+268.2%
Hawaii							
FY 1981	$ 5,435,332	•	•	•	5,435,332	$ 20,576,844	$ 20,556,379
FY 1985	5,275,737	•	•	•	5,275,737	18,592,175	18,549,678
% Change 81–85	−2.9%	•	•	•	−2.9%	−9.6%	−9.8%

State	State General Funds	Other	Children's Trust Funds	Local Funds	Total State and Local Funding	Total Funding (Federal, State, and Local)	Total Funding Less Title IVE
Idaho							
FY 1981	$ 2,950,749	$ 725,910	•	•	$ 3,676,659	$ 11,905,195	$ 11,585,653
FY 1985	2,805,172	587,069	•	•	3,392,241	10,293,964	10,006,033
% Change 81–85	-4.9%	-10.4%			-7.7%	-13.5%	-13.6%
Illinois							
FY 1981	$98,722,989	-0-	-0-	•	$98,722,989	$186,599,854	$182,319,474
FY 1985	54,082,127	$1,056,379	$296,653	•	55,435,159	198,047,688	179,915,133
% Change 81–85	-45.2%	+100%	+100%		-43.8%	+6.1%	-1.3%
Indiana							
FY 1981	$ 7,363	•	•	$21,883,920	$21,891,283	$ 45,465,077	$ 44,221,860
FY 1985	8,564	•	•	25,003,237	25,011,801	46,288,642	45,361,271
% Change 81–85	+16.3%			+14.3%	+14.3%	+1.8%	+2.6%
Iowa							
FY 1981	$18,677,676	•	-0-	$ 306,125	$18,983,801	$ 50,222,135	$ 39,036,089
FY 1985	26,879,776	•	$107,759	1,036,400	28,023,935	46,695,877	45,626,696
% Change 81–85	+43.9%		+100%	+238.6%	+47.6%	-7.0%	+16.9%
Kentucky							
FY 1981	$10,006,424	$1,046,039	-0-	•	$11,052,463	$ 28,597,431	$ 25,990,365
FY 1985	14,785,345	1,087,931	$ 54,310	•	15,927,586	34,880,171	31,325,861
% Change 81–85	+47.8%	+4%	+100%		+44.1%	+21.9%	+20.5%
Louisiana							
FY 1981	$20,145,288	•	•	•	$20,145,288	$ 68,458,767	$ 68,458,767
FY 1985	14,806,320	•	•	•	14,806,320	70,644,109	62,408,290
% Change 81–85	-26.5%				-26.5%	+32.%	-8.8%
Maine							
FY 1981	$ 8,379,015	•	•	•	$ 8,379,015	$ 23,446,467	$ 20,855,461
FY 1985	14,938,793	•	•	•	14,938,793	27,624,999	24,568,965
% Change 81–85	+78.3%				+78.3%	+17.8%	+17.8%
Maryland							
FY 1981	$21,116,318	•	•	•	$21,116,318	$ 89,122,266	$ 88,962,498
FY 1985	35,095,395	•	•	•	35,095,395	59,557,428	56,747,074
% Change 81–85	+66.2%				+66.2%	-33.2%	-36.2%
Michigan							
FY 1981	$78,283,726	•	-0-	•	$78,283,726	$126,264,136	$107,423,665
FY 1985	74,493,103	•	$700,347	•	75,193,450	143,273,017	113,541,983
% Change 81–85	-4.8%		+100%		-3.9%	+13.5%	+5.7%

Table 11C (continued)

State	State General Funds	Other	Children's Trust Funds	Local Funds	Total State and Local Funding	Total Funding (Federal, State, and Local)	Total Funding Less Title IVE
Minnesota							
FY 1981	$ 1,828,373	$50,394,433	...	...	$52,222,806	$109,148,143	$105,991,803
FY 1985	3,465,431	43,958,276	...	...	47,423,707	99,025,850	92,203,354
% Change 81–85	−89.5%	−12.8%	...	...	−9.2%	−9.3%	−13.0%
Mississippi							
FY 1981	$ 6,898,287	...	...	...	$ 6,898,287	$ 28,057,952	$ 26,633,969
FY 1985	5,528,448	...	...	...	5,528,448	23,593,667	22,455,736
% Change 81–85	−19.9%	...	...	...	−19.9%	−15.9%	−15.7%
Missouri							
FY 1981	$24,119,135	...	-0-	...	$24,119,135	$100,437,497	$ 98,856,583
FY 1985	18,820,749	...	$43,103	...	18,863,852	62,073,991	50,620,773
% Change 81–85	−21.9%	...	+100%	...	−21.8%	−38.2%	−48.8%
Montana							
FY 1981	$ 1,872,484	...	...	$ 1,907,816	$ 3,780,300	$ 8,591,328	$ 6,904,390
FY 1985	3,910,086	...	...	1,069,483	4,979,569	9,383,104	8,319,311
% Change 81–85	+108.8%	...	...	−43.9%	+31.7%	+9.2%	+20.5%
Nevada							
FY 1981	$ 3,694,263	$ 328,393	...	$ 118,756	$ 4,141,412	$ 10,209,400	$ 9,780,472
FY 1985	2,506,891	359,448	...	-0-	2,866,339	9,618,703	9,288,146
% Change 81–85	−32.1%	+9.5%	...	−100%	−30.8%	−5.8%	−5.0%
New Jersey							
FY 1981	$28,676,660	$31,581,370	...	$19,117,773	$79,375,803	$121,495,718	$119,354,390
FY 1985	36,998,793	37,954,310	...	14,192,241	89,135,344	125,857,758	121,370,689
% Change 81–85	+28.9%	+20.2%	...	−25.8%	+12.3%	+3.6%	+1.7%
New Mexico							
FY 1981	$ 5,302,946	...	...	$ 2,571,982	$ 7,874,928	$ 16,883,508	$ 16,883,508
FY 1985	7,719,880	...	...	-0-	7,719,880	18,493,118	17,930,559
% Change 81–85	+45.6%	...	...	−100%	−1.9%	+9.5%	+6.2%

State	State General Funds	Other	Children's Trust Funds	Local Funds	Total State and Local Funding	Total Funding (Federal, State, and Local)	Total Funding Less Title IVE
North Dakota							
FY 1981	$ 578,202	• • •	-0-	$ 95,513	$ 673,715	$ 11,413,224	$ 10,733,880
FY 1985	564,915		$43,103	63,272	671,290	8,726,035	8,085,429
% Change 81–85	−2.3%		+100%	−33.8%	−.4%	−23.5%	−24.7%
Pennsylvania							
FY 1981	$106,525,696	• • •	• • •	$ 71,706,638	$178,232,334	$238,686,296	$200,249,465
FY 1985	100,215,517			$ 88,620,690	188,836,207	245,431,035	215,258,621
% Change 81–85	−5.9%			+25.6%	+5.9%	+2.8%	+7.5%
South Carolina							
FY 1981	$ 8,642,398	• • •	• • •	$ 1,298,715	$ 9,941,113	$ 35,199,143	$ 34,603,854
FY 1985	9,283,621			877,586	10,161,207	32,940,517	31,353,448
% Change 81–85	+7.4%			−32.5%	+2.2%	−6.4%	−9.4%
South Dakota							
FY 1981	$ 678,742	$ 302,128	• • •	• • •	$ 980,870	$ 3,787,917	$ 2,834,279
FY 1985	92,186	196,782			288,968	2,380,441	1,681,797
% Change 81–85	−86.4%	−34.9%			−70.5%	−37.2%	−40.7%
Tennessee							
FY 1981	$ 8,950,390	$ 1,885,146	• • •	3,926,112	$ 14,761,648	$ 69,422,070	$ 67,272,222
FY 1985	10,862,182	1,577,048		3,246,563	15,685,793	70,592,044	69,241,355
% Change 81–85	+21.4%	−16.3%		−17.4%	+6.3%	+1.7%	+2.9%
Texas							
FY 1981	$ 21,570,236	$ 1,255,020	• • •	$ 386,152	$100,914,220	$100,914,220	$ 95,330,393
FY 1985	34,898,103	$ 6,347,886		111,668	41,357,657	116,120,935	106,380,351
% Change 81–85	+61.7%	+460.4%		−71.1%	+78.2%	+15.1%	+11.6%
Virginia							
FY 1981	$ 2,915,464	-0-	• • •	$ 5,601,887	$ 8,517,351	$ 37,057,163	$ 34,254,230
FY 1985	1,401,871	$ 689,655		4,339,747	6,431,273	26,309,239	23,847,675
% Change 81–85	−51.9%	+100%		−22.5%	−24.5%	−29.0%	−30.4%
West Virginia							
FY 1981	$ 9,673,448	• • •	• • •	• • •	$ 9,673,448	$ 22,692,720	$ 20,658,459
FY 1985	12,681,034				12,681,034	29,090,517	25,211,207
% Change 81–85	+31.1%				+31.1%	+28.2%	+22.0%
Totals							
FY 1981	$820,839,024	$ 87,518,439	-0-	$129,936,721	$1,038,294,184	$2,145,250,588	$1,978,697,559
FY 1985	$961,529,916	$104,584,008	$1,673,809	$139,711,364	$1,207,499,097	$2,271,680,957	$2,016,393,709
% Change 81–85	+17.1%	+19.5%	+100%	+7.5%	+16.3%	+5.9%	+1.9%

Explanatory Notes for Two Preceding Tables

Alabama
- Title XX includes expenditures for day care services for employment related reasons.
- "Other" (federal) includes WIN (day care).

Arizona
- Title XX includes expenditures for day care services for employment related reasons.
- FY '85 CAPTA amount is from information on child abuse state grants from The National Center on Child Abuse and Neglect, U.S. Department of Health and Human Services. The FY 1985 amount reflects State Grant Part I totals only. Federal FY adjusted to State's FY.
- "Other" (federal) includes Social Security Survivors and Disability benefits (OASDI).
- Arizona Health Care Cost Containment (AHCCCS) is a special state appropriation for child abuse and prevention treatment and is included under state "other."

Arkansas
- Title XX includes funding for day care for employment related reasons.
- FY '85 CAPTA amount is from information on child abuse state grants from the National Center on Child Abuse and Neglect, U.S. Department of Health and Human Services. The FY 1985 amount reflects State Grant Part I totals only. Federal FY adjusted to state's FY.
- Local funds include local contributions and local appropriations.
- Title IVE amount for FY 1981 is from "Background Material and Data on Programs Within the Jurisdiction of the Committee on Ways and Means," U.S. House of Representatives, 98th Congress, 1st Session, February 8, 1983, p. 357. Federal FY adjusted to state's FY.

California
- Title XX does not include expenditures for day care services for employment related reasons, and reflects only CPS services.
- In 1985, all Title XX dollars were spent on adult services.
- FY '81 CAPTA amount is from information on child abuse state grants from the National Center on Child Abuse and Neglect, U.S. Department of Health and Human Services. Federal FY adjusted to state's FY.
- "State General Funds" represent state and local funding.
- "Other" (federal) is an adoption grant—"Joint Assessment Facilitator."
- "Other" (state) includes child abuse prevention funds.

Florida
- Title XX includes expenditures for day care services for employment related reasons.
- FY '81 and FY '85 CAPTA amount is from information on child abuse state grants from the National Center on Child Abuse and Neglect, U.S. Department of Health and Human Services. The FY '85 amount reflects State Grant Part I total only. Federal FY adjusted to state's FY.
- Title IVE amount for FY 1981 is from "Background Material and Data on Programs Within the Jurisdiction of the Committee on Ways and Means," U.S. House of Representatives, 98th Congress, 1st Session, February 8, 1983, p. 357. Federal FY adjusted to state's FY.
- "Other" (federal includes Title IVA and various discretionary grants).

Georgia
- Title XX includes expenditures for day care services for employment and related reasons.
- The large increase in Title XX funds in FY '83 is due to a policy change to contract out most day care services.

Hawaii
- Title XX does not include expenditures for day care services for employment related reasons.
- State General Funds reflect the state's match for Title XX, IVB, IVE, and were summed by the Committee with the state's approval.

Idaho
- Title XX includes expenditures for day care services for employment and related reasons.
- Title XX includes expenditures for child care licensing, and youth rehabilitation.
- Title IVE amount for FY 1981 is from "Background Material and Data on Programs Within the Jurisdiction of the Committee on Ways and Means," U.S. House of Representatives, 98th Congress, 1st Session, February 8, 1983, p. 358. Federal FY adjusted to state's FY.
- "Other" (state) includes receipts (e.g., child support payments, etc.).

Illinois
- Title IVE amount for FY 1981 is from "Background Material and Data on Programs Within the Jurisdiction of the Committee on Ways and Means," U.S. House of Representatives, 98th Congress, 1st Session, February 8, 1983, p. 358. Federal FY adjusted to state's FY.
- "Other" (federal) is federal grants from various sources.
- "Other" (state) is the state child abuse grant program.

Indiana
- Title XX includes expenditures for day care services for employment and related reasons.
- Title IVE amount for FY 1981 is from "Background Material and Data on Programs Within the Jurisdiction of the Committee on Ways and Means," U.S. House of Representatives, 98th Congress, 1st Session, February 8, 1983, p. 358; Ibid, 99th Congress, 1st Session, February 22, 1985, p. 489. Federal FY adjusted to state's FY.
- State does not qualify for CAPTA.
- The county government, rather than the state, administers all child protection services.

Iowa
- Title XX does not include expenditures for day care services for employment and related reasons.
- Title IVB funding information from "Background Material and Data on Programs Within the Jurisdiction of the Committee on Ways and Means," U.S. House of Representatives, 98th Congress, 1st Session, February 8, 1983, p. 358; Ibid, 99th Congress, 1st Session, February 22, 1985, p. 489. Federal FY adjusted to state's FY.
- "Local Funds" represent the local match for day care services.
- "Other" (federal) is Title XIX funding (Medicaid).

Kentucky
- Title XX includes expenditures for day care services for employment and related reasons.
- "Other" (state) is receipts (i.e., child support payments, OASDI payments, etc.).

Louisiana
- Title XX includes expenditures for day care services for employment and related reasons.
- "Other" (federal) includes Low Income Energy Assistance (LIEA) and Title IVA funds.

Maine
- Title XX includes expenditures for day care services for employment and related reasons.

Maryland
- Title XX does not include expenditures for day care services for employment and related reasons.

Michigan
- State system was reorganized in 1983; expenditures for FY '84 and "85 reflect different categories from FY '81 and '82.
- Title IVE and IVB funding information from "Background Material and Data on Programs Within the Jurisdiction of the Committee on Ways and Means," U.S. House of Representatives, 98th Congress, 1st Session, February 8, 1983, p. 358; Ibid, 99th Congress, 1st Session, February 22, 1985, p. 487 and 489. Federal FY adjusted to state's FY

Minnesota
- Title XX includes expenditures for day care services for employment and related reasons.
- Title XX funds are given as block grants to counties.
- Community Social Services Act (CSSA) child protective and child welfare services cannot be separated out of the CSSA.
- Title IVE funding information from "Background Material and Data on Programs Within the Jurisdiction of the Committee on Ways and Means," U.S. House of Representatives, 98th Congress, 1st Session, February 8, 1983, p. 358; Ibid, 99th Congress, 1st Session, February 22, 1985, p. 489. Federal FY adjusted to state's FY.
- "Other" (state) is Community Social Services Act funding.

Mississippi
- Title XX includes expenditures for day care services for employment and related reasons.
- FY 1985 Title XX decrease is the result of the transfer of some programs to other agencies.
- "State General Funds" include both state and local funds.

Missouri
- Title XX includes expenditures for day care services for employment and related reasons.
- Totals are figured by the Select Committee with the state's approval. State had not provided totals due to concern that the state's fiscal year is different from the federal fiscal year. While the state tried to provide an estimate of the same cycle amount some overlapping may occur.

Montana
- Title XX includes expenditures for day care services for employment and related reasons.
- "Other" (federal) includes Refugee Resettlement money.

Nevada
- Title XX does not include expenditures for day care services for employment and related reasons.
- FY '81 CAPTA amount is from information on child abuse state grants from the National Center on Child Abuse and Neglect, U.S. Department of Health and Human Services. Federal FY adjusted to state's FY
- "Other" (state) includes receipts (e.g., child support payments, OASDI payments, etc.).
- "Local Funds" include county participation provider match.

New Jersey
- Title XX includes expenditures for day care services for employment and related reasons.
- "Other" (federal) includes Title XIX (Medicaid) and WIN.
- "Other" (state) includes State Aid; New Jersey law requires funding for emergency care.
- Local Funds—includes counties, private donor funds, receipts (e.g., child support payments, OASDI payments, etc.).

New Mexico
- Title XX does not include expenditures for day care services for employment and related reasons.

– FY '85 CAPTA amount is from information on child abuse state grants from the National Center on Child Abuse and Neglect, U.S. Department of Health and Human Services. The FY '85 amount reflects State Grant Part I total only. Federal FY adjusted to state's FY.

New York

– FY '81 and '85 CAPTA amount is from information on child abuse state grants from the National Center on Child Abuse and Neglect, U.S. Department of Health and Human Services. The FY '85 amount reflects State Grant Part I total only. Federal FY adjusted to state's FY.

North Dakota

– Under "State General Funds" the Committee summed, with the state's approval, two amounts listed on the survey under state funds as Title IVB and IVE, and designated the total as State General Funds. The state indicated the two amounts represented the state match for Title IVB and IVE. Likewise, the state agreed to designating amounts listed under other funds as Title IVE as "Local Funds," since they represented the Local IVE Match.

Pennsylvania

– Title XX includes expenditures for day care services for employment and related reasons.
– "Other" (federal) includes Refugee Resettlement funding.

South Carolina

– Title XX includes expenditures for day care services for employment and related reasons.
– Local Funds include county and match funds from agencies and other private and public providers.

South Dakota

– FY '81 and '85 CAPTA amount is from information on child abuse state grants from the National Center on Child Abuse and Neglect, U.S. Department of Health and Human Services. The FY '85 amount reflects State Grant Part I total only. Federal FY adjusted to state's FY.
– "Other" (federal) includes Bureau of Indian Affairs.
– "Other" (state) includes donations.

Tennessee

– Title XX includes expenditures for day care services for employment and related reasons.
– "Other" (state) includes receipts (e.g., child support payments, OASDI etc.).

Texas

– "Other" (federal) includes Title IVA.
– "Other" (state) includes a Child Welfare Rider, and Child Protection funds to counties—mostly Houston.

Virginia

– Title XX includes expenditures for day care services for employment and related reasons, and includes all Title IVB funding.
– "Other" (state) includes funds for Virginia Family Violence Prevention Program, which is appropriated by the Virginia General Assembly for services to spouse victims and for the prevention of child abuse and neglect.

West Virginia

– Title XX includes expenditures for day care services for employment and related reasons.

12. UNITED NATIONS DECLARATION OF THE RIGHTS OF THE CHILD, 1959

DECLARATION OF THE RIGHTS OF THE CHILD

**Proclaimed by the General Assembly
of the United Nations on 20 November 1959
Resolution 1386 (XIV)**

PREAMBLE

Whereas *the peoples of the United Nations have, in the Charter, reaffirmed their faith in fundamental human rights, and in the dignity and worth of the human person, and have determined to promote social progress and better standards of life in larger freedom,*

Whereas *the United Nations has, in the Universal Declaration of Human Rights, proclaimed that everyone is entitled to all the rights and freedoms set forth therein, without distinction of any kind, such as race, colour, sex, language, religion, political or other opinion, national or social origin, property, birth or other status,*

Whereas *the child, by reason of his physical and mental immaturity, needs special safeguards and care, including appropriate legal protection, before as well as after birth,*

Whereas *the need for such special safeguards has been stated in the Geneva Declaration of the Rights of the Child of 1924, and recognized in the Universal Declaration of Human Rights and in the statutes of specialized agencies and international organizations concerned with the welfare of children,*

Whereas *mankind owes to the child the best it has to give,*

Now therefore,

THE GENERAL ASSEMBLY

Proclaims *this Declaration of the Rights of the Child to the end that he may have a happy childhood and enjoy for his own good and for the good of society the rights and freedoms herein set forth, and calls upon parents, upon men and women as individuals and upon voluntary organizations, local authorities and national Governments to recognize these rights and strive for their observance by legislative and other measures progressively taken in accordance with the following principles:*

PRINCIPLE 1
The child shall enjoy all the rights set forth in this Declaration. All children, without any exception whatsoever, shall be entitled to these rights, without distinction or discrimination on account of race, colour, sex, language, religion, political or other opinion, national or social origin, property, birth or other status, whether of himself or of his family.

PRINCIPLE 2
The child shall enjoy special protection, and shall be given opportunities and facilities, by law and by other means, to enable him to develop physically, mentally, morally, spiritually and socially in a healthy and normal manner and in conditions of freedom and dignity. In the enactment of laws for this purpose the best interests of the child shall be the paramount consideration.

PRINCIPLE 3
The child shall be entitled from his birth to a name and a nationality.

PRINCIPLE 4
The child shall enjoy the benefits of social security. He shall be entitled to grow and develop in health; to this end special care and protection shall be provided both to him and to his mother, including adequate

pre-natal and post-natal care. The child shall have the right to adequate nutrition, housing, recreation and medical services

PRINCIPLE 5
The child who is physically, mentally or socially handicapped shall be given the special treatment, education and care required by his particular condition.

PRINCIPLE 6
The child, for the full and harmonious development of his personality, needs love and understanding. He shall, wherever possible, grow up in the care and under the responsibility of his parents, and in any case in an atmosphere of affection and of moral and material security; a child of tender years shall not, save in exceptional circumstances, be separated from his mother. Society and the public authorities shall have the duty to extend particular care to children without a family and to those without adequate means of support. Payment of State and other assistance towards the maintenance of children of large families is desirable.

PRINCIPLE 7
The child is entitled to receive education, which shall be free and compulsory, at least in the elementary stages. He shall be given an education which will promote his general culture, and enable him on a basis of equal opportunity to develop his abilities, his individual judgement and his sense of moral and social responsibility, and to become a useful member of society.

PRINCIPLE 8
The child shall in all circumstances be among the first to receive protection and relief.

PRINCIPLE 9
The child shall be protected against all forms of neglect cruelty and exploitation. He shall not be the subject of traffic, in any form.

The child shall not be admitted to employment before an appropriate minimum age; he shall in no case be caused or permitted to engage in any occupation or employment which would prejudice his health or education, or interfere with his physical, mental or moral development

PRINCIPLE 10
The child shall be protected from practices which may foster racial, religious and any other form of discrimination. He shall be brought up in a spirit of understanding, tolerance, friendship among peoples, peace and universal brotherhood and in full consciousness that his energy and talents should be devoted to the service of his fellow men.

13. DRAFT UNITED NATIONS CONVENTION ON THE RIGHTS OF THE CHILD

DRAFT CONVENTION ON THE RIGHTS OF THE CHILD

**Text of Articles Adopted by the Open-Ended
Working Group on a Draft Convention on the
Rights of the Child (1987)**

THE STATES PARTIES TO THE CONVENTION

Considering *that in accordance with the principles proclaimed in the Charter of the United Nations, recognition of the inherent dignity and of the equal and inalienable rights of all members of the human family is the foundation of freedom, justice and peace in the world,*

Bearing in mind *that the peoples of the United Nations have, in the Charter, reaffirmed their faith in fundamental human rights and in the dignity and worth of the human person, and have determined to promote social progress and better standards of life in larger freedom,*

Recognizing *that the United Nations has, in the Universal Declaration of Human Rights and in the International Covenants on Human Rights, proclaimed and agreed that everyone is entitled to all the rights and freedoms set forth therein, without distinction of any kind, such as race, colour, sex, language, religion, political or other opinion, national or social origin, property, birth or other status.*

Recalling *that, in the Universal Declaration of Human Rights, the United Nations has proclaimed that childhood is entitled to special care and assistance,*

Convinced *that the family, as the basic unit of society and the natural environment for the growth and well-being of all its members and particularly children, should be afforded the necessary protection and assistance so that it can fully assume its responsibilities within the community,*

Recognizing *that, as indicated in the Declaration of the Rights of the Child adopted in 1959, the child, due to the needs of his physical and mental development, requires particular care and assistance with regard to health, physical, mental, moral and social development, and requires legal protection in conditions of freedom, dignity and security,*

Recognizing *that the child, for the full and harmonious development of his personality, should grow up in a family environment, in an atmosphere of happiness, love and understanding,*

Bearing in mind *that the need for extending particular care to the child has been stated in the Geneva Declaration on the Rights of the Child of 1924 and in the Declaration of the Rights of the Child adopted by the United Nations in 1959 and recognized in the Universal Declaration of Human Rights, in the International Covenant on Civil and Political Rights (in particular in articles 23 and 24), in the International Covenant on Economic, Social and Cultural Rights (in particular in its article 10) and in the statutes of specialized agencies and international organizations concerned with the welfare of children.*

Considering *that the child should be fully prepared to live an individual life in society, and brought up in the spirit of the ideals proclaimed in the Charter of the United Nations, and in particular in the spirit of peace, dignity, tolerance, freedom and brotherhood,*

Have agreed as follows:

ARTICLE 1

According to the present Convention, a child is every human being to the age of 18 years unless, under the law of his State, he has attained his age of majority earlier.

ARTICLE 2

1. The child shall have the right from his birth to a name and to acquire a nationality.

2. The States Parties to the present Convention shall ensure that their legislation recognizes the principle according to which a child shall acquire the nationality of the State in the territory of which he has been born if, at the time of the child's birth, he is not granted nationality by any other State in accordance with its laws.

ARTICLE 3

1. In all actions concerning children, whether undertaken by public or private social welfare institutions, courts of law, or administrative authorities, the best interests of the child shall be a primary consideration.

2. In all judicial or administrative proceedings affecting a child that is capable of forming his own views, an opportunity shall be provided for the views of the child to be heard, either directly or indirectly through a representative, as a party to the proceedings, and those views shall be taken into consideration by the competent authorities, in a manner consistent with the procedures followed in the State Party for the application of its legislation.

3. The States Parties to the present Convention undertake to ensure the child such protection and care as is necessary for his well-being, taking into account the rights and duties of his parents, legal guardians, or other individuals legally responsible for him, and, to this end, shall take all appropriate legislative and administrative measures.

4. The States Parties to the present Convention shall ensure competent supervision of officials and personnel of institutions directly responsible for the care of children.

ARTICLE 4

1. The States Parties to the present Convention shall respect and extend all the rights set forth in this Convention to each child in their territories without distinction of any kind, irrespective of the child's or his parents' or legal guardian's race, colour, sex, language, religion, political or other opinion, national or social origin, family status, ethnic origin, cultural beliefs or practices, property, educational attainment, birth, or any other basis whatever.

2. The States Parties to the present Convention shall take all appropriate measures to ensure that the child is protected against all forms of discrimination or punishment on the basis of the status, activities, expressed opinions, or beliefs of the child's parents, legal guardians, or other family members.

ARTICLE 5

The States Parties to the present Convention shall undertake all appropriate administrative and legislative measures, in accordance with their available resources, and, where needed, within the framework of international co-operation, for the implementation of the rights recognized in this Convention.

ARTICLE 6

1. The States Parties to the present Convention recognize that the child should enjoy parental care and should have his place of residence determined by his parent(s), except as provided herein.

2. States Parties shall ensure that a child shall not be separated from his parents against their will, except when competent authorities subject to judicial review determine, in accordance with applicable law and

procedures, that such separation is necessary for the best interests of the child. Such a determination may be necessary in a particular case such as one involving abuse or neglect of the child by the parents, or one where the parents are living separately and a decision must be made as to the child's place of residence. Such determinations shall not be made until all interested parties have been given an opportunity to participate in the proceedings and to make their views known. Such views shall be taken into account by the competent authorities in making their determination.

3. A child who is separated from one or both parents has the right to maintain personal relations and direct contacts with both parents on a regular basis, save in exceptional circumstances.

4. Where such separation results from any action initiated by a State Party, such as the detention, imprisonment, exile, deportation or death (including death arising from any cause while the person is in the custody of the State) of one or both parents or the child, that State Party shall, upon request, provide the parents, the child or, if appropriate, another member of the family with essential information concerning the whereabouts of the absent member(s) of the family unless the provision of the information would be detrimental to the well-being of the child. State Parties shall further ensure that the submission of such a request shall of itself entail no adverse consequences for the person(s) concerned.

ARTICLE 6 *bis*

1. In accordance with the obligation of States Parties under article 6, paragraph 2, applications by a child or his parents to enter or leave a State Party for the purpose of family reunification shall be dealt with by States Parties in a positive, humane and expeditious manner. States Parties shall further ensure that the submission of such a request shall entail no adverse consequences for the applicants and for the members of their families.

2. A child whose parents reside in different States shall have the right to maintain on a regular basis save in exceptional circumstances personal relations and direct contacts with both parents. Towards that end and in accordance with the obligation of States Parties under Article 6, paragraph 2, States Parties shall respect the right of the child and his parents to leave any country, including their own, and to enter their own country. The right to leave any country shall be subject only to such restrictions as are prescribed by law and which are necessary to protect the national security, public order (*ordre public*), public health or morals or the rights and freedoms of others and are consistent with the other rights recognized in the present Convention.

ARTICLE 6 *ter*

1. The States Parties to the present Convention shall take appropriate measures to combat the illicit transfer and non-return of children abroad.

2. To this end, the States Parties shall promote the conclusion of bilateral or multilateral agreements or accession to existing agreements, as well as the introduction of periodic consultations between the competent national authorities.

ARTICLE 7

The States Parties to the present Convention shall assure to the child who is capable of forming his own views the right to express his opinions freely in all matters, the wishes of the child being given due weight in accordance with his age and maturity.

ARTICLE 7 *bis*

1. The States Parties to the present Convention shall respect the right of the child to freedom of thought, conscience and religion.

2. This right shall include in particular the freedom to have or to adopt a religion or whatsoever belief of his choice and freedom, either individually or in community with others and in public or private, to manifest

his religion or belief, subject only to such limitations as are prescribed by law and are necessary to protect public safety, order, health and morals; and the right to have access to education in the matter of religion or belief.

3. The States Parties shall respect the rights and duties of the parents and, where applicable, legal guardians, to provide direction to the child in the exercise of his right in a manner consistent with the evolving capacities of the child.

4. The States Parties shall equally respect the liberty of the child and his parents and, where applicable, legal guardians, to ensure the religious and moral education of the child in conformity with convictions of their choice.

ARTICLE 8

1. Parents or, as the case may be, guardians, have the primary responsibility for the upbringing and development of the child. The best interests of the child will be their basic concern. States Parties shall use their best efforts to ensure recognition of the principle that both parents have common and similar responsibilities for the upbringing and development of the child.

2. For the purpose of guaranteeing and promoting the rights set forth in this Convention, the States Parties to the present Convention shall render appropriate assistance to parents and guardians in the performance of the child-rearing responsibilities and shall ensure the development of institutions for the care of children.

3. The States Parties shall take all appropriate measures to ensure that children of working parents have the right to benefit from child care services and facilities for which they are eligible.

4. The institutions, services and facilities referred to in paragraphs 2 and 3 of this article shall conform with the standards established by competent authorities particularly in the areas of safety, health, and in the number and suitability on their staff.

ARTICLE 8 *bis*

1. The States Parties to the present Convention shall take all appropriate legislative, administrative, social and educational measures to protect the child from all forms of physical or mental injury or abuse, neglect or negligent treatment, maltreatment or exploitation including sexual abuse, while in the care of parent(s), legal guardian(s) or any other person who has the care of the child.

2. Such protective measures should, as appropriate, include effective procedures for the establishment of social programmes to provide necessary support for the child and for those who have the care of the child, as well as for other forms of prevention and for identification, reporting, referral, investigation, treatment, and follow-up of instances of child maltreatment described heretofore, and, as appropriate, for judicial involvement.

ARTICLE 9

The States Parties to the present Convention recognize the important function performed by the mass media and shall ensure that the child has access to information and material from a diversity of national and international sources, including those aimed at the promoting of his social, spiritual and moral well-being and physical and mental health. To this end, the States Parties shall:

(a) encourage the mass media agencies to disseminate information and material of social and cultural benefit to the child and in accordance with the spirit of article 16;
(b) encourage the production and dissemination of children's books;
(c) encourage international cooperation in the production, exchange and dissemination of such information from a diversity of cultural, national and international sources;

(d)   encourage the mass media agencies to have particular regard to the linguistic needs of the child who belongs to a minority group or an indigenous population; and

(e)   encourage the development of appropriate guidelines for the protectionof thechild frominformationand material potentiallyinjurious tohis well-being bearingin mindthe provisions of article 8.

ARTICLE 9 *bis*

1. The States Parties to the present Convention undertake to respect the right of the child to preserve his or her identity (nationality, name, family relations as recognized by law) without unlawful interference.

2. Where a child is illegally deprived of some or all of the elements of his or her identity, the States Parties shall provide appropriate assistance and protection, with a view to speedily re-establishing his or her identity.

ARTICLE 10

1. A child permanently or temporarily deprived of his family environment for any reason shall be entitled to special protection and assistance provided by the State.

2. The States Parties to the present Convention shall ensure that a child who is parentless, or who is temporarily or permanently deprived of his family environment, or who in his best interests cannot be brought up or allowed to remain in the environment shall be provided with alternative family care which could include, *inter alia*, adoption, foster placement, or placement in suitable institutions for the care of children. When considering alternative family care for the child and the best interests of the child, due regard shall be paid to the desirability of continuity in a child's upbringing and to the child's ethnic, religious or linguistic background.

ARTICLE 11

1. The States Parties to the present Convention shall undertake measures, where appropriate, to facilitate the process of adoption of the child. Adoption of a child shall be authorized only by competent authorities who determine, in accordance with applicable law and procedures and on the basis of all pertinent and reliable information, that the adoption is permissible in view of the child's status concerning parents, relatives and guardians and that, if required, the appropriate persons concerned have given their informed consent to the adoption on the basis of such counselling as may be necessary

2. The States Parties to the present Convention shall take all appropriate measures to secure the best interests of the child who is the subject of intercountry adoption. States Parties shall ensure that placements are made by authorized agencies or appropriate persons under the adequate supervision of competent authorities, providing the same safeguards and standards that are applied in exclusively domestic adoptions. The competent authorities shall make every possible effort to ensure the legal validity of the adoption in the countries involved. States Parties shall endeavour, where appropriate, to promote these objectives by entering into bilateral or multilateral agreements.

ARTICLE 11 *bis*

The States Parties to the present Convention shall take appropriate measures to ensure that a child who is seeking refugee status or who is considered a refugee in accordance with applicable international or domestic law and procedures shall, whether unaccompanied or accompanied by his parents, legal guardians or close relatives, receive appropriate protection and humanitarian assistance in the enjoyment of applicable rights set forth in this Convention and other international human rights or humanitarian instruments to which the said States are Parties. In view of the important functions performed in refugee protection and assistance matters by the United Nations and other competent intergovernmental and non-governmental organizations, the States Parties to the present Convention shall provide appropriate co-operation in any efforts by these organizations to protect and assist such a child and to trace the parents or other close relatives of an unaccompanied refugee child in order to obtain information necessary for reunification with his family. In cases where no parents, legal guardians or close relatives can be found, the child shall be accorded the same protection as any other child permanently or temporarily deprived of his family environment for any reason, as set forth in the present Convention.

ARTICLE 12

1. The States Parties to the present Convention recognize that a mentally or physically disabled child should enjoy a full and decent life in conditions which ensure his dignity, promote his self-reliance, and facilitate his active participation in the community.

2. The States Parties to the present Convention recognize the right of the disabled child to special care and shall encourage and ensure the extension, subject to available resources, to the eligible child and those responsible for his care, of assistance for which application is made and which is appropriate to the child's condition and to the circumstances of the parents or others caring for the child.

3. Recognizing the special needs of a disabled child, assistance extended in accordance with paragraph 2 shall be provided free of charge, whenever possible, taking into account the financial resources of the parents or others caring for the child, and shall be designed to ensure that the disabled child has effective access to and receives education, training, health care services, rehabilitation services, preparation for employment and recreation opportunities in a manner conducive to the child's achieving the fullest possible social integration and individual development, including his cultural and spiritual development.

4. States Parties shall promote in the spirit of international co-operation the exchange of appropriate information in the field of preventive health care and of medical, psychological and functional treatment of disabled children, including dissemination of and access to information concerning methods of rehabilitation education and vocational services, with the aim of enabling States Parties to improve their capabilities and skills and to widen their experience in these areas. In this regard, particular account shall be taken of the needs of developing countries.

ARTICLE 12 *bis*

1. The States Parties to the present Convention recognize the right of the child to the enjoyment of the highest attainable standard of health and to medical and rehabilitation facilities. The States Parties shall strive to ensure that no child is deprived for financial reasons of his right of access to such health care services.

2. The States Parties to the present Convention shall pursue full implementation of this right and in particular, shall take appropriate measure to:

   (a)   diminish infant and child mortality;
   (b)   ensure the provision of necessary medical assistance and health care to all children with emphasis on the development of primary health care;
   (c)   ensure appropriate health care for expectant mothers;
   (d)   encourage the provision of full and accurate information regarding methods of infant nutrition, including the advantages of breast-feeding;
   (e)   ensure the provision of information and training for parents and children in basic health care, sanitation and prevention of accidents; and
   (f)   develop preventive health care and family planning education and services.

3. The States Parties to the present Convention shall seek to take all effective and appropriate measures with a view to abolishing traditional practices prejudicial to the health of children.

4. States Parties to the present Convention undertake to promote and encourage international co-operation with a view to achieving progressively the full realization of the right recognized in this article. In this regard, particular account shall be taken of the needs of developing countries

ARTICLE 12 *ter*

The States Parties to the present Convention recognize the right of a child who has been placed by the competent authorites for the purposes of care, protection, or treatment of his or her physical or mental health, to a periodic review of the treatment provided to the child and all other circumstances relevant to his or her placement.

ARTICLE 13

1. The States Parties to the present Convention shall, in a manner appropripriate to national conditions, recognize for every child the right to benefit from social security and shall take the necessary measures to achieve the full realization of this right.

2. The benefits should, where appropriate, be granted taking into account the national resources available and the resources and the circumstances of the child and persons having responsibility for the maintenance of the child as well as any other consideration relevant to an application for benefits made by or on behalf of the child.

ARTICLE 14

1. The States Parties to the present Convention recognize the right of every child to a standard of living adequate for the child's physical, mental, spiritual, moral and social development.

2. The parent(s) or others responsible for the child have the primary responsibility to secure, within their abilities and financial capacities, the conditions of living necessary for the child's development.

3. The States Parties to the present Convention, in accordance with national conditions and within their means, shall take appropriate measures to assist parents and others responsible for the child to implement this right and shall in case of need provide material assistance and support programmes, particularly with regard to nutrition, clothing and housing.

ARTICLE 15

1. The States Parties to the present Convention recognize the right of the child to education and, with a view to achieving the full realization of this right on the basis of equal opportunity, they shall, in particular:

    (a)   make primary education free and compulsory as early as possible;
    (b)   encourage the development of different forms of secondary education systems, both general and vocational, to make them available and accessible to all children, and take appropriate measures such as the introduction of free education and offering financial assistance in case of need; and
    (c)   make higher education equally accessible to all on the basis of capacity by every appropriate means.

2. The States Parties shall take all appropriate measures to ensure that school discipline is administered in a manner reflective of the child's human dignity.

3. The States Parties to the present Convention shall respect the rights and duties of the parents and, where applicable, legal guardians to provide direction to the child in the exercise of his right to education in a manner consistent with the evolving capacities of the child.

4. The States Parties to the present Convention shall promote and encourage international co-operation in matters relating to education, in particular with a view to contributing to the elimination of ignorance and illiteracy throughout the world and facilitating access to scientific and technical knowledge and modern teaching methods. In this regard, particular account shall be taken of the needs of developing countries.

ARTICLE 16

1. The States Parties to the present Convention agree that the education of the child shall be directed to:

(a) the promotion of the development of the child's personality, talents and mental and physical abilities to their fullest potential and the fostering of respect for all human rights and fundamental freedoms;

(b) the preparation of the child for responsible life in a free society, in the spirit of understanding, peace, tolerance and friendship among all peoples, ethnic and religious groups;

(c) the development of respect for the natural environment and for the principles of the Charter of the United Nations; and

(d) the development of respect for the child's own cultural identity and values, for the national values of the country in which the child is living, for civilizations different from its own, and for human rights and fundamental freedoms.

2. No part of paragraph 1 of this article shall be construed so as to interfere with the liberty of individuals and bodies to establish and direct educational institutions, subject always to the observance of the principles set forth in paragraph 1 and to the requirement that the education given in such institutions shall conform to such minimum standards as may be laid down by the State.

ARTICLE 16 *bis*

In those states in which ethnic, religious or linguistic minorities or indigenous populations exist, a child belonging to such minorities or populations shall not be denied the right, in community with other members of its group, to enjoy its own culture, to profess and practice its own religion, or to use its own language.

ARTICLE 17

1. The States Parties to the present Convention recognize the right of the child to rest and leisure, to engage in play and recreational activities appropriate to the age of the child and to participate freely in cultural life and the arts.

2. The States Parties to the present Convention shall respect and promote the right of the child to fully participate in cultural and artistic life and shall encourage the provision of appropriate and equal opportunities for cultural, artistic, recreational and leisure activity.

ARTICLE 18

1. The States Parties to the present Convention recognize the right of the child to be protected from economic exploitation and from performing any work that is likely to be hazardous or to interfere with the child's education, or to be harmful to the child's health or physical, mental, spiritual, moral or social development.

2. The States Parties to the present Convention shall take legislative and administrative measures to ensure the implementation of this article. To this end, and having regard to the relevant provisions of other international instruments, the States Parties shall in particular:

(a) provide for a minimum age or minimum ages for admission to employment;

(b) provide for appropriate regulation of the hours and conditions of employment; and

(c) provide for appropriate penalties or other sanctions for the effective enforcement of this article.

ARTICLE 18 *bis*

The States Parties to the present Convention shall take all appropriate measures, including legislative, social and educational measures, to protect children from the illegal use of narcotic and psychotropic substances as defined in the relevant international treaties, and to prevent the use of children in the illegal production and trafficking of such substances.

ARTICLE 18 *ter*

The States Parties to the present Convention undertake to protect the child from all forms sexual exploitation and sexual abuse. For these purposes the States Parties shall in particular take all appropriate national, bilateral and multilateral measures to prevent:

(a)   the inducement or coercion of a child to engage in any unlawful sexual activity;
(b)   the exploitative use of children in prostitution or other unlawful sexual practices;
(c)   the exploitative use of children in pornographic performances and materials.

ARTICLE 18 *quater*

The States Parties to the present Convention shall take all appropriate national, bilateral and multilateral measures to prevent the abduction, the sale of or traffic in children for any purpose or in any form.

ARTICLE 18 *quinto*

The States Parties to the present Convention shall protect the child against all other forms of exploitation prejudicial to any aspects of the child's welfare.

ARTICLE 19

1. The States Parties to the present Convention recognize the right of children who are accused or recognized as having infringed the penal law to be treated in a manner which is consistent with promoting their sense of dignity and worth and intensifying their respect for the human rights and fundamental freedoms of others, and which takes into account their age and the desirability of promoting their rehabilitation.

2. To this end, and having regard to the relevant provisions of international instruments, the States Parties to the present Convention shall, in particular, ensure that:

(a)   no child is arbitrarily detained or imprisoned or subjected to torture, cruel, inhuman or degrading treatment or punishment;
(b)   capital punishment or life imprisonment without possibility of release is not imposed for crimes committed by persons below eighteen years of age; and
(c)   children accused of infringing the penal law
    i.   are presumed innocent until proven guilty according to law;
    ii.   are informed promptly of the charges against them and, as of the time of being accused, have legal or other appropriate assistance in the preparation and presentation of their defence;
    iii.   have the matter determined according to law in a fair hearing within a reasonable period of time by an independent and impartial tribunal; and
    iv.   if found guilty are entitled to have their conviction and sentence reviewed by a higher tribunal according to law.

3. An essential aim of treatment of children found guilty of infringing the penal law shall be their reformation and social rehabilitation. A variety of dispositions, including programmes of education and vocational training and alternatives to institutional care shall be available to ensure that children are dealt with in a manner appropriate and proportionate both to their circumstances and the offence.

4. All children deprived of their liberty shall be treated with humanity and respect for the inherent dignity of the human person, and shall in particular:

(a)   be brought as speedily as possible for adjudication;
(b)   be separated from adults accused or convicted of having committed an offence unless it is considered in the child's best interest not to do so, or it is unnecessary for the protection of the child; and

(c)   have the right to maintain contact with their family through correspondence and visits, save in exceptional circumstances.

ARTICLE 20

1. The States Parties to the present Convention undertake to respect and to ensure respect for the rules of international humanitarian law applicable to them in armed conflicts which are relevant to the child.

2. States Parties to the present Convention shall take all feasible measures to ensure that no child takes a direct part in hostilities and they shall refrain in particular from recruiting any child who has not attained the age of fifteen years into their armed forces.

3. In accordance with their obligations under international humanitarian law to protect the civilian population in armed conflicts, States Parties to this Convention shall take all feasible measures to ensure protection and care of children who are affected by an armed conflict.

ARTICLE 21

Nothing in this Convention shall affect any provisions that are more conducive to the realization of the rights of the child and that may be contained in:

(a)   the law of a State Party; or
(b)   any'other international convention, treaty or agreement in force for that State.

ARTICLE 21 *ter*

The States Parties to the present Convention undertake to make the principles and provisions of the Convention widely known, by appropriate and active means, to adults and children alike.

Proposals by Delegations of States

**Considered But Not Yet Adopted
by the Working Group at its 1987 Session**

ARTICLE 5 *bis*

(Proposal by Australia and the United States of America)
To help the child enjoy the rights enumerated in this Convention, States Parties undertake to protect the family as the natural and fundamental unit of society. Parents or legal guardians shall enjoy the primary rights and responsibilities for the care, upbringing and development of the child, having due regard for the importance of allowing the child to develop the skills and knowledge required for an independent adulthood.

ARTICLE 7 *ter* **(formerly considered as Article 18 quater)**

(Proposal by the United States of America)
1. States Parties to the present Convention recognize the rights of the child to freedom of expression, freedom of association and freedom of peaceful assembly.

2. States Parties recognize the right of the child not to be subjected to arbitrary or unlawful interference with his or her privacy, family, home or correspondence.

3. The exercise of the rights to freedom of expression, association and peaceful assembly shall be subject only to those restrictions which are provided by law and which are necessary in a democratic society in the interests of national security, public order (*ordre public*), the protection of public health and the morals or the protection of the rights and freedoms of others.

4. In no case shall a child be subjected to incarceration or other confinement for the legitimate exercise of these rights or other rights recognized in this Convention.

5. This article shall not be interpreted as affecting the lawful rights and duties of parents or legal guardians, which should be exercised in a manner consistent with the evolving capacities of the child.

ARTICLE 14, *new paragraph 4*

(Proposal by Australia)

The States Parties to the present Convention recognize that the responsibilities of the parents or legal guardians, including that of providing appropriate support to the child, continue even when the child is living apart from them, unless a decision to the contrary has been made by a competent body.

ARTICLE 21, *addition of a new paragraph*

(Proposal by Finland)

Nothing in the present Convention may be interpreted as implying for any State Party to the present Convention any right to impose any restriction upon or derogation from any of the fundamental human rights recognized or existing in that State Party by virtue of law, conventions, treaties, agreements, regulations or customs on the pretext that the present Convention does not recognize such rights or that it recognizes them to a lesser extent.

ARTICLE 21 *bis*

(Proposal by the Netherlands, United Kingdom and United States of America)

Nothing in this Convention shall be interpreted as legitimizing any alien's illegal entry into and presence in a State, nor shall any provision be interpreted as restricting the right of any State to promulgate laws and regulations concerning the entry of aliens and the terms and conditions of their stay, or to establish differences between nationals and aliens. However, such laws and regulations shall not be incompatible with the international legal obligations of the State, including those in the field of human rights.

Consolidated Text of Articles 22 and 23

(Submitted by a working party consisting of Canada, Poland, Sweden and the Informal NGO Ad-Hoc Group)

ARTICLE 22

1. For the purpose of **[monitoring the implementation of the provisions of the present Convention] [examining the progress made by States Parties in achieving the realization of the obligations undertaken in the present Convention]** there shall be established a Committee on the Rights of the Child (hereinafter referred to as The Committee).

2. The committee shall consist of **[10-12-15]** experts of high moral standing and recognized competence in the field covered by this Convention. The members of the committee shall be elected by the States Parties from among their nationals and shall serve in their personal capacity, consideration being given to equitable geographical distribution and the representation to the different forms of civilization as well as the principal legal systems.

3. The members of the committee shall be elected by secret ballot from a list of persons nominated by States Parties. Each State Party may nominate one person from among its own nationals.

4. The initial election to the Committee shall be held no later than six months after the date of the entry into force of the present Convention and thereafter every second year. At least four months before the date of each election, the Secretary-General of the United Nations shall address a letter to the States Parties inviting them to submit their nominations within two months. The Secretary-General shall subsequently

prepare a list on alphabetical order of all persons thus nominated, indicating the States Parties which have nominated them, and shall submit it to the States Parties to the present Convention.

5. The elections shall be held at meetings of the States Parties convened by the Secretary-General at United Nations headquarters. At those meetings, for which two thirds of the States Parties shall constitute a quorum, the persons elected to the Committee shall be those who obtain the largest number of votes and an absolute majority of the votes of the representatives of States Parties present and voting.

6. The members of the Committee shall be elected for a term of four years. The term of [ ] of the members elected at the first election shall expire at the end of two years; immediately after the first election the names of these [ ] members shall be chosen by lot by the Chairman of the meeting.

7. If a member of the Committee dies or resigns or for any other cause can no longer perform the duties of the Committee, the State Party which nominated the member shall appoint another expert from among its nationals to serve for the remainder of the term, subject to the approval of the Committee.

8. The Committee shall establish its own rules of procedure.

9. The Committee shall elect its officers for a period of two years.

10. The Secretary-General of the United Nations shall provide the necessary staff and facilities for the effective performance of the functions of the Committee under the present Convention.

11. **[With the approval of the General Assembly, the members of the Committee established under the present Convention shall receive emoluments from the United Nations resources on such terms and conditions as the Assembly may decide.]** or **[States Parties shall be responsible for the expenses of the members of the Committee while they are in performance of Committee duties.]**

ARTICLE 23
1. States Parties to the present Convention undertake to submit to the **[Committee, through the Secretary-General of the United Nations]** **[Secretary-General of the United Nations, for consideration by the Committee,]** reports **[on the measures they have adopted which give effect to the rights recognized herein and on the progress made on the enjoyment of those rights]** **[on the compliance with their obligations under the present Convention]** **[including information about the competent national body or bodies responsible for the implementation of those rights]** **[and assistance they may require from the international community]**
  (a)   within two years of the entry into force of the Convention for the States Parties concerned
  [(b) **thereafter every five years** [or at such longer intervals as the Committee may decide]]
  (b)   **thereafter, after having submitted an initial report, covering all substantive obligations under the Convention, every four years or at such longer intervals as the Committee may decide. Such reports shall be submitted in stages to be established by the Committee within nine months after the entry into force of the Convention.]**
The Committee may request further information from States Parties **[and shall prepare such observations as it may deem appropriate for transmission to the States Parties concerned].**

2. Reports made under this article **[may] [shall]** indicate factors and difficulties **[if any]** affecting the degree of fulfillment of the obligations under the present Convention **[and shall make reference to the measures being taken to extend the rights covered by the Convention to the most disadvantaged children].**

[3. Where relevant information has previously been furnished to the United Nations or to any specialized agency by any State party to the present Convention, it will not be necessary to reproduce that information, but a precise reference to the information so furnished will suffice.]

4. The Committee may decide that a State Party, which has completed a full reporting cycle covering all its substantive obligations under the Convention may limit its further reporting to changes (legal, administrative and in practice) affecting its obligations [and] to [such] questions relating to the obligations of the State Party concerned, which may have been indicated by the Committee [and to continuing factors and difficulties, if any, affecting implementation of the convention].

The following provisions being considered under Article 23 may be merged:
5. The Committee may invite the specialized agencies of the United Nations to be represented at the consideration of the implementation of such provision of the present Convention as fall within the scope of their activities.

6. The Committee may make arrangements with the specialized agencies of the United Nations and with non-governmental organizations in consultative status with the Economic and Social Council in order to receive their views on the implementation of the Convention in areas falling within the scope of their respective activities.

7. The specialized agencies of the United Nations and other international organizations may submit reports to the Committee on the implementation of the present Convention in areas falling within the scope of their activities.

8. States Parties may submit to the Committee their own comments to any observations concerning them by the Committee or by agencies or non-governmental organizations mentioned in paragraph [ ].

9. Reports on the activities of the Committee shall be submitted to the General Assembly [annually] [biennially]. They shall include any observations made under paragraphs [ ] and 6 and any comments under paragraph [ ].

10. The States Parties shall keep their reports widely available to the public.

[11. The Committee may, when it considers it appropriate, initiate a study on specific issues relating to one or more articles of the Convention and their implementation.

12. At the request of a State Party, the Committee shall, if it considers it appropriate, appoint an individual, group or body to assist the State Party in resolving, through inquiry and/or action, a concern expressed by that State Party regarding implementation, within its territory, of one or more provisions of this Convention.]

Further provisions under Article 23 still to be considered:
"[1. In order to foster the effective implementation of the Convention and to encourage international co-operation in the field covered by this Convention, the Committee shall transmit to the United Nations Children's Fund (UNICEF), as the designated lead agency on children, the reports of the States Parties, drawing UNICEF's attention to requests for technical assistance, as well as the Committee's suggestions, recommendations and general comments on States Parties' reports along with States Parties' observations.

2. UNICEF shall collaborate with the specialized agencies and organs of the United Nations and non-governmental organizations to establish and carry out programmes of action to further the implementation of the rights guaranteed by the Convention, giving special attention to requests for assistance submitted by States.

3. The specialized agencies shall keep UNICEF fully informed of measures they have taken either in response to States Parties' requests or within their programmes of action to further the full realization of rights guaranteed by the Convention, and shall bear in mind the importance of responding to States Parties' requests.

4. The States Parties to the present Convention agree that international action for the achievement of the rights recognized in the present Convention includes such methods as the conclusion of conventions, the adoption of recommendations, the furnishing of technical assistance and the holding of regional meetings and technical meetings for the purpose of consultation and study organized in conjunction with the Governments concerned.

5. Nothing in the present Convention shall be interpreted as impairing the provision of the Charter of the United Nations and of the constitutions of the specialized agencies which define the respective responsibilities of the various organs of the United Nations and of the specialized agencies in regard to the matters dealt with in the present Convention.]"

ARTICLE 22

(Alternative proposal by the United States of America—additional sub-paragraph 12)
"[12. The States Parties shall be responsible for expenses incurred in connection with the holding of meetings of the States Parties and of the Committee, including reimbursement to the United Nations for any expenses, such as the cost of staff and facilities, incurred by the United Nations pursuant to paragraph 10 of this Article.]"

Proposals by Delegations of States Not Yet Considered by the Working Group at its 1987 Session

Unnumbered ARTICLE

(Proposal by Norway)
The States Parties to the present Convention shall take all appropriate measures to facilitate the physical, psychological and social rehabilitation of children who have been victims of exploitation or abuse of any kind.

ARTICLE 1

(Proposal by the Netherlands and Austria)
The States Parties to the present Convention shall not provide any discrimination, in particular on the ground of sex, in establishing the age of majority.

ARTICLE 14

(Proposal by Finland)
The States Parties to the present Convention undertake to insure the effective recovery of maintenance from abroad to the child. To this end, States Parties shall promote the conclusion of multilateral or bilateral agreements and the making of any other arrangements relating to the recovery of maintenance.

ARTICLE 16, *paragraph 1, new subparagraph (e)*

(Proposal by the USSR)
Education in the spirit of the inadmissibility of propaganda of war and of any advocacy of national or racial hatred that constitutes incitement to discrimination, hostility or violence.

ARTICLE 24

(Proposal by Poland)

The present Convention shall be open for signature by all States.

ARTICLE 25

(Proposal by Poland)

The present Convention shall be subject to ratification. Instruments of ratification shall be deposited with the Secretary-General of the United Nations.

ARTICLE 26

(Proposal by Poland)

The present Convention shall remain open for accession by any State. Instruments of accession shall be deposited with the Secretary-General of the United Nations.

ARTICLE 27

(Proposal by Poland)

1. The present Convention shall enter into force six months after the date of deposit of the fifteenth instrument of ratification or accession.

2. For each State ratifying or acceding to the present Convention after the deposit of the fifteenth instrument of ratification or accession, the Convention shall enter into force on the thirtieth day after the deposit by such State of its instrument of ratification or accession.

ARTICLE 28

(Proposal by Poland)

As depository of the present Convention, the Secretary-General of the United Nations shall inform all states of:

(a)   signatures, ratifications and accessions under articles 24, 25 and 26;

(b)   the date of the entry into force of the present Convention under article 27.

ARTICLE 29

(Proposal by Poland)

The original of the present Convention, of which the Arabic, Chinese, English, French, Russian and Spanish texts are equally authentic, shall be deposited with the Secretary-General of the United Nations, who shall send certified copies thereof to all States.

ARTICLE 30

(Proposal by Sweden)

1. Reservations shall not be permitted except to Article **[1, 2, 5, 9, 11, 12, 12 *bis*, 13, 14, 15, 16 and 17.]** Such reservations must not be incompatible with the object and purpose of this Convention.

2. No reservation to a provision of this Convention shall affect any obligation undertaken in another international treaty in effect for the concerned State Party.

14. CHILD WELFARE STATUTES—CANADA

CHILD WELFARE STATUTES IN CANADA

British Columbia   *Family and Child Service Act*, Bill 45
                          (not proclaimed in force as of January 1, 1981)
Alberta   *The Child Welfare Act* (R.S.A. 1970, c. 45) as amended
Saskatchewan   *The Family Services Act, 1973* (S.S. c.38) as amended
Manitoba   *The Child Welfare Act* (S.M. 1974, c. 30)
Ontario   *The Child Welfare Act 1978* (S.O. 1978, c. 86) as amended
Quebec   *Youth Protection Act* (S.Q. 1977, c. 20)
Nova Scotia   *Children's Services Act* (S.N.A. 1976 c. 8) as amended
New Brunswick   *Child and Family Services and Family Relations Act*, Bill 43
                          (not proclaimed in force as of January 1, 1981)
Prince Edward Island   *Child Welfare Act*, Bill 57 (First Reading, April 1980)
Newfoundland   *The Child Welfare Act, 1972* (S. Nfld. 1972, Act No. 37) as amended
Yukon   *Child Welfare Ordinance* (R.O. N.W.T. 1974, c. C-3) as amended

15. PROVINCIAL DEFINITIONS OF CHILD IN NEED OF PROTECTION —CANADA

DEFINITIONS OF CHILD IN NEED OF PROTECTION

British Columbia
s.1 "in need of protection" means, in relation to a child, that he is:

a) abused or neglected so that his safety or well being is endangered,
b) abandoned,
c) deprived of necessary care through the death, absence or disability of his parent,
d) deprived of necessary medical attention, or
e) absent from his home in circumstances that endanger his safety or well being.

Alberta
s.14 (e) "neglected child" means a child in need of protection and without restricting the generality of the foregoing includes any child who is within one or more of the following descriptions:

i) a child who is not being properly cared for;
ii) a child who is abandoned or deserted by the person in whose charge he is or who is an orphan who is not being properly cared for;
iii) a child where the person in whose charge he is cannot, by reason of disease of infirmity or misfortune or incompetence or imprisonment or any combination thereof, care properly for him;
iv) a child who is living in an unfit or improper place;
v) a child found associating with an unfit or improper person;
vi) a child found begging in a public place;
vii) a child who, with the consent or connivance of the person in whose charge he is, commits any act that renders him liable to a penalty under any Act of the Parliament of Canada or of the Legislature, or under any municipal by-law;
viii) a child who is misdemeanant by reason of the inadequacy of the control exercised by the person in whose charge he is, or who is being allowed to grow up without salutory parental control or under circumstances tending to make him idle or dissolute;
ix) a child who, without sufficient cause, habitually absents himself from his home or school;
x) a child where the person in whose charge he is neglects or refuses to provide or obtain proper medical, surgical or other remedial care or treatment necessary for his health or well-being, or refuses to permit such care or treatment to be supplied to the child when it is recommended by a duly qualified medical practitioner;
xi) the child whose emotional or mental development is endangered because of emotional rejection or deprivation of affection by the person in whose charge he is;
xii) a child whose life, health or morals may be endangered by the conduct of the person in whose charge he is;
xiii) a child who is being cared for by and at the expense of someone other than his parents and in circumstances which indicate that his parents are not performing their parental duties toward him;
xiv) a child who is not under proper guardianship or who has no parent
  A) capable of exercising, or
  B) willing to exercise, or
  C) capable of exercising and willing to exercise, proper parental control over the child;
xv) a child whose parent wishes to divest himself of his parental responsibilities toward the child.

Saskatchewan
s.15 Definition of child in need of protection. A child is in need of protection when:

a) he is without proper or competent supervision;
b) he is living in circumstances that are unfit or improper for him;

c)   he is in the custody of a person who is unable or unwilling to exercise proper control over the child;

d)   his life, health or emotional welfare is endangered by the conduct of the person who has custody of the child;

e)   the person in whose custody he is neglects or refuses to provide or obtain proper medical, surgical or other recognized remedial care or treatment necessary for his health or well-being or normal development, or refuses to permit such care or treatment to be supplied to the child when it is considered essential by a duly qualified medical practitioner;

f)   his parent is unfit, unable or unwilling to care for him.

Manitoba

s.1 In this Act:

a)   "abuse" means acts of commission or omission on the part of the parent or the person in whose charge a child is which results in injury to the child but is not necessarily restricted to physical beating, physical assault, sexual abuse and failure to provide reasonable protection for the child from physical harm.

s.16 In this Act, a child in need of protection means:

a)   a child who is an orphan or who has been abandoned or deserted by his parents and:
    i)   who is not being properly cared for by anyone, or
    ii)   who with the consent of the person in whose charge he is, is brought before a judge to be dealt with under this Act;

b)   a child where the parent or person in whose charge he is cannot, by reason of disease, infirmity, misfortune, incompetence, imprisonment, or any combination thereof, care properly for him;

c)   a child whose life, physical or mental health, or morals may be endangered by the conduct of the person in whose charge he is;

d)   a child who is beyond the control of his parents or person in whose charge he is;

e)   a child whose behavior, condition, environment or association is injurious to himself or others;

el)   a pregnant child who refuses or is unable to provide properly and adequately for the health and welfare needs of herself or her child both before and after birth of the child;

f)   a child born to parents not married to each other whose mother is unable or unwilling to care for him;

g)   a child where the parent or person in whose charge he is neglects or refuses to provide or obtain proper medical, surgical, or other remedial care or treatment necessary for health and well-being of the child, or refuses to permit such care or treatment to be supplied to the child when it is recommended by a duly qualified medical practitioner;

h)   a child whose emotional or mental development is endangered because of emotional rejection or deprivation of affection by the person in whose charge the child is;

i)   a child under the age of 12 years who is left unattended for an unreasonable length of time without making reasonable provision for the supervision and safety of the child; or

j)   a child subjected to abuse.

Ontario

s.19—1 b) "child in need of protection" means:

i)   a child who is brought, with the consent of the person in whose charge the child is, before a court to be dealt with under this Part;

ii)   a child who is deserted by the person in whose charge the child is;

iii) a child where the person, in whose charge the child is, cannot for any reason care properly for the child, or where that person has died and there is no suitable person to care for the child;

iv)   a child who is living in an unfit or improper place;

v)   a child found associating with an unfit or improper person;

vi)   a child found begging or receiving charity in a public place;

vii)   a child where the person in whose charge the child is is unable to control the child;

viii)   a child who without sufficient cause is habitually absent from home or school;

ix)   a child where the person in whose charge the child is neglects or refuses to provide or obtain proper medical, surgical or other recognized remedial care or treatment necessary for the child's health or well-being, or refuses to permit such care or treatment to be supplied to the child when it is recommended by a legally qualified medical practitioner, or otherwise fails to protect the child adequately;

x)   a child whose emotional or mental development is endangered because of emotional rejection or deprivation of affection by the person in whose charge the child is;

xi)   a child whose life, health or morals may be endangered by the conduct of the person in whose charge the child is.

Quebec

s.38 Security of child endangerd. For the purposes of this act, the security or development of a child is considered to be in danger where in particular:

a)   his parents are dead, no longer take care of him or seek to be rid of him and no other person is taking care of him;

b)   his mental or emotional development or his health is threatened by the isolation in which he is maintained or the lack of appropriate care;

c)   he is deprived of the material conditions of life appropriate to his needs and to the resources of his family;

d)   he is in the custody of a person whose behaviour or way of life creates a risk of moral or physical danger for the child;

e)   he is of school age and does not attend school or is frequently absent without reason;

f)   he is the victim of sexual assault or he is subject to physical ill-treatment through violence or neglect;

g)   he has serious behaviour disturbances;

h)   he is forced or induced to beg, to do work disproportionate to his strength or to perform for the public in a manner that is unacceptable for his age;

i)   he leaves a reception centre, a foster family or his own home without authorization.

New Brunswick

s.31 When security or development of child is in danger—(1) The security or development of a child may be in danger when:

a)   the child is without adequate care, supervision or control;

b)   the child is living in unfit or improper circumstances;

c)   the child is in the care of a person who is unable or unwilling to provide adequate care, supervision or control of the child;

d)   the child is in the care of a person whose conduct endangers the life, health or emotional well-being of the child;

e)   the child is physically or sexually abused, physically or emotionally neglected, sexually exploited or in danger of such treatment;

f)   the child is living in a situation where there is severe domestic violence;

g)   the child is in the care of a person who neglects or refuses to provide or obtain proper medical, surgical or other remedial care or treatment necessary for the health or well-being of the child or refuses to permit such care or treatment to be supplied to the child;

h)   the child is beyond the control of the person caring for him;

i)   the child by his behavior, condition, environment or association, is likely to injure himself or others;

j)   the child is in the care of a person who does not have a right to custody of the child, without the consent of a person having such right;

k)   the child is in the care of a person who neglects of refuses to ensure that the child attends school; or

l)   the child has committed an offence

Nova Scotia
S.2 (m) "child in need of protection" means

i)   a child who is without proper supervision or control;
ii)   a child who is living in circumstances that are unfit or improper for the child;
iii) a child in the care or custody of a person who is unfit, unable or unwilling to exercise proper care over the child;
iv)   a child whose life, health or emotional welfare is endangered;
v)   a child who is in the care or custody of a person who fails to provide for his education;
vi)   a child who is committed pursuant to paragraph (h) or (i) of subsection (1) of Section 20 of the Juvenile Delinquents Act (Canada); or
vii) child who is in the care or custody of a person who refuses or fails:
   A)   to provide or obtain proper medical or other recognized remedial care or treatment necessary for the health or well-being of the child, or
   B)   to permit such care and treatment to be supplied to the child when it is considered essential by a duly qualified medical practitioner.

Prince Edward Island
s.1 (2) For the purposes of this Act a child may be in need of protection when:

a)   the child is without adequate care, supervision or control;
b)   the child is living in unfit or improper circumstances;
c)   the child is in the care of a person who is unable or unwilling to provide adequate care, supervision or control of the child;
d)   the child is in the care of a person whose conduct endangers the life, health or emotional well-being of the child;
e)   the child is physically or sexually abused, physically or emotionally neglected, sexually exploited or in danger of such treatment;
f)   the child is living in a situation where there is severe domestic violence;
g)   the child is in the care of a person who neglects or refuses to provide or obtain proper medical, surgical or other remedial care or treatment necessary for the health and well-being of the child or refuses to permit such care or treatment to be supplied to the child;
h)   the child is beyond the control of the person caring for him;
i)   the child by his behavior, condition, environment or association, is likely to injure himself or others;
j)   the child is in the care of a person who neglects or refuses to ensure that the child attends school; or
k)   the child has committed an offence

Newfoundland
s.2 (p) "neglected child" means

i)   a child who is without proper supervision or control;
ii)   a child who is living in circumstances that are unfit or improper for the child;

iii)   a child in the care or custody of a person who is unfit, unable or unwilling to exercise proper care over the child;

iv)   a child whose life, health, or emotional welfare is endangered;

v)   a child who is in the care and custody of a person:
   A)   who fails to provide for his education, or
   B)   who does not try to prevent habitual absences of the child from school when there is no valid reason for the absence;

vi)   a child in respect of whom an offence has been committed under subsection (4) or (5) of section 4 of the Adoption of Children Act, 1972, or under an equivalent statutory provision in force before that Act;

vii)   a child who has no living parents and who has no person willing to assume responsibility or with a legal responsibility for his maintenance;

viii)   a child who is in the care or custody of a person who refuses or fails:
   A)   to provide or obtain proper medical or other recognized remedial care or treatment necessary for the health or well-being of the child, or
   B)   to permit such care and treatment to be supplied to the child when it is considered essential by a duly qualified medical practitioner.

Yukon Territory

s.6 When child is in need of protection—(1) For the purpose of this Part a child is deemed to be in need of protection when:

a)   Orphan—he is an orphan who is not being properly cared for;

b)   Desertion—he is deserted by the person in whose charge he is;

c)   Incapacity—the person in whose charge he is cannot care properly for him;

d)   Consent—he is brought, with the consent of the person in whose charge he is, before a justice to be dealt with under this Part;

e)   Abandonment—he is under the age of twelve years and is frequently left by the person in whose charge he is without care and supervision of an older person or when such older person fails to give him proper and adequate care and supervision;

f)   Unfit home—his home by reason of neglect or depravity on the part of the person in whose charge he is, is an unfit or improper place for him;

g)   Unfit associate—he is found associating with an unfit or improper person who is not his parent;

h)   Begging—he is found begging in any street, house or place of public resort, whether actually begging or under the pretext of selling or offering anything for sale or is found loitering in a public place;

i)   Criminal connivance—with the consent or connivance of the person in whose charge he is, he commits any act that renders him liable to a penalty under any ordinance, Act of Parliament of Canada or municipal by-law;

j)   Inadequate control—by reason of the inadequacy of the control exercised by the person in whose charge he is, he is being allowed to grow up under circumstances tending to make him idle, dissolute, delinquent or incorrigible, or without a proper education;

k)   Truancy—he habitually absents himself from the home of the person in whose charge he is, or from school when he is within the compulsory school attendance age, without sufficient cause;

l)   Neglect of health care—the person in whose charge he is neglects or refuses to provide or secure proper medical, surgical or other remedial care or treatment for his health or well being, or refuses to permit such care or treatment to be supplied to the child when it is recommended by a medical practitioner;

m)   Lack of affection—is deprived of affection by the person in whose charge he is, to a degree that is sufficient to hinder his emotional and mental development;

n) Ill-treatment—he is by reason of the ill-treatment, cruelty, frequent personal injury, grave misconduct or frequent intemperance of or by the person in whose charge he is, in danger of loss of life, health or morality;

o) Lack of control—the person in whose charge he is, is incapable of exercising or unwilling to exercise proper parental control;

p) Consent—he is a child born out of wedlock whose mother consents to him being brought before a justice for the purpose of transferring his guardianship to the Director;

q) Absence of parents—his parents or only parent is undergoing imprisonment or is a patient in a hospital for the mentally ill, a tuberculosis sanatorium, or rehabilitation centre for physical restoration of the disabled.

Northwest Territories
s.14 Child deemed to be in need of protection—(1) For the purposes of this Part a child is deemed to be in need of protection when:

a) he is an orphan who is not being properly cared for or is brought, with the consent of the person in whose charge he is, before a justice to be dealt with under this Part;

b) he has been born out of wedlock and his mother has delivered him to the Superintendent for adoption;

c) he is deserted by the person in whose charge he is, or that person has died or is unable to care properly for him;

d) the person in whose charge he is cannot, by reason of disease, infirmity, misfortune, incompetence, imprisonment or any combination thereof, care properly for him;

e) his home, by reason of neglect, cruelty or depravity on the part of the person in whose charge he is, is an unfit and improper place for him;

f) he is found associating with an unfit or improper person;

g) he is found begging in a public place;

h) with the consent or connivance of the person in whose charge he is, he commits any act that renders him liable to a penalty under any Ordinance, Act of the Parliament of Canada or municipal by-law;

i) he is delinquent or incorrigible by reason of the inadequacy of the control exercised by the person in whose charge he is, or he is being allowed to grow up under circumstances tending to make him dissolute;

j) he habitually absents himself from the home of the person in whose charge he is without sufficient cause;

k) the person in whose charge he is neglects or refuses to provide or secure proper medical, surgical or other remedial care or treatment necessary for his health or well-being, or refuses to permit such care or treatment to be supplied to the child when it is recommended by a duly qualified medical practitioner; or

l) he is deprived of affection by the person in whose charge he is to a degree that, on the evidence of a psychiatrist, is sufficient to endanger his emotional and mental development.

BIBLIOGRAPHY

Abel, Ernest L., *Fetal Alcohol Syndrome and Fetal Alcohol Effects*. New York: Plenum Press, 1984.

Adams, William, Neil Barone and Patrick Tooman, "The Dilemma of Anonymous Reporting in Child Protective Services " *Child Welfare*, 61:1(January 1982), 3-14

Adams-Tucker, Christine, "Defense Mechanisms Used by Sexually Abused Children," *Children Today*, (January-February 1985): 9-34

Agathonos, Helen, "First European Congress on Child Abuse and Neglect, Rhodes, Greece, April 6-10, 1987 " *Child Abuse & Neglect*, 12(1988): 123-128.

Agopian, Michael W., *Parental Child Stealing*. Lexington, Mass.: D.C. Heath, 1981.

Alfaro, J., "Report on the Relationship Between Child Abuse and Neglect and Later Socially Deviant Behavior," Paper presented at Exploring the Relationship Between Child Abuse and Delinquency Symposium, University of Washington, Seattle, 1977.

Alleyne, G.A.O. et al., *Protein-Energy Malnutrition*. London: Edward Arnold, 1977.

American Association for Protecting Children, *Highlights of Official Child Neglect and Abuse Reporting, 1986*. Denver: American Humane Association, 1988.

————, *Highlights of Official Child Neglect and Abuse Reporting, 1983*. Denver: American Humane Association, 1985

————, *Highlights of Official Child Neglect and Abuse Reporting, 1981*. Denver: American Humane Association, 1983.

American Humane Association, *National Analysis of Official Child Neglect and Abuse Reporting, 1980*. Denver: American Humane Association, 1982.

Antler, Stephen, ed., *Child Abuse and Child Protection: Policy and Practice*. Silver Spring, Md.: National Association of Social Workers, 1982.

Arthur, Lindsay G., "Child Sexual Abuse: Improving the System's Responses," *Juvenile and Family Court Journal*, 37:2(1986).

Baher, R.E. et al., *At Risk: An Account of the Work of the Battered Child Research Department*. London: Routledge and Kegan Paul, 1976.

Baily, Thelma F. and Walter H. Baily, *Criminal or Social Intervention in Child Sexual Abuse: A Review and a Viewpoint*. Denver: American Humane Association, 1983.

Bakan, David, *Slaughter of the Innocents*. San Francisco: Jossey-Bass, 1971

Bassuk, Ellen and Lenore Rubin, "Homeless Children: A Neglected Population," *American Journal of Orthopsychiatry*, 57:2(April 1987), 279-286.

Baugh, W.E., *Introduction to the Social Services*. London: Macmillan, 1973

Behlmer, George K., *Child Abuse and Moral Reform in England, 1870-1908*. Stanford, Calif.: Stanford University Press, 1982.

Bennie, E. and A. Sclare, "The Battered Child Syndrome," *American Journal of Psychiatry*, 125(7): 1969, pp. 975-979.

Besharov, Douglas J., "An Overdose of Concern: Child Abuse and the Overreporting Problem," *Regulation* (November-December 1985):25-28.

———, "Policy Guidelines for Decision Making in Child Abuse and Neglect," *Children Today* (November-December 1985).

———, "Child Welfare Liability: The Need for Immunity Legislation," *Children Today* (September-October 1986).

Biller, Henry B. and Richard S. Solomon, *Child Maltreatment and Paternal Deprivation*. Lexington, Mass.: Lexington Books, 1986.

Black, Henry C., *Black's Law Dictionary*, 5th ed. St. Paul, Minn.: West Publishing Co., 1979.

Bolton, F.G., J. Reich, and S.E. Guiterres, "Delinquency Patterns in Maltreated Children with Siblings," *Victimology*, 2(1977), pp. 349- 357.

Bourne, Richard and Eli H. Newberger, eds., *Critical Perspectives on Child Abuse*. Lexington, Mass.: Lexington Books, 1979.

Broadhurst, D.D., M. Edmunds and R.A. MacDicken, *Early Childhood Programs and the Prevention and Treatment of Child Abuse and Neglect* (The User Manual Series). Washington, D.C.: U.S. Government Printing Office, 1979.

Burgdorf, K., *Recognition and Reporting of Child Maltreatment*. Rockville, Md.: Westat, 1980.

Burgess, A.W. et al., *Sexual Assault of Children and Adolescents*. Lexington, Mass.: Lexington Books, 1978.

Caffey, John, "Multiple Fractures in the Long Bones of Infants Suffering from Chronic Subdural Hematoma," *American Journal of Roentgenology, Radium Therapy, and Nuclear Medicine*, 56(1946), pp. 163- 173.

———, "On the Theory and Practice of Shaking Infants," *American Journal of Diseases of Children*, 124:2(1972): 161-169.

———, "Some Traumatic Lesions in Growing Bones Other Than Fractures and Dislocations," *British Journal of Radiology*, 23(1957), 225-238.

———, "The Whiplash Shaken Infant Syndrome: Manual Shaking by the Extremities With Whiplash-Induced Intracranial and Intraocular Bleedings, Linked With Residual Permanent Brain Damage and Mental Retardation," *Pediatrics*, 54:4(1974), 396-403.

Carmi, A. and H. Zimrin, eds., *Child Abuse*. Berlin: Springer-Verlag, 1984

Carr, A., *Reported Child Maltreatment in Florida: The Operation of Public Child Protective Service Systems*, a report submitted to the Administration on Children, Youth and Families, National Center on Child Abuse and Neglect, Department of Health, Education, and Welfare. Kingston, R.I.: mimeographed, 1979.

Caulfield, Barbara A., *Child Abuse and the Law: A Legal Primer for Social Workers*. Chicago: National Committee for Prevention of Child Abuse, 1979.

Chesler, Phyllis, *Mothers on Trial, The Battle for Custody and Children*. New York: McGraw-Hill, 1986.

Children's Defense Fund, *Children Without Homes*. Washington, D.C.: Children's Defense Fund, 1978.

Cohen, Emmeline W., *English Social Services*. London: Allen & Unwin, 1949.

Cohen, S. and A. Sussman, *The Incidence of Child Abuse in the United States*. Unpublished manuscript, 1975.

Committee on Education and Labor, House of Representatives, One Hundredth Congress, First Session, *The Chairman's Report on Children in America: A Strategy for the 100th Congress*, vol. 1 (Committee Print), October 7, 1987. Washington, D.C.: U.S. Government Printing Office, 1987.

———, *The Chairman's Report on Children in America: A Strategy for the 100th Congress, A Guide to Federal Programs that Affect Children*, vol. 2 (Committee Print), October 7, 1987. Washington, D.C.: U.S. Government Printing Office, 1987.

Cook, Joanne Valiant and Roy Tyler Bowles, eds., *Child Abuse and Neglect: Commission and Omission*. Toronto: Butterworths, 1980.

Coser, L.A., *Continuities in the Study of Social Conflicts*. New York: Free Press, 1967.

Cox, Daniel J. and Reid J. Daitzman, *Exhibitionism: Description, Assessment and Treatment*. New York: Garland Press, 1980.

Daigle, Patricia, "Opposing Corporal Punishment in 2 Lands," *Contra Costa Times* (December 13, 1986).

Defense for Children International-USA Collective, *The Children's Clarion, Database on the Rights of the Child, 1987*. Brooklyn, New York: DCI-USA, 1987.

De Francis, Vincent, *The Fundamentals of Child Protection*. Denver: American Humane Association, 1978.

———, *Speaking Out for Child Protection*. Denver: American Humane Association, Children's Division, 1973.

———, "Testimony at the hearing before the subcommittee on children and youth of the committee on labor and public welfare," U.S. Senate, 93rd Congress, First Session (On S1191 Child Abuse Prevention and Treatment Act). Washington, D.C.: GPO, 1973.

De Mause, L., "Our Forbears Made Childhood a Nightmare," *Psychology Today* (April 1975), pp. 85-87.

De Mause, L., ed., *The History of Childhood*. New York: Psychohistory Press, 1974.

Derdeyn, Andre P., "A Case for Permanent Foster Placement of Dependent, Neglected, and Abused Children," *American Journal of Orthopsychiatry*, 47(1977):604-614.

Dickey, Susan and Margruetta Hall, "The Results of Data Analysis of 50 Pregnancy and Addiction Studies, 1965-1977," Arnold J. Schecter, ed., in *Biomedical Issues*, vol. 1 of Drug Dependence and Alcoholism. New York: Plenum Press, 1978.

Drinan, Robert F., "The Supreme Court and Baby Jane Doe," *America* (March 8, 1986):180-182.

Dykes, Lucinda J., "The Whiplash Shaken Infant Syndrome: What Has Been Learned?" *Child Abuse and Neglect*, 10:2(1986), 211-221.

Ebeling, Nancy B. and Deborah A. Hill, *Child Abuse and Neglect*. Acton, Mass: PSG Inc., 1983.

Eberle, Paul and Shirley, *The Politics of Child Abuse*. Secaucus, N.J.: Lyle Stuart, 1987.

Eckenrode, J., J. Powers, J. Doris, J. Munsh and N. Bolger, "Substantiation of Child Abuse and Neglect Reports," *Journal of Consulting and Clinical Psychology*, 56:1(1988), pp. 9-16.

Egeland, B., D. Jacobvitz and K. Papatola, "Intergenerational Continuity of Abuse," in R. Gelles and Lancaster, eds., *Child Abuse and Neglect: Biosocial Dimensions*. Hawthorne, N.Y.: Aldine deGruyter, 1987.

Ellerstein, Norman S., ed., *Child Abuse and Neglect: A Medical Reference*. New York: John Wiley, 1981.

Elmer, E., *Children in Jeopardy: A Study of Abused Minors and Their Families*. Pittsburgh: University of Pittsburgh Press, 1967.

Elmer E., and G.S. Gregg. "Developmental Characteristics of Abused Children," *Pediatrics*, 40(1967):596-602.

Ennew, Judith, *The Sexual Exploitation of Children*. Cambridge, U.K.: Polity Press, 1986.

Family Welfare Association, *Guide to the Social Services 1987*, 75th ed. London: Family Welfare Association, 1987.

———, *Guide to Social Services 1988*, 76th ed., London: Family Welfare Association, 1988.

Federal Bureau of Investigation, *Uniform Crime Report*. Washington, D.C.: United States Department of Justice, 1986.

Finkelhor, David, *Child Sexual Abuse*. New York: Free Press, 1984.

———, *Sexually Victimized Children*. New York: Free Press, 1979.

———, *A Sourcebook on Child Sexual Abuse*. Beverly Hills, Calif.: Sage Publications, 1986.

Finkelhor, David and J. Korbin, "Child Abuse as an International Issue," *Child Abuse and Neglect: The International Journal*, 12:1(1988), 3-23.

Finkelhor, David et al., eds, *The Dark Side of Families*. Beverly Hills, Calif.: Sage Publications, 1983.

Fontana, Vincent, *Somewhere a Child is Crying: Maltreatment—Causes and Prevention.* New York: Macmillan, 1973.

Fortune, Christopher, "Help for Abused Parents," *MacLean's* (October 6, 1986):10-12.

Forward, Susan and Craig Buck, *Betrayal of Innocence.* New York: Penguin, 1979.

Frankenburg, William K., Robert N. Emde and Joseph W. Sullivan, *Early Identification of Children at Risk.* New York: Plenum Press, 1985.

Franklin, Alfred White, ed., *Concerning Child Abuse: Papers Presented by the Tunbridge Wells Study Group on Non-accidental Injury to Children.* Edinburgh: Churchill Livingstone, 1975.

Franklin, Bob, ed., *The Rights of Children.* Oxford: Basil Blackwell, 1986.

Friedrich, W. and J. Boriskin, "The Role of the Child in Abuse: A Review of Literature," *American Journal of Orthopsychiatry*, 46:4(1976), 580-590.

Galdston, R., "Observations of Children Who Have Been Physically Abused By Their Parents," *American Journal of Psychiatry*, 122:4(1965), 440-443.

Gallagher, J.P., *The Price of Charity.* London: Robert Hale, 1975.

Galtney, Liz, "Mothers on the Run," *U.S. News and World Report* (June 13, 1988):22-33.

Garbarino, James, "The Human Ecology of Child Maltreatment," *Journal of Marriage and Family*, 39(1977):721-735.

Garbarino, James and G. Gilliam, *Understanding Abusive Families.* Lexington, Mass.: D.C. Heath, 1980.

Garbarino, James, Edna Guttmann and Janis Wilson Seeley, *The Psychologically Battered Child.* San Francisco: Jossey-Bass, 1986.

Garbarino, James et al., *Troubled Youth, Troubled Families.* Hawthorne, N.Y.: Aldine, 1986.

Garner, Bryan A., *A Dictionary of Modern Legal Usage.* New York: Oxford University Press, 1987

Gelles, Richard J., "Child Abuse as Psychopathology: A Sociological Critique and Reformulation," *American Journal of Orthopsychiatry*, 43(July 1973):611-621.

————, "An Exchange/Social Control Theory," in D. Finkelhor, R. Gelles, M. Straus and G. Hotaling, *The Dark Side of Families: Current Family Violence Research.* Beverly Hills, Calif.: Sage Publications, 1983.

————, "Parental Child Snatching: A Preliminary Estimate of the National Incidence," *Journal of Marriage and the Family*, 46:3(August 1984), 735-739.

————, "The Social Construction of Child Abuse," *American Journal of Orthopsychiatry*, 45(April 1975):363-371.

————, "Violence in the Family: A Review of Research in the Seventies," *Journal of Marriage and Family*, 42(November 1980):873-885.

————, "Violence towards Children in the United States," *American Journal of Orthopsychiatry*, 48(October 1978):580-592.

Gelles, Richard J. and Claire Pedrick Cornell, eds., *International Perspectives on Family Violence*. Lexington, Mass.: Lexington Books, 1983.

Gelles, Richard J. and Ake W. Edfeldt, "Violence Towards Children in the United States and Sweden," *Child Abuse and Neglect*, 10(1986):501-510.

Gelles, Richard J. and Murray Straus, "Determinants of Violence in the Family: Toward a Theoretical Integration," in W. Burr et al., eds., *Contemporary Theories About the Family*, vol. 1. New York: Free Press, 1979.

————, *Intimate Violence*. New York: Simon and Schuster, 1988.

————, "Is Violence Towards Children Increasing? A Comparison of 1975 and 1985 National Survey Rates," *Journal of Interpersonal Violence*, 2(June 1987):212-222.

Gelles, Richard J., Murray Straus and J.W. Harrop, "Has Family Violence Decreased? A Response to J. Timothy Stocks," *Journal of Marriage and the Family*, 50:1(1988), 286-291.

Gerbner, George, Catherine J. Ross and Edward Zigler, eds., *Child Abuse: An Agenda for Action*. New York: Oxford University Press, 1980.

Gil, David G., "Unraveling Child Abuse," *American Journal of Orthopsychiatry*, 45(April 1975):358-364.

————, *Violence Against Children: Physical Child Abuse in the United States*, Cambridge, Mass.: Harvard University Press, 1970.

Giovannoni, Jeanne M. and Rosina M. Becerra, *Defining Child Abuse*. New York: Free Press, 1979.

Goldstein, Joseph, Anna Freud and Albert J. Solnit, *Beyond the Best Interests of the Child*, new ed. New York: The Free Press, 1979.

Goldstein, Seth L., *The Sexual Exploitation of Children*. New York: Elsevier, 1987.

Gordon, Thomas, *Parent Effectiveness Training*. New York: Peter H. Wyden, 1970.

Green, Arthur H., *Child Maltreatment*. New York: Jason Aronson, 1980.

Guntheroth, Warren G., *Crib Death: The Sudden Infant Death Syndrome*. Mount Kisco, N.Y.: Futura, 1982.

Hawes, Joseph M., *Children in Urban Society*. New York: Oxford University Press, 1977.

Hawes, Joseph M. and N. Ray Hiner, *American Childhood, A Research Guide and Historical Handbook*. Westport, Conn.: Greenwood Press, 1985.

Herrenkohl, R.C., E.C. Herrenkohl, B.P. Egolf and M. Sibley, *Executive Summary*, vol. 1 of Child Abuse and Social Competence. Bethlehem, Pa.: Lehigh University Center for Social Research, 1984.

Holden, Constance, "Baby Doe Regs Set," *Science*, 228(May 3, 1985):564.

Holder, Wayne M. and Cynthia Mohr, eds., *Helping in Child Protective Services*. Denver: American Humane Association, 1980.

Hunter, R. and N. Kilstrom, "Breaking the Cycle of Abusive Families,"*American Journal of Psychiatry*, 136(1979):1320-1322

Hyman, Irwin A. and James D. Wise, eds., *Corporal Punishment in American Education*. Philadelphia· Temple University Press, 1979.

Jackson-Nakano, Ann, "Our Long History of Hating Children," *The Sydney Morning Herald* (April 12, 1988):19.

Johnson, B. and H. Morse, "Injured Children and Their Parents," *Children*, 15(1968):147-152.

Johnson, Toni Cavanaugh, "Child Perpetrators—Children Who Molest Other Children: Preliminary Findings," *Child Abuse and Neglect* 12(1988):219-229.

Kadushin, Alfred, *Child Welfare Services*, 2nd ed. New York: Macmillan, 1974.

Katz, Michael B., *In the Shadow of the Poorhouse*. New York: Basic Books, 1986.

———, *Poverty and Policy in American History*. New York: Academic Press, 1983.

Katz, Sanford N., *Child Snatching: The Legal Response to the Abduction of Children*. Chicago: ABA Press, 1981.

Katz, Sedelle and Mary Ann Mazur, *Understanding the Rape Victim*. New York: Wiley and Sons, 1979.

Kaufman, Joan and Edward Zigler, "Do Abused Children Become Abusive Parents?" *American Journal of Orthopsychiatry*, 57:2(April 1987), 186-192.

Kelly, Jeffrey A., *Treating Child-Abusive Families*. New York: Plenum Press, 1983.

Kempe, C. Henry, "Pediatric Implications of the Battered Baby Syndrome,"*Archives of Disease in Children*, 46(1971):28-37.

Kempe, C. Henry and Ray E. Helfer, Editors. *The Battered Child, 3rd Edition*. University of Chicago Press Chicago, 1980.

Kempe, C. Henry et al., "The Battered-Child Syndrome," *Journal of the American Medical Association*, 181(1962):17-24.

Kinard, E. Milling, *Emotional Development in Physically Abused Children*, R and E Research Associates, Palo Alto, CA, 1978.

———, "The Psychological Consequences of Abuse for the Child," *Journal of Social Issues*, 35:2(1979) 82-100.

Korbin, Jill E., ed., *Child Abuse and Neglect: Cross-Cultural Perspectives*. Berkeley: University of California Press, 1981.

Lacayo, Richard, "Sexual Abuse or Abuse of Justice," *Time* (May 11, 1987):49

Laird, Joan and Ann Hartman, *A Handbook of Child Welfare*. New York: Free Press, 1985.

Lawrence, Bobbi and Olivia Taylor-Young, *The Child Snatchers*. Boston: Charles River Books, 1983.

Layzer, Jean I., Barbara D. Goodson and Christine deLange, "Children in Shelters," *Children Today*, (March-April 1986):6- 11.

Lines, David Robin, "The Effectiveness of Parent Aides in the Tertiary Prevention of Child Abuse in South Australia," *Child Abuse and Neglect*, 11(1987):507-512.

Lynch, Margaret A. and Jacqueline Roberts, *Consequences of Child Abuse*. London: Academic Press, 1982.

MacKeith, R., "Speculations on Non-Accidental Injury as a Cause of Chronic Brain Disorder," *Developmental Medicine and Child Neurology*, 16(1974):216-218.

MacNamara, Donal E. and Edward Sagarin, *Sex, Crime, and the Law*. New York: Free Press, 1977.

Maden, Marc F., *The Disposition of Reported Child Abuse*. Saratoga, Calif.: Century Twenty One, 1980.

Maden, Marc F. and D.F. Wrench, "Significant Findings in Child Abuse Research," *Victimology*, 2(1977):196-224.

Maidman, Frank, ed., *Child Welfare*. New York: Child Welfare League of America, 1984.

Maltz, Wendy and Beverly Holman, *Incest and Sexuality*. Lexington, Mass.: Lexington Books, 1987.

Marks, John, *The Vitamins, Their Role in Medical Practice*. Lancaster, England: MTP Press, 1985.

Martin, H.P., "The Child and His Development," in C.H. Kempe and R.E. Helfer, eds., *Helping the Battered Child and His Family*. Philadelphia: Lippincott, 1972.

Martin, H.P. et al., "The Development of Abused Children," *Advances in Pediatrics*, 21(1974):25-73.

Mayer, Adele, *Sexual Abuse*. Holmes Beach, Fla.: Learning Publications, 1985.

Mayhall, Pamela and Katherine E. Norgard, *Child Abuse and Neglect*. New York: MacMillan, 1986.

McCormack, Arlene, Mark-David Janus and Ann Wolbert Burgess, "Runaway Youths and Sexual Victimization: Gender Differences in an Adolescent Runaway Population," *Child Abuse and Neglect* 10(1986):387-395.

Meriwether, Margaret H., "Child Abuse Reporting Laws: Time for a Change," *Family Law Quarterly*, 20:2(Summer 1986), 141-171.

Merton, R. and R. Nisbet, *Contemporary Social Problems*, 4th ed. New York: Harcourt Brace Jovanovich, 1976.

Mnookin, Robert H. *Child, Family and State: Problems and Materials on Children and the Law*. Boston: Little, Brown, 1978.

Moore, Jean G., "Yo-Yo Children—Victims of Matrimonial Violence," *Child Welfare*, 54:8(1975), 557-566.

Morgan, Robin and Gloria Steinem, "The International Crime of Genital Mutilation," *Ms.* (March 1980).

Morgan, Sharon R., *Abuse and Neglect of Handicapped Children.* Boston: College-Hill Press, 1987.

Morse, C., O.J.Z. Sahler and S. Friedman, "A Three-year Follow-up Study of Abused and Neglected Children," *American Journal of the Disabilities of Children,* 120(November 1970):439- 446.

Myers, John E.B., "A Survey of Child Abuse and Neglect Reporting Statutes," *Journal of Juvenile Law,* 10:1(1986), 1-72.

Nagi, S., "Child Abuse and Neglect Programs: A National Overview," *Children Today,* 4(May-June 1975):13-17.

National College of District Attorneys, *Child Abuse and Neglect.* Houston: Prosecutors Child Abuse Project, National College of District Attorneys, 1977.

Nelson, Barbara J., *Making an Issue of Child Abuse.* Chicago: University of Chicago Press, 1984.

Newberger, Eli and Richard Bourne, eds., *Unhappy Families.* Flushing, N.Y.: PSG Publishing, 1985.

Newberger, Eli et al., "Pediatric Social Illness: Toward an Etiologic Classification," *Pediatrics,* 60(August 1977):178-185.

Nightingale, Benedict, *Charities.* London: Allen Lane/Penguin Books, 1973.

Oates, Kim, *Child Abuse and Neglect: What Happens Eventually.* New York: Brunner/Mazel, 1986.

O'Donnell, Carol and Jan Craney, eds., *Family Violence in Australia.* Melbourne: Longman Cheshire Pty. Ltd., 1982.

Ordovensky, Pat, "Texas Tops USA School Spankings," *USA Today* (March 7, 1988):1.

Palmer, Shushma and Shirley Ekvall, eds., *Pediatric Nutrition in Developmental Disorders.* Springfield, Ill.: Charles C. Thomas, 1978.

Parke, R.D. and C.W. Collmer, "Child Abuse: An Interdisciplinary Analysis," in Mavis Hetherington, ed., *Review of Child Development Research,* vol. 5. Chicago: University of Chicago Press, 1975.

Parker, Deborah, "Child Sex Abuse," *The Recorder* (Greenfield, Mass.) (January 12, 13, 1987):1.

Parton, Nigel, *The Politics of Child Abuse.* New York: St. Martin's Press, 1985.

Pelton, Leroy H., "Child Abuse and Neglect: The Myth of Classlessness," *American Journal of Orthopsychiatry,* 48(October 1978):607-617.

————, *The Social Context of Child Abuse and Neglect.* New York: Human Sciences Press, 1981.

Plant, Moira, *Women, Drinking and Pregnancy.* London: Tavistock Publications, 1985.

Polansky, Norman A. et al., *Damaged Parents.* Chicago: University of Chicago Press, 1981.

Pollitt, Ernesto and Rudolph Leibel, "Biological and Social Correlates of Failure to Thrive," in Lawrence Green and Francis Johnston, eds., *Social and Biological Predicators of Nutritional Status, Physical Growth and Neurological Development.* New York: Academic Press, 1980.

Potts, D. and S. Herzberger, "Child Abuse: A Cross-generational Pattern of Child Rearing?" paper presented at the annual meeting of the Midwest Psychological Association, Chicago, 1979.

Radbill, S., "A History of Child Abuse and Infanticide," in Ray Helfer and C. Henry Kempe, eds., *The Battered Child*, 3rd ed. Chicago: University of Chicago Press, 1980.

Redden, Kenneth R. and Enid L. Vernon, *Modern Legal Glossary.* Charlottesville, Va.: Michie Company, 1980.

Richter, Ralph W., ed., *Medical Aspects of Drug Abuse.* Hagerstown, Md.: Harper and Row, 1975.

Robertshaw, Corinne, *Child Protection in Canada*, discussion paper. Ottawa: Social Services Division, Department of National Health and Welfare, 1981.

Robin, M., "Historical Introduction: Sheltering Arms, The Roots of Child Protection," in Eli Newberger, ed., *Child Abuse.* Boston: Little, Brown, 1980.

Rodriguez, Alejandro, *Handbook of Child Abuse and Neglect.* Flushing, N.Y.: Medical Examination Publishing Co., 1977.

Rosenheim, Margaret K., *Pursuing Justice for the Child.* Chicago: University of Chicago Press, 1976.

Rosenthal, James A., "Patterns of Reported Child Abuse and Neglect," *Child Abuse and Neglect*, 12(1988):263-271.

Ross, C.J., "The Lessons of the Past: Defining and Controlling Child Abuse in the United States," in G. Gerbner et al., eds., *Child Abuse: An Agenda for Action.* New York: Oxford University Press, 1980.

Rubin, Eva R., *The Supreme Court and the American Family.* New York: Greenwood Press, 1986.

Rush, Florence, *The Best Kept Secret: Sexual Abuse of Children.* Englewood Cliffs, N.J.: Prentice-Hall, 1980.

Russel, Alene Bycer and Cynthia Mahr Trainor, *Trends in Child Abuse and Neglect: A National Perspective.* Denver: American Humane Association, Children's Division, 1984.

Ryan, Gail, "Annotated Bibliography: Adolescent Perpetrators of Sexual Molestation of Children," *Child Abuse and Neglect*, 10(1986):125-131.

Samuda, Garythe M., "Child Discipline and Abuse in Hong Kong," *Child Abuse and Neglect*, 12(1988):283-287.

Sandgrund, A., R. Gaines and A. Green, "Child Abuse and Mental Retardation: A Problem of Cause and Effect," *American Journal of Mental Deficiency*, 79:3(1975), 327-330.

Schaefer, Charles E., *Childhood Encopresis and Enuresis: Causes and Therapy.* New York: Van Nostrand Reinhold, 1979.

Schetky, Diane H. and Elissa P. Benedek, *Emerging Issues in Child Psychiatry and the Law*. New York Brunner/Mazel, 1985

Select Committee on Children, Youth and Families, U.S. House of Representatives, *Abused Children in America: Victims of Official Neglect*. Washington, D.C : U.S. Government Printing Office, 1987

————, *Child Abuse and Neglect in America: The Problem and the Response*, hearing held in Washington, D.C., March 3, 1987. Washington, D.C.: U.S. Government Printing Office, 1987.

Silverman, Peter, *Who Speaks for the Children?* Don Mills, Ontario: Musson Book Company, 1978.

Sloan, Irving, *Child Abuse: Governing Law and Legislation*. New York: Oceana Publications, 1983.

————, *Youth and the Law*, 4th ed. New York: Oceana, 1981.

Smith Charles P., David J. Berkman and Warren M. Fraser, *Reports of the National Juvenile Justice Assessment Centers, A Preliminary National Assessment of Child Abuse and Neglect and the Juvenile Justice System: The Shadows of Distress*. Washington, D.C.: National Institute for Juvenile Justice & Delinquency Prevention, 1979.

Smith, Holly, with Edie Israel, "Sibling Incest: A Study of the Dynamics of 25 Cases," *Child Abuse and Neglect*, 11(1987):101-108.

Smith, S., *The Battered Child Syndrome*. London: Butterworths, 1975.

Smith, Selwyn M., ed., *The Maltreatment of Children*. Baltimore: University Park Press, 1978.

Smith, Steven R. and Robert G. Meyer, "Child Abuse Reporting Laws and Psychotherapy: A Time for Reconsideration," *International Journal of Law and Psychiatry*, 7(1984):351-356

Spinetta, J. and D. Rigler, "The Abusing Parent: A Psychological Review," *Psychological Bulletin*, 77(April 1972):296-304

Spitz, Rene A., "Hospitalism," *The Psychoanalytic Study of the Child*, 1(1945):53

————, "Hospitalism: a follow-up report," *The Psychoanalytic Study of the Child*, 2(1946):113

Steele, Brandt F., "The Child Abuser,' in I. Kutash et al., eds., *Violence: Perspectives on Murder and Aggression*. San Francisco: Jossey-Bass, 1978.

————, "Notes on the Lasting Effects of Early Child Abuse throughout the Life Cycle," *Child Abuse and Neglect*, 10(1986):283-291.

Steele, Brandt F. and C. Pollock, "A Psychiatric Study of Parents Who Abuse Infants and Small Children," in R. Helfer and C.H. Kempe, eds., *The Battered Child*, 2nd ed. Chicago: University of Chicago Press 1974.

Steinmetz, Susan K., "Violence Between Family Members," *Marriage and Family Review*, 1:3(1978), 1-16.

Stewart, V. Lorne, *The Changing Faces of Juvenile Justice*. New York: New York University Press, 1978

Straus, Murray, "Leveling, Civility, and Violence in the Family," *Journal of Marriage and the Family*, 36(February1974):13-29; plus addendum in August 1974 issue

———, "Measuring Intrafamily Conflict and Violence: The Conflict Tactics (CT) Scales," *Journal of Marriage and the Family*, 41(February 1979):75-88.

———, "A Sociological Perspective on the Causes of Family Violence," in M. Green, ed., *Violence and the Family*. Boulder, Colo.: Westview Press, 1980.

Straus, Murray A. and Richard J. Gelles, "Societal Change and Change in Family Violence From 1975 to 1985 As Revealed by Two National Surveys," *Journal of Marriage and the Family*, 48(August 1986):465-479.

Straus, Murray A., Richard J. Gelles and Susan Steinmetz, *Behind Closed Doors: Violence in the American Family*. New York: Doubleday/Anchor, 1980.

Strouse, Evelyn, *Incest: Family Problem, Community Concern*. New York: Public Affairs Pamphlets, 1985.

Subcommittee on Public Assistance of the Committee on Finance, United States Senate, Ninety-sixth Congress, First Session, on H.R. 3434, *Proposals Related to Social and Child Welfare Services, Adoption Assistance and Foster Care*, hearing held in Washington, D.C., Sept. 24, 1979. Washington, D.C.: U.S. Government Printing Office, 1979

Subcommittee on Select Education of the Committee on Education and Labor, House of Representatives, One Hundredth Congress, First Session, *Reauthorization of the Child Abuse Prevention and Treatment Act*, hearing held in New York, April 3, 1987. Washington, D.C.: U.S. Government Printing Office, 1987.

Tangen, Ottar, *The Rights of the Abused Child*. Olstykke, Denmark: Medical Publishing Company, 1981.

Tower, Cynthia Crosson, *Child Abuse and Neglect: A Teacher's Handbook for Detection, Reporting and Classroom Management*. Washington, D.C.: National Education Association, 1984.

Tower, Cynthia Crosson, ed., *Questions Teachers Ask About Legal Aspects of Reporting Child Abuse and Neglect* Washington, D.C : National Education Association, 1984.

Trenshaw, Domeena C., *Incest: Understanding and Treatment*. Boston: Little Brown, 1982.

Turbett, J.P. and R. O'Toole, "Physicians' Recognition of Child Abuse," paper presented at annual meeting of American Sociological Association. New York, 1980.

United Nations Department of Public Information, *Everyone's United Nations*, 10th ed. New York: United Nations, 1986.

U.S. Department of Health, Education and Welfare, Office of Human Development Services, Administration for Children, Youth and Families, Children's Bureau, National Center on Child Abuse and Neglect, *Child Abuse and Neglect in Residential Institutions: Selected Readings on Prevention, Investigation, and Correction*. Washington, D.C.. Government Printing Office, 1978; (OHDS) 78-30160.

———, *Child Abuse & Neglect, State Reporting Laws*. Washington, D.C.: Government Printing Office, 1979; (OHDS) 80-30265

————, *Child Protective Services: A Guide for Workers*. Washington, D.C.: Government Printing Office, 1979; (OHDS) 79-30203.

————, *Selected Readings on Mother-Infant Bonding*. Washington, D.C.: Government Printing Office, 1979; (OHDS) 79-30225.

————, *State Child Abuse and Neglect Laws: A Comparative Analysis, 1985*. Washington, D.C.: Clearinghouse on Child Abuse and Neglect Information, April 1987.

U.S. Department of Health and Human Services, Office of Human Development Services, Administration for Children, Youth and Families, Children's Bureau, National Center on Child Abuse and Neglect, *Child Abuse and Neglect: An Informed Approach to a Shared Concern*. Washington, D.C.: Government Printing Office, 1986

————, *Child Protection: The Role of the Courts*. Washington, D.C.: Government Printing Office, 1980; (OHDS) 80-30256.

————, *Executive Summary: National Study of the Incidence and Severity of Child Abuse and Neglect*. Washington, D.C.: Government Printing Office, 1981; (OHDS) 81-30329.

————, *Interdisciplinary Glossary on Child Abuse and Neglect*. Washington, D.C.: Government Printing Office, 1980; (OHDS) 80-30137.

————, *Literature Review of Sexual Abuse*. Washington, D.C.: Clearinghouse on Child Abuse and Neglect Information, August 1986; (OHDS) 87-30553.

————, *Perspectives on Child Maltreatment in the Mid '80s*. Washington, D.C.: Government Printing Office, 1984.

Van Stolk, Mary, *The Battered Child In Canada*. Toronto: McClelland and Stewart, 1978.

Vander Mey, Brenda J. and Ronald L. Neff, *Incest as Child Abuse*. New York: Praeger, 1986.

Volpe, Richard, Margot Breton and Judith Mitton, *Maltreatment of the School-Aged Child*. Lexington, Mass.: D.C. Heath, 1980.

Wald, Michael S. and Sophia Cohen, "Preventing Child Abuse—What Will It Take," *Family Law Quarterly*, 20:2(Summer 1986), 281-302.

Wells, Dorothy P., *Child Abuse: An Annotated Bibliography*. Metuchen, N.J.: Scarecrow Press, 1980.

Welsh, Ralph S., "Spanking: A Grand Old American Tradition?" *Children Today* (January-February 1985):25-29.

West Publishing Co., *The Guide to American Law Yearbook, 1987*. St. Paul, Minn.: West Publishing Co., 1987.

Whitman, David, "The Numbers Game: When More is Less," *U.S. News and World Report* (April 27, 1987):39-40.

Williams, Gertrude J. and John Money, eds., *Traumatic Abuse and Neglect of Children at Home*. Baltimore: Johns Hopkins University Press, 1980.

Woolley, P. and W. Evans, "Significance of Skeletal Lesions Resembling Those of Traumatic Origin," *Journal of the American Medical Association*, 158(1955):539-543.

World Health Organization, *The Treatment and Management of Severe Protein-Energy Malnutrition*. Geneva: World Health Organization, 1981.

Wringe, C.A., *Children's Rights*. London: Routledge & Kegan Paul, 1981.

INDEX

J

K